Choosing Our Religion

Choosing Our Religion

The Spiritual Lives of America's Nones

ELIZABETH DRESCHER

OXFORD
UNIVERSITY PRESS

OXFORD
UNIVERSITY PRESS

Oxford University Press is a department of the University of Oxford. It furthers
the University's objective of excellence in research, scholarship, and education
by publishing worldwide. Oxford is a registered trade mark of Oxford University
Press in the UK and certain other countries.

Published in the United States of America by Oxford University Press
198 Madison Avenue, New York, NY 10016, United States of America.

Library of Congress Cataloging-in-Publication Data
Names: Drescher, Elizabeth.
Title: Choosing our religion : the spiritual lives of America's Nones /
Elizabeth Drescher.
Description: New York : Oxford University Press, 2016. | Includes
bibliographical references.
Identifiers: LCCN 2015034053 | ISBN 978–0–19–934122–1 (cloth : alk. paper)
Subjects: LCSH: Spiritual biography—United States—History and criticism.
Classification: LCC BL71.5 .D74 2016 | DDC 200.973—dc23 LC record available
at http://lccn.loc.gov/2015034053

5 7 9 8 6
Printed by Sheridan, USA

And we all have a duty to do good. And this commandment for everyone to do good, I think, is a beautiful path towards peace. If we, each doing our own part, if we do good to others, if we meet there, doing good, and we go slowly, gently, little by little, we will make that culture of encounter: we need that so much. We must meet one another doing good. "But I don't believe, Father. I am an atheist!" But do good. We will meet one another there.

—Pope Francis, remarks at morning mass, May 22, 2013

CONTENTS

TABLES AND FIGURES

Tables

Figures

ACKNOWLEDGMENTS

I begin this pilgrimage across the changing American spiritual landscape by exploring the diversity of religious unaffiliation as it is characterized by the demographic data that have tended to define "Nones" in the popular imagination over the last decade, moving from there into the complex contours of the everyday spiritual lives of Nones. Such a journey, of course, is never undertaken alone, so before sharing its details further, I would like to acknowledge the individuals and institutions that have contributed to and supported me along the way. It is usually the case that one wants to avoid ranking the contribution of any particular person or group in acknowledgments. Yet in a project such as this one it is certain that, while any failures in what follows are entirely my own, with regard to any insight I have been able to offer on changing American religious and spiritual landscape, I am most deeply indebted to the many Nones who gave up hours of their time to talk with me about their spiritual lives, to allow me to observe their spiritual practices, and to connect me to others in their spiritual networks. Likewise, the project was considerably enriched by the many "Somes"—as I've come to refer to the religiously affiliated—who reached out to me at speaking engagements, via email, Facebook, Twitter, on planes and trains, as well as at neighborhood gatherings and church coffee hours, to share their own perspectives on religious affiliation and unaffiliation.

Because I have been able to interview many people in their own communities, and often in their homes, the portrait of American religion and spirituality that emerges from this opportunity is inflected by differences in geography, culture, personal background, and so on, that are not often a part of qualitative studies such as this one. My ability to travel considerably during the project was supported by grant funding as well as through a number of speaking engagements that gave me access to Nones well beyond the usual urban, coastal locales in which they are most often studied. In the former case, I am deeply grateful for a fellowship from the Social Science Research Council as part of its "New

Directions in the Study of Prayer" (NDSP) initiative and for the encouragement of Paul Bloom, Courtney Bender, Fenella Cannell, Taline Cox, Anna Glade, Robert Orsi, Jonathan VanAntwerpen, and the array of challenging, insightful colleagues with whom the NDSP initiative put me in conversation. Likewise, funding through a Hackworth Grant from the Markkula Center for Applied Ethics at Santa Clara University supported focused research on the ethical practices of Nones.

A number of speaking and consulting engagements also allowed me to interview Nones across the United States, to share my early findings, and to test my preliminary thinking with congenial groups of the (mostly) religiously affiliated. I am grateful for the hospitality of following organizations: The Episcopal Diocese of Northwestern Pennsylvania, Bradford, Pennsylvania; The Episcopal Diocese of California, San Francisco, California; St. Michael and All Angels Episcopal Church, Mission, Kansas; Luther Seminary, St. Paul, Minnesota; The Episcopal Church in Almaden, San Jose, California; Princeton Theological Seminary, Princeton, New Jersey; The Association of Lutheran Church Musicians at Valparaiso University, Valparaiso, Indiana; The BTS Center, Portland, Maine; General Theological Seminary, New York, New York; Upper Dublin Lutheran Church, Ambler, Pennsylvania; Sunnyvale Presbyterian Church, Sunnyvale, California; St. Jude's Episcopal Church, Cupertino, California; The Lilly Endowment Web Consultation at Duke University, Durham, North Carolina; The Episcopal Diocese of Arizona, Phoenix, Arizona; Andover-Newton Theological School, Boston, Massachusetts; the New England Synod of the Evangelical Lutheran Church in America, Worcester, Massachusetts; Bellarmine College Preparatory, San Jose, California; St. Ignatius College Preparatory School, San Francisco, California; Le Moyne College, Syracuse, New York; Brite Divinity School, Forth Worth, Texas; and the Forum for Theological Exploration Transition-Into-Ministry Gathering, Indianapolis, Indiana.

The presentation of academic papers at the 2012 Annual Meeting of the American Academy of Religion in Chicago and at the Religion, Politics, and Globalization Program (RPGP) at the University of California, Berkeley, in the spring of 2013 also provided opportunities to interview Nones and to hone my thinking among challenging and encouraging colleagues. Likewise, articles written for *America*, The BTS Center *Bearings* blog, *The Narthex, Religion Dispatches, Salon*, the *Washington Post*, and elsewhere, as well as interviews with *The Atlantic, The Deseret News*, Confirm Not Conform, and Collegeville Institute, have allowed me to test my findings and refine my ideas with the varied and enthusiastic readers who very often shared their own perspectives on religion and spirituality through comments, posts, tweets, and emails.

My colleagues in Religious Studies and the Graduate Program in Pastoral Ministry at Santa Clara University have been characteristically supportive as I have wended my way through this project. I would like to thank especially Gary Macy, William J. Dohar, James Bennett, J. David Pleins, and Vicky Gonzalez. Much gratitude is owed to Deborah Lohse and Deepa Arora in SCU's outstanding Media Relations department. My teaching and research life was likewise made immeasurably easier by the efforts of my stalwart graduate teaching and research assistant at Santa Clara University, Danyelle Kelly. Much gratitude is owed, as well, to undergraduate research assistant Gillian Kratzer, of the Pennsylvania State University, whose enthusiasm for the project and attention to detail considerably lightened the load of early bibliographic research.

It is a delight and an honor to have been able to complete this project with Oxford University Press. I am grateful for the guidance, support, and, especially, the patience of Cynthia Read, the OUP editorial and marketing staff, and the anonymous proposal reviewers who pressed me to sharpen my research and writing plan at the earliest stages of the project. Anonymous reviewers of the final manuscript likewise helped tremendously to improve the work that follows.

A wide network of colleagues, friends, and other supporters of my work have made the writing of this book much easier than it could possibly have been without them. It is impossible for me to list here all those whose kind words, thoughtful comments, and generosity with background resources helped me along the way. Nonetheless, I would like to thank in particular Keith Anderson, Jennifer Alboim Anderson, Steven Bauman, Diane Bowers, Pat Carr, Hans-Christian Kasper, Bettie Davis, Kenda Creasy-Dean, Mary Gray-Reeves, Robert Grove-Markwood, Susan Grove-Markwood, James Estes, Matt Fisher, Donna Freitas, Mary Hess, Anita Houck, Arthur Holder, Alyssa Lodewick, Rebecca Lyman, Jeff Oakes, Nathaniel Porter, Ellen McGrath Smith, Kirk Smith, and Greg Troxell. As always, Kelly Simons has added much to the spiritual richness of my own everyday life throughout this project.

At the end of the day, I am reasonably certain that religion and spirituality—however we might understand them—would not have come to be such enduring forces in diverse human cultures across the millennia were it not for experiences of suffering and loss encountered in every life. As I was working on this book, I lost a dear friend and spiritual companion, Bill Vodzak (1957–2013). This book is dedicated to the memory of Bill's kindness, compassion, and encouragement of others, whoever they happened to be and wherever they might be heading on their particular pilgrimage.

Choosing Our Religion

Introduction

An American Spiritual Pilgrimage

Faith is not the clinging to a shrine but an endless pilgrimage of the heart.

—Abraham Joshua Heschel

Once you see the boundaries of your environment, they are no longer the boundaries of your environment.

—Marshall McLuhan

By noon on a bright Saturday in July, it was already scorchingly hot as Dorit Brauer drove us to the top of the leafy Chatham University campus in Pittsburgh. We were on our way to Jessica's Labyrinth, a meditative memorial site on a small rise in front of an administrative building at the far side of campus. A brochure explains that "the landscaping hides the labyrinth at eye level, allowing it to be gradually discovered by visitors as they walk the slight incline from Woodland Road to the entry path." For the uninitiated, it is a secret waiting to be revealed, a tranquil spiritual oasis on the urban university campus. But the labyrinth at Chatham is no mystery to Brauer, who in recent years has become something of an expert on the spirituality of the winding sites for walking meditation, typically modeled on medieval designs that were meant to provide a localized experience of pilgrimage to the Holy Land.

Labyrinths were popularized in the United States in the 1990s through installations at a number of churches—Grace Episcopal Cathedral in San Francisco among the earliest and most noted in this movement—along with the development of specialized training in the construction of labyrinths and the facilitation of prayer and walking meditation on them.[1] Brauer's fascination with the spirituality of labyrinths inspired a midlife, cross-country motorcycle pilgrimage from one labyrinth site to the next. This journey forms the structural frame for a self-published memoir, which had just been released the summer we walked Jessica's Labyrinth.[2] For Brauer, walking these "sacred circles" functions not merely as an embodied metaphor for the larger spiritual journey across time and geography, though it is that, too. Labyrinths for her are also places where "prayer happens as the body connects with the earth. It is not just words—the words spoken, the words in your head," she explained to me as we parked the car and swam into the summer's heat. "The words—or even just one word—can guide you or focus you. But the word is not the prayer, you know. The walking is not the prayer. Walking on the ground, on the earth, with a heart open to the divine, to God, if you want to call it that—this is the prayer of a labyrinth."

I had walked my share of labyrinths—the famous thirteenth-century Chartres Cathedral labyrinth in my teens; years later, a remarkable square labyrinth at Ely Cathedral in England; more recently, the Grace Cathedral labyrinth in my own neck of the woods; and, not for nothing, a number of more or less impromptu, "crowd-sourced" turf labyrinths in the Oakland Hills in Northern California, where my dog and I walked when I lived in the area as a graduate student. On my fortieth birthday, I built a labyrinth on a beach in Isla Mujeres, Mexico, with companions on a women's retreat. Some months after Brauer and I walked together through the summer heat, I visited several labyrinths in Sedona, Arizona, these often presented as pre-, post-, or otherwise extra-Christian designs. I was familiar with the form and with the grounded and embodied contemplative practices they host. Labyrinths are in many ways the perfect symbol for the spiritual lives of many Americans today, appearing as they do in traditional religious settings as well as in the increasingly ad hoc spiritualities of people affiliated with institutional religions as well as those whose spiritual lives unfold largely outside the doors of churches, synagogues, mosques, and temples.

My aim in meeting with Dorit Brauer, however, was not to swap notes on labyrinth spiritualities but rather to reconnect with one of the first people I had known as a serious practitioner of "alternative" or "New Age" spiritualities. She seemed the perfect resource at the beginning of my own cross-country pilgrimage into the spiritual lives of the religiously unaffiliated in America—and no few of the affiliated as well. Throughout more than two years, I traveled from Maui to Maine to collect the stories of these so-called "Nones"[3]—people who answer "none" when asked with what religious group they are a member or with which they identify—seeking to add flesh and spirit to the bare-bones demographic data that have poured into academic research and popular media with increasing frequency over the past few years.

I first met Dorit Brauer, then in her mid-thirties, in the 1990s, when she taught a series of guided meditation classes offered through a wellness program at the corporation where I worked. In addition to teaching these classes and maintaining an active practice as a reflexologist,[4] she had been part of a study on "alternative medicine" sponsored by the National Institutes of Health through the Center for Integrative Medicine at the University of Pittsburgh Medical Center.

There, her meditation classes with cardiac patients, people with cancer, and others with high-risk illnesses exacerbated by stress were regularly evaluated for their impact on the overall well-being of participants. I also recalled that Brauer shared a number of other spiritual practices—chanting, drumming, crystal healing bowls, and a spiritualized version of family systems counseling[5]—with various groups and individuals as part of her "holistic living" practice, "Live Your Best Life, Inc." The labyrinth meditation was a new addition to her extensive spiritual repertoire, as was her focus on various forms of spiritual writing. But neither was a surprise to me in a woman with an expansive spiritual curiosity and seemingly boundless energy—not just for experimenting with but for working to master new practices that would deepen her own spirituality and allow her to offer a wider array of spiritual teachings, practices, and healing options for her clients.

We had not been in touch for more than a decade, yet early in my exploration of the spiritual lives of America's Nones I felt compelled to reconnect with Brauer. She seemed to represent the sort of person who comes to mind for many people when they think about the religiously unaffiliated: spiritually eclectic, practicing outside or on the margins of institutional religions, self-authorizing and idiosyncratic in choosing or constructing modes of spiritual practice, and often connected to commercialized modes of such practice. My brief studies with her had contributed to my own interest in the varieties of lived spirituality and religion in America. Conventional academic and demographic assessments tend to focus on people's belief in a personal god or higher power; their formal, membership-based affiliation with an institutional religious group; their attendance at worship services in intuitional religious settings; and the frequency with which they pray. Even before I began researching the spiritual lives of those who are and those who are not affiliated with institutional religions, my experience studying with Brauer and observing others in her classes made clear that spirituality and religion in American life could hardly be understood in all their diversity and richness by focusing exclusively on what happens in relation to churches, mosques, synagogues, and temples or the various administrative and educational institutions that support them.

In many ways, Dorit Brauer typifies an extra-institutional spirituality, the nuances of which are often marginalized in studies of religion. She is a self-identified "seeker"[6] with an eclectic toolkit of spiritual practices drawn from diverse religious and spiritual traditions, which she has shaped into a self-authorized mode of meaning-making.[7] Still, though she does not affiliate with an institutional religion, she nonetheless draws upon traditional religious practices (like labyrinth walking). She often conducts her own spiritual practices and classes in traditional religious sites and generally argues for transhistorical, universalist connections among religions. Brauer has long been a practitioner of spiritually infused alternative healing methodologies, drawing liberally upon the language and methods of empirical science to validate these practices. Her teaching and writing are punctuated with clinical research findings on the efficacy of meditation, the measurement of energy emanating from the body's meridians, and so on.[8] Brauer posted on Facebook a scientifically infused appeal to her nearly three thousand friends and followers to "meditate away" the dramatic effects of climate change, including severe winter weather throughout the East Coast and Midwest:

> Dear Friends, do you believe it's possible to collectively meditate this away? Millions of people focused on fear and worry, not a good thing. Scientific research shows that the practice of meditation in high crime areas of Philadelphia and DC statistically lowered the crime rate for the length of the study (3 months). Imagine what can be accomplished with the power of thought if millions of people focus simultaneously on a positive outcome. What do you think?[9]

Such practices and perspectives have meandered through academic literature on the religiously unaffiliated, which has begun to shape an articulation of a distinctly American spiritual-religiosity with long and tangled historical roots. American extra-institutional engagement with seen and unseen spiritual forces winds through the paradoxes of the Puritan piety and Enlightenment thinking that shaped the founding of the nation. Through the nineteenth century, it appears in the New England metaphysical thought associated with Ralph Waldo Emerson and Emanuel Swedenborg and in New Thought movements like Divine Science and Religious Science identified with Ralph Waldo Trine and later Mary Baker Eddy and Christian Science. Elsewhere, in a very different register, the eighteenth-century Evangelical Awakening stirred by George Whitefield, Jonathan Edwards, and others re-emerged in the nineteenth century through camp meetings that spread the Spirit to the masses, including blacks and women, through the powerful preaching and missionary outreach of Charles Finney, Jarena Lee, and Ellen G. White.[10] These diverse strands of lived spirituality converge in the ubiquitous "Spiritual-But-Not-Religious" moniker adopted by many of the unaffiliated themselves and applied to them by those who study and comment on their spiritual lives.[11] Brauer's spiritual pilgrimage takes her through much of this genealogy.

The Spiritual-But-Not-Religious label, often reduced to the acronym SBNR, was not an exact fit for Dorit Brauer, however. When I asked her how she would respond to someone who asked what her religion was, she said, "I would say I am 'spiritual,' but," she continued,

I am interested in religion, too. I don't worry so much about the labels. You know, a long time ago, I couldn't go into a church and feel comfortable. But that has changed for me over time. Now I can go to a Catholic mass with my mother and it's a very spiritual experience—and a religious experience, I guess. But that is not the core of my spirituality, of course.

The Church of the Risen None—Or Not

Her self-description and her relative comfort with conventional religion notwithstanding, it seems likely that many would lump Brauer in with the "Spiritual-But-Not-Religious," some adding the unflattering assessment of the spiritual lives pursued by people like Brauer as "individualistic," "narcissistic," "uncommitted," "unbelieving," "consumerist," "superficial," and otherwise less serious and meaningful than those of people who anchor their spiritual identity to formal membership in institutional religious organizations.[12]

Dorit Brauer may indeed correspond to a certain *stereotype* of the religiously unaffiliated in America, and she may be somewhat typical of some Nones of a certain age, class, ethnic, and religious background. This was part of my initial interest in reconnecting with her as I began this project. But as will become clear in the pages ahead, Brauer is hardly an *archetype* for the wide array of Americans who select "none of the above" on surveys of religious affiliation. The tremendous diversity of self-identification of American Nones is among the most difficult things for commentators—academic, journalistic, and religious alike—to grasp about a demographic category that does not, in fact, describe a distinct social group. "None" is a "negative definition." It describes people who *do not* identify as belonging to a specific group, who *are not* affiliated with one institutional religion or another.[13] It was thus not surprising that nearly all of the people I interviewed for this book at one point or another mentioned, as did Brauer, a discomfort with the labels, and the practice of labeling itself, as supposed ways of understanding the religion and spirituality of individuals or groups.

However they have described themselves or have been labeled by others, Nones have periodically been objects of curiosity, compassion, derision, and sometimes outright hostility throughout the life of the nation.[14] Surveys from the Pew Research Center and researchers at Trinity College have identified a particularly significant jump in the population of Nones from the 1990s through the beginning of the new millennium.[15] The near doubling in the percentage of Nones—from around 9% in 1990 to just over 16% in 2008—briefly drew the attention of the popular media and religious leaders.

But a survey from Pew and the Religion & Ethics Newsweekly program, "Nones on the Rise," released just before the 2012 presidential election, stirred considerably more conversation across religious, political, and media organizations. In addition to foregrounding the generally more liberal political leanings of Nones, the new data showed further dramatic growth in the population of the religiously unaffiliated. One in five Americans overall—20%—now claimed no religious affiliation. And among people under the age of 30, a full 30%—one in three—were unaffiliated.[16] By 2015, a new Pew survey marked a further uptick in unaffiliated Americans to nearly 23%.[17] A full 35% of American adults under age 30 are unaffiliated.[18] This newly reported increase in unaffiliation outpaced a projection by Pew only a month earlier that suggested the rate of unaffiliation in the North America would reach nearly 26% by 2050.[19] Clearly, Nones are the overachievers of the US religious landscape.

All of the numbers tell us that if the unaffiliated gathered into a formal religious organization, it would be larger than any Protestant denomination and *all* Mainline Protestant denominations combined. Though there is of course no Church of the Risen None, no Affiliation for the Religiously Unaffiliated, the increase in Nones raises questions about contemporary American culture that merit our attention: Are Americans giving up on God? Is the United States becoming more fully secularized, along the lines of most Western European nations? Or, is something altogether different happening? Are the meanings of "religion" and "religious affiliation" themselves changing in profound and enduring ways?

For a nation whose history, politics, legal and educational systems, and wide swaths of the broader culture have been profoundly influenced by religion, the questions raised by the recent growth in the population of Nones are not unimportant, regardless of how we do or do not practice religion. What do the Nones tell us about the changing American spiritual and religious ethos at the beginning of the twenty-first century? What are the implications of a growing population of religiously unaffiliated Americans for social cohesion, ethics and morals, existential meaning-making, charitable giving, social justice action, volunteerism, and other phenomena associated with religion as it has been traditionally understood?

Choosing Our Religion: The Spiritual Lives of America's Nones offers an exploration of this newly fascinating demographic category. Through interviews with a diversity of Nones across the United States, the book explores who Nones are, how they came to their unaffiliated status, their spiritual influences and exemplars, and how they live out their spiritualities, individually and with others. The book moves through and then beyond the statistical reports that have been as anxiety-provoking to religious leaders and many in their flocks as they have been compelling to social commentators and political operatives who hanker for the support of a newly defined constituency.

In Chapter 1, I explore recent demographic data on Nones. But I also consider the role of such demography itself in a certain theologically and ideologically compartmentalized, market-based, and institutionally oriented understanding of American religion and spirituality. Ultimately, this book contests this view through its more sustained attention to the spiritual narratives of the unaffiliated themselves. This initial discussion, then, is meant to open a more expansive understanding of the population of Nones that moves beyond the ideas of lack and loss—lack of faith, loss of belief, lack of commitment, loss of community, and so on—that more often than not characterize conversations about the unaffiliated within institutional religious communities and many academic circles. Chapter 1 sets up what I have taken as the primary challenge of the book: to present Nones as other than a homogeneous group or "tribe"[20] in competition with the religiously affiliated. The book, thus, situates Nones as diverse participants in an increasingly vibrant, historically rich, and religiously pluralistic landscape within which conventional measures like institutional affiliation, worship attendance, and belief in God or a Higher Power are increasingly less meaningful indicators of the extent or depth of American religiosity or spirituality. In many ways, even among "Somes"—as I have come to call the religiously affiliated—exclusive participation in institutional religious groups is now becoming something of an "alternative" religious practice itself in a world where more diversely resourced, everyday spiritualities are becoming the norm.

Given the complexity of this landscape, Chapter 1 also takes up the question of what we mean when we talk about "spirituality" and "religion" in the United States today. The two terms have a complex and often conflicted history that flows through various streams of religious, academic, and popular discourse. This history is inflected by the claims of secularism, religious pluralism, religiously infused politics, and consumer culture, among other factors. I suggest that the ongoing debate about what counts as the "spiritual" and what is more properly "religious" reveals more about who is using these words than about the terms themselves or, perhaps more significantly, than it does about the spiritual and/or religious experiences and commitments of ordinary Americans in the midst of everyday lives.

Chapter 1 also explores the idea of "the spiritual life" as defined by *practices* rather than *beliefs*, though I do not set these two phenomena in opposition to one another—thoughts against actions. Rather, I consider a richer understanding of "practice" in the context of religious and spiritual identity as a dynamic blend of actions, attitudes, preferences, material objects, feelings, and thoughts that forms coherent ways of living with others in the world. Practice, in this sense, both shapes and is shaped by the experiences of everyday life within networks of relationships. Practices are the raw material for stories of the self that narrate what a person understands as her or his own identity, including spiritual or religious identity.

Based on narrative surveys with more than a thousand affiliated and unaffiliated Americans, and extended interviews with more than one hundred Nones across the country,[21] *Choosing Our Religion* invites readers to listen in on the stories of Nones themselves as they describe their spiritual lives: the paths they followed to their current approach to spirituality (Chapter 2); the writers, thinkers, gurus, teachers, and other influencers of their spirituality (Chapter 3); the specific practices they find spiritually enriching or otherwise meaningful (Chapters 4); how prayer among the unaffiliated bridges traditional religious understandings and new spiritual self-understandings (Chapter 5); the ways in which the spirituality of Nones influences their ethical values and moral practices (Chapter 6); and how they approach the spiritual and moral formation of their children (Chapter 7). In the end, this is not a book *about* Nones, but a book *of* Nones and their stories. The pages that follow, in which Nones themselves are extensively quoted, hardly map the whole of unaffiliated spirituality across the country and within complex and changing lives. Still, my hope is that the wide variety of unaffiliated Americans will recognize important elements of their own stories here as well.

The book is more than this, however, for it situates Nones in relationship to Somes in the midst of their lives in common. The spiritualities of Nones are hardly distinct or isolated from the spiritualities of Somes with whom they share much of their everyday lives, including experiences and practices that both the affiliated and the unaffiliated alike would mark as "spirituality significant." Rituals associated with life transitions such as births, graduations, marriages, and deaths, as well as seasonal celebrations and holidays, bring Nones and Somes into frequent spiritual proximity. Although they may approach and interpret these occasions differently, and though cultural norms frequently limit sustained discussion of the spiritual meaning of such shared experiences,[22] my interviews with Nones as well as my conversations with many Somes make clear that most of us, regardless of how we see ourselves in terms of affiliation and unaffiliation, are actively attentive to and curious about each other's spiritual or religious practices (even when we may be overtly dismissive or otherwise critical of them). For many Americans, the resources this curiosity brings to consciousness will find their way, directly or perhaps more obliquely, into their own spiritualities.

In addition, the recent data on religious affiliation in America tell us that more than 70% of Nones were raised in families affiliated with institutional religions, this background generally having been in a Christian denomination.[23] This hard fact has churned considerable interest and angst among religious leaders and congregants, generating something of a cottage industry for guides to re-engaging or, more troublingly, "capturing" Nones.[24] This book is not such a guide. Its focus is not on why Nones left the churches of their childhoods or what they do not like about religious institutions of one sort or another. These details do come up in the context of descriptions of how people came to self-identify as Nones. But, though I expect that those concerned about the viability of institutional religion can learn much from the stories of Nones that follow, the book does not specifically offer advice on how to shape worship, formation, service, and so on, in ways that might be more attractive to the unaffiliated.

Yet no matter how Nones come to engage religious traditions within their adult spiritual lives, this background will surely have shaped features of their spirituality or religiosity. While Nones are characterized by the fact that they do not claim formal, membership-based affiliation with institutional religious groups, many of those I interviewed periodically—indeed, in some cases quite regularly—attended services in one or more church, shanga, synagogue, temple, or other religious community.[25] Many Nones also participate in volunteer work sponsored by religious groups. Not infrequently, then, Nones sit next to Somes on the pews of a neighborhood church. They lend a hand along with Somes to care for people experiencing homelessness, poverty, illness, the effects of natural disasters, and so on.

Many of the Nones we will meet in the pages ahead actively carry beliefs, rituals, artifacts, and other elements of their religious upbringing and of the religious tenor of American culture in general into their adult spiritual lives. Even among Nones who were adamant that their spirituality had nothing to do with conventional religion, many seemingly self-styled practices have discernible echoes of the practitioners' religious upbringings. The practice of prayer, for instance, continues to be a meaningful practice for many Nones, including those who describe themselves as Atheists or Agnostics. Take, Judith Leonard,[26] a 61-year-old None living in New York City, who left the Catholic Church in her mid-thirties after a painful divorce. When I first talked with her over coffee at a Greenwich Village cafe, she insisted, "I put everything Catholic behind me. All of it: the beliefs, the rituals, the icons, and twelve years of Catholic school discipline that taught me never to trust myself." Yet each morning, Judith, who described herself as an "Agnostic with a lot of Atheist seasoning," lays out a small collection of photos on her breakfast table. She explained:

> Every morning, I take out the pictures of my daughters and my granddaughters. I say their names, and I think what they mean to me and how proud I am of them. I want them to have good lives—to do good. I say it's a "prayer," but a priest wouldn't call it that. I don't think something happens just because I want good things for them. I don't believe in

some god who will protect or reward my loved ones and not someone who didn't ask.

I remarked that Judith's photos, and the practice she calls "prayer" despite her lack of belief that a supernatural being might intervene on her behalf for the sake of her loved ones, brought to mind Catholic prayer cards—portable, playing-card-sized devotional images of a holy person or other religious figure on one side and a short prayer or Bible verse on the other.[27] She was plainly surprised by the connection I had made, and eventually dismissive. "Oh, it's nothing like that," she said, waving her hand, "mumbo-jumbo to made-up saints in heaven. Kids traded them like baseball cards when I was in school. The nuns gave them as prizes. This is me thinking about the kids, is all. Bringing them to mind with pictures of them before I start the day."

I take Judith at her word with regard to her own understanding of her morning prayer and its sources. Yet the practice of making the absent present through regular, ritualized contemplation of a visual image, and the tactile experience of holding each photo in her hands has, even without desired supernatural intervention, much in common with the traditional religious practice. If, as Robert Orsi claims, "religion is the practice of making the invisible visible,"[28] Judith's prayer ritual seems certainly to make a recognizably religious claim.

Such arguably traditional religious echoes in the spiritual practices of many of the Nones I interviewed only amplified what the recent deluge of demographic data often obscures: the boundaries between the affiliated and the unaffiliated are remarkably porous. In terms of spiritual and religious practice; the thinkers and teachers who serve as guides to spiritual knowledge and enrichment; the material objects that represent, memorialize, and often anchor spiritual activities; and the language used to narrate these practices and their meanings—the whole expansive idiom of what scholars have come to call "lived" or "everyday religion"[29]—the spiritual paths of Nones and Somes parallel and intersect on a regular basis. A None may periodically attend a chanted Taizé service offered by a local Presbyterian church—such Protestant locales themselves an appropriation of Roman Catholic liturgical practice—without feeling the need to become a member. By the same token, a "cradle Episcopalian" may from time to time attend a mindfulness meditation group at a Buddhist center without feeling obligated to give up or hyphenate what she thinks of as her "Anglican identity." If it is the case that some trace of institutional religious identity lingers within many Nones, so, too, a free-floating cultural "Noneness" infuses the spirituality of many of the affiliated. The terms "unaffiliated/affiliated," "Nones/Somes," are best understood, then, not as fixed categories in themselves, but as markers on a wide continuum of American religiosity and spirituality, the fluidity of which has become, if not in fact greater, at least increasingly more visible in recent years as a vastly expanded broadcast media landscape and new digital social media practices have given all of us much more access to the smallest details of everyday life, including its spiritual contours. Most recently, digital social media practices in particular have expanded our capacity to construct and present our own spiritual selves to others and to ourselves.[30]

Spirituality Well Beyond Belief

This point was brought sharply into focus during the course of my research when those who would seem to be furthest apart on the religious continuum—Atheists and highly active churchgoers—reached out to me to share their own spiritual insights. This happened after I published a short article that highlighted books that might help people to understand a subset of the religiously unaffiliated, so-called "religious Nones."[31] These are Nones who claim no religious affiliation but who nonetheless profess a belief in a god, a higher power, or life force; who engage in spiritual practices like prayer, meditation, or yoga; and who may, periodically at least, attend services of traditional religious groups. At the time, it had seemed reasonable to narrow my research focus to these religious Nones, excluding those who self-identify as more fully in Atheist, Agnostic, or Secular Humanist categories, and who, I assumed, would not see themselves as either "spiritual" or "religious."

To my surprise, I received a number of emails from self-identified Atheists, Secular Humanists, and other "non-religious" or "secular" Nones wondering why I had not highlighted any titles related to their spiritual lives. One man wrote,

> I don't have any belief in a supernatural being, higher power, or Star Wars "force." I think of myself as within the humanist tradition that relies on reason and experience to understand life. But because of that, I believe in the human spirit, and in the progressive development of humane capacity in people so that the world we live in and the world we leave behind are better. This the only "eternity" that exists. There is a long, proud history of this humanist, atheist, and freethinking tradition in America, starting with our founders like Thomas Jefferson, James Madison, and Thomas Paine. It is predictable that the "spirituality" of these "nones" would be ignored by mainstream press writers, but I would think that [this publication] would be more inclusive in their coverage of religion and spirituality.

Chastened and intrigued, I expanded my research to include Nones who do not believe in a divinity, higher power, or life force, or, as many of my conversation partners put it, "whatever." I attended meetings of Secular Humanist groups and a newly emerging "Atheist Church." I also invited Atheists to participate in the narrative "Nones Beyond the Numbers" survey I had developed in order to identify and screen potential interview subjects. I conducted extended interviews with a number of self-identified Atheists, Secular Humanists, and other non-religious Nones through the course of my research.

The following spring, when I wrote about the prayer practices of Nones, making sure to include perspectives from non-religious Nones, I received feedback from both religiously affiliated and unbelieving unaffiliated readers who argued, with remarkable consistency across these two typically opposed categories, that it was "impossible" for an Atheist to "pray." Religiously affiliated commenters tended to wonder to whom unbelieving Nones prayed and what they expected as results of their "godless petitions." An Atheist commenter went so far as to call the suggestion that an Atheist would pray "an act of slander against freethinking people."[32] As noted earlier, and as I will discuss further in Chapter 5, prayer turns out to be a particularly durable spiritual practice among the unaffiliated, including non-believing Nones. Its spiritual value, as we will see, often has less to do with a supernatural being to whom one might pray or an expected result, but rather in the capacity of the word "prayer" itself to express a complex experience of vulnerability, often imbued with conflicting emotions—anxiety and hope, for instance—and to situate the one who prays in a closer emotional relationship to the person or condition for which she prays.

At the other end of the spectrum—among highly active churchgoers of the sort who attend conferences on religion and spirituality at which I sometimes speak—the permeable boundaries of affiliated and unaffiliated religion likewise revealed themselves. When I talked at seminaries or with church groups during the early stages of my research, many Somes (always off to the side, outside the formal presentation) expressed considerable shame that their own adult children were not churchgoers and were not, therefore, raising their own children in a church tradition. By the midpoint of the project, however, as the word "None" became more a part of the popular lexicon through regular reporting well beyond religious and academic publications, and as my early findings provided somewhat more nuanced glimpses into the spiritual lives of the unaffiliated, these "confessions" began to change. Often in question and answer sessions at the end of presentations, Somes in their fifties and well beyond would express relief that they could now understand their teenaged and adult children who no longer affiliated with the churches of their childhood as "Nones" rather than "lapsed," "unchurched," or (apparently worse for many who whispered these terms) "atheist" or "agnostic."

By the end of the project, a different manner of "confession" from Somes began occurring after my talks. In these, Somes would seek me out during a break or happen upon me in a hotel lobby. On these occasions, however, Somes were not confessing on behalf of their children or because of what they feared was their failed religious parenting, but rather on their own behalf. At a conference for church musicians I was approached by the music director of a mid-sized Lutheran church in Maryland. "I love the choir. I love singing every week at choir practice and at the Sunday service," she told me. Then she continued in a rather different tone:

> I've done it for almost twenty years—since I was in college, which means that I've been around church for long enough to know that most of it is a lot of crap. I don't believe very much of it. But I like to sing, and I couldn't do that if I told everyone I'm probably a None. A Lutheran-None. So, I keep quiet. I get to sing with people I really like every week, and I don't have to deal with the rest of it.

"Maybe I'm really an Agnostic," a twenty-something youth minister working a large, mostly white, Methodist congregation outside Atlanta told me at a conference in New Jersey. "You know, it's not like I have all the answers," he said. "It's not like I want to. I don't really have to, right? So, yeah, now I really do think I'm a None. That makes more sense."

On the flight home from the same engagement, I happened to be seated beside a 40-year-old Presbyterian minister, who, when he learned about my study, quickly offered his own None-ish confession:

> If I'm really honest and ask myself if I'd go to church regularly if I weren't clergy, I have to say, "no." It just doesn't always feed me spiritually. I can only half imagine what it must be like for people without a vocational anchor to give up everything else that might be spiritually meaningful on a Sunday morning to go to church.

It seems certain that the mountain of mainstream reporting on an even larger mountain of polling data from Pew, Gallup, the General Social Survey (GSS), Harris, the Public Religion Research Institute (PRRI), and others that formed during the course of my research played a role in the shifting self-understandings and self-descriptions of both Nones and Somes.[33] The experience also reshaped my own understanding of religion in the United States and my approach to the project I had undertaken. Thus, while *Choosing Our Religion: The Spiritual Lives of America's Nones* focuses most directly on the unaffiliated as they narrate their own spiritual stories, it is also a book about the changing currents of American religion and spirituality more broadly. Again and again in my research—in interviews with Nones certainly, but no less in a number of telling conversations with the religiously affiliated themselves—the "Noneness" of contemporary American religion in its institutional forms, alongside spirituality in its everyday practice, was apparent.

Rather than expressing itself through traditional modes of *believing, belonging,* and *behaving* that have fueled much recent discussion within religions about how to engage the unaffiliated and to retain current members, this broader Noneness appeared among the Nones I interviewed in narratives that emphasized experiences of *being* and *becoming.*[34] As elaborated in the chapters that follow, for the majority of Nones who talked with me, the spiritual life is seen as emerging organically from the whole of life in relation to a diversity of others, rather being structured through categories of propositional beliefs, affiliational patterns, and the associated ritual and social actions of defined religious groups. In contrast to the thin, internalized, self-referential quality that is often ascribed to spiritualities pursued outside institutional contexts, a spirituality of being and becoming includes a number of robust practices that unfold in the context of everyday life. Among the characteristic categories of practice explored in the chapters that follow are

- *gathering* and *relationship-tending* with families, friends, local communities, and others across social networks increasingly expanded and diversified through digital social media;
- exploring the perceived wisdom of a wide array of *spiritual teachers*—self-identified as such or not—within and beyond conventionally recognized spiritual and religious categories;
- engaging in formal and informal *rituals* that both mark and move the boundaries of *sacred space and time* across the various domestic, commercial, natural, cultural, and other landscapes of everyday experience;
- honoring the role of human *bodies* themselves as creative and expressive sites of the sacred;
- grounding *ethical action* in *care for others* and *appreciation of difference*, rather than on reinforcing assumed commonalities; and
- narrating the spiritual life though a *distinctive discourse* that highlights fluidity, provisionality, diversity, unpredictability, wonder, and awe in human experience over time.[35]

Here again, it is important to note that what I have come to understand as the durably malleable character of American religion and spirituality appears to be as much a part of the lives of the religiously affiliated and the institutions where they center much of their spiritual practice as it is of the spiritual lives of the unaffiliated. Because of this, though *Choosing Our Religion* remains "a book of Nones," I discuss in the Conclusion some implications of the "none-ing" of America for religious *and* non-religious institutions whose long-term viability depends in some measure on continued meaningful engagement with Nones. Here, I reflect on what it might mean for both religious and non-religious people and institutions to act out of a deeper understanding of the intersecting lived religious and spiritual realities of Nones and Somes alike today. And, I consider how a largely deinstitutionalized American spirituality structures itself along the lines of the networked, relational culture shaped over the past decade by new digital practices. How institutional religions engage without attempting to colonize the multiple, overlapping networks of American Noneness is, I conclude, the key challenge for American religion in the decades ahead.

1

Nones beyond the Numbers

Do I contradict myself? Very well, then I contradict myself, (I am large,
I contain multitudes.)

— Walt Whitman, *"Song of Myself"*

Even "agnostic" or "atheist" carry a lot of cultural baggage that I just
don't want to take on. I don't want you to be thinking of me in terms
of spirituality or religion. Not my religion—if I have one—not your
religion. These designations just should not be part of how we relate to
each other no matter what we believe. So, you can go ahead and call me
"none." But only if you know I really mean "none" by that.

— Dmitri Kraznos, *age 20, Oberlin, Ohio, "None"*

"Oh, so they're like canaries in the cathedral," said Sean Rowe, the bishop of the
Episcopal Diocese of Northwestern Pennsylvania, after a talk I gave very early in
my research on the unaffiliated. "Yes," I agreed, "except they're not in the cathedral very much. They've flown away."

I'd been talking about the percentage of the unaffiliated—nearly three-
quarters—who were raised in families with some religious affiliation, generally in
a Christian denomination. The exodus is most pronounced among Protestants.
Some 44% of Nones were raised in a Protestant tradition; 27% were raised as
Roman Catholics. Among Protestant denominations, progressive Protestant
denominations (Disciples of Christ, Episcopalian, United Church of Christ) are
tied in the percentage of their contributions to the ranks of the unaffiliated:[1] 20%
of young people raised in each of these traditions become unaffiliated as adults.
The losses are only slightly lower for Nondenominational Protestants at 19%.
Among those raised as Roman Catholics, 14% become Nones, but their larger
population overall, along with that of more conservative Protestant denominations, means that numerically more Nones come from Catholic and Evangelical
backgrounds[2] than from Mainline Protestant traditions (see Table 1.1).

That was cold comfort to Bishop Rowe, who could see that the spiritual lives
constructed by Nones outside the churches of their childhood pointed not just
to problems with institutional religion in general and Christianity in particular.

Table 1.1 **Change in Childhood Religion by Religious Group**

Religious Group of Upbringing	Percent Who Stay as Adult		Percent Who Leave as Adult		Percent Who Become Nones	
	2007	2014	2007	2014	2007	2014
Adventist	59%	51%	41%	69%	10%	15%
Anabaptist	40%	52%	60%	48%	7%	5%
Baptist	60%	57%	40%	63%	11%	15%
Buddhist	50%	39%	50%	61%	28%	40%
Catholic	68%	59%	32%	41%	14%	20%
Congregationalist	37%	31%	63%	69%	20%	28%
Episcopalian / Anglican	45%	39%	55%	61%	20%	27%
Hindu	84%	80%	16%	20%	8%	18%
Historically Black Protestant	NA	70%	NA	23%	NA	13%
Holiness	32%	32%	68%	68%	13%	18%
Jewish	76%	75%	24%	25%	8%	18%
Lutheran	59%	51%	41%	49%	13%	20%
Methodist	47%	40%	53%	60%	12%	19%
Mormon	70%	64%	30%	36%	14%	21%
Muslim	NA	77%	NA	23%	NA	15%
Nondenominational Protestant	44%	47%	56%	53%	NA	19%
Orthodox	73%	53%	21%	47%	7%	24%
Pentecostal	47%	50%	53%	50%	12%	15%
Presbyterian	40%	34%	60%	66%	14%	25%

Data adapted from Pew, "2008 U.S. Religious Landscape Survey," 30–31, and Pew, "America's Changing Religious Landscape," 39, 42. The "2008 U.S. Religious Landscape Survey" did not track retention of members for Muslims, Nondenominational Protestants, or Historically Black Protestants.

They also pointed to broader changes in religious and spiritual practice in the United States that institutional religions seemed ill prepared to engage.

This is not a book about how churches or other religious groups might retool in order to gather Nones back into the fold or keep wavering Somes from leaving. But Bishop Rowe was right to suggest that the unaffiliated are telling us all something important about the very nature of religion in America.

Understanding how American Nones fit into a wider religious and spiritual landscape that also includes increasingly diverse varieties of Somes requires addressing a few basic questions: Who are the Nones in demographic terms and as they identify themselves? What do we mean when we talk about "religious" or "spiritual" identity, and how is this related to affiliation or unaffiliation? What is the difference between "religion" and "spirituality," anyway? And, how is "the spiritual life" related to other aspects of everyday life in general? This chapter explores these questions, taking the wealth of demographic data that has appeared in the past decade as a starting point. However, it moves quickly beyond survey data to consider more complex concepts of identity, affiliation, spirituality, and religion in light of the way Nones themselves tell the story of their spiritual lives.

Who Are the Nones?

In some ways, it seems such a simple question. According to the 2015 "America's Changing Religious Landscape" report from the Pew Research Center, nearly a quarter (23.9%) of all Americans say that they have no religious affiliation. This finding amplifies data from the 2012 "Nones on the Rise" report from Pew, as well as the General Social Survey (GSS), a national survey of American adults conducted by the Sociology Program of the National Science Foundation since 1972.[3]

In previous generations, religious unaffiliation tended to be geographically centered around urban, coastal areas of the United States, especially in the so-called "None Zone" of the Pacific Northwest.[4] More recent data shows growth in the percentage of Nones in every region of the country. The Mountain states, which in 1990 had the lowest level of religious unaffiliation in the nation (less than 5%) had among the highest (26%) in 2014. From 2007 to 2014, though religious affiliation remained higher in the Bible Belt states of the US South than elsewhere in the country, the percentage of Nones more than doubled, growing from less than 6% to 16%.[5] In Mississippi alone, which boasted the highest level of religious affiliation in 2007 (96%), unaffiliation grew a whopping 133%. Nones, it turns out, are everywhere. (Figure 1.1 shows the percentage of Nones in each of the nine US Census regions. Figure 1.2 shows the percentage of growth in each region from 2007 to 2014.)

Nones are pretty much *everyone* as well. It remains the case that women are more likely to be affiliated with a religious group than are men. There are more women (52%) than men in US population overall, but Nones are significantly more likely to be men (57%) than are women (43%). So, too, unaffiliation spans racial and ethnic categories, though it remains a much more distinctly white

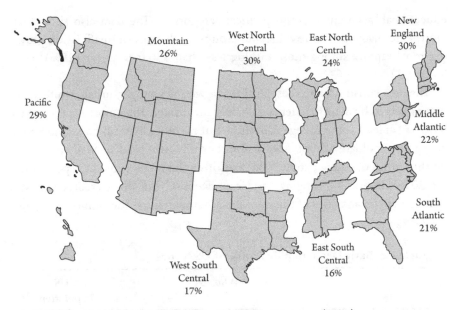

Figure 1.1 Percentage of Nones in Nine US Census Divisions (2014)

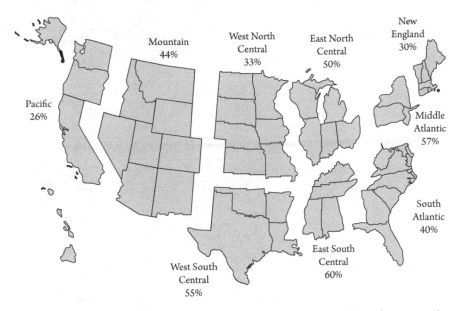

Figure 1.2 Growth in the Percentage of Nones in Nine US Census Divisions (2007–2014)

phenomenon. More than two-thirds (68%) of the unaffiliated are white, down slightly from 2007 (73%). But the unaffiliated population included slightly more Asians (5%, up from 4% in 2007) and Latina/os (13%, up from 11% in 2007) in 2014. Blacks among the unaffiliated dropped from 9% in 2007 to 8% in 2014.[6] Still, religious unaffiliation has grown across all gender, racial, ethnic, educational, geographical, and political categories.[7] The data also show that Nones are distributed across income groups, with rates of unaffiliation growing most rapidly among those making less than $30,000 a year (29%)[8] (see Table 1.2).

The data construct a stereotypical None who is younger, urban, white, a bit more likely to be male than female, slightly more likely than most Americans to have had at least some college education, but no more likely to have completed college or graduate school. Media reports on Nones tend to focus primarily on the stories of young people.[9] This was often the focus of media reports after the 2015 "America's Changing Landscape Report." But this stereotype speaks as much to the anxieties of the over-age-50 crowd at the top of most religious

Table 1.2 **Basic Demographic Profile of US Nones**

	% of Nones Who Are		% of US Population
Gender	Female	43%	52%
	Male	57%	48%
Age	18–29	35%	22%
	30–49	37%	35%
	50–64	19%	26%
	65+	9%	18%
Race and Ethnicity	White	68%	66%
	Black	9%	11%
	Hispanic	13%	15%
	Asian	5%	5%
	Other/Mixed	4%	2%
Educational Level	High School Grad	38%	43%
	Some College	32%	29%
	College Grad	18%	19%
	Post-Grad	11%	10%
Income Level	Under $30,000	33%	36%
	$30,000–$74,999	20%	34%
	$75,000–$99,999	26%	12%
	$100,000 or More	21%	17%

Data adapted from Pew, "America's Changing Religious Landscape," 56, 57, and Appendix D: Detailed Tables, 118.

institutions about the defection of younger people than it does about the reality of unaffiliation as it extends across all age groups.

Young people in America, it is true, are much more likely to be Nones than are their over-age-30 parents, other relatives, professors, employers, and so on.[10] But in a counterintuitive bit of demographic math, there are actually more Nones over 30 than under 30. Why? Because numbers: nearly 80% of the US population is *over* age 30. More than 40% of the population is *over* age 50.[11] So, while individuals under age 30 are more likely to be religiously unaffiliated, older Nones make up the bulk of the unaffiliated population because there are simply more of them. This means that the story of religious change in America is incompletely told when it focuses primarily on amplified rates of unaffiliation among the young.

We can see from the data that, far from being a fringe phenomenon among the "unchurched" in overeducated, latte-slinging corridors of the country, unaffiliation is part of the religious and spiritual structure of every social sector. Furthermore, sustained growth in unaffiliation since at least the early 1970s shows that it is not a passing trend. The data mark a significant religious and spiritual shift in the United States across the last three generations.[12]

But the data also confuse the matter in a number of ways, inviting depictions that misrepresent not only who the unaffiliated are, but also how they participate in the wider religious and spiritual culture. These misrepresentations have to do with beliefs, actions, commitments, and networks of relationships that shape the spiritual lives of many Nones and influence the practice of religion and spirituality in United States more generally. Ground zero of this frequent misunderstanding has to do with the diverse ways in which Nones themselves understand and describe their own spiritual identities.

No Labels Except No Labels

As it turns out, all Nones are not the same—very often by wide margins. Schemes to categorize and label them fail to understand a basic value expressed by the majority of Nones who shared their stories with me. For many Nones, including Dmitri Kraznos, the young man quoted at the beginning of this chapter, self-identification is an important part of the spiritual life itself. Those who insist that all Nones are Atheists or other unbelievers,[13] Spiritual-But-Not-Religious,[14] or once-affiliated "dropouts" and "prodigals" longing for a way back home[15] ignore the distinctiveness of the unaffiliated across a religious and spiritual continuum that also includes the religiously affiliated. The 2012 Pew data, for instance, show that a plurality of the unaffiliated—37%—identify as "Spiritual-But-Not-Religious." This is not a small percentage, but it is hardly the entire population of

Nones. Beyond this, it is worth noting, first, that nearly one in five Nones (18%) described themselves as "a religious person." Second, at the affiliated end of the spectrum, where, unsurprisingly, the majority describe themselves as "a religious person" (75%), 15% nevertheless identify as Spiritual-But-Not-Religious.[16] Religion and spirituality in America turn out to be sliding-scale phenomena.

Boston University sociologist Nancy Ammerman has shown that formal church members and those whose spiritualities unfold largely outside religious institutions share much in terms of their understanding of "the spiritual" as it plays out not in churches, synagogues, or mosques, but rather in the contexts of everyday life—home, work, neighborhoods, healthcare settings, and nature. Their spiritual narratives, Ammerman and colleagues revealed, draw upon a range of theistic and extra-theistic language that makes it impossible to draw hard lines between the affiliated and the unaffiliated beyond the relatively minor fact, in terms of their day-to-day spiritual experience, of institutional member-ship. Says Ammerman of the affiliated:

> What we discover is that some religious participants employ a robust set of Extra-theistic meanings *along with* their wide array of Theistic ones. They are perfectly conversant with the spiritual language of their traditions, but they also see spirituality in experiences beyond those tra-ditions, even interpreting each in light of the other. The churches them-selves promote just this sort of crossover, offering classes in meditation or yoga, for instance, that are framed in generic ways that obscure their roots outside of Christianity and emphasize instead the development of one's interior self. The permeable boundaries between some Christian communities and the larger culture can be seen in this mixed discursive field.[17]

By the same token, as we saw with Dorit Brauer and Judith Leonard, language and rituals associated with conventional religious practice make their way, inten-tionally or otherwise, into the spiritualities of the unaffiliated.[18] Unfortunately, since the release of the "2008 U.S. Religious Landscape Survey," the "American Religious Identification Survey," and the "Nones on the Rise" reports, Nones have increasingly been described as though they form a homogeneous social group that can be directly compared and contrasted to members of institutional religious groups. This is hardly the case.

Technically speaking, Nones are members only of a demographic *category* made up of people who share similar characteristics but "who do not necessarily interact or identify with one another." They are not part of a *group* proper, which would require that they meet at least periodically with one or more other Nones expressly on the basis of their shared "noneness" and that together they would act on the basis of that common identity.[19] They would do "none-like" things together, whatever that might turn out to be, as Presbyterians do specifically Calvinist sorts of things or Episcopalians for Anglican sorts of things. But Nones don't generally do that precisely because they're Nones. That is, demographically speaking, what Nones have in common is that they *do not* share a specific set of beliefs with others in groups of which they are members. Further, Nones tend to see their rejection of commonly held beliefs and practices as a core element of their identification as Nones.[20]

This may seem like so much wonky sociological hairsplitting, but it's a distinction with a meaningful difference. The population of Nones in the United States can be categorized according to gender, race, ethnicity, age, educational level, geographic location, and other personal characteristics. But they do not form a cohesive social or ideological group, as do Buddhists, Jews, Catholics, or Protestants, despite the fact that these, too, can be categorized in terms of the same characteristics.

It's different with Somes. The religiously affiliated, by definition, join religious groups, and membership in itself functions as an additional demographic characteristic. Like Nones, the affiliated are male and female, young and old, gay and straight, black and white. But they are also Buddhist, Catholic, Episcopalian, Evangelical, Hindu, Jewish, Lutheran, Presbyterian, and so on, and they tend to hang out at least periodically with people who identify religiously in the same way. Not so with Nones. However much academic researchers and mainstream media writers may like to corral them into group-like classifications, the unaffiliated resist such herding not only as a matter of demographic correctness but also as a matter of spiritual identity and practice. Embracing the very noneness of Nones is critical for those attempting to understand the spiritual lives of the unaffiliated and an important starting point for understanding how American religion and spirituality are changing in general.

It was the compulsion to group and label people who are not members of a traditional institutional religion that so exasperated Dmitri Kraznos, a 20-year-old college student in Ohio. Dmitri's parents immigrated to the United States from Russia when he was only two. He has no direct memory of the dramatic religious shifts that followed the breakup of the former Soviet Union in 1991, two years before he was born. But for his college professor parents, both Atheists, the "re-Christianization" of Russia was a frequent topic of conversation at home, as was the political influence of the Christian Right in America. "For people who don't believe in a god," Dmitri sighed, "they talk about god and religion all the time." The constant din of religious conversation among his parents and their friends, as well as what he experienced as insistence among his schoolmates in the Cleveland suburb where he grew up that everyone "pledge allegiance to one religion or another, or even to nothing" turned Dmitri off to any even nominal identification with religion, spirituality, or the lack thereof.

"I truly don't get why this matters so much to everyone," he said. "Why are these labels necessary? Do they really tell anyone anything important?"

It was something of a surprise, then, that he had responded to the online narrative survey I conducted through most of 2013 on the spiritual practices of the religiously unaffiliated, and that he had agreed to be interviewed about his spiritual life. A friend of his mother had mentioned the survey, which Dmitri completed "because why not?" he told me. I wondered how periodic attendance at a Friends Meeting House near his college campus, which he had reported in the survey, factored into what he presented as something of a strident None perspective.

"For one thing," he laughed, "the Quakers are quiet."

Dmitri had attended the Friends meeting, along with a few other students, as part of a requirement for a freshman seminar. But, even after the course was over, he found himself drawn from time to time to what he saw as the peaceful simplicity of the gathering. He also appreciated that no one seemed interested in "making me into a Quaker." Dmitri explained,

> I don't know if all of the Quakers are like this, but these are very wel-
> coming but not in an overwhelming way. They invite you in, explain a
> little how the meeting goes, and then kind of leave you alone. It's very
> peaceful, which is good when things are very stressful with school. You
> know, I know they believe that the Holy Spirit or God or something is
> moving around the circle. I don't think about it that way, but no one has
> asked me about it either. They'll ask if they can pray for me once in a
> while, which is fine. . . . The main thing is that whatever I'm thinking or
> feeling about if there is or isn't a god or whatever, whatever I believe at
> that particular moment, doesn't define me as a human being. I'm not a
> Quaker. I'm not an Agnostic or an Atheist. I'm a None who once in a
> while goes to church and most of the time doesn't. I'm just this guy,
> Dmitri, to them. I'm pretty sure I won't do this for the rest of my life.
> I feel like they respect that.

The apparent conflict when Nones like Dmitri insist on an utter lack of identification or affiliation but also at least periodically participate in a wor-shipping community often confounds both researchers and the general pub-lic. But considered more carefully, Dmitri's relationship with the Quaker meeting nuances what is often a fairly flat reading of an often-cited data point in the 2012 "Nones on the Rise" report on the desire for affiliation among the unaffiliated. Pew researchers asked people, "Are you looking for a religion that would be right for you?" A whopping 88% of Nones indicated that they were not.[21] Dmitri would almost certainly have been among them. "People are not looking for religion. They are not seekers," Pew senior researcher Carey Funk told the *Huffington Post* when the report came out,[22] distinguishing Nones today from the Baby Boomers profiled by Wade Clark Roof in the early 1990s.[23] This is clearly true of Nones like Dmitri—he is not looking for a religious home for life. Nonetheless, it is also true that he happened upon something of value in the Friends' meeting that draws him to repeated attendance.

The many religious leaders who were alarmed by these data might be forgiven for concluding that Nones had no interest in engaging with *any* religious group in *any way*. "Yes" or "no" survey questions may well show Nones' lack of interest in settling into a *single* religious tradition for the rest of their lives. But that's not the whole story. A 2009 poll, also conducted by Pew, showed that a third of unaffiliated respondents attended a worship service, usually in a church or other house of worship, at least yearly.[24] As Dan Li, a 33-year-old None from Waimea, Hawaii, put it, "There's something about selecting one religion, one path, in the narrow way that I was brought up that seems so wrong, so unhelpful. The world is filled with wisdom. Human history is filled with wisdom. Why would I close myself off to that?" As a part of what he saw as his own "humanistic spiritual development" as a former Evangelical "brought up to judge and exclude people who didn't believe the way we believed," Dan makes a practice of attending worship services and other events in different religious groups from time to time. He explained:

> I guess I still have a lot of religion in me, you could say. It just comes out differently now. I feel comfortable in a church for the most part, or in a Buddhist temple, or whatever even if I don't exactly believe what they believe. I think it is good when people pray together and sing. All religions have something good in them, even the most small-minded of them. I like that. I like to be open to all of it.

Dan is surely not "looking for a religion that would be right" for him—at least not in the shape of formal membership in a particular church or temple. Still, his identification as a None does not include an unwillingness to participate in traditional religious services, in the way that identifying as Buddhist or Muslim suggests that a person is likely to center religious practice in the worship services of a named religious group (though the same Pew survey noted above found that more than 40% of Protestants and Catholics also attend services in other traditions).[25] Religious and spiritual identification can be seen, then, as something of a spiritual practice in itself. Identification as a None can mean that a person is entirely indifferent or even hostile to religion. But it often signals interest in participating in an expanded array of traditional and untraditional practices.

Nones by Many Other Names

Pew and other polling organizations tend to slot Nones into a few categories: Atheist, Agnostic, Nothing-in-Particular and, more recently, Spiritual-But-Not-Religious. However, people described their spiritual or religious identities through a much wider array of labels when I asked, "How would you respond to someone who asked you what your religion is?" Even these labels had a somewhat provisional, utilitarian quality to them. Interviewees would shift labels in the course of an interview, sometimes widely. "I was an Atheist back then," Megan Coleman, a 27-year-old None from Salem, Alabama, said of her early spiritual life. "But now I'd say I'm more of an Agnostic. I think I have less certainty about everything, and that applies to my spiritual life and whatever I might think about the idea of a divinity."

"I guess I'm a seeker . . . ," 46-year-old Glenda Storey said, "but I wouldn't call myself that exactly now. I really would say I'm Spiritual-But-Not-Religious, which includes seeking as part of just what you do." For both women, describing changing spiritual identification offered a lens through which their spiritual lives could be seen as more complex and dynamic features of their evolving life story.

Still others made clear that their religious identification played out strategically, relationally, and experientially. Alicia Iyers-Marks, a 42-year-old social services executive from Chicago who self-identified as an Atheist put it this way: "I joke that my take on spiritually is that I can go from stone cold Atheist to Pentecostal tingly and back again in sixty seconds." Alicia, who was raised in a conservative Evangelical household with a particularly strict and judgmental father, explained that she was actively rebellious about religion through college and graduate school. But after her father died she felt less pressure to distinguish herself spiritually from her mother and aunts. "I don't really have an argument with them," she said.

> They're over trying to influence my life choices actively. You know, they'll pray for me, I'm sure, but they don't harangue me anymore about going to church or meeting a nice Christian boy. And I've come to respect that their religion means a lot to them. It doesn't cost me anything to pray with them over a meal or to listen with real caring when an auntie tells me about how "god spoke to her" through a Bible verse. Okay, that happened for you. It doesn't happen for me when I read the Bible, but what does happen is that my listening, my acceptance,

deepens our relationship. That's spiritual for me. I'd feel okay using that word to describe it.

On other occasions, Nones seemed to be testing various labels within the interview itself, or asking for my designation based on what they had shared. "Maybe that makes me more of an Agnostic," said 19-year-old Priscilla Danford, a college student from Bloomington, Indiana, as she described her understanding of god or a higher power:

> I mean, I do think there's *something*, but I don't know what it is. I don't think anyone can be sure, you know? No one can <u>prove</u> it. And I sure don't think it matters, you know, in terms of how most of the world works—like the government or businesses. I mean, I *feel* really spiritual sometimes, and I've done yoga and other things that I think are really spiritual. But it's not part of, like, my school, or work, or anything. I mean, I don't pray or meditate while I'm shelving books in the library. So, does that mean I'm Secular instead of Spiritual? Can I be both at the same time? What would you call me?

She concluded, if tentatively:

> I really think I'm mostly just Spiritual. That's how I would describe myself if you asked. But, you know, a lot of the time it's kind of like in the background. You know, like I'm Irish, too, on my dad's side. But I'm not like at work going, "You're book's due on May 30. I'm Irish! I'm Irish!"

Those who spoke with me reported sometimes using the "None" designation as a shield against religious labeling generally. "This obsession with labeling everyone—putting me in this category and you over there—I just don't get it," Robbie Smith, a 29-year-old from Auburn, Georgia, told me. "I want to be known as who I am, by how I relate to you, by what I do in the world. Not by some designation that's meant to tell everyone everything about me and never change over time."

Still, labeling the unaffiliated has been something of a national pastime since the founding of the country. Despite rates of formal religious affiliation often well below 20% and equally limited church attendance, even during the revivals of the eighteenth and nineteenth centuries, the openly unaffiliated were judged harshly against the ideal America as a Christian nation.[26] Through the mid-twentieth century, charitable commentators referred to the unaffiliated as the "unchurched," the "unsaved," or the "churchless." More pejoratively, Nones

were called out as "publicans," "pagans," "heathens," and "infidels." The unaffiliated themselves claimed their own identifying labels, presenting themselves as
"metaphysicals," "freethinkers," and "nothingagarians."

More recently, the unaffiliated have been less likely to self-define or to be
defined by others (outside certain church circles) in relation to institutional
religion—as "un"-this, or that-"less." But Nones have nonetheless collected a
wide range of labels. Among those most often claimed by *Choosing Our Religion*
interviewees:

- Atheist: someone who does not believe in a supernatural, transcendent being
  (God or gods) or force that governs the universe.[27]
- Weak (or Soft) Agnostic: someone who has persistent doubts about the existence of a supernatural, transcendent being or force, but who is not entirely
  closed to the idea and is interested in exploring the possibility.[28]
- Strong (or Hard) Agnostic: someone who believes that it is not possible for
  anyone to know whether there is or is not a supernatural, transcendent being
  or force, and who, thus, is not particularly interested in exploring the question
  further.[29]
- Secular Humanist: someone influenced, knowingly or not, by Enlightenment
  models of humanist discourse that highlight the essential goodness of the
  human person and the application of human reason in the light of scientific
  knowledge as the root of human flourishing and mutual good in the world.
  Secular humanists may or may not believe in a supernatural, transcendent
  being, but they incline toward agnostic or deist understandings of a distant
  deity not involved in human history.
- Humanist: someone similar to the Secular Humanist, but with less interest
  in the political implications of secularity and more interest in extra-religious
  projects of human flourishing.
- Secular: someone self-described as concerned with the separation of religion
  from public life. (They are generally characterized by more conservative reli-
  gionists as atheistic in orientation, though this is not always the case.)
- Spiritual: someone who pursues some level of practice oriented toward nurturing spiritual development, deepening relationships with others, and experiencing what Charles Taylor has described as a greater sense of "fullness" in
  the context of everyday life.[30]
- Spiritual-But-Not-Religious (SBNR): someone who generally believes in
  some form of a supernatural, transcendent being or force, and who is likely to
  take up various practices from traditional religions and metaphysical teachings. Unaffiliated SBNRs are typically not interested in sustained engagement
  with institutional religious organizations, doctrine, or dogma.[31]

- Neopagan/Wiccan: someone who participates in any of a number of widely varied adaptations of ancient and postmodern traditions, generally those outside Christian and other Western religious traditions; typically polytheistic in belief, with strong influences from environmental and feminist ideologies. Neopagans of the Wiccan variety often see women and the earth as sources of enrichment, healing, and ethical practice, orienting spiritual practice around a mother goddess associated with the sacredness of the earth.[32]
- Nothing-in-Particular: someone who doesn't rule out the possibility of a supernatural, transcendent being, and may engage in various spiritual practices, but who is wary of labels and narrow classifications of religious or spiritual identity.
- All of the Above: someone who understands existential meaning-making as moving throughout life through different modes of spiritual, religious, or non-religious self-understanding with associated differences in affiliation and unaffiliation, exploration of and indifference to religion.
- None/None of the Above: someone who answers "none" or "none of the above" when asked about religious preference, affiliation, or identity. Nones may also claim other more nuanced spiritual self-descriptions outside survey contexts.

This list is hardly exhaustive of the various ways Nones describe themselves, but it represents the most common labels those who talked with me used in their self-descriptions. Such naming is hardly an insignificant gesture in the spiritual lives of Nones, any more than claiming a denominational identity marker is for Somes.

What's in a Religious or Spiritual Name?

How we are named or name ourselves personally, professionally, and politically, as well as religiously or spiritually, of course matters a great deal. "A proper name," according to Roland Barthes, "should always be carefully questioned, for the proper name is . . . the prince of signifiers; its connotations are rich, social and symbolic."[33] Acts of naming and being named are key moments in the sacred narratives of many religions. The power that the God of the Hebrew Bible confers on Adam to name the plants and animals in the Garden of Eden (Gen. 2:19–20) helps humans to understand their surroundings and their place in the newly created world. The renaming of Abram as Abraham (Gen. 17:1–14) expresses his new, covenantal relationship to God and marks the future trajectory of his lineage. Likewise, the renaming of Yathrib to al-Madinah al-Nabi (usually referred to as Medina, "the town of the Prophet") at the end of Muhammad's migration from Mecca marks the beginning of the Islamic calendar, shifting time itself to mark religious identity. Indeed, in many religions, choosing a name that expresses a close coherence between self-identity and religious identity and affiliation (or having one conferred) is a defining ritual feature, as in the Sikh Nam Karam ceremony for naming a child according to the first letter of a sacred hymn.[34]

To claim "None" as the label for one's spiritual identity is to refuse to participate in the normative system of religious identification, where labels suggest general agreement with beliefs, values, and practices that distinguish one religious institution from another. The power of religious naming extends beyond institutional designations, too. As Dmitri made clear when he asserted that "Even 'agnostic' or 'atheist' carry a lot of cultural baggage that I just don't want to take on . . .," refusing the religiously and often politically charged label of Atheist or Agnostic is no less a declaration of spiritual independence than is shedding the label "Catholic," "Mormon," or "Presbyterian."

The routine use of religious labels by pollsters, academics, journalists, religious leaders, and the population in general suggests that being religious is in some way a "natural" part of being human. Everyone has a religious marker that must be revealed, even if it's "no religion." What's more, the various labels for Nones—not least the label "*un*affiliated" itself—insist that genuine spiritual or religious identity can only be shaped and named in relation to institutional religion. Given this, labeling one's own spiritual identity as outside institutional religion is both to resist a long-standing cultural insistence on at least the pretense of religious affiliation and to identify as an outsider, an other—an "un"—within the normative religious culture.

But even new religious and spiritual self-identifications are not often idiosyncratic novelties. Rather, they emerge from wider cultural influences. Thus, very early in my research I regularly had to explain to people, including many of the unaffiliated themselves, what "None" meant in demographic and sociological terms. After the data from the 2012 "Nones on the Rise" report were popularized through mainstream media, however, people regularly presented themselves pre-labeled as Nones. For example, Julia Xavier excitedly told me that she was "relieved" that she could call herself a None now:

> I never really knew what to say to people. I'm not really an Atheist or Agnostic, but I can think along those lines at times. And I don't want to come off as all woo-woo if I talk about "spirituality." All this None stuff in the news lately has made it so much easier.

To the extent that, like Julia, few people self-identified as a "None" before October 2012, it can be argued that the various surveys and polls from Pew,

Gallup, Harris, and others that find their way into news re
commentaries do not merely tally up members of a preexistin
also can be seen as conjuring or constructing this population.
wonder to what extent the increase in Nones marked in the 2(
do with the greater familiarity people have with the terminol

Terms like "pagan" or "heathen," or even the more pastoral unc.....
"unsaved," were meant to demean, shame, or perhaps invite the unaffiliated into
institutional religious communities. But "None" carries little of the stigma once
associated with these terms. In a sense, claiming the label "None" can be seen as
a "queering" gesture, as when lesbians, gay men, bisexuals, and transgendered
people embrace heterosexist slurs such as "queer," "dyke," and "faggot."[36] "None"
seems to open up spiritual possibility, flexibility, fluidity, porousness, and variation over time for an increasing number of people.

The extent of this shift from shaming to claiming unaffiliated status was perhaps made clearest to me by the oldest interviewee in my study, Jack Bell, an
83-year-old from a suburb of Kansas City, Kansas, who emailed me after he
heard his pastor son complain about an article I'd written about controversies
surrounding the National Day of Prayer. A retired engineer with considerable
internet savvy, Jack found his way to my website, where I was just beginning to
write about my research on Nones. He contacted me to share his experience
as a "strong Agnostic"—his own self-designation—who had spent his life as a
reasonably active member of a local Free Methodist church as part of a marriage
agreement with his late wife.

"I've hidden my whole life as an unbeliever," Jack wrote. "No one but my wife
knew. Not our family or friends, not our children. That was the promise I made
to her when we married. It didn't seem such a big thing at the time. But it ate at
me over the years."

The following summer, I arranged to meet with Jack at a library near a bus-
tling suburban shopping mall in Overland Park, Kansas, for a long conversation
about his experience has a None-in-Some's-Clothing. Jack shared the story of an
unbeliever who lived on the edge of the Bible Belt for all of his life except for a
brief stint in the Air Force during the Korean War and six years at the University
of Michigan, where he had earned undergraduate and graduate degrees. When
he came back to Kansas to settle down with his high school sweetheart, raising
three children and working at a large technology company, "it felt like I was from
outer space a lot of the time," Jack said. "Everything I'd experienced in the Air
Force and everything I'd studied had confirmed what I'd long suspected growing
up: There's no way of knowing there is or isn't a god. Religion is a social club.
Church is moral finishing school."

Devoted to his wife, however—"she believed enough for both of us," he told
me—he kept mum about his own beliefs and attended church with her and their

enough to keep us off the radar" of neighbors who might be inclined to gossip about too many absences. He continued:

> I never full-out lied about my beliefs if someone asked. I just didn't talk
> about it at all. I'd say, "Oh, Marilyn is the theologian in our household,"
> and change the subject. In church, I never sang the hymns; never prayed
> along with the service. I just sat and stood when I was supposed to, and
> maybe nodded a little during the sermon. That wasn't such a big deal,
> especially for men in those days.

This social performance of conventional religious belief, however, was deeply troubling to Jack, especially in the context of his relationships with his children. He shared his story with apparent heaviness, sighing often, looking down at his clasped hands, gazing out the window for short spells, and shaking his head to punctuate what he saw as his own moral failures in light of the religious farce he had lived out within his family and community:

> I also never talked to my kids about any of it—that there are other ways
> of thinking about things. There are options. And it's not just, you're
> a Christian or you're going to hell. I hate to think that's what they'd
> think about me if they knew who I really am. I hate that basically, I lied
> to them my whole life. Maybe I did it for what were good reasons at
> the time, but, still, you want your own kids to know who you are, what
> you believe in. So, I'm trying to figure out how to talk about it now. It
> took me a longer time to get to this place than maybe a younger person.
> When I came up, you went to church or you had the good sense to say
> you meant to. And it mattered to my wife, on a social level, sure, but also
> spiritually. I know it comforted her, and I know she was a true believer
> to the end. But I always questioned. I always doubted. I never really
> believed. Now I'm at the end of my life, and I can finally talk about that...
> a little.

For Jack, the opportunity to claim "Strong Agnostic" allowed him to begin—at least within the context of our conversation—to think of different ways of relating to others in his life. "I think I ought to at least write this all down for them," he told me at the end of the interview. A few weeks later, Jack emailed me to report that he had stopped attending church with his son's family. "I told them it wasn't what I needed right now," he wrote, "which they took to mean I am still grieving. But I'll get out more of the true reason a little bit at a time."

Beyond the refusal of the kinds of social constraints on authentic religious identification illustrated by Jack's story, interview subjects often expressed offense at being labeled by others not only because the label wasn't correct. Many of the Nones who talked with me refused to be set within religious, political, and academic categories that could allow them to be used as weapons in religiously infused culture wars or to be in any way pegged within a particular religious, ideological, political, social, or other fixed worldview. For many interviewees, claiming the status of "None" allowed them to strategically obscure or reveal their religious perspectives and practices within the context of different relationships and social settings.

"I grew up in a really, really liberal household," said Lance Everett, a 38-year-old lawyer from Chicago who described himself as a None. "We went to a really, really liberal Episcopal church where everybody was pretty much on the same page about gay marriage and legal abortion, or the right for women to be priests, and all that. And everyone was really against Pat Robertson, and Rick Warren, and those types." He continued,

> But when I got to college and grad school, people were all over the map with their views. It's not like I didn't want to talk with them about our differences over gay marriage or something. I just got tired of the religion thing being the center of that. It would always come down to, "Well, it just goes against my faith," on the one hand, or "Jesus loves everybody, no exceptions," on the other. I'd be like, "hey, could we talk about this at the level of public policy?" . . . I wouldn't say I lost my religion then exactly. I have kids, so, you know, you kind of find yourself praying whether you want to or not. And my wife goes to a Lutheran church, so sometimes I go with her. But I did give up any and all religious labels. I just think they make things worse, make it harder to engage human being to human being.

Likewise, what interviewees often seemed to be after in their spiritual self-description was not so much a sense of demographic precision, but rather a way of signaling a process of spiritual growth and change across the course of their lives. Catherine Neville, a 49-year-old None from Bellevue, Washington, described her spiritual journey in this way:

> I like to think I've grown spiritually over the years. Sometimes I look at some of the things I used to be into—"The Angel Years" when I was in my twenties, for instance, or the Native American drumming—and I can't imagine putting my energy into that today. But at the time, it meant something. It helped me, I guess, to feel that I was surrounded by all these "angels." I learned some things, including that believing in angels is like believing in magic fairies. You know, I was such a "New

Ager." I was into that for sure. . . . And then I moved on. I tried different things—Twelve-Step groups, therapeutic touch, meditation. I was
an Episcopalian, sort of, for a couple years. Now I practice yoga and
I meditate regularly. I'm really a None. Or, maybe an All-of-the-Above.
I guess None is what's working now. But parts of all of the rest are still
there one way or another. If I need them, if they make sense, they're
there for me.

The self-designations claimed by the unaffiliated, including the term "None"
itself, press against descriptors that seek to fix them categorically in relation to
more religiously normative, institutionally affiliated people. Self-naming also
contests the idea of a single religious identity as an unchanging element of the
self that can be tracked and measured over time. Nones, like their forebear Walt
Whitman, do indeed contradict themselves, but not out of the sort of narcissistic
fickleness often called out by their critics. They may not "contain multitudes,"
spiritually speaking, but their lives seem to contain at various times both more
and less than can be contained in one lifelong spiritual or religious designation.

In this, they are not entirely different from the affiliated. No few Somes also
vary their spiritual or religious self-designation in different social settings. With
the affiliated, however, more provisional, experimental, or less fixed identity
markers are often used as qualifiers to an affiliational identity that is assumed to
be stable over time and to fairly represent the range of beliefs and actions that
make up their spirituality. Somes, it seems, start with institutional affiliation as
an identity base, then progressively temper problematic elements by adding
resources from other spiritual traditions or from personal experience to express
what they see as a more authentic, often hyphenated religious identity. "I'm
Catholic, but I don't go to church much. I don't believe all the teachings," one
of my undergraduates told me. "I'm really more spiritual. I find God in lots of
different places other than church. So, I'm kind of a Cultural Catholic, because
I was raised that way, but I'm really Spiritual when you get down to it." Likewise,
a colleague reported, "I'm a classic Jew-Bu. The Buddhist practice allows me to
let go of the Jewish guilt and neuroses so I can focus more on the beauty of my
natal tradition. Buddhism is like a spiritual palate cleanser for me. I couldn't be
a good Jew without it."

Complicating the picture further, many people who describe themselves
as Nones have what would be seen as somewhat conventional approaches to
religion and spirituality that play out extensively in relationship to traditional
institutional religion. Anna Solomon, for instance, a 27-year-old, self-described
Atheist living near Jamestown, New York, was raised as a moderately observant
Conservative Jew. "We kept kosher at home," she told me, "but the world outside
was literally our oyster!" Anna reported that she was never a strong believer in

Judaism as a religion, but the culture of the Jews and their history of persecution and triumph fascinated her. She studied religion as an undergraduate, then completed a master's degree in Jewish studies, focusing on the development of identity among diaspora Jews. For her thesis, she did field research at a number of synagogues outside areas with large Jewish populations. She met her husband at a Reform synagogue that was one of her research sites.

"It was funny," she said, "he was exactly like me in not being much interested in the religion part—and yet where did we meet? In a synagogue! We both believe it's important to engage the culture, to do our part to keep the history alive. But, you know, all the rules and the biblical teachings, it's just not for us."

Nonetheless, Anna, who was eight months pregnant when I first interviewed her, was certain that she and her husband would raise their soon-to-be-born daughter as a Jew. I wondered what that meant, given her self-identification as an Atheist and her indifference to Jewish practice.

"You really only get the culture if you're in a synagogue, with a community— especially out here," she said, highlighting the scarcity of Jews in rural Western New York. "So, we'll join one."

"And then you'll be affiliated?" I asked. Anna assured me,

> We're not going to change our beliefs. We're not going to lie to our kid.
> But we want her to be around other Jews, to be around Jewishness. You
> know, when she visits with her grandparents or plays with her cousins,
> we want her to understand that this is a basic thing that makes us a fam-
> ily. It connects us. We want her to have that experience as a part of who
> she is no matter what she ends up believing or not believing. In this part
> of the world, that's going to happen at a synagogue or it's not going to
> happen. But I'll still be an Atheist. That won't change.

For Zachary Thomas, a 19-year-old college student from Marietta, Georgia, identifying as a None rather than as a Christian had nothing to do with rejecting the teachings of Jesus Christ. For Zachary, whom I met near Mission, Kansas, at a conference for worship leaders, being a None allowed him to keep a strategic distance from institutional Evangelical Christianity and many of the conservative ideologies with which he had grown to disagree. "I try to follow Jesus," he told me. "It's that simple. And I guess that hard. I don't want someone to see me as self-righteous or judgmental. I don't want them to assume I hate gays or think there were dinosaurs on Noah's ark. And I mean that for people in churches as much—maybe more—than I do for people I just meet on the street or whatever."

Zachary worked part-time as a youth leader at an Evangelical mega-church. When I asked if he was a member of that church, he assured me that he was not. "I don't belong to any church. I won't," he said. "I just don't believe that's what Jesus wanted—these institutions, these corporations." He explained that, because he was still in college, there was little pressure on him to formally join or pledge financially. "They know what they pay me," he laughed, "so they know I'm broke." He continued,

> It's not about that, though. I'm not hostile to churches, really. And I do feel a call to ministry. But, when I read the gospels, I just don't see that Jesus was about, you know, let's raise $10,000 so we can get a new sound system for the youth auditorium. I'll give my money, when I have it, where I see that it's helping "the least of these."[37] But I'm not interested in a program with, you know, an executive director and a staff of twenty people. I'll buy a homeless guy a sandwich, you know. I'll mow an old lady's yard. I want to help people who really need help. I don't know that, for me or most people my age, "Christian" means that anymore. For me, saying I'm a Jesus Follower or a None means I get to live as best I can as a disciple of Jesus without taking on all the other stuff that pushes people away from his gospel.

As I was working on this project, the perspective shared by Zachary came into public view when the front man for the popular band Mumford & Sons, 27-year-old Marcus Mumford, shocked the Evangelical world by coming out as something of a post-Evangelical None. Mumford is the son of Eleanor and John Mumford, leaders of the emergent, evangelical Vineyard church in the United Kingdom.[38] The group's music is standard fare among hipster Evangelicals and many other Christians across a wider ideological spectrum. Yet in a *Rolling Stone* interview, Mumford said, "I don't really like that word [Christian] . . . I think the word just conjures up all these religious images that I don't really like. I have my personal views about the person of Jesus and who he was. Like, you ask a Muslim and they'll say, 'Jesus was awesome'—they're not Christians, but they still love Jesus. I've kind of separated myself from the culture of Christianity."[39]

Narrating the Unaffiliated Self

What we see in all of this is that religious and spiritual identity is by no means an uncomplicated concept. Indeed, scholars routinely debate what we mean when we're talking about "identity" in any sense. Is it primarily a *social category*, indicating the groups to which a person belongs and suggesting cultural characteristics assumed to belong to social groups? Or is it a *personal characteristic*, referring to inherent or developed traits in individuals? Is identity something that develops more or less from the inside out through personal maturation and self-reflection? Or is it something conferred upon a person from the outside in? Is identity a reasonably fixed phenomenon, or does it change and develop across a lifetime? Can elements of identity be chosen by a person or discarded if they no longer seem to fit? In recent years we've seen the stakes at play as these questions are explored in the public debate over LGBT rights, which often centers on whether a person chooses to be lesbian, gay, bisexual, transgender, or heterosexual, or if she is, as the Lady Gaga song goes, "born this way."

It probably goes without saying that the answers to these questions vary widely, depending on who's doing the answering. But the LGBT rights experience in America has tended to solidify the public perception that identity is primarily personal and essential, emerging from the individual as a set of more or less fixed characteristics that don't change much after adulthood. To a significant degree, the common understanding derives from Erik Erikson's notion, developed in the 1950s, of "identity" as

> ... a unique unification of what is *irreversibly given*—that is, body type and temperament, giftedness and vulnerability, infantile models and acquired ideals with the *open choices* provided in available roles, occupational possibilities, values offered, mentors met, friendships made, and first sexual encounters.[40]

It is from Erikson that we get the idea of an "identity crisis." The idea that forces outside the self that tell us who we *should be* might come into conflict with who we *really are* has shaped popular notions of "identity" as something that authentically expresses "what is irreversibly given" in a person. But Erikson saw identity as tied to complex social relationships that contributed to a process of conscious and unconscious "being and becoming" throughout life, and scholars have continued to see identity as a much more complex entanglement of the social and the personal, of predispositions and choices, of relatively fixed characteristics and more dynamic features of the self.

In recent decades, scholars have tended to focus less on what identity is or is not, and more on how individuals and the groups with which they interact develop, claim, contest, and otherwise use identity to live what they come to think of as more or less "good" or "meaningful" lives.[41] In this view, identity is neither a given nor a choice, but rather a process that continues throughout a lifetime, sometimes changing, sometimes not so much. Many scholars see this process as primarily discursive, or narrative—as a story of the self that unfolds over time, influencing the practice of everyday life. This narrative understanding of identity has important implications for how we understand religious or spiritual identity among Nones and Somes.

Who we understand ourselves to be as religious or spiritual persons has most often been expressed in relation to the religious institutions with which we were affiliated. It is the enduring correlation between institutional affiliation and religious identity that prompts the many "un" and "less" descriptions of Nones discussed previously. Indeed, many more conventionally religious people have expressed confusion and dismay to me over the "None" designation. One minister insisted vehemently on my Facebook wall, "They're not *nothing*! When you call someone 'none,' you're saying they're nothing." What she seemed unable to get past was the idea that Nones choose, to the extent possible within a culture steeped in religious symbols, rituals, and labels, not to identify their spirituality through institutional religious designations. This often includes even less pejorative labels like "seeker" or "Spiritual-But-Not-Religious." Claiming the label "None" does not mean that a person sees herself as "nothing" spiritually, but that she elects not to describe her spirituality either in institutional religious terms or fraught categories like Atheist or Agnostic. "I'm none of *that*," she is saying, even when much of "that" may factor into her own spirituality and the story it allows her to tell about who she is in the world.

Such stories are central to the development of personal identity, social identity, and a coherent understanding of life, including its spiritual and religious nuances and meanings. According to philosopher Paul Ricoeur, we are the stories we tell about ourselves in the ever changing, complexly networked context of our lives. The development of identity though narrative, Ricoeur argues, means that who we are and how we live our lives are ultimately projects of imaginative self-transformation that we narrate over time. He explains,

> Narrative identity is not a stable or seamless identity. . . . Just as it is possible to compose several plots on the subject of the same incidents . . . so it is always possible to weave different, even opposed, plots about our lives. . . . In this sense, narrative identity continues to make and unmake itself. . . .[42]

Ricoeur describes two elements of the identity narrative: a *stable self* made up of those parts of our stories that stay much the same over time—our birthdays, genders, personal and family names, and so on—and a more malleable, *reflexive identity* that, like musical notes on the lines of the staff, hum, trill, and harmonize with others to create an ongoing song of the self. Religious affiliation has for a very long time been understood to be the baseline of the more static, stable self-identity, but it is more and more just one part in a grand self-identity opera with many different spiritual and religious variations.[43]

The sense we have of "being ourselves" in changing situations over time depends on the degree to which the diverse elements that form the identity can be harmonized with the more fixed elements of the self. When people cannot easily carry elements of religious experience into other aspects of their lives, there is less narrative coherence—the story stops making sense. If the values, symbols, and rituals found in a religion seem not to fit into everyday life, the stability of religious identities can be undermined. If, for instance, your religion teaches that certain kinds of people are to be avoided, but it turns out that you work with some of those people and they seem perfectly lovely, it becomes harder to include religious teachings and practices in the story of the self in much of your life. Religion may be bracketed out as something that happens only in a specific religious setting, at specific times, and only with people from that religious group. Or, it may come to be understood as a cultural practice more than a spiritual one. In any case, it is often going to become a less significant part of the story of the self-as-spiritual. For many people, including the religiously affiliated, the institutional religious storyline largely goes away.

The reverse is true as well. When other elements of personal identity cannot be integrated into religious narratives, as when the leadership and decision-making capabilities that women exercise every day at work and at home are diminished, or the healthy relationships of LGBT people are demeaned in religious contexts, identity coherence is difficult to sustain. To make sense of ourselves, that is, the narrative must translate with relative fluency from home, to work, to the yoga studio, to weekend activities with friends and family, and, if institutional religion is to be an integral part of the story, to church, mosque, or synagogue. It is this need for narrative coherence across all of the contexts and relationships in our lives that prompts many scholars to argue that the feelings we have of "being authentic" aren't entirely about discovering and revealing unchanging truths about our unique selves. Rather, authenticity is about the degree to which we understand and can express to others how we change while remaining the same across the different stages of our lives, within various relationships, and in the diverse settings of everyday experience.

The sociologist Anthony Giddens explains it in this way: "A person's identity is not to be found in behaviour, nor—important though this is—in the reactions of others, but in the capacity to *keep a particular narrative going.*"[44] Where the narrative of self cannot be sustained, as when Nones like Jack feel uncomfortable expressing religious difference or doubt, there can be a profound sense of risk to relationships, social status, psychological and physical safety, and so on. Whether or not these inconsistencies provoke a full identity crisis, there is at the very least what many Nones experienced as an uncomfortable and often painful spiritual inauthenticity. As Kenda Jackson, a 27-year-old Agnostic from Arlington, Texas, put it, "I live in the Bible Belt in close proximity to my very religious family, and I probably spend 90% of the day pretending to be a Christian." Similarly, Railey Haines, a 29-year-old Humanist living in Columbia, South Carolina, told me,

"I edit myself a lot around here. It's just easier that way." That kind of "pretending" or "editing" is obviously unpleasant; it can also undermine the development of a coherence story of self.

The well-meaning efforts of many religious groups to engage the unaffiliated may thus fall flat because they invite the kind of "self-editing" that many Nones hope to avoid. For instance, a number of churches have attempted to shift toward gestures of unconditional belonging in their worship and away from affirmations of creedal beliefs and seemingly judgmental assessments of behavior. Some progressive Protestant Christian traditions have "open communion" rituals in which the unbaptized or those with no Christian background at all are welcomed to receive the bread and wine offered in remembrance of the final meal shared by Jesus and his disciples.[45] These efforts may be perceived by some Nones as gracious and hospitable. But others are put off by what can easily be read as pressure to participate in a practice that is incoherent within a personal narrative that does not include a particular church, its practices, or theologies.

This was the experience of Eric Allemande, a 28-year-old graduate student originally from Lansing, Michigan. Eric told me of a Sunday when he indulged his partner by attending an Episcopal church near their Berkeley, California, campus. During the service Eric carried much of his anxiety-provoking Evangelical background into his understanding of what "communion" might mean:

> The whole thing seemed very Catholic to me, and, you know, I was brought up that those people weren't even Christian. But I knew that the Episcopals [sic] were okay with gays, and my boyfriend told me that one of the priests was a lesbian. And it was important to him, so I went. But when the whole communion part came up, it really freaked me out. Kind of in two ways. First, it seemed so, you know, cannibalistic. But also, because I knew I was reacting as an Evangelical, and I didn't know how to stop that in my head.

The experience got worse when an enthusiastic usher pressed Eric to join everyone in the small congregation, who had gathered around the altar for the Eucharist:

> He was so nice, really. "You're welcome to join us. Everybody's welcome," he said, and he put his hand on my arm to urge me up there. I kind of said "no thank you" at first, and he was a little insistent. He said "It's really okay" or something. I just started crying. I mean I didn't even know this guy. He had no idea who I was or what my story is. It was a mess. My boyfriend came down when he saw. He was kind of mortified. I just kept thinking, "What am I doing here? This is so not

me." You know, my boyfriend keeps telling me how nice everyone is and how concerned they are about me. But at least now he does the whole church thing on his own and I can take the dogs to the park or walk in the hills—either of which feel more spiritual to me anyhow.

Obviously, there were a number of narrative clashes in Eric's experience that made for a spiritually unsettling experience. Neither his Evangelical religious upbringing nor his claim of unaffiliation as an adult made spiritual sense in the context of the Episcopal service. Through the fervor of the usher, a Eucharistic ritual adapted with the aim of enhancing a sense of belonging turned out to further alienate Eric from what was an important element in his partner's spirituality that he wanted to support. Walking the dogs or enjoying nature did not present the identity incoherence that resulted in feelings of risk and insecurity for Eric.

Outside institutional religious settings, many Nones are much more easily able to translate their unaffiliated spiritualities into different social contexts. For Gretchen Drew, a 52-year-old Spiritual-But-Not-Religious and Agnostic None from Mount Lebanon, Pennsylvania, focusing on experiences of gratitude, insight, and inspiration allows her to carry her spirituality into relationships without referring to beliefs or religious rituals. "I'm not a theist," she explained, "but I don't really talk about myself in that way with my family or with most of my friends." She made clear,

> I'm not hiding out. People in my life know I don't go to church or any-thing. It's more that I'm not really fixated on defining myself in terms of particular beliefs or labels that I think get in the way a lot of the time. When I talk about experiences—just everyday things—I don't know, these moments of insight, or gratitude, or connection that come up anywhere—at the grocery store, or taking a walk, even at work. You know, when someone says "I don't know how I came up with this idea but . . ."—that's when it's happening, too, I think—that kind of inspiration that you share with someone. I count that as "spiritual," and I can talk about that with most people.

Benjamin Altos, a 44-year-old from Danbury, Connecticut, who described himself as "a Spiritual Agnostic," actively worked at rearticulating his spiritual self-understanding when his twin daughters were born. Raised as a Methodist, he had stopped attending church when he went to college. When we met over coffee, Benjamin told me that through most of his adult life he been in church only for funerals and for weddings (including his own wedding, in a Roman Catholic church–his wife's religious background).

"Here's how not a part of our lives religion was," he explained, "we literally didn't talk about it once in the four years between our wedding and the week before the girls were born." That week, anxious and excited about the care of their new family, Benjamin said,

> My wife is, like, nuts over, "Should we baptize the babies? Should we not baptize them?" I mean we're terrible, right? We hadn't given it a thought. And that tells you something, right? But we go through all the "What will people say?" crap for a while, and the "How will they get their morals?" stuff anyway. "What will we tell them about Christmas?" You know, it went on and on. You can imagine.

I could. Eventually, however, Benjamin and his wife decided to defer the decision until well after the birth of their daughters, once the couple was settled into something of a manageable routine with the new babies. It was in the course of that adjustment period, Benjamin reported, that he came to understand, "I'm spiritual enough. We're all spiritual enough right here." He continued,

> For feedings, you know, I'd hold one of the girls and Kate would feed the other one. We'd all just be in those rocking chairs, and it would smell all milky and sweet. You know, wow! You get that this is everything. This is perfect. There's no sin to wash off these girls. And just when I'm thinking that—that very moment—Kate says, "I don't think we need to baptize them." And we were both, like, yeah, we're just not doing the whole religion thing, and we just worked it out from there.

"Working it out" involved a number of intricacies, given that both Benjamin's family and his wife's included people (not least their parents) who had expected that the couple would join a church after they had kids. Benjamin and Kate put some time into how they wanted to support their daughters' development as moral people. But their claim of a spiritual significance in everyday experiences like feeding the new babies or enjoying time with family generally, without need of formal religious validation, is common among Nones.

The Four Fs of Contemporary Spirituality

The role of the everyday in spiritual identity revealed itself very early in my research. I began with a test survey on practices that people found spiritually meaningful. I was trying both to get a handle on basic issues in American spirituality and to develop greater fluency with the demographic research. The test survey was meant to take the spiritual pulse of what I hoped would turn out to be a couple hundred people and to help me to shape robust questions for interviews.

The survey drew from my experience teaching classes on spirituality in light of studies that tracked practices such as "attending worship," "studying scripture," and "praying" along with "belief in God or a Higher Power" as indicators of the level of religiosity in the United States. When I asked students to name activities that were "spiritually meaningful" to them, even seminarians and other graduate students in religion *never* included things like Bible study or going to church. Prayer did sometimes appear (eventually), but it was clear that the standard affiliation- and belief-based orientation in the study of religion in the United States obscures diverse and rich spiritualities that unfold primarily in everyday life, largely avoiding the church or synagogue down the road. My initial survey was an attempt to get a better sense of what people really did see as the most important activities, ideas, and influences in their spiritual lives.

When I contacted 20 friends and colleagues and asked them to share my test survey with 10 or 12 contacts unknown to me, I was surprised at the volume of the response. The survey was completed by more than a thousand Somes and Nones over a weekend.[46] Respondents ranked "enjoying time with family," "enjoying time with pets or other animals," "enjoying time with friends," and "preparing or sharing food" as among the most "spiritually meaningful practices" in an inventory that also included the conventionally measured practices of "attending worship," "studying sacred texts," and "praying" (see Table 1.3).

Table 1.3 **The Four Fs of Contemporary Spirituality**

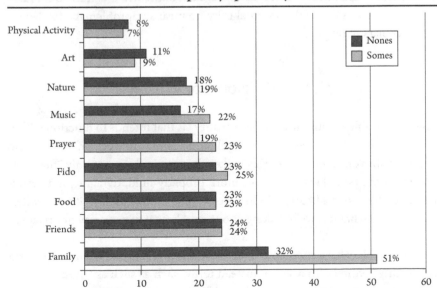

Among conventional religious practices, only prayer made it to the top of the list, coming in at number five behind what I have come to call "The Four Fs of Contemporary American Spirituality": Family, Fido, Friends, and Food. At the bottom of the ranking were those things most measured by pollsters: "attending worship" and "studying sacred scriptures." Significantly, this ranking was consistent whether respondents identified as religiously affiliated or not.

The test survey made it clear that everyday experiences are the core resources of spiritual narratives, even for those affiliated with traditional religious institutions. The sense Benjamin had while he and his wife were feeding their daughters that "[t]his is everything" is largely bracketed out of institutional religious practice or is narrowly contained within initiation rituals like a baptism or a bris. Quotidian experience is often segregated structurally as infants, children, teens, young adults, parents, and older adults are separated for distinct practices of formation, worship, and service. Brittney Samuels, a 54-year-old former Lutheran from Omaha, Nebraska, who now identifies as a Humanist, put it this way: "I treasure the relationships in my life—with my husband, my kids, my friends, our pets. When we went to church regularly, I was mostly cut off from that. The kids went to Sunday school, my husband was in the choir. I had no real friends there. Now, Sundays are precious time for me when I can really connect with everyone I love." Church in this case acted as a barrier to relationship and actually diminished the sense of the spiritual in Brittney's life.

The experience of the spiritual in everyday life feels more authentic for many Nones (and, remembering Nancy Ammerman's research, also no few Somes). This routine experience of the spiritual tends to sharpen the distinction between "religion" and "spirituality" that is now prevalent in the wider culture. But bracketing the religious out of the spiritual is by no means unproblematic for Nones or for scholars of religion.

Spiritual, Religious, "or Whatever"

One basic problem with the term "spirituality" is that it tends to function within an intermediate space between "the religious" and "the secular." But it also inhabits both zones separately. This makes the terminology not only "fuzzy," as one group of researchers put it, but more properly fluid, dynamic, indeterminate, and often contradictory.[47] When we talk about "spirituality," it's difficult to know exactly what it is we're talking about, and how it may or may not relate to "religion."

Some scholars have attempted to get past this fuzziness by avoiding the term "spirituality" entirely. They adopt instead terms such as such as "lived religion," "everyday religion," or the more awkward "religion as lived"[48] to describe "how particular people, in particular places and times, live in, with, though, and against the religious idioms available to them in culture. . ."[49] Lived religion is distinguished from the practices of "official religion" that take place under the authority of formal religious leaders in officially designated religious spaces and times with authorized rituals, symbols, and doctrines. This study of lived religion has enriched our understanding of how ordinary people engage questions of meaning and value, deepen their self-understanding in relation to others, cope with suffering and loss, ritualize life transitions and other moments of existential significance, frame their ethical commitments and actions, and otherwise engage in practices that have not, until quite recently, been the focus of either religious studies scholars or confessional theologians.

But calling these everyday phenomena "lived religion" can also seem like a strategy for academics to avoid being tainted by characterizations of "spirituality" as inherently irrational, solipsistic, syncretistic, materialistic, consumeristic, and, very often, feminine. Scholars of lived religion, that is, stake a claim in the traditional fields of "religion" or "religious studies," signaling their intellectual robustness, doctrinal precision, and masculinized authority.[50] I would argue, however, that it is important to distinguish "spirituality" from "religion" in all of its uses (ecclesial, academic, political) precisely because this is how the ordinary people of interest to scholars of "lived religion" most often describe their experience and how they understand themselves.[51] Whatever else spirituality may be in America today, it is for most people *not religion*—official, lived, or otherwise.

In this light, the history of the two terms is no mere "pothole," as one recent essay put it,[52] in the discussion of their current usage. Words are haunted in the present by the past we imagine for them.[53] For Nones, "religion" carries historical, ideological, and political baggage that is imagined as having traveled into contemporary life like a grumpy, argumentative uncle from the old country—stilted language, silly costumes, dated music, and an assumed (but by now largely evacuated) authority in tow. Freighted with a troubled past and an often problematic present, "religion" seems irredeemable as an institutional structure, concept, history, and terminology to the majority of Nones who talked with me.[54]

Many Nones trotted out standard complaints, such as religion being responsible for more suffering, war, and death in the world than any other force. Most noted the litany of sins associated with religious leaders: hypocrisy, greed, judgmentalism, sexual abuse, sexism, homophobia, anti-scientific ignorance, and so on. But most, like the majority of the unaffiliated represented in the "Nones on the Rise" survey, also acknowledged the contributions of religious groups, or at least religious individuals working together, in addressing issues like poverty, hunger, and homelessness.[55] Often "religion" failed for Nones not only because it was seen as dull, formulaic, rule-bound, or corrupt, but also because it tended to overwrite self-identity in ways that seemed to compromise personal integrity and authenticity. Where "religion" seemed to make individuals passive objects within a rigidly unchangeable structure, "spirituality" allowed for creativity, flexibility, and change by individuals situated as active agents in their own lives. Hugo Carmen, a 33-year-old Agnostic from Miami, Florida, who sometimes stops to pray at a local Catholic church, described the problem this way:

> So, if I tell you I'm "religious," or if I say I am "Catholic," you will already have all these preconceived notions of what I believe and what I do. But I don't believe all that stuff. I mean, some of it I do, but a lot of it—most of what you think a quote-unquote "Catholic" or a "religious person" would believe—I just don't. And I don't do all that stuff either. You know, sometimes I go into the church, I don't know, because I feel like it. Because it seems like that's what I need to do right then. It's more of the aesthetics of the experiences I get from the church I like in my neighborhood. It's quiet and usually cool inside. You can hear the kids playing in the schoolyard sometimes.

A visual artist by profession, Hugo connects his experience in the church, at least in part, to a wider and more primary segment of his life and identity:

> For an artist, this kind of space—the light, the sounds, the smells, you know, just the experience of sitting quietly there for twenty or thirty minutes, maybe lighting a couple candles—is very provocative for me. It can inspire me. I mean, that's not everything. You know, I don't go there to quote-unquote "get inspired." It's spiritually important to me in other ways, too. But, you know, if I tell you I'm Catholic, you're going think about me worshipping the pope or whatever. You're going to make me into whatever your version of "a Catholic" is, good or bad. You're not going to know anything about who I really am as a person and why a guy like me is lighting candles in a Catholic church on a Tuesday afternoon.

The church Hugo sometimes visits can be woven into his identity narrative as an artist, but religious affiliation as a Catholic (even if that were consistent with his beliefs) would tend to overwrite a more complex story in which the artistic and the spiritual intersect, diverge, blend, complement, and contradict one another. Where Catholic or another affiliational identity might at one time have offered a sense of security by signaling commonalities with others who claim the same identity, for Nones like Hugo, the use of religious designations in the construction and presentation of identity is destabilizing. They seem to misrepresent the self and thereby inhibit the development of trust, intimacy, and other positive qualities in relationships with others.

But "spirituality" is not entirely free of the problems Nones have with the word "religion." In addition to its historical associations with institutional religions, in recent decades "spirituality" has accrued some connotations of its own that rankle with many Nones. Like the construction of "religion," the genealogy of "spirituality" is also primarily Christian and Western.[56] In the early stages of Pauline Christianity, "spirituality" was mainly understood as movement of the Holy Spirit of God, the *Spiritus Dei*. In relatively short order, however, "spirituality" took on an institutionalized meaning referring to "ecclesiastical jurisdiction or persons executing such jurisdiction" as "*spiritualitas* or 'lords spiritual'" as well as property under the control of said lords.[57] Thus, when the troublesome late medieval English lay mystic Margery Kempe (c. 1373–1441) boasted that she was protected by "friends in the spirituality," she was appealing to this institutional authority.[58]

At the same time—and here a self-styled lay "religious" like Kempe is an important pre-Reformation marker—as the Christian Church was perhaps at the fullest expression of the kinds of institutionalized control, conformity, and repression that turn many Nones away from religion today, the meaning of "spirituality" began to go rogue. Against the idealized model of enclosed mystics like Julian of Norwich, Kempe is known for her insistence on speaking of scripture in public, the chaste marriage she negotiated with her husband, her adoption of the white clothes of the vowed religious virgin (this despite having borne 14 children), her pilgrimages through England and to the Holy Land, her public weeping and keening over the suffering of Christ, and her rebuke of moral error among clergy and lay alike. These practices begin to fray the very institutional "spiritual" authority to which she appeals and expand it into the domain of the personal, the experiential, the everyday.[59] By the time, after the Protestant Reformation, that the Roman Catholic church was cracking down on the likes of the French quietist mystic Madame Guyon (1648–1717) for heterodox approaches to prayer centered on clerically unmediated union with God,[60] "spirituality" had flown the institutional religious coop, and would in relatively short order become "a subset of a broader category that is neither confined to nor defined by Christianity or even by religion."[61] Since the seventeenth century, "spirituality" has been shadowed by the specter of its Christian past. Nonetheless, it has had a certain durability in American culture in connoting a range of extra-institutional, experiential, experimental, eclectic, and quotidian activities, ideas, and dispositions that include understandings of "the spirit" as a divine force or being, as well as those that attempt to avoid religious references entirely.

Given this more expansive understanding of "spirituality," a number of Atheists, Humanists, Secularists, and stronger Agnostics I interviewed expressed little discomfort using the word in the context of their own stories. Caitlin Withers, a 21-year-old university student and self-described "Spiritual Humanist" from Thornton, Colorado, explained it this way:

> "Spiritual" or "spirituality" can be religious, but it doesn't have to be. It isn't for me. It's about the human spirit, the spirit of nature—the thing that makes us alive. You don't have to believe in god to understand that there's something that animates us, something that makes the wind blow, and makes plants grow. Some people think of that, I guess, as a kind of energy, which it certainly is. I'm not all that metaphysical about it. But I do think that there are things you can do—mindfulness meditation is something that I do, for example—that can, I don't know, focus that spirit—make it function better. And there are ways that you can help to better the human spirit in general, like when we do after-school tutoring with at-risk kids. That's contributing to the whole human spirit, to improving it for humanity. That's not a god thing for me. It's a human thing.

That said, more than half of the people I interviewed also used the placeholder "or whatever" along with their use of the terms "spiritual" or "spirituality."[62] "I don't think of myself as religious at all," said Kimberley Arthur, a 22-year-old Secular Humanist from Phoenix, Arizona. "I'd say I'm more spiritual, or whatever."

Linguists describe filler words and phrases like "or whatever" as "discourse markers" or "vague category identifiers." They tend to project a thought not yet entirely known or understood, which is suggested by the surrounding words but not fully expressed by them. Such phrases "can play a strategic role in an unfolding utterance" that can be developed over time in conversation with others.[63] These utterances "provide a way for the speaker to indicate that the thought she has in mind is more complex than is being expressed and to appeal to the listener to construct the relevant members of the evoked set."[64] "Spirituality, or whatever" is thus not necessarily a dismissive gesture indicating that the words used do not matter.[65] The phrase "or whatever" can signal a speaker's inarticulateness, but it can also indicate that the available terminology is inadequate to the many thoughts the speaker has about a particular concept or concern.

When I asked Kimberley what she meant by "or whatever," she referred to what for her was the troubling Christian genealogy of the word "spiritual" as well as the negative connotations it can carry (superficial, uncommitted, narcissistic, etc.). But she also highlighted a limitation of the term as a signifier for the aggregated actions, ideas, attitudes, sensations, material artifacts, and so on that are typically associated with the word "spirituality":

> Well, I mean, when you say you're "spiritual," then people kind of auto-matically link that to religion and Christianity—you know, that you mean "the Holy Spirit." Or, they think you're into energy fields or some witchy stuff you made up yourself. So, the "spirit" part is a problem, kind of, because people don't think of it as the human spirit, but as some-thing supernatural, which I don't, personally. Even Humanists I know will sometimes talk about "the human spirit" like it's a sort of magical thing. That doesn't really work for me. And also, it doesn't include the natural world and the experiences you have there. It's almost like you kind of flip a switch when you say that word, "spirituality," that takes you down a kind of religious path whether you want to go or not. So, I guess maybe it's really the experiences you have that people call "spiri-tual" that I'm talking about. You know, when I say, "or whatever," it's because "spirituality" isn't exactly what I'm experiencing, but I don't know what else you would call it. I mean, it's just hard to explain when all the words are so loaded. I've never really thought about it a whole lot, I guess, what would be a better word. I don't even know if there is one.

Kimberley's description of what she might mean by "spirituality, or whatever" highlights limitations in research on religion and spirituality that Abby Day and Gordon Lynch have noted in their studies of young people in the United Kingdom. They argue that, "[r]esearch interventions such as surveys and inter-views encourage young people to articulate beliefs in ways that they may not have done before."[66] Their descriptions and explanations develop in the process of coming to know and finding language for spiritual or religious experience, that is, rather than as explications of what is already known and easily communicated through standard religious discourse.

The problem Day and Lynch note, which I think we can fairly assume applies at least to some extent across age groups, is further complicated when people like Kimberley are attempting to describe not propositional religious beliefs but lived, felt experiences that are, as such, known substantially in sensate and emotional rather than cognitive terms. Indeed, I would suggest that some of the murkiness researchers find in people's spiritual narratives may emerge from the strain of attempting to translate felt experience into statements of propositional belief. As the experiences of Hugo Carmen in his neighborhood church make clear, and as Talal Asad has explained, ". . . the senses themselves do not *neces-sarily* require meanings. . . . [I]t is possible for someone to encounter something unpredictably that transforms her, to be gripped through her senses by a force (whether immanent or transcendent) *without having to interpret anything.*"[67]

A particular challenge for those who do want to interpret such experiences, or offer them to others for interpretation, is that the available language is, as Kimberley notes, primarily drawn from religious, and more specifically Christian, contexts. To a large extent it is literally the case that *there simply are no words* in the available lexicon to describe experiences of the unaffiliated that would traditionally have been described as "religious" or "spiritual" from an institutional perspective. "Spirituality" comes to stand for that which is "not religious." But, paradoxically, it may also stand for that which is *"not spiritual"* in the senses associated with religion, whether or not the speaker adds "or whatever." The word "spirituality," then, is as much a marker of its conflicted genealogy and contemporary usages as of individual experience.

"We must reclaim the word 'spirituality' from the religions," proclaimed a speaker addressing a meeting of a Humanist group in Palo Alto, California, on the benefits of a "secular spirituality."[68] Likewise, at a meeting of the Sunday Assembly in San Jose, California, a chapter of a recently formed "godless church," as the leader invited the group into a period of silence, he allowed that "it's okay if you think of this as 'spiritual.' You can use whatever language works for you."[69] But for many Nones, appropriating language with obvious religious connotations adds to the challenge of sustaining a coherent spiritual identity that feels authentic. "It's a slippery slope," grumbled one man at the coffee hour after the Humanist presentation. "Once you pick up [religious] words, they're in your mind. You can't shake that. I just don't think it's a good idea."

Traditional Western conceptions of what constitutes "religion" or "spirituality" situate the words and the experiences they describe in conflict with the primarily secular lives most people live, within which many, if not most, "unpredictable encounters" experienced as "transformative" or otherwise significant occur. As with the label "None," the trouble is not that there is nothing there, that nothing happened. It is that much of the readily available language can actually work against articulating, interpreting, and sharing whatever did happen with others.

Occasionally in our conversations, Nones would attempt to press past this discursive barrier. Brandon Metcalfe, a 45-year-old from Stamford, Connecticut, who described himself as "a secular existentialist" searched for other metaphors for the experiences he had described to me as "spiritual, or whatever":

> You could almost think of it—and I know this sounds a little flakey—
> as "the music of life." What I mean by that is that there are things we
> know music is—sound waves, rhythms, harmonies made by a voice or

another instrument that come into the ears. But, if you've ever heard really incredible music, where it almost makes you feel like you're floating, or it stays in your head for days, you know it's more than that, too. You know, it was the music but also what was going on in your life that night, who you were with, or what the weather was like. You don't worry about explaining it so much, but you do find ways to repeat that experience if you can. Sometimes you can and sometimes you can't, but that doesn't mean it wasn't real. When I say, "spirituality, or whatever," I guess I'm getting at what you could call "the music of life"—dorky though that may sound. Someone else might think of it as "the poetry of life" or the "dance of life." These aren't good ways of describing it, I guess, because they aren't universal enough. But they get closer, I think, than maybe the word "spirituality" really does anymore.

This metaphor had its own limitations, however, as indicated by Brandon's concern that phrases like "the music of life" or "the dance of life" might "sound a little flakey" or "dorky." I asked him if he had used the phrase "the music of life" among family, friends, coworkers, and strangers. "I don't think I ever have," he said.

"Would you?" I wondered.

"I'm going to say probably not," he confessed, "except maybe with my girl-friend. After a couple drinks. I don't know that other people would necessarily read it as I mean it. I guess I would say 'spiritual' or 'spirituality' to most people, and then kind of elaborate from there."

It may not be true that "religion" (along with its "lived," "everyday" varia-tions), as Jonathan Z. Smith has famously argued, "is solely the creation of the scholar's study. It is created for the scholar's analytic purposes by his imagina-tive acts of comparison and generalization. Religion has no existence apart from the academy."[70] But it does seem that "spirituality" in America today is the still incomplete creation of the religiously unaffiliated. The "elaboration" that Brandon speaks of has begun to reshape the meaning of "spirituality" further. Perhaps such elaborations will produce new ways to describe experiences that have long been associated with the word. In the meantime, "spirituality," as it is variously articulated, moves throughout the lives of Nones as they craft stories that (1) are embedded in everyday life; (2) center primarily on relationships rather than individualistic pursuits or institutionalized rituals; and (3) are com-posed of practices focused on the integration of body, mind, and spirit. Over time, these stories make up "the spiritual life."

We will, then, explore the spiritual lives of American Nones through narra-tives of lived, everyday practice. First, however, we will explore in the next chap-ter the ways in which Nones understand their own development as religiously unaffiliated. These stories of becoming None certainly touch on themes of dissatisfaction with traditional religion and with expressions of religious and political dissent. But they are more illuminating in their emphasis on personal discovery, creativity, authenticity, and changes in relationships with others. Ultimately, for most Nones the unaffiliated spiritual life is not defined by what may have been left behind, but rather by what was found.

2

Becoming None

Religiously Manufactured Spiritual Self-Invention

I feel like [going to church] is not something I need as an adult. You know, it taught me a lot about being a good person, I guess. But I don't need to hear that lesson every week. I got it.
—Noelle Lamb, *age 26, Eugene, Oregon, "Spiritual"*

There's this thing on [the radio] about Darwin and religion—about how he was a skeptic, maybe, but that he wasn't hostile toward religion. . . . It just kept making more and more sense to me. And then I thought, "Hey, what else did they lie to me about?" That was more or less the beginning of the end.
—William Lim, *age 29, Augusta, Maine, "Agnostic"*

I didn't leave Catholicism. The church left me. It abandoned me. It cast me out. And I was heartbroken.
—Natalie Darling, *age 41, St. Paul, Minnesota, "Spiritual"*

What does it mean to be None? How does someone become None? In the most literal sense, to be unaffiliated means simply that a person is not a member of an institutional religious group. But we have seen that being None is also a matter of social identity—of who a person understands herself most authentically to be in relation to others. This self-understanding develops over time as circumstances—relationships, intellectual and physiological development, geographic location, education and employment, economic realities, technologies, and so on—inflect, amplify, redirect, and sometimes substantially reconfigure an ongoing narrative of the self.

"The process of religious change that takes place in a dynamic force field of people, events, ideologies, institutions, expectations, and orientations," as Lewis Rambo defines "religious conversion,"[1] can begin in a sudden flash of insight, or it may unfold gradually. It is sometimes emotionally and interpersonally dramatic; other times, shifts in affiliation occur with little immediately noticeable effect on self-understanding or primary relationships. For Christians, the blinding conversion of the apostle Paul on the road to Damascus[2] and the extended philosophical explorations and moral transformation of Augustine of Hippo[3] are paradigmatic. For Buddhists, the prince-turned-roaming-pauper Siddhartha Gautama's night of awakening while sitting under the Bodhi tree, illuminated by a full moon, is the archetypal moment of mature awareness and liberation that characterizes the enlightened person.[4] Narratives tracing the process of becoming None are harder to come by in the popular culture—at least until quite recently, when the New Atheist movement, centered on Richard Dawkins, Christopher Hitchens, and Sam Harris, gained notoriety.[5] Despite the robust sales of books by these authors, few tales of unaffiliation are found within the canons of "classic literature." In fact, stories of the unaffiliated are more often told by the religiously affiliated. Typically, these are presented as cautionary tales cast in terms of loss and failure, the tragedy of religious change mitigated only by the hope that the prodigals will eventually return.[6]

Stories of unaffiliation told by Nones themselves form a rather slim and recent genre that focuses mainly on the experiences of Atheists and emphasizes propositional beliefs over the practices that many Nones, often including Atheists, think of as "spiritual."[7] This chapter focuses on how Nones themselves describe the way in which their identification as religiously unaffiliated of one sort or another came to be. Within religious institutions the process of moving from one religious tradition to another, or to none, is usually defined as "conversion" or, often more pejoratively when people leave institutional religion entirely, as "deconversion."[8] The overwhelming influence of the Christian tradition makes it difficult to avoid words like "conversion" or "formation" that seem to suggest that people are passive objects in their own spiritual lives rather than authors of an ongoing spiritual story. For the most part, those who shared their stories with me did not describe the process of becoming Nones in terms of conversion or deconversion. Still, as with the Nones quoted in the epigraphs above, their identification as "unaffiliated" does frequently occur in relation to conventional religious institutions and practices. And, at least among Nones from Christian backgrounds, the emotions associated with the shift from affiliated to unaffiliated tend to map in distinctive ways to the religious tradition in which a person was raised.[9]

The Nones who talked with me consistently saw themselves as active creators in the story of their own spiritual lives. Their narratives were populated with the language of "discovery," "freedom," "escape," "liberation," "maturation," "journeying," "enlightenment," and "self-realization," or "growth" in "awareness," "knowledge," "self-understanding," or "insight." Whether their self-identification as None occurred suddenly or, as was more often the case, unfolded over a longer time frame, they presented themselves as inherently predisposed toward "questioning," "challenging," "exploring," "curiosity," "experimentation," and "seeking." Ethan Quinn, a 45-year-old Atheist from Washington, D.C., who had been raised in a Mormon family in Nevada, put it this way:

Religion dictated so much of my life as a child. Not just what we believed, but really who we were against the rest of the world and how we were with each other. It was like no one was ever really just themself [*sic*]. We were Mormons first, from five generations of Mormons. But, I was always asking questions. Why do we do it this way? Why can't I have a Coke? And mom or dad would say, "You have to have faith." I knew enough to shut up. And, you know, as a kid, I didn't really disagree exactly. I just wanted to know why. I was always like that. I asked questions about everything. Ask too much about the church, though—that was about the worst sin you could do. So, I went after answers on my own, first at the local library, and then, when we got the internet—oh, man, I couldn't get enough. All the windows started to open. All the lights went on.

As Ethan's story makes clear, Nones do not come to see themselves as such out of nowhere. Something may stir inside their hearts as a faint calling toward other ways of being spiritual. They may have doubts and questions that fester unanswered. Or, as in the case of William Lim, the 29-year-old former Pentecostal quoted at the opening of this chapter, new information or experiences may come into a life as if from another universe. Likewise, as we will see, troubling experiences with institutional religions may push someone toward unaffiliation. However they come to understand themselves as Nones, the unaffiliated have only the resources available within their own backgrounds and what they know of the wider culture from which to construct their unaffiliated identities. It is important to bear in mind, especially in the face of the significant growth in unaffiliation that has been tracked over the last two decades, that religious unaffiliation is never a *sui generous* phenomenon. It is always made up of existing ideas, artifacts, traditions, rituals, and modes of interpreting experience, however idiosyncratically they may be pieced together. Elements of the larger religious culture play into narratives of religious change at the personal and local level—for individuals, families, and other personal social networks. Each individual None, as she rearticulates the story of the spiritual self to family, friends, and the occasional researcher, in turn contributes something to the changing narrative of religion and spirituality in America.

The Religious and Spiritual Ecosystem

The narratives of individual Nones are not entirely singular stories, that is. They are shaped by a variety of historical and contemporary forces, the roots and effects of which cannot always be traced or untangled. Scholars point to a number of factors that contribute to changes in the religious and spiritual climate across history. While no single factor in itself can be isolated as a root cause, together they contribute to the development of a social environment in which becoming None seems to be a more viable option in relation to personal disposi- tions, social relationships, and other commitments. Historical, social, technical, and ideological dynamics result in the production of new resources—ideas, ways of acting, modes of interpretation, artifacts, technologies, and the like—for con- structing and understanding the self, including the self as spiritual or religious.

Importantly, I am not suggesting here that increasing unaffiliation is caused by "the culture" as a sort of vague, nefarious force that overtakes the spiritu- ally weak-willed or inattentive. Rather, I making the fairly obvious point that changes in religious affiliation, while not determined by cultural factors alone, are enabled or constrained by culture. Still, this point is often obscured by the Western embrace of Enlightenment ideas of individual autonomy, rationality, and freedom, along with associated Reformation Protestant notions of a "per- sonal god," [10] that shape a modern outlook, within which unaffiliation is seen primarily as a matter of individual choice in the "religious marketplace."[11] We must remember that ideas of religion as personal and private are relatively recent in the grand sweep of religious history, but they have had a profound impact on how we currently understand religion, spirituality, and their various meanings and significances in our lives. As sociologist Thomas Luckman put it,

> Once religion is defined as a "private affair" the individual may choose
> from the assortment of "ultimate" meanings as he sees fit—guided
> only by the preferences that are determined by his social biography.
> An important consequence of this situation is that the individual con-
> structs not only his personal identity but also his individual system of
> "ultimate" significance.[12]

Given a cultural climate after the Enlightenment that was more sustaining of individualized approaches to the spiritual, a number of scholars contend that alternatives to institutional religion have flowed through the wider currents of American life since the earliest days of the nation.[13] Courtney Bender and Leigh Eric Schmidt have traced contemporary unaffiliated spiritual practices, mentali- ties, and identities back to eighteenth-century spiritualism, nineteenth-century New England Transcendental and New Thought movements, William James's psychological exploration of religion and mysticism, and progressive political sensibilities that developed through the early twentieth century. In this view, growing unaffiliation, especially as it tracks to increasing political progressivism, is but one effect of a "cosmopolitan spirituality as an inheritance in American religious life."[14] This distinctly American spirituality unfolds in the diverse locales of everyday life, "including," writes Bender, "many that we do not con-sider religious."[15] Yet the homes, neighborhoods, workplaces, markets, and other locales that Americans themselves have long counted as important sites of spiri-tual engagement and meaning have often been ignored or devalued by scholars of religion and leaders of religious institutions, making it difficult to fully take stock of the extent or diversity of religious or spiritual practice. Further, Bender argues, by placing spiritual pursuits in the realm of the private and seeing spiri-tuality as an interior phenomenon, they are further marginalized in our under-standing of the wider, extra-ecclesial scope of religious life among the religiously affiliated and unaffiliated alike.

Buying into Unaffiliation

Consumer culture is also part of this more expansive spiritual and religious reality. Book publishing plays a particularly significant role in this regard. In the early to mid-twentieth century, a new "middlebrow" mass-market book culture aimed to revitalize religion by imbuing the wider, purportedly secular, culture with the spiritual and ethical gifts of progressive Protestantism. "Liberal Protestantism since the nineteenth century," says University of Virginia religion professor Matthew S. Hedstrom, "had sought to redeem the culture through full participation in it."[16] Helped by well-placed Protestant publishing executives and booksellers, a wide array of books promoting "personal betterment in matters of psyche and spirit"[17] contributed to new conceptions of spirituality that spread from individuals across extra-institutional clusters of reading practitioners who gathered in book clubs as often as in churches. Hedstrom suggests that the "rise of the Nones" is the direct extension of this brand of progressive Protestantism, shaped by popular religious and spiritual literature. This liberal cultural strain of Protestantism was experienced by ordinary Americans as "intellectually engaged, psychologically oriented, and focused on personal experience"[18]—qualities that continue to be valued by many of the religiously unaffiliated. Historian David A. Hollinger, likewise, argues that the "egalitarian impulses and the capacities for self-interrogation" embraced by progressive Mainline Protestants "enacted acceptance of ethnoracial, sexual, religious, and cultural diversity" in the nation in general, and allowed that institutional religious affiliation was not a require-ment for ethical practice.[19] This liberalizing spiritual and ethical push was assisted by the gradually disseminated results of empirical scientific research, including the theory of evolution, that at once highlighted the role of individual rationality in determining what is "true" about reality and challenged the long held, largely biblically grounded religious monopoly on "truth."

The market-based spiritualities inspired by book publishers have been vastly expanded through contemporary broadcast media and associated commercial enterprises.[20] Yale religious studies scholar Kathryn Lofton offers a compelling depiction of a spiritualized consumer culture through the media icon Oprah Winfrey. Lofton argues that "the Winfrey project"—a phenomenon that extends well beyond the celebrity herself, including the products and gurus she endorses, as well as modes of spiritualized life practice—deploys modes of nineteenth-century revival preaching and confessional conversion practices, along with ritualistic "makeovers" of various social underdogs (poor women, unappreciated mothers, overweight women), to shape a spirituality of "redemption" through personal buying choices. This consumerist spirituality assiduously avoids any critique of the social structures that create the conditions in which many in the Oprah audience are unable to "live their best life."[21] For Lofton, Oprah is the cruelest sort of "false Messiah,"[22] offering hope for change through misdirected personal initiative, reinforcing notions of spiritual autonomy in relation to popular media consumption and consumerist practices. Media personalities, of whom Oprah is a dominant archetype, are repackaging American religion and spirituality for commercial gain.

Fordham University theologian Tom Beaudoin has also connected consumer practice to the construction of religious and spiritual identity. But while Lofton's disdain for "the Oprah"[23] is palpable, Beaudoin sees commercial brands as potential resources in the construction of authentic postmodern spiritual identities. "The world of our products is . . . spiritually volatile," he acknowledges. "Through our relation to products we become more faithful, hopeful, and loving—or more covetous and self-enclosed."[24] Lofton and Beaudoin show American consumer culture as providing significant imaginative and material resources for the construction of a spiritual self both within and well outside institutional religious affiliations. Through consumer spiritualities such as those offered by Oprah, quips Lofton, Americans learn that "[w]e can choose whether to go to church or not, we can worship as we please—or we can lounge in bed on a Sunday morning, wearing the very cutest underwear."[25]

Religious change, including religious unaffiliation, is shaped by economic factors that affect the supply of institutional religious options available to "consumers." The religious marketplace also offers varieties of products to which consumers attach religious and spiritual significance, whether religiously institutional or (mostly) otherwise. Consuming in itself—selecting branded items that express some element of religious identity and associated commitments, going to a mall or other shopping venue as "retail therapy," selecting locally produced or organic products on the basis of ethical values, as well as tending purchases, displaying them, or giving them to family and friends—has become a spiritual practice. Of course, the role of commercialism in American religiosity and spirituality raises questions about the effects of globalization.[26] Media practices, widely globalized as they have become, are implicated as well.

The climate warmed again for extra-institutional spiritual practices that were, it turns out, always a resilient feature of the American religious and spiritual life during the political and cultural upheavals of the 1960s. According to sociologist Wade Clark Roof, the experiences and politics of the era—participating in or protesting the unpopular Vietnam War; the civil rights, feminist, and early gay rights movements; the sexual revolution; and cultural events such as the Woodstock Music Festival and the Summer of Love in San Francisco—shaped the Baby Boomers as "a generation of seekers" who were "touched in ways that led to many differing, and even alternative, spiritual and religious trajectories."[27] Even as the Religious Right gained political power through the 1980s, the intertwined legacies of Enlightenment rationality and individuality, Transcendentalist spiritual eclecticism and experimentation, and a resistant strand of religious indifference continued to weave themselves through American culture.

Increasing politicization of religion by conservative Evangelicals reinforced the alienation from institutional religion experienced by many in the Baby Boomer generation and modeled discontent to subsequent generations. Michael Hout and Claude S. Fisher argue that "part of the increase in 'nones' can be viewed as a symbolic statement against the Religious Right."[28] In the bestselling *Bowling Alone*, Robert D. Putnam argued that, at the end of the twentieth century, unaffiliation was related to a wider trend of social disconnection and anti-institutionalism.[29] The impact of social isolation related to factors such as suburban living, broadcast media consumption, pre-social media internet use, and an ideological underpinning of American individualism made itself felt by the Elks and Kiwanis—along with their bowling leagues—no less than by the neighborhood church and synagogue.

It is important to note that more recent changes in communications technologies have revolutionized our ability to engage information and entertainment in ways that mitigate the increasing isolation Putnam identified as a byproduct of a late broadcast age, pre-social media culture. Recent data do suggest that younger adults in particular are "unattached to organized politics and religion" and other institutionalized elements of culture, but they nonetheless form multiple, overlapping friendship networks, mediated through digital social platforms like Facebook, Instagram, and Snapchat that are increasingly mobile and integrated into daily life.[30] The social structure of institutionalized religious affiliation, which flows from a pattern of gathering large groups of people into religious institutional categories—Protestants, Catholics, Jews, in Will Herberg's classic conservative configuration[31]—simply makes less sense in light of the digitally integrated social networks through which adults in the United States today, especially those under the age of 40, connect and gather with others online and offline. New digital technologies and social media practices, like books and broadcast technologies before them, have reconfigured the ways in which people relate to one another socially, including practices of affiliation.[32]

Hints of this social reconfiguration could be seen early in the new media age, especially among young adults. In an intriguing study of public mourning after the death of Pope John Paul II in 2005, sociologist Grzegorz Brzozowski found that "public rituals and moments of shared identification with sacred forms can . . . bring young people together into temporary communities that are not premised on a single set of beliefs or mode of believing."[33] Like an earlier study by sociologist Enzo Pace that highlighted Catholic World Youth Day celebrations as opportunities for vaguely spiritualized sexual encounters among young people,[34] Brzozowski contends that religious occasions and the physical spaces they occupy function as temporary sites of provisional spiritual affiliation. People come together not because they believe the same things or practice their spirituality in the same ways. They come together to share the same kind of experience, however differently they may interpret it or translate it into spiritual or religious meanings. This is not a matter of thin relational or ideological commitments, according to sociologist Abby Day, but of experiences of authenticity in the context of meaningful social networks. "I did not find that young people were drifting through an a-moral universe or were unable to cope with life's challenges in the absence of grand meta-narratives," says Day of her research with young adults in the United Kingdom. "They were informed and sustained by relationships and contexts where they felt they belonged."[35]

The response of one young woman to an article I wrote on high levels of support for prayer at public meetings shows that Day's point can be extended to include social media practice. In the article, I suggested that changing definitions of prayer and a more fluid approach to difference among young people might account for the support for public prayer as much as would traditional religiosity. Referring to two Nones I had quoted in the article, she wrote, "Both people have a refreshing way of allowing others to express their beliefs without feeling pressured by them. The next generation is used to seeing many different opinions and feelings float by on their Facebook page. They can deal with the differences."[36] In the new media age, difference is less a distinguishing barrier between groups of individuals than it is an invitation to engage and explore the lives of diverse others.

Unaffiliated Religious Secularism

Some academics, religious leaders, and members of the general public see growing unaffiliation as evidence of increasing American secularism, not unlike that seen in formerly majority Christian European nations.[37] This European model is based on the idea of religious subtraction. As philosopher Charles Taylor explains, this version of secularism is understood by the general public as the evacuation of religion from the public sphere, in the work of government, education, health care, and other social institutions that were once closely associated with, if not entirely controlled by, the Church.[38] Related to this subtraction theory is an idea of secularization as reflected in increasing individual disengagement from organized religion and the pluralization and privatization of religious practice. Here, "secularism comes to be defined as a form of pluralism with metaphysical foundations and not . . . as a replacement of religious values by irreligious ones."[39] That is, it is not that people become less religious or spiritual, or that religion is entirely absent from public life. But religion's public role is limited to those functions that support common civil, political, and commercial life regardless of religion—national days of prayer, for instance, or celebrations of gift-giving and food-sharing holy days. Other practices that tend to highlight religious difference—wearing religious garb like a hijab or a turban, or observing special dietary practices—appear to undermine civil unity. Secularity in this view is not the absence of religion, but rather official religion's institutionalizing and privatizing enforcer.[40] Here, the trend toward religious unaffiliation can be seen as an unintended consequence of Enlightenment notions of religion as a matter of individual choice, best kept private or tightly restricted to defined religious spaces and limited public expressions.

On the other hand, unaffiliation in the postmodern, new media age can be seen as primarily influenced not so much by wider access to information about different religious options.[41] Rather, new media practices of seeing others, seeing difference, expressing difference, and being in variously distributed relationships with religiously diverse others have an effect on how people regard religious difference in increasingly overlapping zones of private and public life. What I post on Facebook may feel like private expression that is acceptable in a "secular" social media community. I may be addressing a specific friend or cluster of friends when I post a quote from Dorothy Day or Pema Chödrön. But, as we are rapidly learning, this expression is of course public, extending across my self-selected digital social network, to the networks of all those to whom I have connected, and on through their networks, and so on.

The blending of the public and private here requires a disposition of the cosmopolitan equanimity shown by the young woman who insisted that members of her generation "can deal with the differences." In fact, it is by *not dealing with them*, by letting them "float by" without engaging them interpersonally, without looking for commonalities or exploring differences, that social harmony is maintained in the context of dramatically increased, widely globalized, everyday diversity. In this new, digitally integrated social world, participation in many of the practices of everyday life—including the Four F's of Contemporary Spirituality—invites self-presentation not simply as secular. We see glimpses of your religious or spiritual self on your Facebook page and Pinterest boards. But the logic of digitally integrated social practice encourages self-representations in which affiliational commitments are muted, expressing religious and spiritual perspectives in ways that signal a lack or a loosening of institutional, doctrinal, and ritual rigidity that might undermine social harmony and stability. No small part of this muting practice includes the selection of networks of mostly like-minded people who are apt to reinforce each other's perspectives. Still, social media technologies are designed in such a way that no individual participant can ensure—even in enclaves assumed to be private—that her content will not find its way via networked interactions (I saw your post on my friend's Facebook wall even though I am not in your network; your friend copied your post to a more public area of the platform, etc.) into more diverse contexts of engagement.

Thus, in digitally integrated culture, where proximity to many others with different perspectives and life situations is a regular occurrence, unaffiliation can also be seen as an expression of what we might call a "strategic cosmopolitanism" in which differences are not muted directly, but rather are allowed to "float by" without making any claim on the attention of others or generating conflict. We see an offline version of this behavior in the way many people conduct cellphone conversations in close proximity to others, under the apparent assumption that others cannot hear—an assumption often borne out by the studied indifference to others' conversations affected by those in earshot.

A cultural climate for unaffiliation is shaped by currents that have moved from the European Enlightenment and Protestant Reformation into American transcendentalist religious experimentation and liberal Protestant social ideologies and practices—all popularized through book culture and, later, broadcast media. Commercial and consumer practices have warmed the climate for religious "branding" and self-invention. Likewise, a modern secular versus religious structuring of social life has contributed to the idea of religion as a matter of personal choice and private practice. Most recently, changing communication media have begun to confuse the public-private boundaries thus constructed. To this list I would add one further factor: changes in human longevity.

With the geographically concentrated devastation of two World Wars in the past, the development of new medical approaches to disease prevention and treatment, and sustained periods of economic stability that allowed most Westerners to enjoy regular healthy meals and access to education and health care, people live much longer lives in greater comfort. In 2009, average life expectancy in the United States was 78.5 years. Women in most ethnic groups could expect to live beyond their eightieth birthdays.[42] A hundred years earlier, in 1909, it was nearly half that—52.1 years on average; 34.2 years if you were an African American man.[43] A century or two earlier, in colonial times, life expectancy was in the mid-thirties.[44]

Today, things are of course dramatically different across the American populace. It will apparently be the case that many people alive in the United States
today will live well into the nineties or one hundreds. By both historical and
current global standards, these long American lives will unfold extensively in
conditions of relative affluence that allow access to abundant food, reasonably
reliable medical care, extensive educational resources, and comparatively inex-
pensive national and global travel. Further, outbreaks of religiously infused violence (for example, in the case of the 2012 shooting rampage at a Sikh temple
in Oak Park, Wisconsin), recurrent Ku Klux Klan violence, or anti-abortion and
anti-gay violence notwithstanding, few Americans live actively with the threat
of violence in cases of religious nonconformity. This changes profoundly how
the narrative of the self is kept going over the course of a life. People live longer
and are exposed to more intellectual, experiential, and material resources over
the course of an expanded number of life stages,[45] as well as through more frequent career and vocational changes.[46] We are more likely to relocate to different
geographical areas with different religious demographics.[47] Postmodern shifts in
relationship configurations, redefinitions of racial, ethnic, and gender identities,
and so on, are all augmented by greater access to information and the means to
produce and distribute knowledge than were possible, let alone imaginable, for
ordinary people in previous eras. What all of this suggests is that people are less
formally religious today not necessarily, or at least not entirely, because of any
particular ideological shift or change in scientific knowledge, however influential these factors may be. People today are less traditionally religious because, in
terms of personal authority and the time to enact that authority with regard to
religion and spirituality, *they can be.*

As religion or spirituality factors into identity, then, institutional affiliation
is now but one resource that might shape the story of the self-as-spiritual. The
religious and spiritual environment is warmed and cooled, made fertile or bar-
ren, by a variety of forces, of which institutional religion, while perhaps the
most obvious, is no longer the most influential—if, in fact, it ever really was.
As we will see, for the majority of Nones who were raised in traditional religious backgrounds, institutional religion simply did not translate into their
adult lives in coherent and durable ways. Instead, any number of other spiritual
resources—elements of other religious traditions, insights from nonreligious
fields like quantum physics or cognitive psychology, entertainment media figures and narrative products (books, television shows, movies, music, etc.), and
personal and communal experiences interpreted as "spiritual" without need of
institutional religious sanction—find their way into narratives that give the unaffiliated a greater "capacity to use the 'I' in the shifting contexts" of everyday life.
This capacity, says Anthony Giddens, "is the most elemental feature of reflexive
conceptions of personhood."[48] Being unaffiliated, that is, allows many people to

experience themselves more authentically as they move from one part of life to another, regardless of how benign their prior institutional religious experience may have been. This seems especially to be the case for Nones who were raised in Mainline Protestant traditions.

Becoming None from Mainline Protestant Some

For Corrie Milliman, a 33-year-old None from Larkspur, California, the experience of growing up in an Episcopalian family was "perfectly fine." Corrie, a painter and sculptor, enjoyed the "aesthetic ethos" of her mostly white, liberal church community. "Everyone was so supportive and kind," she told me. "From a very young age, people understood that I had an artistic vocation, and they really affirmed that. I'm so grateful to have been nurtured spiritually and artistically in that community." Still, Corrie reported that she never exactly believed Christian doctrine, though, like many Nones, she appreciated the stories of Jesus. "It just never really resonated for me," she said. "I mean, I loved the pageantry of the liturgy and all the altar dressings. And the language of the *Book of Common Prayer* can be really beautiful. But at the level of spiritual feeling, it just didn't happen for me in that context."

When Corrie went to art school on the East Coast, she "just sort of drifted off" from the religion of her childhood, though she continued to have what she described as a "strong spiritual center." She developed a network of friends who were involved in environmentally oriented art projects, such as creating "art gardens" in various urban settings, especially in economically disadvantaged areas. "It was spiritually intense in a way I had never experienced," Corrie told me. "We were not just bringing beauty into these distressed areas, but finding beauty and honoring it there."

The experience of creating art in a small, closely knit community of activist artists was also inspiring for Corrie. A few of the artists were involved in a local Neopagan[49] circle. Corrie explained that these friends shared a similar "sacred aesthetic" that bonded them as a group and facilitated her eventual more formal identification as Wiccan Neopagan:

> It was really centered in the art, this transformation for me, which
> makes sense because that's the center of me, right? It's who I am at the
> deepest level. My art is who I am. But it's also more than that. It's who
> I am in the world, connected to everyone and everything I encounter.
> I guess that sounds a little grand, but it's a powerful experience to be in
> that wave of creation when I pick up the brush. The idea as it's forming,

the ritual, the color and light, the giving of it to someone or a group of strangers or friends—all of that is sacred experience for me.

My family and the people in the church community I grew up in appreciated my art. They encouraged me. They loved me. But I don't think they really got the deeper spiritual part. The Neopagan art community is really diverse and, you know, we're all over. There's not one specific kind of Neopagan. But we all have that chord, so we're always connected that way. It seemed like such a natural thing. You know, we don't call it "conversion" when you enter a Neopagan community. You're not "joining" an organization. You're not turning yourself into something else. You're recognizing your people. There's a synchronicity to it. We call it "coming home." It was absolutely like that for me.

Like other Nones who started out as Mainline Protestants, Corrie felt little stress about "drifting off" from the religion of her childhood. In part, this was because spiritual exploration was encouraged in her church. "They trusted us," Corrie explained, "to work out what we believed and how we wanted to pursue our spiritual lives. I really didn't feel any pressure. I mean, my parents are kind of Episcopalian by accident. Dad was a disillusioned Catholic. Mom didn't have much religious background. They liked the church down the block, so they stayed. Now that I think of it, I kind of did the same thing in my own way."

The affiliational drift for other Nones from Mainline Protestant backgrounds is less a matter of identity alignment and more a matter of spiritual ennui. As with Noelle Lamb, the 26-year-old None quoted at the beginning of the chapter who was raised as a Lutheran, for many former Mainline Nones, church teachings and practices seemed unnecessarily repetitive, perhaps even childish. Noelle, we will recall, felt that participating in an institutional religion was "not something I need as an adult." Noelle told me, "I liked my church growing up. It was fun to do vacation bible school and, later, mission trips. I still go with my parents sometimes at the holidays." However, her periodic church visits with her parents are more a matter of reinforcing family ties than religious ones. "It's like a thing we do from the past that we can still do together once in a while," she said.

Michael Clancy, a 53-year-old former United Methodist from Valparaiso, Indiana, found that participating in a church did not add meaningfully to family life once what he saw as the basic "do unto others" teachings of Christianity were instilled in his children. Michael describes himself as Agnostic now. His drift into the ranks of the unaffiliated was not unlike Noelle's, though it was activated from a parental perspective. Michael excused his three children—ages 9, 10, and 14—from church when he came to an awareness that the experience was not meaningful in their spiritual or moral development. He recalled,

It just struck me one Sunday: I mean, how many times do they need to hear "do unto others" and Jesus is the Good Shepherd? You know, they're good kids—well-behaved, smart, friendly. They're not going to, like, turn to a life of crime without church. I just thought, "What are they really getting out of this that we're not teaching them at home?" You know, I was raised Methodist. My wife, too. Setting aside that there's so much I just flat out don't believe and a lot I question—not to mention that we were both sick of fighting to get them there every week—I think we've got the rest of it—the moral, ethical parts—down. So, my wife and I talked about, and then we asked them if they'd rather stay at home on Sunday mornings, if they would miss going to church. It was like a thirty second conversation: "No, no, no. Thank you very much!" We went back that Christmas, but it was a little awkward. We kept up our pledge for another year or so. But now we don't go at all. It's really better for all of us. We end up spending more time together as a family.

It seemed to me that Michael may have projected some of his own disinterest in the church experience onto his kids, so I asked him if there was anything he missed about being affiliated with a church. "Zero," he said quickly. "Honestly, we only went for the kids. And, I guess, because it's just what you do in a place like this. But I was never really into it myself, even as a kid. Why put my kids through that for the sake of show once they've gotten the idea that you're supposed to be a good person—you know, do unto others. . . ."

Railey Haines, a Humanist from Columbia, South Carolina, sounded a similar note with regard to the ethical grounding provided by religions. Railey had been raised in the United Church of Christ in Upstate New York, and said he "had nothing to complain about" with regard to his religious upbringing. "It gives you a structure," he said, "to start thinking on your own about how you think you should behave and what's right and wrong." But he did not think this moral framework required repeated reinforcement. "I know some people like the community they feel at church, but I have that in other parts of my life," Railey said. He runs with a group a couple times a week, and on weekends they often get together for brunch after a long run. A doctoral candidate in information science, he spends lots of time with academic colleagues both working on shared projects and gathering socially. As he put it, "I've got plenty of options for coffee and doughnuts through the week." He added, "I do appreciate the humanist underpinnings of Christianity. But, you know, I'm not real spiritual in that emotional way some people have. I'm pretty practical. I wasn't learning anything new. After I went to college, it just wasn't necessary."

Corrie, Noelle, Michael, and Railey were raised in different Mainline Protestant denominations, in different parts of the country. And, their experience and identification as unaffiliated are different—Neopagan, Spiritual, Agnostic, Humanist, respectively. But they have much in common nonetheless. They all were raised in what they described as economically comfortable families. They are all white, and their church communities generally were as well. None of them experienced the religion of their childhood as repressive. They all felt free to give up the religious tradition in which they were raised and to explore other options—or not—as this made sense in their adult lives. There is a sense, perhaps, of middle-class entitlement here. Church is a discretionary activity, not an essential one. When it fails to feed or enrich the self, or when its work in the moral education of children is complete, other spiritual or non-spiritual options can easily replace it.

Corrie's path to unaffiliation was oriented around her development as an artist, and her experience with the Neopagan art community seemed to offer more opportunities to engage others within and outside that group. Noelle, Michael, and Railey expressed what I think is fair to describe as a certain boredom with the experience of church. "I got it," each of them said at one point or another about their understanding of the basic moral teachings of their Christian denomination. Noelle and Railey seemed to outgrow the experience of church; Michael and his wife anticipated that their children would as well. This theme of boredom with the repetitiveness of religious teachings in the context of regular church attendance was consistent among the former Mainline Protestant Nones who talked with me. Indeed, during the course of my research with the unaffiliated, I also happened to meet with separate groups of teens at a Presbyterian and an Episcopal church. I asked teens in both groups—active youth group members, mission trip and service project alumni, who regularly attended Sunday services with their parents—how they saw their engagement with their churches playing out in their adult lives. Teens in both groups, unsurprisingly by then, waxed eloquent about how their church experience had helped to shape them as "good people" who could "be ethical." But when I asked if they saw themselves continuing to attend church as college students and beyond, there was an awkward pause in both groups. Finally, one boy spoke up. "I see [the church] as getting us all ready morally and spiritually to go out into the world, and to do good things like caring about social justice and poverty. I don't think I'll need to keep going over and over it."

Many former Mainline Protestant Nones expressed disagreement with Christian doctrine, but, as in these examples, this disagreement was generally presented in rather mild terms. Michael "set aside" the elements of the tradition he was raised in that he "just flat out [didn't] believe" as he considered leaving the church. Such disagreements seemed not to be a part of the decision-making

process. Railey tempered any theological misgivings in a tepid acknowledge-
ment of "the humanist underpinnings of Christianity." For her part, Noelle actually indicated a general agreement with Christian teachings when we talked.
"I mean, you can't take it all literally," she said, "but if it didn't have some
important truth in it, it wouldn't have lasted so long." It just was not a truth that
needed reinforcement past adulthood, in Noelle's view. Corrie found "much
beauty" in the Anglican/Episcopal tradition, and she told me she had "great
respect" for the teachings of Jesus. She also noted that early Christians had
adopted many Pagan ideas and practices, the "ancient resonances" of which
she felt still connected her to her childhood faith. For these and many other
former Mainline Nones, church was mostly fine while you were growing up.
It helped to establish a moral framework for adulthood. Then you move on.

Former Lutheran Priscilla Danford, a 19-year-old college student in Chicago
who described herself as "just spiritual," talked about a series of summer mission
trips—one to New Orleans, one to Kentucky, one to Guatemala—as "probably
the most significant things I ever did." She also described a number of youth
group projects that she found meaningful, and reported that she still had a number of close friends from youth group. All of that, she told me, "really helped
make me who I am now and kind of laid out the person that I want to be in the
future." But she didn't see church affiliation or participation as necessary for that.

Lily Hampton, age 23, was brought up in an Episcopalian family in St.
Louis, Missouri. Now a first-year law school student in California, Lily identifies as Agnostic. Here again, her intellectual and behavioral distancing from
the faith of her childhood did not involve any particular existential crisis or
clash of beliefs. "Strictly speaking," Lily said, "I'm pretty sure most people in
my church weren't, like, hard core 'believers' with a capital 'B' in, you know,
'Jesus is Lord,' or whatever. It was more about establishing values and doing
justice. That influenced me a lot, but it's not really relevant in a practical sense
in my life now. Once I got to college, I had kind of grown out of it."

Some former Mainline Nones did report that their parents had some concerns about their unaffiliated status, but not one talked about it in terms of significant conflict. Jordan Cascade, a 30-year-old Humanist from San Antonio,
Texas, who was raised as a Presbyterian was fairly typical in this regard. He told
me his mother worried about him when he stopped attending church in college.
"She thought it was a phase," he told me. "I think she still does. She's waiting for
me to settle down and come back to the fold, I guess. She'll ask about it once
in a while, but it's not like we argue about it." Similarly, Win Nguyen, who grew
up in a mostly Asian United Methodist church, now identifies as Agnostic. "I
know my mom is disappointed," she said when we talked. "It's kind of hard to
miss that. But it hasn't come between us. It hasn't hurt our relationship. It's just
something we don't agree on. You know, she doesn't like my boyfriend either."

Becoming None, it seems, is a relatively untroubled passage for many Mainline Protestants. They seem to shed denominational identity like an old coat—maybe one they used to like a great deal, but which no longer fits into their adult lives. They become bored with the repetitiveness of the church experiences, even if they appreciated the ethical grounding these experiences gave them. They graduate into what feels like a better fitting spiritual identity— hence retired Episcopal bishop John Shelby Spong's characterization of former Mainliners as "the church alumni association."[50]

Becoming None from Conservative/Evangelical Protestant Some

Nones from other Christian backgrounds were often much less nonchalant about the process of becoming unaffiliated. Nones from more conservative Protestant backgrounds—Evangelicals, Jehovah's Witnesses, Mormons, Pentecostals, Seventh-day Adventists, and conservative Baptists, among those I interviewed—tended to express anger and frustration with both the teachings and practices of their childhood churches as a significant part of their identification as unaffiliated. Unlike Mainline Protestants who shared their stories with me, the process of becoming None for these former Christians (whom I generally characterize here as "Evangelical" or "conservative") was often precipitated by a specific crisis or conflict.

For instance, 40-year-old Caleb Capra, from Pine Bluff, Arkansas, left a nondenominational Evangelical church of which he had been a member for more than a decade "in a heartbeat" when he learned that the senior pastor had been embezzling donations to the church to finance the purchase of vacation homes out of state, expensive cars, and other luxuries well beyond the means of the congregants whose money he took. Indeed, at the time he learned about the fraud, Caleb had been unemployed for the better part of a year and had been volunteering at the church several days a week to keep himself occupied and "to try to keep my hope up." The news "was a cold slap in the face. It was my 'Damascus Road experience,' only in reverse," said Caleb, who now describes himself as a "Jesus Follower." He continued,

> I wasn't blinded. My eyes were opened. In that very instant, I knew I would never be part of a church again. I was done with it. I walked out the door, and I never came back. Never will. Thinking about it still makes by blood pressure spike. I literally mowed that man's lawn while he was stealing my unemployment money out of my pocket. I gave a

bunch of tithe money that I'd sure love to have in my bank account right now. But, you know, maybe it was worth it, because now I know that my relationship with God is something I have to work on myself everyday. It's a personal thing that I can only show by how I treat others—not by going to church to be seen every Sunday or giving money to support some corrupt charlatan. I do good in my own way where I live, and when I see the fruit of that it helps me not to be bitter so much, to forgive a little bit. But I'm not going to forget. You can be sure of that.

Caleb's anger at his pastor and the church he believed was "basically set up to benefit the leaders" and the sense that William Lim, the None quoted in the epigraph to the chapter, had of having been lied to about Darwin are fairly characteristic among the Nones I interviewed who had come from Evangelical, fundamentalist, or other conservative religious backgrounds. For William, getting to college from his childhood home in Virginia with "a backpack full of stories and bullshit about creationism" was "humiliating." Homeschooled by his mother, William was intellectually gifted. He excelled at developing video games and, eventually, smartphone applications, including several with creationist biblical themes. "I never thought about the science of it," he told me. "I was into the story and the technology. I got so much praise for my stuff that it never occurred to me to doubt." But when he started taking classes in biology and geology, instead of the math and computer science classes for which he had originally registered, William explained,

> I felt like a chump. There I was thinking I was so smart. You know, all the parents always brag about how much better homeschooled kids do on standardized tests. I did so well on the SATs. I actually had a full academic scholarship. I was that smart. And I also thought the universe was six thousand years old. I actually believed that.

William's anger quickly came to the surface as we talked:

> Who the fuck sends their kids into the world thinking that? What was wrong with my parents that they believed these domineering, self-deluded church leaders who told them to teach us this stuff? And, how the hell did they think I was going to go out into the real world where the information, the truth, isn't hidden—you know, me, a really smart kid—and not trip over the plain facts that exposed everything I was raised with as one big, giant lie?

In contrast to Caleb's experience, however, becoming None was more gradual for William, despite his anger. College was a process of intellectual and religious discovery that progressively drew him away from the Pentecostal tradition in which he had been raised, leaving behind a deep resentment that continues to trouble him:

> I try to not blame my parents. I know they love me and they were try-
> ing to "raise me up right," as my mom would say. I mean, I was this
> geeky half-Asian kid with thick glasses, and they made me feel special.
> You know, I would have had a permanent wedgy if I'd gone to secular
> schools. But I do know I missed a lot that I shouldn't have. Does that
> make me angry? Yes, yes it does. I mean, I basically had to reprogram
> myself intellectually, and that eventually made it impossible for me to
> be religious at all. I tried to connect with more liberal Evangelicals for
> a while, but I think in the end you either believe what the Bible says on
> some level or you don't. I just don't. And, you know, I just don't have
> the time and energy for religion now. I wasted too much of that already.

Former Evangelical Glenda Storey now identifies as Spiritual-But-Not-Religious. Glenda was raised in Orange Country, California, where her family attended a well-known Evangelical mega-church with a number of celebrity preachers. "I hated it," she blurted out when I asked what her childhood experience of church was. "I just hated it for as long as I could remember. I used to pretend I was sick as often as I could get away with so I didn't have to go." What put Glenda off so intensely? "Oh, the hypocrisy," she groaned, continuing:

> Everything was for show. The music. The lights. How people dressed. It
> was just Disneyland for Jesus freaks. And, you know, it was pretty much
> lily white, conservative Republican—which suited my parents fine. But,
> it was all pretty much fake. Like, my mom would host a women's Bible
> study, and they'd all talk about other women from church. Or they'd
> have this really fancy religious jewelry. They actually had jewelry parties
> where you could buy—oh, I don't know—diamond studded crosses,
> and stuff. Everything was big, and loud, and flashy. I just never went in
> for any of that. You know, I was a quiet kid. I liked to read and ride my
> bike around the park, under the trees. Even when I was maybe seven or
> eight, I knew they were all fakes—unfortunately, my parents included.

What troubled Glenda in particular, as she pedaled around town, was how many homeless people she saw outside the gated communities where her family and those of most of their church friends lived. She asked her parents if the church was helping any of the people she had seen:

> My mom goes, "Oh, sweetie, they have to *want help* first. They have to help themselves." And, my dad nods. "You can't give people handouts. They won't value work then," he says. I mean, I had seen old people— really old people—sleeping in the park, going through the trash. You know, it was an everyday thing, and [my parents] had nothing. Nothing. Well, I guess I shouldn't say that. They told me I should pray for the people I'd seen. You know, the whole thing was that it didn't matter if you *were* good. It mattered if you *felt good* and if you *looked good*. Praise Jesus for liposuction!

Her concern about the homeless notwithstanding, it seems fair to say that Glenda, an only child, had a difficult relationship with her parents on a number of levels. Our conversation overall made it clear that she never quite felt in step with the affluent Orange Country culture in which she grew up. Religion seemed but one more way that Glenda, who also described herself as "chronically non-normative" with regard to her weight, felt different. Religion played into that experience as well. The family church also sponsored a weight loss program centered on Bible study, prayer, and scripture memorization. When she was 16, Glenda's parents signed her up for a 10-week summer program for teens, the goal of which was to "lose 30 pounds by getting closer to God."[51]

"It would have been bad enough," Glenda told me, "if it was just, like, an eating plan and support group. But they made it about you failing God by being overweight—you 'profaning the temple of your body.' It was incredibly shaming, especially because other kids would see all of us going to that part of the campus—'the fat lands,' they called it." The experience was deeply scarring for Glenda, and further alienated her from her parents. Halfway through the summer, she attempted suicide. She spent most of the next year in and out of treatment facilities, where her exposure to self-help literature by the likes of Melody Beattie and John Bradshaw offered her new ways of exploring her spirituality outside the Evangelical tradition.[52] "Ironically, it was my miracle," she said of the experience overall. "I guess I had always had an intuition that there were other, more compassionate ways of being in the world. Who knows how long it would have taken me to escape from that Evangelical mind control cult."

Now a massage therapist and Reiki practitioner, Glenda lives in Oak Creek, Arizona, the heart of the spiritually resonant Sedona "Red Rock" region.[53] She says she continues to work through resentments about the way her parents used religion to shame her and "make me hate my beautiful, generous body." She has traded in forced daily Bible readings for daily meditation, and tries to "listen to the anger to see what I can learn from it" when it wells up. And the homeless who so concerned Glenda as a young girl? I wondered if they were on her mind and how they factored into her spiritual life today.

"That's complicated here," she smiled, "because a lot of the people you see around here that you'd think were homeless somewhere else are really not. They're just working out their lives in different ways. We all take care of each other, though. Most of the cafes share food at the end of the day, and they're always giving people water when it's hot."

"What about you?" I asked. "How do you help out?"

"Oh, I do Reiki," she said quickly. "When I see someone who really seems to need healing—be it physical, psychological, or spiritual—I align with them energetically by visualizing healing light all around us. I ask the universe to keep sending healing energy to the person, or sometimes to, you know, everyone in the area who needs it."

"It sounds a little like you're praying for them," I said.

Glenda sighed, only a little impatient. "I can see how you might think that," she indulged me, "but it's nothing like prayer in the sense that my parents and their church prays [*sic*]. Those prayers are just wishes—mostly for material things. Reiki really moves energy. It really changes the energy around us and in a person. It's not an idea or a dogma. It's a real thing that happens."

"Oh," I nodded.

"That's how I got all of the anger, the poison of my childhood religious upbringing, out of me. Reiki literally healed me. It turned all that anger into nothing but good so I can try to help in healing others now."

Among Nones from Evangelical and other more conservative Christian traditions who talked with me, frustration and anger featured frequently in stories of becoming None. This often had to do with the circumstances of the change in their religious and spiritual self-identity. For Caleb and Glenda, for instance, the shift was borne out of particular crises that had many other dimensions beyond religion. In some sense, arguably, religious affiliation mediated other problematic relational dynamics, becoming another casualty as the relationship frayed. In both cases, healing from these painful experiences has been a longer process. William, by contrast, while still angry about feeling that his parents had lied to him about evolution and other scientific information, seems to have had a strong enough relationship with his parents to be willing to work through his anger with them. In all of these examples, however, becoming None was not the kind of drift I tended to see among former Mainline Protestants. It took a certain spark to prompt change, even among those who had questioned or doubted before leaving their churches. Becoming None came, in many cases, through the pull of an outside circumstance, rather than the push an inward doubt, question, or desire.

Becoming None from Roman Catholic Some

A push toward unaffiliation rather than an inward pull was likewise the case for many of the former Roman Catholic Nones who shared their stories with me. Among the 18 Catholics I interviewed, however, anger was not generally the most pronounced affect. Rather, most of them expressed feelings of loss, hurt, and pain. Nones who had been raised as Catholics, more than those from any other religious background, talked about what they missed from their earlier religious experience. They told of Catholic exemplars they continued to admire—Dorothy Day or Thomas Merton, for example. Even when they were critical of Catholic teachings on sexuality, the role of women in religious leadership, or the response of the church to clergy sexual abuse, they were consistently appreciative of Catholic spiritual, liturgical, and social justice practices. It should perhaps not be surprising, then, that fully half of the Catholics I talked with said that they felt pushed out of the church. Like Natalie Darling, the former Catholic None quoted at the beginning of the chapter, who felt "cast out" from and "abandoned" by the Catholic Church, other former Catholic Nones used words like "exile" and "exclusion" to a degree I did not hear among Nones raised in any other religious tradition.

In the case of 41-year-old Natalie, who was raised as a Catholic and attended Catholic schools and universities all the way through graduate school, the process of becoming None unfolded slowly. Becoming None was not a rejection of the Catholic tradition per se. "I just loved so much of it—the sacraments, the rituals, the seasons of the liturgical year. I still do. I loved Lent, especially," she told me. "For a while I even thought I might be a nun." A growing feminist consciousness, however, challenged her ability to accept church teachings on women, especially in religious leadership.

> There are Catholic feminists. There are lots of women who are trying to change the church "from within." You know, they'll say, "we can't let them"—the male hierarchy—"push us out of our own church." I was like that for a long time. I didn't want to go. I wanted to help make a change.

Finally, however, after she had come out as a lesbian in her early thirties, Natalie came to feel that "there was no place for me once I really knew who I was." When Catholic bishops joined Mormons and Evangelicals in campaigns against marriage equality for same-sex couples, Natalie felt "exiled" from the church:

> You know, I stood by the church even through all the sex abuse scandals. At the time, I tried to focus on all the good that was done for the poor by people in Catholic churches—by women religious, especially.

I didn't excuse the abuse, but I didn't want to throw away all the good, too. I knew—still know—wonderful priests and brothers who are remarkable servants of God's people. But I knew the church wouldn't stand by me, let alone stand up for me. I knew they were willing to throw out all the good done by faithful Catholic lesbians and gays just so they could win this fight. I mean, the letters they sent to be read in the churches on Sundays. The things they mailed to our homes. It was horrible. It broke my heart. I literally cried for days. How could they have so much hate for us? Eventually, I knew it was time. I just had to find my own way spiritually. I couldn't call myself "Catholic" anymore. I couldn't call myself anything. And, I didn't really want to be anything else—you know, Episcopalian or something. I'm just Spiritual now. I'm finding my own way.

Natalie's "own way" does involve periodic participation in church services. She attends a monthly chanted prayer, or Taizé, service at a Benedictine monastery in the area. And, still having many Catholic friends, including a number of women religious, she does volunteer work with a social service agency affiliated with the local diocese. But, she told me, "I know I'm just a visitor there. I don't take communion. I don't pretend I'm one of them. I know I'm not."

The push for Frank Brunner, a 37-year-old from Erie, Pennsylvania, who described himself as "Spiritual-But-Not-Religious," came from a somewhat different direction, but it was nonetheless hurtful at a very personal level. In Frank's case, the church's stands on contraception, assisted conception, and stem cell research turned him away from the church. Unlike former Pentecostal William Lim, however, this was not a matter of coming into new scientific knowledge. Rather, Frank's transition from Catholic to None was initiated by conflicts between Catholic teachings and very personal life-and-death experiences in his close-knit family. Like Natalie, Frank had grown up in the church and had been educated in Catholic schools through high school. He and his wife, who remains Catholic, had been married in the church. The couple baptized their two children in the local church of which they, along with both sets of their parents and a number of their siblings, were also members. Frank told me, "I figured we'd all be buried there." Two family crises, however, caused Frank to reconsider, and ultimately end, his relationship to the church. The change was not immediate. Rather, he explained, "It kind of played out over a few years, first when my sister couldn't have a baby and then when my Uncle Frank, who I was named for, died of Parkinson's."

In the first case, Frank's younger sister had experienced a series of devastating miscarriages, and eventually had surgery in the hopes of improving her chances of carrying a child to term. When that failed, Frank's sister and her husband

decided to use a surrogate, who would be impregnated through in vitro fertiliza-
tion. When the family priest found out, he counseled strenuously against surro-
gacy. The priest's intervention had a destabilizing effect on the whole extended
family. Frank narrated a painful drama that erupted when the priest became
aware of the couple's decision:

> Father comes over the house, and he tells her that she can't do this, that
> it's a sin. He says she won't be able to go to communion if she does
> it. And, you know, my mom is crying and my sister is crying. It was
> like somebody died when these kids just want to have a baby, right? It
> was crazy, the whole thing. And I just remember thinking, "Man, this
> is really coldhearted." It was almost like *The Scarlet Letter*, because, you
> know, if our whole family stops going to mass, people are going to want
> to know why, right? So, then everybody starts arguing about whether
> we should listen to Father or should we go to another church or not go
> at all. It was awful. Just awful.

In the end, Frank's sister did use a surrogate to carry her baby, and the baby
was eventually baptized in the church. Though there was a period of awkward-
ness within the family and between the family, the priest, and other members of
the parish community, the drama eventually settled down. But the episode "got
me to thinking," Frank told me, about his relationship to the parish, the Catholic
Church, and religion in general. "It's funny," he said,

> what a big part of my life that church was, but when it got right down to
> it, it didn't really have my values. Not in itself. It was what we brought
> to it as a family. That's what was really "spiritual" to me—that this was
> the church we all grew up in, and got married, and baptized our kids.
> But with this thing with my sister, you could see the priest and a lot of
> people in the church who heard about it, didn't care about her and her
> husband. They didn't care that this was tearing them up. It just kind
> of ate at me. When I'd go after that, even when it all had pretty much
> settled down, I'd get upset. I had to go outside a couple times.

The local church had been a social nexus for Frank, his extended family, and a
large number of friends who had also grown up in the church and had remained
in the area. "I started to think I was going for the wrong reasons," Frank said.
He felt his affiliation was really more about his relationship with his family and
community than about a commitment to the Catholic Church and its teachings
as such. "Once I really started looking at what the church teaches, I didn't agree
with a lot of it. I mean, we use contraception, right? That's just being responsible.

But it makes us sinners in the eyes of the church. I don't think my wife and I are sinners because we're responsible adults. I don't think my sister and her husband sinned. So what am I doing there?"

Still, Frank stayed in the church for some time, his feelings about the priest's callow and judgmental response toward his sister and the difference between many of his own beliefs and Catholic teachings stirring within him. The final push came when his beloved uncle succumbed to complications from Parkinson's disease. This again brought the family into closer engagement with the parish priest as they organized the funeral mass. The priest's offense this time around? He objected to the family's request that funds be donated in Uncle Frank's name to a Parkinson's organization that sponsored stem cell research. Uncle Frank himself had supported the organization. The younger Frank was furious at the insensitivity and arrogance of the priest, who lectured the family in the lobby of the funeral home about "being Catholics when it's convenient," referencing the incident with Frank's sister. Ultimately, however, Frank's anger turned into a surprisingly compassionate sadness:

> He stood there, wagging his finger, saying something like, "When you receive communion, you receive the whole church and all of its teachings, not just the ones that suit your lifestyle." It just sunk into me, he thinks he's better than all of us—more moral, more holy. But also I got he resented us—our family, I think, and how we care about each other. You know, the church is supposed to be so "pro-family." But I think he had no idea what it really means to love someone when they're going through what my sister went through or losing someone like Uncle Frank. It's not about a bunch of rules. It's about how you love people. I knew I didn't need to be part of that church to love my family. I still pray. I still believe there's something out there, you know, higher than us. But I don't need the church to tell me they know everything about how that all works. No one does. And I don't need them telling me how to run my life.

For Judith Leonard, the New Yorker we met in the Introduction, anger about her church experience was still a palpable emotion, but the underlying pain when she found herself "tossed to the curb" by the Catholic Church after a divorce was also clear. In her late thirties at the time, with two teenaged daughters, Judith had turned to a pastoral assistant, who happened to be a Dominican sister, when her alcoholic, abusive, and philandering husband filed for divorce. "I thought she, as a woman, would understand better," Judith sighed bitterly. "But, you know, those women are just manufactured on the other end of the factory from the priests. It was like talking to a stone."

Judith had been a stay-at-home mother, and had no immediate employment prospects. In addition, despite the fact that he had initiated the divorce and was living with another woman, her husband continued to come by the apartment, usually drunk and often violent. Judith had hoped that the church would help her in both spiritual and practical ways through the divorce.

> I was desperate. I didn't know what to do. I needed to find an apart-
> ment that he couldn't find and that I could afford. I needed to figure
> out where he had moved our money. I needed to get child support.
> I needed to find a job. But, mostly, I think, I wanted someone to, I don't
> know, tell me God still loved me—that it wasn't my fault. You know, he
> had cracked me in the face in front of my girls. There's no fixing that. But
> what does she say to me? She says—right hand to whoever you want—
> she says "it's no good making everything into a soap opera." She told me
> I was being "dramatic," that I wanted attention. She tells me I should—
> get this—"pray to the blessed virgin" for help saving my marriage and
> then go to confession. And, this was not, let me point out, in nineteen-
> fifty-something. This is in the late 1980s, when you have to be an idiot
> to think like that. In Long Island, New York! It devastated me. It really
> just devastated me the way she just tossed me to the curb like that.

In 2012, the Roman Catholic Diocese of Trenton, New Jersey, conducted a survey of "lapsed" Catholics to try to determine why they had left the church.[54] As in the examples of former Catholic Nones mentioned here, and as with many former Mainline Protestant Nones, the researchers found that most of the peo-ple they surveyed did not cite doctrinal concerns as a primary reason for leaving. People did note disagreements with Catholic stances on abortion, contracep-tion, divorce, women clergy, married clergy, homosexuality, and confession to a priest. But these disagreements did not generally cause the anger displayed by many Nones who had been raised in conservative Evangelical churches. Like most Mainline Protestant denominations, Roman Catholicism—at least in America—has a degree of theological diversity and flexibility that generally includes space for wrestling with doubts and questions. Plenty of Catholics, as survey upon survey makes clear, actively disagree with the church on one or more doctrinal matters. Yet, as with Natalie Darling's feminist friends who hoped to "change the church from within," they continue to identify and prac-tice as Catholic.[55]

Unlike former Mainliners, however, Nones from Catholic backgrounds who talked with me did not simply drift away from the faith. This was likewise the case among the 300 former Catholics surveyed in the Trenton Diocese. Rather, as with Natalie, Frank, and Judith, something drove them away—something more painfully personal than abstractly theological. Questions and doubts were not addressed with respect and complexity. Concerns were dismissed or demeaned. Spiritual experience was diminished. Hence, half of the former Catholics from the Trenton diocese reported that they were put off by the "arrogant, distant, unavailable, and uncaring" actions of parish clergy. Doctrine might have been faulty for many former Catholics, but relationships were what ultimately failed.

Thus, perhaps a reflection of a deeper integration of Catholic identity in the story of the self overall, the "none-ing" of most of the former Roman Catholics who talked with me typically played out over time. Even Judith, stunned and "devastated" by the response she received from the pastoral associate and further embarrassed when word leaked out to others in the parish about the divorce— "I can still feel how people looked at me," she told me—took her daughters to church regularly through the next year. She made sure her younger daughter completed the Confirmation rite that marks the movement of young teens into early adulthood as Catholic Christians. For Judith and Natalie, leaving the Catholic Church was not unlike leaving an abusive marriage. Frank described it as being like giving up an addiction. For all three, the transition from affiliated to unaffiliated took time. The shift had consequences within networks of relationships that wove through the church. Frank's mother, he said, still cries about his decision to leave the Catholic Church. His wife remains Catholic, though she now belongs to a different parish. She worries, Frank reported, about how their kids will interpret his rejection of the church. For her part, Natalie remains connected to many Catholic friends, but "it's different now," she told me. "I'm not one of them anymore." Overall, the process of becoming Nones was been tremendously painful for many of the former Catholics who talked with me.

A Caution on Denominational Type Casting

Bored Mainliners, Angry Evangelicals, Wounded Catholics—these are obviously broad generalizations that do not apply in each, individual instance of former Christians becoming Nones. There is no simple typology here, as emotions overlap and circumstances diverge. It is also important to bear in mind that all of the people who agreed to be interviewed for *Choosing Our Religion* wanted to share their stories. There are many motivations for that, but the plethora of blogs by and for former Evangelicals and former Roman Catholics in particular, whether or not they became Nones, and the tone of many of the posts to those blogs do suggest that angry former Evangelicals, Mormons, and other more conservative Christians and wounded Roman Catholics yearn for outlets to tell their stories. Bored, drifting, or seeking former Catholics and Evangelicals seem mostly to have floated away from the wider conversation, and this may explain the distinctive denominational tones that generally emerged from the interviews. Indeed, the youngest of the former Catholic Nones I interviewed, 18-year-old Roberto Torres, an Agnostic from Quincy, Massachusetts, sounded much more like the former Mainline Nones who talked with me:

> Oh, I just got sick of it after 12 years of Catholic school. "Love your neighbor"—check! "Help the poor"—check! "Respect life"—okay, I don't really agree with how they see that. But, sure, check! The thing is, I'm on my own now in college. Is there a god? Isn't there? That, I could not tell you. But I think I'm a good person. It's my job to figure the rest of it out. That's what you go to college for.

Roberto seems much like the majority of the undergraduates in my religion classes at a Jesuit university. Whether or not they were raised as Catholics, most of my students identify as some variety of None in college, and few of them trouble much over leaving their religious past behind.[56] The transition from Some to None seems almost unintentional. On reflection, it may raise some identity questions, but these do not provoke the anguish we saw in Frank, Judith, or Natalie. One student put it this way in a paper about her religious identity:

> I wasn't really against being Catholic. Nobody believes in all of it, and there are things I did personally disagree with. I don't think I really ever got much out of going to mass, to tell the truth. But it was more like there was so much going on here [at college], and so many other ways to express my spirituality that I just kind of set it aside. I almost sort of forgot I used to be Catholic. If people ask me, I just say I'm not religious. Technically, that would mean I'm not Catholic, but I guess probably part of me still is in a way just because that is my religious background, so it's how I sort of was trained to think about values and spirituality. It was how my moral compass was set up.[57]

Like the former Mainline Protestant Nones we met earlier in the chapter, Roberto and my student exhibited something of a sense of benign entitlement with regard to religious and spiritual choices. Considered from a wider cultural perspective, this is perhaps not surprising. The irony of the long-standing normative leaning of the United States as "culturally Protestant"[58] is that it has allowed what was once a more dominant religious group in terms of numbers and sociopolitical influence to neglect the reinforcement of denominational identities by way of church attendance or affiliation. But the more pervasive Protestant ethos of American culture in fact reinforces at least a tepid form of these values through various media, educational structures and practices, and political rhetoric. Researchers have found, for example, that the majority of weddings on television and movies are Protestant.[59] Those from other religious groups do not enjoy—or, perhaps, suffer from—this level of general cultural reinforcement of their religious backgrounds. But they do absorb a version of cultural Protestantism from the media-infused reality of everyday life. Thus, a national, longitudinal study of young people revealed what researchers referred to as "the dominant religion among US teenagers": "moralistic therapeutic deism," or MTD. Christian Smith and Melinda Lundquist Denton identify five characteristics of MTD through interviews with 267 teens:

1. A God exists who orders and created the world and watches over human life on earth.
2. God wants people to be good, nice, and fair to each other, as taught in the Bible and by most world religions.
3. The central goal of life is to feel good about oneself.
4. God does not need to be particularly involved in one's life except when God is needed to resolve a problem.
5. Good people go to heaven when they die.[60]

Smith and Denton express a certain frustrated cynicism about this view as wholly a different religion from the institutional religions in which their teenaged subjects were raised. Yet it does not take much of a stretch to see in MTD something of an over-generalized and theologically weakened form of the progressive Mainline Protestantism that Matthew Hedstrom and David A. Hollinger argue successfully permeated the wider culture in the beginning of the twentieth century, and which Kathryn Lofton, much more pessimistically, saw amplified in the spiritual offerings of media icons like Oprah Winfrey.[61] Indeed, in a follow-up study on the data from which Smith and Denton's conclusions are drawn, Kenda Creasy Dean makes clear that these findings do not depict a generation of prodigals gone lost from the true faith of the elders. Rather, says Dean, "The National Study of Youth and Religion reveals a theological fault line running underneath American churches: an adherence to a do-good, feel-good spirituality that has little to do with the Triune God of Christian tradition and even less to do with loving Jesus Christ enough to follow him into the world."[62] She tells fellow Christian leaders, educators, and parents, "We're responsible" for the drift that MTD allows young adults raised in Christian churches to make into unaffiliation.[63] But it is important to understand that the muted Protestant ideologies that have been shaped, in Dean's view, by Christians themselves into moral therapeutic deism extend well beyond Christian communities as a postmodern version of progressive Protestantism that is distributed through the culture, without consideration of religious distinctions.[64]

One implication of cultural Protestantism has traditionally been that non-normative religious groups had to work harder to reinforce religious identity and affiliation. Given the more marginal cultural status of Catholics, Evangelicals, Mormons, Jews, Muslims, Buddhists, and so on, the decision to leave could often be more dramatic—a breach of community and culture as much as of religious practice. In this light, Mainline Protestants who become Nones have had the luxury of being more sanguine about their gradual drift into unaffiliation. Morally, socially, psychologically, and spiritually, the consequences of change often feel more significant for Catholics and conservative Protestants, especially those over age 40 or 50.

But it now seems that younger Catholics from families more fully assimilated in the still vaguely Protestantized mainstream America feel, like their Mainline Protestant peers, a greater sense of spiritual and religious self-determination than did Catholics in previous generations and than many Evangelicals still do. Less obviously anchored to ethnic and class identity than in previous eras, Catholicism today is less reinforced by other elements of social self-identity. It is, thus, less integrated into other parts of life and moves less fluidly through the narrative of the self. We have seen this disambiguation of religious, ethnic, cultural, and other elements of social identity among American Latinos, a group traditionally thought of as resiliently Catholic. Though more than half of American Latinos identify as Roman Catholic, one in four Latinos is a former Catholic. And, as with Americans overall, nearly 20% of Latinos are now religiously unaffiliated.[65]

Marginally Religious Nones and Nones from the Margins

As noted in the Introduction, consistent with the religious make-up of the US population, the majority of the participants in the surveys and interviews I conducted were from Christian backgrounds. I would not feel comfortable generalizing about the six people who talked with me who had been raised as Jews. I interviewed only one person raised as a Buddhist, one raised as an Atheist (Dmitri, whom we met in the Introduction), and two who came from a household with no religious practice at all. No Nones who had been raised as Muslims or Hindus participated in the "Nones Beyond the Numbers" survey or were interviewed. Further, it is important to remember that all Mainline Protestants, conservative or Evangelical Christians, or Roman Catholics are not alike. Some were raised in only nominally religious households. Again, this reality insists that much caution should be taken in applying the "bored, angry, sad" schema wholesale. Likewise, it suggests that we consider religious unaffiliation as much in its diverse particularity as in any temporary typology that might be developed on the basis of characteristics like religious background, which we may assume to have common characteristics but which in fact often do not.

"Technically, we were Christian," 22-year-old Adam Noonan from Huntington Beach, California, told me. "But we went to church maybe three times a year. You know, at Christmas, Easter, and one more time because my mom felt bad about going just on Christmas and Easter." Said Adam, who now identifies simply as Spiritual, "what I know about Christianity you could literally put in a thimble." For Adam, becoming None could hardly be called a "drift" at all. He was, arguably, a None in all but name throughout his life.

So, too, Bliss Winter, a 19-year-old Spiritual-But-Not-Religious None from Phoenix, Arizona, came from a nominally Christian background. "I think we were Presbyterian," she told me. "And maybe Methodist. I know my grandma on my mom's side is Presbyterian, and we would go there when I was little. But my dad was Methodist, I'm pretty sure." Bliss describes herself as having been Spiritual-But-Not-Religious "pretty much for as long as I can remember." Similarly, though a discernible tone could be heard in interviews with Nones who emerged from Catholic backgrounds, there were other outliers like Roberto. Paolo Morelli, a 23-year-old Agnostic from Baltimore, Maryland, reported that being Catholic "came with the territory" of having an Italian father and a Portuguese mother. Unlike Roberto, however, in Paolo's family, this Catholic cultural background came with little actual religious practice. "My mom and dad were never really strict about it," he told me. "It was more for the benefit of my grandparents. I was baptized Catholic, but we only ever went to church with them."

Thirty-two-year-old Agnostic Leslie Powers, from Upper Darby, Pennsylvania, went to a United Church of Christ congregation as a child. Her parents divorced when she was 10, however. Leslie explained, "My mom went back to school to get her nursing degree. Then she had to work on Sundays a lot, so we more or less stopped going. But when we had time together on a weekend, it was really the most spiritual thing. I still feel that way spending time with her."

Divorce likewise factored into 33-year-old Colton Sarver's lack of familiarity with the Episcopal tradition that was a vague part of his childhood religious experience. "I would ask my mom if we were still—I couldn't even pronounce it—Epi-SCOP-al," he said. "She'd say, 'Your dad is. But we aren't anymore,' so I let it go. When my mom remarried when I was in college, she joined the church my step-dad went to. I'm just spiritual now."

While these former nominally Christian Nones do not share the "bored, angry, sad" tone of other former Christians who talked with me, they do have in common that they are under the age of 40. Most of their parents were attached to an institutional religious tradition, but the connection was clearly thin. They passed bits and pieces of Christian gospel stories and moral teachings to their children, but also allowed a considerable amount of spiritual exploration—or not—by their kids. Generally, these Nones did not have the sense of active spiritual "seeking" that Wade Clark Roof described among their Boomer parents or grandparents. Rather, they seemed much more settled into the idea that the spiritual life is something you sort out for yourself, guided by your own curiosity and passions or the suggestions of friends and family members. Bliss Winter captured something of this young None approach as it grew from the marginally religious backgrounds of her parents and grandparents when she told me,

> I think for my mom, you had to lock down your religion or give it up. She kind of gave it up. I don't feel that either-or about it. I mean, I'm open to a lot of different things, but I'm not anything in particular myself. Like, my boyfriend is African American, and he goes to this Baptist gospel church where they sing, and praise, and all that. They were really big in civil rights in the 60s, I guess. I really like all that. I like going. A lot, actually. But I don't feel pressure to *be that*. Like, I have friends who are Buddhist or just more spiritual like me, and I think we really appreciate each other. No one wants to convert anyone. That would really, I don't know, make me sad, I guess, if someone felt like we couldn't be friends unless we were *exactly alike* in terms of religion. I mean, we can share, like my boyfriend does, how it feels to do it these different ways.

Nones from marginally religious backgrounds have not, it seems, so much drifted into noneness as they have attached a culturally current label for the unaffiliated to fluid spiritualities that have evolved throughout their lives. By contrast, Nones who come from religious backgrounds that have historically been more marginalized in "Christian America" and the very small number of Nones from Jewish and Buddhist backgrounds who talked with me may move into unaffiliation somewhat differently. We will recall that Anna Solomon, who identifies as an Atheist, nonetheless saw her own ethnic, political, and historical identity as a Jew as something sufficiently significant in itself that she intends to raise her daughter in a Jewish community.

Forty-three-year-old Aaron Jacobson likewise believes that Jewish culture and history are important. An Agnostic from Elizabeth, New Jersey, Aaron was raised in a "secular Jewish" household. That is, his family did not generally observe the Sabbath, adhere to kosher dietary rules, or celebrate Jewish holidays like Yom Kippur, Passover, and Hanukkah. More than 20% of Jews see themselves as secular rather than religious, and, as with the US populace in general, the percentage jumps to above 30% among Jews under age 30. Nearly two-thirds of Jews—including many of those who see themselves as religious rather than secular—report that culture and ancestry are the most important elements of

Jewish identity, over religion.[66] Like Anna, Aaron values this cultural identity. He attended Hebrew school until he was 13—the year Jewish boys complete the Bar Mitzvah ritual and girls complete the Bat Mitzvah, signaling the transition to adulthood. "You have to know where you come from, what your roots are," he told me. "I'm glad now I understand more, but, man, I hated it at the time." Nonetheless, Aaron and his husband, also from a secular Jewish background, have no plans to send their four-year-old daughter and two-year-old son to Hebrew school. "There's no need to put them through that," he insisted, continuing:

> Their dads are Jewish. Their grandparents are Jewish. Their aunts, and uncles, and cousins are Jewish. And, we live where we live. There's a lot of Jewish culture around, I'm saying. We'll teach them where they come from and the important stuff—you know, Passover, Yom Kippur—as part of their culture. But we just don't see a need to run them through the whole Hebrew school gauntlet for the sake of saying we did it and having a big party.

I wondered, since Aaron had identified himself in the "Nones Beyond the Numbers" survey as Agnostic (though he noted his Jewish background in comments), if he saw himself as more Agnostic than Jewish. "It's apples and oranges," he said. "You wouldn't ask an Italian guy that, right? Do you see yourself more Italian or Catholic?"

"Well," I noted, " 'Italian' isn't a religion as well as a cultural tradition."

"Sure, okay," Aaron briefly conceded,

> But for me it's almost the same. I'm not going to say I'm not Jewish, because that's what I am. My parents, my grandparents, my great-grandparents—all Jewish. And, you know, it will happen that from time to time someone will say something anti-Semitic. I'm real Jewish then. But it's not my religion. So, if you ask me my religion, I'm going to say "none," or "nothing," or "Agnostic." I'm not going to say "Jewish." So, sure, religiously speaking, I am more Agnostic than Jewish. I'm always still Jewish. It's not like a "conversion."

Where cultural, ethnic, and ancestral identity is connected to a religious tradition—as, for example, with many Irish American or Italian American Nones from Roman Catholic families—formally claiming the label of one kind of None or another can be complicated. It is perhaps unproblematic to think of Jordan Cascade as a "former Presbyterian" or of Colton Sarver as a "former Episcopalian." But, even from the outside looking in, it can be challenging to consider Anna or Aaron "former Jews" given the degree to which their cultural identity as Jews and their religious self-understanding as Nones weave through the narrative of the self—often with considerable ease. Jessica Werner, a 34-year-old from Chevy Chase, Maryland, explained the mixing of her Jewish and Agnostic identity this way:

> Jews have balanced fitting in and not fitting in for centuries. That's how we've survived. We've had to have dual identities just to get by, so I don't think it's such a big deal to be Jewish and Agnostic, or Jewish and Buddhist, or whatever, in the way that it would be if someone Catholic was also an Atheist. It wouldn't work because I think Christians are more about affirming very specific beliefs more than they are about being a part of a historical community. Also, in my case, my grandmother wouldn't let me say I'm not Jewish. I could say I'm Agnostic all day. She'd wave her hand and say, "Whatever. You were born a Jew. You're a Jew." So, you know, we make different, blended, mixed, maybe a little messed up work for us.

"Mixed up" though unaffiliated religious and spiritual identity blended with Jewish cultural identity may be, none of those from Jewish backgrounds experienced transition to being a None as particularly fraught. "My grandmother worried about me not marrying a Jewish man," Jessica told me, "but she didn't really care if he was religious or not. Once I hit 30, she just worried about me getting married at all."

Glen Schmidt, a 50-year-old Agnostic from Prescott, Arizona, was raised in a religious Jewish family in Pittsburgh, Pennsylvania. He said he had never been religious himself, and he had given up any religious practice in college. "I didn't even join the Jewish fraternity," he told me. Still, because he knew it would hurt his mother and grandmother, he participated in religious rituals when he visited with his family. After college, he took a job on the West Coast, then eventually settled in Arizona in his early thirties, marrying a non-practicing Christian woman. Only then, when the couple was planning a "mostly not religious" wedding at a resort in Mexico, did he tell his family he had not been a practicing Jew for a very long time. "Were they upset? Well, sure," he told me. "But it blew over. Once we had kids, they were just happy about that. It's not like we're the only people in the family who don't practice." Unlike Anna and Aaron, however, Glen and his wife have not stressed religion in their children's upbringing. "They know our religious background, and they know both of us are up in the air about the God thing," he told me. "We want them to come to their own conclusions. We try not to push them one way or another."

For 34-year-old Agnostic Nick Darien, the only None from a Buddhist back-ground who talked with me, becoming unaffiliated was not an entirely untrou-bled process. Rather, he saw it as moving away from "drama" in the Buddhist community in which his family were members, rather than "being caught up in crazy all the time." Nick was raised in Los Angeles, where his parents were, and continue to be, active in a Tibetan Buddhist community. Nick and his two sisters regularly attended group meditation sessions, lectures, and other events at the Buddhist center with their parents. Nick "didn't mind" the meditative practice, and he told me he remains attached to the story of the historical Buddha. But, as he grew up, he became suspicious of the "cult of personality" that he believed had formed around some of the teachers at the center, especially the most senior teacher, or Lama, who had great ambitions to establish similar centers across the world. Nick told me:

> It just seemed like Christian evangelism to me. You know, my mom and
> dad were—still are—so devoted to him. They can't hear any criticism. I
> mean, they make up these, you have to call them "myths" about the lineage
> of the leaders going back to ancient Tibetan kings and queens. I mean,
> they're like gods, really. They're not human. It just didn't make any
> sense when you thought of it logically. I don't know, maybe it was just
> an L.A. thing, too. There was always just a lot of drama, a lot of celebrity.
> It was kind of ironic given how most people think of Buddhism as all
> silence and chanting. But it was just like any other religion. There was
> a lot of craziness and controversy all the time. After I was a kid, like in
> high school, and I could see more of what was going on, it just didn't
> work for me. My parents weren't happy about it at all, but I actually
> used the Buddhist teaching that "no two monks travel the same road" to
> convince them that it was okay for me to follow my own path.

Now a conference marketing director in Chicago, Nick reported that he meditates regularly, but doesn't otherwise engage the Buddhist community or culture. "You know, I'm not Asian, so no one expects me to be Buddhist," he said. "It just would never come up unless I brought it up, which I usually don't. I tell people I'm Agnostic if they ask. Some friends know I meditate, but, you know, everybody meditates."

Though he did have his share of frustrations about the hierarchy of the Buddhist tradition in which his family practiced, Nick expressed little of the boredom, anger, or sadness shared by many of the Nones from Christian back-grounds who talked with me. And, he did not feel part of a wider historical and cultural construction of Buddhism. Mostly, he seemed interested in distancing himself from his Buddhist upbringing and from American understandings of

Buddhism. "You hear people talking about Buddhism like it's all Keanu Reeves sitting under a tree and Richard Gere hanging out with the Dalai Lama. It's nothing like that," Nick sighed. "But, from what I know about other religions, they're nothing like what they project either. Buddhism is no worse, I guess. But it's not any better either."

Again, it is impossible to make any generalizations based on so slim a group of Nones from outside the mainstream Christian currents of American religion and spirituality. But their stories do make clear that becoming None is not as simple as "losing religion." It is not simply about rejection, loss, and dissent. Becoming None does not erase or overwrite whatever came before it, whether that includes elements of cultural identity, spiritual practices, moral values, or reconfigured personal relationships. There is a certain amount of layering that happens—a spiritual palimpsest begins to form, as with Judith Leonard's "praying" with photos of her daughters and granddaughters and the Catholic prayer cards she traded in grade school or the link I could not help making between Glenda Storey's practice of sending "healing energy" to troubled people around her and the suggestion her mother made when she was young to pray for the homeless. In the end, becoming a None, as Aaron Jacobson put it, is "not like a 'conversion'" for most of the people who talked with me, even when it was easier to set former religious identities and practices outside the reach of daily consciousness. Echoes remain, Corrie Milliman reminds us as she hears "ancient resonances" between her Christian upbringing and her current Neopagan practice. The religious past whispers in the ear of the spiritual present. We will hear many of these echoes in the chapters that follow, as we move from this exploration of *becoming* None to consideration of what *being* None means in the daily lives of the people who talked with me. We begin in the next chapter by meeting many of the companions—authors, teachers, gurus, and other influencers— who help shape and nurture the spiritual outlooks of Nones. By engaging, adapting, and otherwise appropriating the thinking and practices of these influencers, we will see, Nones shape spiritualities that alternately boundary and bridge their religious past and present. Such influencers help Nones to re-mediate the sacred in their everyday lives, decentering institutional religion in their own practice and, arguably, in the wider culture.

3

Companions on the Journey

Resources for Unaffiliated Affiliation

I'm just interested in things that will help me to grow spiritually as a person, you know, from whatever perspective—religious or philosophical. Growing up, we just had the Bible, and I wasn't really into that. Then I found out there was so much more, so many teachers. I mean, wow!
—Terri Poole, *age 28, Phoenix, Arizona, "Spiritual"*

You might say that rationality is my religion. I believe in thought, in rational argument. That is a kind of self-transcendence, right? Considering someone else's ideas? . . . I "worship," if you like, online where Atheists meet to exchange ideas and information about what's wrong with religion and how it can be challenged by thinking people.
—Neil Grosse, *age 61, Brooklyn, New York, "Atheist"*

Music is where I turn for inspiration . . . I think there's just something about art in general that isn't about offering up all the answers. You know, you listen to Mos Def or someone like [Immortal] Technique, you're going to come away with a lot of questions. But they're the right questions for people like me, my generation—the questions you can't ask in a church about why the world is how it is today. You know, *real* sin and not much salvation.
—Anthony West, *age 33, Akron, Ohio, "Agnostic"*

Early in my research, I attended an academic meeting at which I presented very preliminary findings from the first series of interviews with Nones I had completed the previous summer. My focus in the presentation was on the ways the unaffiliated self-identify and how this compares to how they have been described by the affiliated throughout American history, especially in news and other popular media. During the question and answer segment, someone—a psychologist, I think, though I never actually met him—asked with great intensity, "But what do they *read*, your Nones? How do they inform themselves? What shapes their minds?"

It was not a surprising question in an academic setting. After all, most scholars are shaped significantly by our reading. Further, the traditional model of the lone researcher or writer toiling at her desk, surrounded by piles of books and articles, reflects a normative understanding of academic identity formation as almost entirely a one-to-one cognitive exchange between words on scholarly pages and gray matter in scholars' brains. The same could be said of religious professionals as well, surrounded with sacred texts and isolated in solitary cells. It was not a stretch, then, for an academic to assume that a particular canon of texts would inform and shape a particular variety, or varieties, of unaffiliated minds. And I must confess that, though I was not considering only written texts, when I asked Nones what resources were meaningful to them in their spiritual lives—books, teachers, music, material objects, and so on—I had a particular set of images in my head. The crudest configuration of this would be something along the lines of Lofton's Oprah-infused Spiritual-But-Not-Religious consumerists; Dawkins-Hitchens-style angry New Atheists; *Da Vinci Code* "conspiritualitiests" who meld conspiracy theory and New Age spiritualities;[1] fans of whatever the latest versions of Yanni or Enya might be; and collectors of angels-among-us artifacts. Some of that did appear, though seldom within the narrow stereotypes I initially indulged. Instead, I found that the resources Nones considered "important" or "influential" mapped distinctive spiritual networks that expressed and shaped identity in the context of community—of a sort. As I spoke with Nones about who and what inspired them through their spiritual lives, what emerged were influences shared across local, distributed, and digitally integrated social networks and communities that could be characterized as a form of unaffiliated affiliation. These networks function as social contexts for spiritual enrichment, growth, support, and identity formation.[2] This chapter looks at the resources Nones use to explore, express, interpret, and otherwise shape spiritual and social experience and identity beyond the bounds of institutional religion. We'll also consider how these resources shape loose affiliations that function something like communities.

A case in point is 28-year-old Terri Poole, who described herself as "just spiritual." I met Terri entirely by chance. But she wouldn't see it that way.

During an unplanned, five-hour layover at the Phoenix airport, I happened upon a "recharging lounge" sponsored by a local hotel and settled into a chair at a long bar table fixed with electrical outlets for powering up mobile devices and decorated down the center with a row of waving artificial grasses. Terri, who was reading a book when I sat down across from her, was one of two lounge hosts employed by the hotel. She greeted me warmly. "We're here to help you be as relaxed and comfortable as you can be when you're traveling," she told me as I began plugging my cellphone, iPad, and laptop into the power strip.

"We're kind of an oasis," she added. When I noted that drinks were not served in the lounge, as one might expect of an "oasis," she amended her description, with an endearing patience, given how many cranky travelers like me she must encounter on any given day: "We're more like a *spiritual* oasis."

"Oh?" I wondered. "How does that work?"

I could see that the question threw her a little at first. She worried that the word "spiritual" had made me uncomfortable. "I mean, we're not a religion," she was quick to assure me. "We're a hotel. But, we do our best to be present to people in the moment. We're a spiritual oasis in that way," Terri explained.

"Tell me more," I encouraged, curious now about who exactly this random encounter might have brought into my research orbit now that I had a few extra hours to spare. Terri continued:

> You know, people come in from really hectic travel situations, and we try to help them experience "the Now" with less discomfort. So, your flight was delayed. You want to be home or wherever you're supposed to be going. You're attached to what you thought would be next. Your mind is doing that. So, you're not present in "the Now," and that's pain-ful. We're saying, "You're here, now. You're only ever exactly where you are." We try to make "the Now" and its gifts more apparent to you.

"Wow. That's your hotel's philosophy?" I asked.

"I guess it's my philosophy as I'm working for the hotel," Terri said, without a trace of guile. "They would want you to think about staying at [the hotel] the next time you're in Phoenix. I would hope you're really in 'the Now' wherever you are, which could be our really comfortable hotel."

She offered me a brochure and a free luggage tag.

"Gee," I said, "You have a really spiritual approach to your work."

Terri nodded, apparently reassured that I would not be put off by religious or spiritual talk. She pointed to a page in the book she was reading, Eckhart Tolle's bestselling *The Power of Now: A Guide to Spiritual Enlightenment*. "I highlighted this part this morning, which is exactly where I think my work and my spiritual-ity meet," she said, reading out Tolle's wisdom:

> Make the Now the primary focus of your life. Whereas before you dwelt in time and paid brief visits to the Now, have your dwelling place in the Now and pay brief visits to past and future when required to deal with the practical aspects of your life situation.[3]

She added, "I guess I try to help people have a dwelling place in 'the Now.'"

Over the course of the next four hours, after having explained the nature of my research, and with regular pauses as Terri and her coworker, Kimberley Arthur, tended to other travelers plugging in at the lounge, the two women shared experiences and insights from the perspective of two rather different Nones, each highlighting different influences in their spiritual life. In Terri's case, writers like Eckhart Tolle (a guru to media mogul Oprah Winfrey), Deepak Chopra, Caroline Myss, and, in a slightly different self-help register, Brené Brown[4] were frequent go-to resources for "inspiration and illumination." She told me she also participated from time to time in courses and services offered at a local Center for Spiritual Living. The Center is part of a network of some 450 spiritual communities[5] founded by followers of *Science of the Mind* author and popular turn-of-the-twentieth-century New Thought lecturer, Ernest Holmes.[6]

"I'll go to a class for a few weeks, and maybe a service on Sunday once in a while," Terri said of her relationship to the Center, "but I wouldn't say I 'belong' to it. It doesn't own me. I'm empowered through the work I do there." Regardless of the irregular nature of her attendance and the informality of her relationship with the Center, Terri reported that she had found there a supportive spiritual community and teachers, including the Center's senior minister and a licensed Practitioner of Religious Science, who helped her "find healing in a difficult family situation."

Imagining Unaffiliated Affiliation

An assortment of resources—books, classes, spiritual counselors, loose networks of like-minded seekers, and informal participation in events at the more institutional Center for Spiritual Living—were important in Terri's shaping of a spirituality focused on personal growth through the "opening of consciousness." Through such resources, Nones such as Terri find other ways to connect with people who will affirm, enrich, and support their spiritualities outside traditional religious congregational membership structures. Thus, though much of the rhetoric of contemporary extra-institutional spirituality is framed in the language of individual empowerment, discovery, and authenticity, the network of resources drawn upon by Nones like Terri holds the potential to connect her to other Nones (and sympathetic Somes) with similar spiritual leanings.

Such networks are part of an established tradition of extra-institutional American spirituality. From luminaries such as Emanuel Swedenborg, Ralph Waldo Emerson, Phineas Quimby, and Ernest Holmes, to Mary Baker Eddy, Emma Curtis Hopkins, Norman Vincent Peale, and on to well-known twenty-first-century spiritual teachers like Tolle, Americans have had no shortage of guides to spiritual life outside organized religion. Throughout much of American history, formal and informal communities have formed around these teachers, their ideas, and their practices.[7]

A friend had introduced Terri to the Center for Spiritual Living during the "family situation" she mentioned, and she began spiritual counseling with a "practitioner"—a spiritual counselor who has "enjoyed the teachings of Religious Science, and [has] taken classes and deepened their ability to use the Principles effectively in their own life."[8] The practitioner encouraged Terri to attend a women's "real love" group that would, according to the Center's website, help her to "open [her] heart and mind to unconditional love."[9] Other women in the group, a couple of whom became close friends, introduced Terri to the teachings of Chopra, Tolle, Myss, Brown, and others. "The teaching really helps to keep me open," Terri told me. "It's just really easy to close yourself off to the real potential for love and joy that is always present. You know, we offer each other these gifts of wisdom as we come upon them, and that's really influenced me a lot—I mean both the teachings and the way people share and really want to give this wisdom to everyone."

As books and other resources meant to extend spiritual learning into daily life—classes, music, visual art, music, and products from journals and jewelry to incense burners, glass affirmation stones, and (in Andrew Weil's chain of wellness stores) chewing gum—are shared among friends and acquaintances, a form of spiritual community is formed. Within such communities, what makes a resource important or influential is not so much the words on the page, or the color and shape of a set of prayer beads, as it is the experience of finding it, often through the recommendations or gifts of friends, exploring it with others, passing it along, and so on.[10] Communications scholars Danielle Fuller and DeNel Rehberg Sedo note that in a culture in which new media and broadcast media come together to shape interactive reading practice, "a book can act as a cultural mediator or a kind of engine for social gatherings" like book clubs, discussion groups, or online conversations.[11] These gatherings need not be formalized in the sense of having regular meeting times, identified leaders, or defined agendas. Often there are entirely ad hoc, especially as Nones explore spiritual resources online. Tweet the title of the latest Brené Brown offering, and you'll quickly find yourself in a dynamic conversation with hundreds of people with similar interests and spiritual outlooks.

Oprah's #SoulSunday on Twitter or Pinterest is a spiritual community that engages her weekly television program through social media. A "community" in this sense is shaped as people share resources, along with constantly developing, mutually reinforcing interpretations that mark both the resource and its meanings as particular to a loose social network of individuals with similar spiritual sensibilities. The test of this idea is simple enough. Look on the bookshelves of a few of your friends or close associates and you're likely to find that your reading lists have much overlap in both specific titles and the general kinds of books you read. The same is likely to be true for the kinds of television shows you watch, the movies you see, and so on.

The community defines both the function of something designated "valuable" or "important" (it "keeps one open") and its meaning (that "real potential for love and joy is always present"). Acceptance and reinforcement of these meanings identify one as within or outside the community. Thus, somewhat ironically, the "openness" to new insights and meanings that Terri highlights is in practice closed down as an authoritative canon is constructed across her spiritual network. In Terri's spiritual community we might expect an "openness" to the writings of, say, Wayne Dyer or Marianne Williamson. They may perhaps slide in a slightly more Christian direction toward Richard Rohr or Anne Lamott—apocryphal texts intersecting the more typical canon to the extent that they reinforce the values of "openness" or "ever present potential for joy." But those in Terri's community are not likely to feel as comfortable with, say, the writings of Parker Palmer (around whom communities have likewise formed) and self-enrichment practices such as modified Quaker clearness committees, or the theories of secularism and religion offered up by anthropologist Saba Mahmood and the conversations that swirl around her work in academic networks.

While not tightly boundaried, different clusters of the unaffiliated thus come to have distinctive canons of literature, music, film, art, commercial products, and so on, which express, shape, and define their perspectives. When Nones refer to these canonical resources in social settings, they send a signal to others that invites conversation and connection.[12] What might be seen as "misfires" in this signaling also allow people in differing communities to withdraw from what might be socially awkward conversation. I was aware of the specialized way Terri was using "the Now," which she drew from the work of Eckhart Tolle. I engaged that language as a researcher, but would likely not have in a different social setting. The way different clusters of Nones talk about their spirituality and the resources they reference form distinctive "spiritual genres" that cue fellow travelers that they've found a companion and signal spiritual outsiders that they've crossed into a strange neighborhood.[13] The social structuring that takes place, or breaks down, through signaling with resources in a particular spiritual genre was clear as Kimberley, a Secular Humanist who worked alongside Terri at the recharge lounge, periodically rolled her eyes discreetly or sighed a bit as Terri described the resources she found influential.

"So, you're not much into Tolle's work?" I asked Kimberley as Terri was greeting a new group of visitors to the lounge.

She smiled slightly. "I can't honestly say I've read him," she said. "But I'm pretty sure I wouldn't. It's just not really my sort of thing."

"What is?" I wondered.

"I tend to have a more rational approach to things," Kimberley explained. "I'm not so 'touchy-feely.' I like to think my way through things."

Even so, this "thinking through things" was no more an independent, individualistic approach for Kimberley than it was for Terri. Her boyfriend, a law student, had introduced her to the writings of Noam Chomsky and brought her into a community of activists associated with the Occupy movement, where the writings of Salman Rushdie and Slavoj Žižek were regularly shared. These associations greatly expanded the resources she drew on to develop her self-understanding as a Secular Humanist. At the same time, other college friends recommended books by Margaret Atwood, Umberto Eco, Zadie Smith, and Alice Walker that introduced a literary aesthetic to her rationalism. For Kimberley, who had recently completed an undergraduate degree in marketing but was considering a somewhat different direction for graduate school—law or literature, she told me—rational consideration of existential questions and aesthetic experience hinged on individual agency:

> Literature shows how thinking and feeling come together as a natural function of human reasoning without the need to invent some sort of ethereal otherworld to connect it all. For me, literature *is* spirituality; politics *is* spirituality. They are the human spirit at work. And, because they're creative work—from an individual perspective—you engage them as a unique individual with your own perspectives.

We see in Kimberley's and Terri's reflections elements of the social distinctions that sociologist Pierre Bourdieu has described as driving factors in the development of "personal" taste. Bourdieu argues that taste is not merely a matter of personal preference, but rather that it adapts and reinforces social categories such as class, gender, religion, and so on.[14] Taste, in Bourdieu's schema, contributes to a distinctive way of being in the world through people's patterns of consumption—the books they buy, teachers they admire, films they watch, and so on. These become symbols through which members of a social network, however informally affiliated, recognize one another.[15] Kimberley made clear that Tolle et al. were "not my sort of thing," despite her further admission that she had not read them. The lexical markers Terri used—air-quoting selected words and phrases such as "the Now"—indicated to Kimberley that this resource was outside her intellectualized Secular Humanist canon. Later, Terri came back to the conversation as Kimberley and I were talking about Atwood's *The Handmaid's Tale*, protesting that "it's all over my head." Each woman distinguished herself, her community, and its canonical resources from the other, both directly and more subtly. Yet just as Terri's embrace of "openness" as a value actually closes her to certain spiritual resources and associated practices that would not be valued within her community, Kimberley's valuing of "individual perspective" is shaped by a wider, collective viewpoint. The resources each uses to support and enrich her unaffiliated spirituality function as a mode of affiliation. Teachers, books, movies, music, journals, statues, and the like that are valued across loose networks of spiritual affiliation not only provide Nones with content—ideas, inspirations, and suggestions for more authentic living. They also allow Nones to imagine a wider community of like-minded people and, through digital social networking especially, to connect with them with greater ease and regularity than would have been possible in the past.[16]

The complexity of this kind of intertwined interpretive, resource-dependent structuring of community is illuminated when Nones move from one spiritual community to another—or to none at all, as with Natalie Darling, the former Catholic introduced in the previous chapter. As she worked to get over the feeling of having been "cast out" of the church, Natalie retained a number of relationships within the church and continued a measure of practice by attending Taizé services periodically and participating in a food-sharing program. But, however much she continued relationships with Catholic friends, she came to see herself as "not one of them." In this time of spiritual transition, Natalie began to seek out other resources for understanding and nourishing her developing spiritual identity and enriching her spiritual practice. Her starting point was other religious traditions. She explained:

> I always knew, of course, some things about other world religions— probably especially Judaism. As a social worker, you know, I had to have sensitivity about other religions. We have a large Muslim population in the Twin Cities, and lots of Sikhs, too. So, I wasn't ignorant. But, I think I'd say that when I was Catholic, I understood other religions almost entirely in relation to Catholicism. To understand them, I guess, I would look for commonalities and sort of ignore the major differences. Even if different elements interested me, I wasn't really inclined to go too deep. . . . But after a while—after I started to feel less upset about religion in general, I guess—I started really trying to look at other religions as much as I could on their own terms. Not "How is this like/not like Catholicism?" But, "What do these people believe? How do they act? What can that bring to my spirituality?"

"It was an interesting experiment and I really think I learned a lot," Natalie concluded. "But I wasn't going to become some other kind of religion. I kept looking—I'm still looking—for things that can help me to grow spiritually and for some kind of community where I'm comfortable, where there are people more like me. I really miss that." In the end, learning about other religious

traditions, interesting though that might have been, didn't allow Natalie to identify a community of "people more like me." Still, her exploration of writings on
different religious traditions is an important part of Natalie's efforts to imagine
herself into such a community.

It's worth noting that the communities imagined by Nones as they move
from affiliation to unaffiliation are hardly hallucinatory; these imagined collec-
tivities have very real social effects. The same is true when Somes understand
themselves as Methodist or Hindu. They don't personally know every other
Methodist or Hindu, but their imagined community nonetheless has concrete
effects when they identify with its values, cultural practices, mytho-histories,
and, in some cases, ethnicities. The reality of these largely imagined connections
gives them their political import, which also extends to economic, religious,
and other effects in the wider society. Thus, in January 2013, on the heels of
the release of the "Nones on the Rise" report, which highlighted Nones' more
generally liberal outlooks and voting practices, an annual meeting of leaders of
Humanist, Atheist, and other non-religious organizations convened "to chart a
path forward and discuss the most important issues facing 'nones' today." The
group was concerned to "consolidate [the] cultural presence" of Nones to "gain
broader social acceptance" and to amplify their wider cultural and political influence.[17] Based on new demographic data, the leaders had imagined a collective
with interests that aligned with their own, and thus sought to gather and mobi-
lize them toward assumed common political goals.

As we've seen, Nones are *by definition* not affiliated with a group with leaders
who might chart a unified course for a widely dispersed and ideologically diverse
population. But imagining Nones as such does begin to form a community distinct from the larger structures of power. The imagination of such communities
has allowed unconnected individuals with no formal, institutionalized connections to have tremendous impact on laws, policies, commercial practices, and
culture in general. What we see, then, is spiritual, intellectual, and other cultural
artifacts—certain books and teachers, rainbow flags or god's eyes, social practices such as participating in meditation groups or online networks—define,
secure, and reproduce individual and collective identities over time. Nones recognize themselves in collective representations even if they differ in particulars,
just as Buddhists see themselves in certain generalized stereotypes that they
know do not apply to all members of their distributed communities.

Terri Poole draws her imagining of an unaffiliated community, with a subtle
and most likely unintentional proselytizing styling, through the lens of "quantum spirituality"—the application of principles of quantum mechanics to spiritual cosmology.[18] I might learn all about this, Terri told me, through the films
What the Bleep Do We Know (a dramatized documentary film) and *Cloud Atlas*
(a dramatic feature film). These films argue that quantum physics explains how

human consciousness shapes material reality and posit the inherent interconnectedness of all being. Unsurprisingly, "being open" to the possibilities that become available when we recognize the reality of various quantum dimensions is a critical practice encouraged in both films. When I expressed some surprise that I had happened upon her "randomly" at the airport, Terri, applying the quantum spirituality interpretive frame of her community, insisted that our encounter was no accident:

> Quantum physics tells us that, really, we're all connected. And, we know that we manifest the "reality" of our experience through our inner thoughts. So, you know, something in you manifested me, and something in me manifested you, and we both manifested this place. That's kind of what I believe "fate" is. We create our fate within ourselves. It's not an outside force. I mean, except that the ideas of "inside" and "outside" are an illusion, too.

The resources cited by Terri, Kimberley, and other Nones do not generally represent doctrinal propositional beliefs. Terri doesn't "believe in" Eckhart Tolle or that particles are waves and vice versa, as quantum mechanics apparently theorizes.[19] Rather, resources set those who use them within configurations of community in at least three ways:

1. They provide common interpretive lenses.
2. They structure social relationships as resources are created, accessed, interpreted, and shared across loosely configured, often widely distributed, networks of people with similar interests and sensibilities.
3. They invite the imagining of a collective similar to oneself in most dimensions because of sharing one or perhaps a few dimensions (Spiritual-But-Not-Religious, Secular Humanist, Atheist, etc.). This collective can never be verified, but it nonetheless is understood and experienced as "real," as "people like me."

The way in which spiritual resources function socially across communities illuminates how "unaffiliated affiliation" is practiced outside traditional institutional structures and formal membership in religious groups. The unaffiliated indeed do affiliate, just not in the ways that would click a demographer's counter. Oprah or Tolle might be "institutions" in a certain sense, but those for whom their teachings are important do not form an institutional group. Unaffiliated affiliations are looser, more provisional, shifting across social settings depending on changing norms and needs for engagement from one context to another. Here, too, affiliation does not define spiritual or religious identity as "a singular guiding 'core' that shapes how others respond to us and how we guide our own behavior."[20] It is, rather, part of the language of spiritual experience through which the story of a spiritual life is told.

The Invisible Unaffiliated Religious Landscape

Beyond the broad generalizations about Nones filtered through popular media, distributed networks of unaffiliated affiliations are often invisible to the traditionally religiously affiliated, whose own social-spiritual networks are concretized in formal memberships and physical locales. However much traditional religions have understood themselves primarily in terms of beliefs, the locus of traditional religious affiliation has long been geographical place. People do not join a church just because they believe; they believe because they are members of a church. And the physical locale has very much to do with creating the opportunity to develop and nurture social bonds that reinforce identification with wider communities of Somes.

Mostly absent formally defined public spaces within which to practice their spirituality, the unaffiliated have gathered across various imagined communities of spiritual practice. The things that shape these communities have been books, magazines, films, television programs, and occasional engagements with venerated teachers, rather than specific physical places. Nones might visit natural or prehistoric sites like the Great Serpent Mound in Ohio or Stonehenge in England; they may gather at venues like Esalen Institute in Big Sur, California and other retreat centers, attend festivals like South-by-Southwest Interactive in Austin, Texas, where spirituality is an increasingly popular theme among technology, music, and art enthusiasts. Or, they can simply hang out at esoteric bookshops and cafés that are plentify in even fairly small cities across the country. Some may participate in meditation, yoga, or other spiritual practice groups. But these do not generally have the week-to-week regularity in gathering associated with the institutional identities that characterize the religiously affiliated. Even yoga studios, where people often do meet with some regularity, are not, to use traditional religious language, "sacralized" for specific religious or spiritual purposes—the space in itself does not generally contribute to the spiritual significance of the experience.[21] Instead, for many Nones, broader spiritual networks, the relationships that sustain them, and the content they share often take on the aura of the sacred.

In the past decade, these distributed sacred spaces have been expanded greatly by new digital social media practices and the resources and relationships made real through online engagements. For Neil Grosse, a 61-year-old Atheist from Brooklyn, the internet and participation in a range of Atheist digital social

networks have made "the world of rational thought against religious supersti-
tion" available. Social media also made a wider range of conversation partners
available to Neil. He explained:

> It's New York, so it's not like everyone's all Jesusy-religion all the time.
> But there's a lot of churches around here, and I came up Catholic
> myself and was around churches in the neighborhood all my life. Even
> still, mostly people didn't talk about it, and if I brought up something
> about being an Atheist, there was a kind of what I would call ignorant
> conversation about it, by which I mean people are generally just very
> uneducated about religion and freethinking. You try to have a reason-
> able conversation even with people who aren't real personally religious,
> and you end up spending half an hour just going over very, very basic
> stuff. Who has time?

Neil, a limousine driver who has spent years earning "a PhD of the streets" by
reading voraciously while waiting for clients, was grateful to find "reliable, cre-
dentialed information" on online sites like Atheist Nexus, maintained by former
fundamentalist Christian and public speaker on atheism, Richard Haynes,[22] and
a social forum, ThinkAtheist, where Neil connected with other Atheists around
the world.[23] He also enjoyed online research and policy advocacy sites like the
Center for Inquiry[24] and the Humanist Society.[25] The list of thinkers, books,
and organizations that Neil told me shaped his thinking would fill a volume of
its own. In books alone, he traveled in our conversation from "New Atheists"
Richard Dawkins, Sam Harris, and Christopher Hitchens—"not really our fin-
est advocates," he shrugged—to the political writings of Thomas Paine and Karl
Marx and on to Kurt Vonnegut and humorists Dave Barry and Julia Sweeney.
Neil waxed eloquent about the great canon of non-theistic philosophy "erased
from American education, even for most Atheists." This reading, he insisted,
"isn't a hobby for me. It's a necessity in a world where my perspective is mostly
kept out of public view. We're only able to speak for ourselves." His reading likewise included books by religious writers challenging Atheists or attempting
to call the non-religious back to faith. Recently, for instance, he had read Ray
Comfort's *God Doesn't Believe in Atheists*. "You have to know what's out there,"
Neil said, when I wondered about his interest in the book. "And," he added,
"you're not really a *free* thinker if you're locked on Atheist dogma any more than
if everything is Jesus and the Pope. I mean, I'm not going to turn Evangelical, but
you have to keep an eye on what they're saying about Atheist thought. You got
to give them their due."

Most of these resources Neil found in the public library, and he liked having a
"proper book" or two along with him in the car. He got lots of recommendations

from people he had met in online social networks, and he enjoyed discussing what they were reading, but he mostly participated in these digital communities because, he said, "they give me the chance to be myself—an Atheist in Brooklyn—a couple, three hours a week with a group of really good people." When I noted that his participation in online Atheist communities sounded, well, a little bit "religious," he agreed:

> You might say that rationality is my religion. I believe in thought, in rational argument. That is a kind of self-transcendence, right? Considering someone else's ideas? You know, getting out of your own head. That really is what religion is about, yeah? The idea is you have Jesus in your head—you follow Jesus—instead of your own, independent thinking. I never, from when I'm a kid, went in for that kind of total brainwashing. But there is something to be said for good conversation with decent people you respect, who are going to force you to consider your own thinking, maybe get you to see it a different way. And, when I talk with Atheists online, I get a lot of real insight into how to talk better with theists instead of just arguing. The Friendly Atheist is the perfect example of that.[26] So, sure, I "worship," if you like, online where Atheists meet to exchange ideas and information about what's wrong with religion and how it can be challenged by thinking people. But we also have real personal relationships, too. We get together. You know, guys online will ping me when they're in town to get them at JFK. We'll get a drink, or something. We stay in touch. So, it's a real community all around.

For Neil, the experience of community moves into more regular personal engagement, precisely because it is significantly enacted online. Network theorists would say that his online community is more "efficient" than the happenstance of offline engagements would be because it costs him less in terms of time, effort, and aggravation to connect with people with similar outlooks.[27] Whereas before the internet an Atheist here and an Atheist there would have a hard time finding each other, especially outside metropolitan areas, digital connections allow geographically dispersed Atheists, Agnostics, SBNRs, Humanists, and so on, to cluster together. While intellectual and spiritual resources are important in these communities, relationships are perhaps even more so. And, they extend globally, at least across the English-speaking world for Neil, as he participates in online forums hosted outside the United States, in the United Kingdom and elsewhere. In this way, intellectual, technological, social, and spiritual resources come together to define unaffiliated communities with common, quasi-ritual practices and values. The same kind of clustering can happen in local contexts like meditation classes or running groups, as well as in regional, national, or international conferences, retreats, and events such as the annual Burning Man Festival in the Nevada dessert,[28] the South-by-Southwest conference, with its expanding attentiveness to the eclectic spiritualities at the intersection of high tech and arts communities,[29] or the Summer Solstice celebration at Stonehenge in England.

Unaffiliated Community Near and Far

While such networks of spiritual affiliation are meaningful to many Nones, they are difficult to sustain. They do not translate readily into local practices of community modeled on religious and civic institutions. This was clear even at a longstanding Humanist Society meeting I attended near Stanford University, where organizers fretted as a much as any pastor of a declining church over how to draw new, especially younger, members and how to sustain funding. Likewise, at early meetings of a local chapter of the Sunday Assembly, a so-called "Atheist church" founded in 2013 by British comedians Pippa Evans and Sanderson Jones, the challenge was even more pronounced, this despite the fact that the new organization has attracted large groups in England and has expanded into the United States and other English-speaking countries. In late 2013, Sunday Assembly launched a worldwide growth campaign, starting assemblies in Europe, North America, Australia, New Zealand, and South Africa, and extending its online presence significantly.[30]

When I attended a meeting of the recently formed Silicon Valley Assembly in January 2014, the often reported enthusiasm of such gatherings was not initially evident. Small clusters of people who appeared to have arrived together—some of them families, some friends, some apparently couples—settled into rows of chairs in an early nineteenth-century meeting hall in downtown San Jose. Those who, like me, ambled in unaccompanied sat somewhat awkwardly until the service started. When the Assembly leader came forward to greet the hundred-plus people gathered, however, the group showed more energy, especially when led into a somewhat wobbly rendition of the Beatles' song "Ob-La-Di, Ob-La-Da (Life Goes On)," accompanied by a small band of local musicians.

The motto for the "godless congregation" is "live better, help often, wonder more," and its creed consists of similarly pithy slogans like "all the best bits of church, but with no religion and awesome pop songs."[31] Sunday Assembly consciously draws on the liturgical practices of Christian megachurches, referring organizers of new Assemblies to Rick Warren's *The Purpose Driven Life* for lessons in the effective integration of motivational teaching, self-help practices, pop culture, and religion (or the lack thereof) for the purpose of attracting non-believers in particular.[32] All of these came into play in the very tightly

choreographed service, where *bon mots* from Evans and Jones were regularly called out by the facilitator, who did his best to mimic Jones's Monty
Pythonesque demeanor before introducing the day's speaker, a researcher on
regenerative medicine. The service moved from there into another song, followed by a period of silence. A final speaker shared a personal reflection as part
of a standard segment, "Doing My Best," a form of testimony that involves a
confession of one's human failings—missed appointments, flawed parenting,
cranky moods, et cetera—and a counterbalancing expression of acceptance of
human limitedness. The segment concluded with participants affirming that
the speaker was, indeed, "doing her best." After a somewhat painful Reggae
cover of "Over the Rainbow," participants were invited to mingle over coffee
and cookies, old school church style.

It was here, in the coffee hour, loosed from the tight liturgical structure of
the service, that the challenge of institutionalized, local affiliation was most
pronounced.

"Do you know other people here?" I asked Jonathan Waits, a 28-year-old
Humanist from Menlo Park, California, who was waiting with me in the line
for tea.

"No," he said, explaining, "I came to the first one with a friend. But she couldn't
make it today. I think there are groups, or committees, or something you can join
if you want to meet people. I'm not sure I really want to." He laughed, "Oh, I'm
horrible, right? I just mean I have a lot going on outside of here."

I assured Jonathan that I was confident that he was "doing his best," then
asked him how he and his friend came to find the Sunday Assembly.

"Online," he said quickly. "I think one of my friends posted an article on
Facebook about Sanderson and Pippa, and then I googled 'Sunday Assembly'
and found a whole bunch more articles. One of them said they were coming
here, so my friend and I went when they were in Oakland."

After briefly introducing myself and describing my research, I asked Jonathan
if he would tell me more about his interest in Sunday Assembly and his spiritual life more generally. A few days later, we met outside a library at Stanford
University, near where he works as a medical research analyst. Since one of the
prominent data points in the Pew "Nones on the Rise" report, we will recall, was
that the majority of the unaffiliated are "not looking for a religion that is right
for [them],"[33] I wondered if Jonathan thought the high negative response to the
question was because the unaffiliated have few options for affiliation in groups
that fit their religious or spiritual outlooks. Would that change, did he think, with
the availability of more non-religious groups like Sunday Assembly?

"For me, no, that wouldn't be the case," Jonathan said. "I'm not really looking
for that kind of group on a—what?—you know, lifetime basis. I think that's what
the 'church' part is about."

I was curious about why Jonathan had gone not only to the launch of the Silicon Valley congregation, but also came back to a subsequent service. "I was interested in the speaker," he told me, because the stem cell research discussed related indirectly to research underway at the lab where Jonathan works. "I wanted to see how [the speaker] was relating that to spirituality, or whatever. I'm interested in how you present those sorts of ideas together. But, I don't know if I'll go next time," he shrugged. "It's on love or something like that, right? If the topic looks interesting, I'll probably go again. Or if a friend wants to go, I would." He added, "Sanderson and Pippa are a real draw. I'd go when they're back in town."

I can hardly claim, of course, that Jonathan is representative of everyone who attends Sunday Assembly services across the country. Though I did talk with other attendees at the three services I attended, Jonathan was the only one with whom I had an extended conversation. And, as the organization is very new, I would hesitate to speculate on the long-term durability of the relationships of individuals to each other and to the nascent institution. Still, my limited observation raised questions about how patterns and practices of affiliation are changing, and how this is related to shared engagement with canonical resources.

One prominent question is related to the "draw" of comedians Pippa Evans and Sanderson Jones, which points to the role of entertainment of the spirit along with, or perhaps instead of, its enrichment. In this regard, the advice to new Sunday Assembly leaders to read Rick Warren's work and study his ministry style is telling. Warren, like other megachurch celebrities, combines a larger-than-life charismatic personality with self-help spirituality (notwithstanding his own claim that *The Purpose Driven Life* is an "anti-self-help book" in its call for reliance on God for real and lasting change[34]). On the inside cover of the journal available as a companion to *The Purpose Driven Life*, Warren promises that his approach can "reduce your stress, increase your satisfaction, help you make better decisions, and most importantly prepare you for eternity."[35]

Warren's expansive ministry follows a "seeker-sensitive" approach[36] aimed to appeal to the unchurched, the religiously disengaged, and non-Christians in general. Thus, though Warren professes conservative principles of biblical literalism and inerrancy, a masculine divinity, opposition to homosexual practice, and so on, the marketing of his churches has focused more on self-improvement, life transformation, finding community, and social engagement than on rigid theological doctrine. Services are shaped by dual influences of customer-satisfaction research encouraged by Warren's mentor, management guru Peter Drucker, and entertainment metrics he learned as an advisor to the animated film *Prince of Egypt*.[37] To appeal to non-religious participants, services are characterized by "contemporary music, theatrical presentations, and friendly environments devoid of religious imagery."[38]

It is not difficult to see why this evangelical approach to common worship would be attractive to the founders of Sunday Assembly. Indeed, the Assembly has sought to widen its appeal to broader categories of seekers by downplaying its early emphasis on being an "Atheist church." At the services I attended, a period of silent reflection was introduced as open to whatever a participant might want to bring to it—silence, meditation, contemplation, "or even prayer," according to the facilitator. This has provoked complaints that Evans and Jones are pushing the Assembly away from its atheistic roots. "I'd like to make this as un-atheistic as possible. Atheism is boring. We're both post-religious," Sanderson told a reporter.[39] In response, a rival group has begun offering "A Godless Revival" as an expressly Atheist alternative to the growing Sunday Assembly brand.[40]

How this Warren-esque, seeker-friendly styling of unaffiliated affiliation will play out remains to be seen. But it does seem clear that what Sunday Assembly organizers miss in their embrace of megachurch practices is that, ultimately, despite the toning down of Christian language, symbols, and doctrine, the goal of seeker-driven ministries like Warren's is to draw unbelievers or disengaged ones into the community of Christianity. Participants are being invited into a universal metanarrative centered on the Christian gospels. Christian scripture and an Evangelical version of Christian tradition dictate the structure of worship/entertainment. People come seeking "purpose," which, despite an emphasis on personal uniqueness, will play out around a single resource—the Christian Gospels—presented in multimedia packaging through sermons, podcasts, books, CDs, music, events, and the like through the lens of an authoritative mediator of the teachings of Jesus Christ—Rick Warren.

When Jonathan came to Sunday Assembly, he was not looking for "purpose" or the guidance of spiritual teachers. His initial curiosity was fueled by friends, and his subsequent visit was motivated by a very specific interest in the speaker for that Sunday. Jonathan reported that Evans and Jones were "a draw," highlighting their celebrity status. (Indeed, I ran into Jonathan again when Jones returned to San Jose a few months later.) In this respect, Jonathan approached Sunday Assembly as spiritually or intellectually enriching entertainment, not unlike that offered through the "Cosmic Masses" offered by Matthew Fox's University of Creation Spirituality in Oakland, California,[41] or weekly lectures by *A Course in Miracles* guru Marianne Williamson on Monday evenings in Los Angeles.[42] He attended without particularly expecting to find community, beyond what he brought with him by way of personal friends and the network of resources they share. For many Nones like Jonathan, community is structured around commonly valued cultural resources, rather than particular spaces or institutional groupings. Shared experience—be it youth masses with the Pope, a Macklemore & Lewis concert, or a gathering with Atheist comedians—itself becomes a resource for spiritual enrichment. However, these events rarely prompt formal affiliation, even within the loose configuration of an "Atheist church." People "belong" in a specific moment, and that feeling of "belonging" has to do with being in the same place with people of similar interests, rather than with a shared commitment to making the event and its relational encounters continue through practices of institutionalization. (Hence, perhaps, the failure so far of the popularity of Pope Francis to move the needle much on Catholic affiliation in the United States or Europe.)

Entertaining the American Spirit

Despite Neil Postman's pained 1985 argument that we have privileged entertainment and diversion over real analysis and reflection,[43] for large swaths of human history, religion *was* entertainment. Philosophers and theologians may have had the luxury of sustained, deep thought, but the mostly unlearned, worker-bee masses spent much of their limited discretionary time on whatever the historically appropriate equivalent of *The Real Housewives of . . .* might have been, including religious and spiritual versions thereof. From ancient, wine-infused dancing, dining, singing, and sexual abandon during Dionysian Mystery festivals, where the Hellenic deities were worshipped,[44] to the famous medieval York Corpus Christi Plays, which allowed laypeople in a carnival atmosphere to act out religious authority they could not claim within the Church,[45] social, aesthetic, embodied, and entertainment experience has been no small part of religious practice. This was only amplified through the mass media practices of the modern era as a feature in spiritual practice, identity formation, and affiliation. That Oprah, Rick Warren, and the Sunday Assembly would partake of this legacy is hardly a historical accident.

Nor should it surprise us that resources drawn from the world of entertainment are important in the spiritual lives of the unaffiliated (and affiliated) as sources of meaning, enrichment, comfort, and a camaraderie that together function as a mode of loosely networked affiliation. In this light, we must allow, as Fordham University theologian Tom Beaudoin has argued, that engagement with popular media and commercial products need not be superficial. "There is spiritual power in these branded objects," Beaudoin insists, including aesthetic products like music, movies, television shows, and visual art.[46] Among Nones who talked with me, music was among the most important, influential, and inspirational "branded object" named as a "significant resource in your spiritual life." A case in point is Anthony West, a 33-year-old Agnostic originally from Akron, Ohio, who had recently moved to Oakland, California, to pursue a career in music. For Anthony, rap and hip-hop music and culture were central in his spiritual identity and practice. He explained,

> My mom and my aunties are always turning to the Bible for answers, and I respect that. I know that comforts them. It's their community. For a long time, I guess I played along. I went to church. I was a good kid. But, as I grew, I just couldn't make it all line up for me, personally. And, you know, the pastor would say you should "turn to Jesus" or "read the Good Word" when you needed help or inspiration, but it never did say anything to me. Music is where I turn for inspiration because it speaks to my heart in a language that is my language, that is how me and my friends talk it out. . . . I think there's just something about art in general that isn't about offering up all the answers. You know, you listen to Mos Def or someone like [Immortal] Technique, you're going to come away with a lot of questions. But they're the right questions for people like me, my generation—the questions you can't ask in a church about why the world is how it is today. You know, *real* sin and not much salvation.

Anthony assured me that the spiritual engagement he felt listening to music was "deep," shaping his identity, touching the concerns of greatest significance to him, and engaging him in community with new insight. He explained that one of his favorite artists, the rapper Immortal Technique, "is an activist, and his activism, I would say, is very much an act of faith, but, you know, not in God. In *you*—in you as you're listening." Anthony continued,

> On a track like "Dance with the Devil,"[47] he's reaching out to dudes on the street, and he's preaching hard for them not to get caught up in the gang life, right? Not to disrespect women and our communities. I mean, "the devil" is not some abstract "Satan" they tell you at church. It is in you—it's that temptation to go out and be a big man by joining a gang, selling drugs on the corner, raping women. And it's all the ones that have gone that way and the whole system that makes it seem like that's the only option. All of that is "the devil." Then, and this is, you know, genius, he pulls in beats from "Love Story"—from Henry f-ing Mancini. He's got all of that in there, and I'm like, "wow, this guy *moves me*. This is 'the way, the truth, and the life' for me and my generation."

Throughout Anthony's description of the music that influences, teaches, and inspires him, there are repeated references to local and distributed communities: "me and my friends," "our communities," "my generation," "me and my generation." Through artists like Immortal Technique, Anthony affiliates with others whose tastes, outlooks, practices, and generational grouping he imagines to be similar to his own. The reality of this spiritual cohort is affirmed, Anthony reported, when he gathers with friends to listen to music, when he DJs at local clubs and parties, and when he performs his own music:

> Rap, hip-hop comes from the African blues and soul tradition, right? And that comes from the old slavery spirituals. And those came about because slaves had no other way really to pray together. And those prayers were also codes to help each other escape, avoid the master, stay alive. So, for me, this music is religion in the sense that "religion" is what keeps you alive. You know, those slaves bent over in the field might have been singing about some chariot from heaven coming to save them, but underneath the words, they were making plans to break free, to be alive. So, God is just an idea that helped with that, as I see it. The music, singing, singing out your reality, that's what made it happen. When I'm at a club, whether it's my own thing or I'm playing somebody else, you know people are feeling that spirit all the way back. Maybe they don't talk about it like that, but it's there to see if you know how to look for it. You see how people move, how they respond to different things in a track, be it words, or a beat, or something you can't quite put your finger on. You just know they're "feeling it." That's religion, the way I see it.

In 2003 sociologist Robert Wuthnow surveyed 1,530 Americans and talked with several hundred Christian clergy and laypeople in interviews and focus groups by way of exploring the relationship between the arts, (institutional) religion, and (personal) spirituality. He saw music as a resource critical to the vitality of American congregational life. (Wuthnow's work did not extend beyond Christianity, though he noted Eastern influences from time to time.) Though his sample did not include admirers of rap and hip-hop music like Anthony, Wuthnow confirmed a close association between people's interest in spirituality and their interest in the arts, especially music, which was seen as important in mediating divine presence both by those who deliberately included music as part of their spiritual practice and those who did not.[48] Wuthnow concludes that "there appears to be a strong relationship between artistic interests in general and an orientation toward spiritual growth." Music and art, he continues, are animating features not only of institutional religions, but of the spiritual experience of everyday life. This quotidian spiritual experience is, he says, "there for the taking. It requires little in the way of doctrinal understanding, serving instead as personal affirmation of the divine. Just as in the political meaning of *democracy*, spiritual democracy is thus one in which all persons have a voice"[49] (even if that voice raps or sings in a hip-hop register).

This was true to a certain extent for those who participated in my initial spiritual practices test survey. Nones and Somes alike ranked "creating or enjoying music" and "creating or enjoying art" as among the top 10 most spiritually meaningful activities in their lives.[50] As with Anthony, music and art were sources of information and inspiration of various sorts—spiritual, artistic, political— as well as bridges to the historical experience of African Americans. Anthony makes a historical link between Immortal Technique's work and early African American musical traditions that connect to subversive slave communication practices and, in his immediate context, to the beating hearts and the living spirits of people in the clubs where he performs. Rather than being simply a consumerist behavior through which identity and social status are vaguely spiritualized,[51] engagement with music as a spiritual resource situates Anthony within a "community of memory."[52] The historical resonances of this community engage both local and more distributed relationships, including those with people of similar sensibilities who never meet face to face, to construct a broad spiritual affiliation.

In the case of Paul Harland, a 54-year-old None from Fargo, North Dakota, the spiritual affiliation shaped by music was more immediate, and clearly unfolded well beyond consumerist spiritual practice. Paul, who had been raised Episcopalian, stopped going to church when his three children were relatively young because, he said, "it just got logistically complicated for us. I don't have a better answer than that." He paused, adding, "Other than that what was going on at church at the time, which was a lot of bickering over gays, didn't really seem worth the effort it took to get three kids dressed and in the car." Still, Paul missed having been part of a small acoustic music group that sometimes played at services. He kept in touch with a couple of the others in the group for a while after he and his family stopped going. Eventually they decided to get together with a few other friends to play music together. Paul recounted the formation of what he referred to as "The Lost Souls Saturday Night Jam Band and Potluck" as a warm, spiritually rich, and deeply relational practice:

> We all had kids, and none of us could afford babysitters, so we decided to do a potluck at one guy's house who has a huge backyard. So, that became a big part of it, too: the kids and the food. But we get there, and, you know, we'd been playing church music together for a few years, and we really didn't know anything else that we could do together. I mean, we're all amateurs, except a friend of one of the guys, who teaches high school music. But that's where we started anyway—you know, right out of *Lift Every Voice*,[53] the hymnal we used a lot at church for "non-traditional" services.

As he described the experience to me, in a small coffee shop in Chicago, Paul became visibly emotional, shaking his head and laughing at himself as he blinked away a tear. "Jesus, I'm *that guy*," he said, "but, you know, it was really something else. It really was." A deep breath and a few sips of coffee later, Paul continued:

> So, we're trying to get going, and the kids are like crazy running around the yard, and I'm thinking, "This is such a bad idea." One of the guys brought his girlfriend, who he said was a great singer, and she's going through the hymnal turning up her nose, saying, "I can't sing this! I can't sing this!" And, really, I'm just like, "Well, okay, this is not going to happen," looking for a beer, when she says she knows "Wayfaring Stranger" if we can do it slow, which, really, is the only way we could do anything at that point. . . . So, we finally get going, and, man, she really can sing. It's incredible. I mean, everything just hushes down—the kids, and everything. And then, you know, I feel something on my leg, and I look down, and my littlest girl is just hugging my leg, rocking along with the music. And she stayed right up with me the whole night. Man, I mean, that would never, never happen in church. It just wouldn't. I knew this was just, you know, the whole thing in one moment.

A version of the group has played together most every month for the past decade, Paul reported, changing over time as new people joined and others drifted away, moved, or, in one case, died. The group has never lost its spiritual meaning for Paul, and he says he's "learned more about how God works through the music than I ever did in church." While they don't always play specifically spiritual or religious music, the relational spirituality of the gathering remains an important element of the shared experience. What is more, the music brought by new participants into the group has expanded Paul's own religious and spiritual thinking. The music of Peter Mayer,[54] for example, a former Catholic seminarian popular among many Spiritual-But-Not-Religious unaffiliated, has been influential, pressing Paul to consider the spirituality of environmental justice work. As well, a new participant in the group recently suggested the music of indie-rock, "Atheist band" Quiet Company.[55] The group's 2011 album, "We Are All Where We Belong," explores front man Taylor Muse's embrace of Humanism after a "crisis of faith" with regard to the Southern Baptist Christianity in which he had been raised.[56] "I don't know where we're going to go with that," Paul shook his head, "but we started with 'lift every voice' as a kind of motto and we're sticking with it."

For both Anthony and Paul, music functioned as a spiritual resource on both cognitive and affective levels, both personally and socially. Likewise, for both men, engaging music within the register of the spiritual and religious offered a measure of spiritual agency they had not experienced in church settings, shaping their spiritual identities in new ways and within different communities of practice. Whatever meaning each man drew from particular pieces emerged not merely from the lyrics, the musical form, or the embodied practice of performing, but through all of these elements as they unfolded in social and relational contexts that could be seen as catalysts for spiritual experience. Further, their discussion of the role of music in their spiritual lives articulated clear social and ethical values and concerns. Importantly, both Anthony and Paul themselves named the intersections of thinking and feeling, of the personal and the communal, of the spiritual and the ethical, as these were created by performing and enjoying music as an experience of spiritual insight, growth, and connectedness. For both, music is not a soundtrack for spiritual life, or even a tableau upon which it plays out, but a dynamic agent in the construction and nurturing of identity, social relationships, meanings, and values.

In Anthony's case, the lyrics of rap music provided historical, political, and religious information, symbols, and contexts that contributed to his identification as an African American Agnostic for whom the spiritual was most richly lived outside of church. But his sense of people in the audiences for his performances "feeling it"—the "it" being both the music and the history of the music within the context of contemporary African American urban experience—points as well to what sociologist of music Tia De Nora has highlighted as experiences of music "[doing] emotional work" that helps musicians and listeners feel more connected and empowered in particular social and cultural contexts.[57] That is, music invites people to feel together, and that shared feeling, independent of any particular shared belief sets or common institutional backgrounds, registers as spiritual. The felt sense of the musical-social experience was abundantly clear both in Paul's description of his daughter's affectionate response to the music and his own emotional reaction to the memory of that experience. It is this affective aspect of the social experience of music that prompts theologian Gordon Lynch to ask, "Is the process of religious identity-formation through popular music actually as much a process of learning to *feel* about one's self and the world in particular ways, as one of learning to *think* about it in certain ways?"[58]

For Anthony and Paul, the setting of the musical performances they described—a crowded urban club, a casual suburban backyard potluck—contributed to the experience of the occasion as "spiritual" or "religious" as much as did the lyrical and structural content of the music itself or the community present as it was performed. The public, social, and relational settings of these experiences, as we have seen elsewhere, challenge notions of spirituality that highlight interiority and private experience.

Still, music is also often performed and enjoyed privately, its nuances infusing personal rather than immediately relational spiritualities. For Wendy Patterson, a 31-year-old Spiritual None from South Harbor, Maine, the role of music in spiritual life played out in what would seem very conventional forms. Wendy was raised as a Christian Scientist, where prayer intersected powerfully with physical healing. Although she left the church in her teens, she continued to focus on healing in her spiritual practice, working as a massage therapist with training in Reiki and reflexology. As part of a network of spiritual healing practitioners in northern New England, Wendy became acquainted with chanting practices drawn from Buddhist and Native American traditions. While she attended chanting workshops, she told me she used chanting as a part of her "personal spirituality" rather than within the repertoire of healing practices she shared with others. "This is what I do to get in touch with my deeper self," Wendy said. "It helps me get ready for the work I do and, you know, to heal myself from the effects of having my hands and heart in other people's ailments." She laughed, referring to her work in the spa at a local resort, "You know, lots of tourists with lots of issues."

Before she goes to work, and when she gets home most evenings, Wendy, who has the good fortune to live in a small cottage on a pond, sits on her deck and chants:

> It just clears you out, it does. I mean, at night I really feel everything heavy and hurtful leaving my body. In the morning, it goes the other way. It opens me up. You know, there are kind of clinical elements of this, I guess. You know, you're breathing very rhythmically and that will lower your heart rate and calm you. But there's something more to it for me. I mean, I don't believe in a god the way I did when I was younger, but I do feel this as really "spiritual" more than just physical. It's like something deep inside me is, I don't know, adjusted in more than a physical or psychological way. I can't explain it exactly, but it doesn't happen the same way for me with any of the other practices I do. I mean, it's not just that I'm calmer and more focused when I chant, which I am. It's that I'm more myself. You know, that part of you that hums in your sternum when you sing? That's just such an energy center, and I just know it's "on" in a different way because I chant regularly. That's kind of why I keep it for myself.

Wendy also listens to recorded chanting and other "spiritual music" on her way to and from work. De Nora argues that such private musical practices are "technologies of the self" through which individuals "regulate, elaborate, and substantiate themselves as social agents."[59] In this sense, even private, solitary musical practices like Wendy's chanting are social in that they prime her for future relational engagements and help her process, in an embodied fashion, prior engagements. In De Nora's conception, listening to or practicing music can be a disciplining technology rather than a spiritual practice per se. Through the intervention of music, the self-as-spiritual is a more compliant, obedient self, able to engage with diverse others in complex social settings with minimal stress. Wendy, who had a diverse and sophisticated range of technologies for managing mood, disposition, physical energy, and so on at her disposal, didn't seem to see it in quite that way:

> I try to be careful about this language because it has religious baggage that I know people misread, and, honestly, is a difficult part of my past on some levels, but the chanting is "prayerful" for me. It restores me and brings me back myself, to the people I care for, to the earth in just a different way than, say, mental meditation, which I'm not great with. And, I think because I do it every day—twice, every day—I mean, I'm really on edge on days when I just can't, you know, like, I was traveling with a friend last month to a conference in Boston, and there just wasn't any way to do it. Anyway, because I do it every day, it's not just like a gimmick or, I don't know, an exercise regimen.

As with Anthony and Paul, place was significant in Wendy's spiritual understanding of her musical practice:

> You know, it's almost like a monastery out on the lake. For most of the year, there's just no one around. So, the chanting is me connecting to all that in this really deep, personal way. Bringing it into me, and me into it. I don't believe anymore in a personal god, but I think that's what people mean when they say they have that sort of relationship. But it's not like "talking to god." I'm not asking for anything or really even saying anything. Most of the chants don't have words, exactly. So, as you're chanting you're being spirit and being spirit-filled, and amazing things happen. Sometimes I literally feel like I'm swimming in the water while I'm chanting or floating above the trees. I don't really know how else to say it. I get carried in the chant.

As Wendy seemed to understand it, chanting is a resource in her spirituality with an almost independent agency. It affirms, nurtures, heals, and transforms the self. Certainly, the ritual of chanting each morning and evening structures Wendy's day and situates her as "a spiritual healer through the body." But it also shapes a sense of interiority that gives her a clearer sense of authority over the self who works with "lots of tourists with lots of issues." After affecting a demeanor of patience, courteousness, and boundaried compassion, as Wendy must on a daily basis, in order to reclaim the self in relation to the world it most values—the edge of the lake, surrounded by trees—the private use of music would, indeed, be transformational on a daily basis. De Nora describes this ongoing, transformative identity work in this way:

> Music can be used as a device for the reflexive process of remembering/constructing who one is, a technology for spinning the apparently continuous tale of who one is. To the extent that music is used in this way it is not only . . . a device of artefactual memory . . . it is a device for the generation of future identity and action structures, a mediator of future existence.[60]

Whether private or public, music engages the spiritual self in relation to real and imagined social networks. Indeed, because of new digital formats and online platforms for creating and sharing music across unbounded global space and time, these networks have extended dramatically in recent years. While private spiritual practice may highlight traditional modes of spirituality as "man in his solitude," as William James famously put it, they nonetheless nurture this interiority for the benefit of future existing and imagined relationships. As a spiritual resource, then, music is no less affiliational than are texts.

A similar cognitive-affective-affiliational practice is associated with the visual arts, as was the experience of Corrie Milliman. And certain material objects— gifts from important people, items found in nature, talismans of various sorts— were also important resources for some Nones. Karen Dade, a 32-year-old Spiritual None from Spring Hill, Florida, collected small stones, pine cones, bird feathers, snakeskins, and other items found on regular hikes through a wildlife sanctuary near her home. "I think the earth teaches you things," she told me, "with the beauty it lays out in front of you, with what it leaves behind for you to find." She sets her "findings" on a stone wall at the back of her yard. "I don't keep them forever. It's not a shrine or an altar," she said. "They're just there as long as they are. My husband will notice something I didn't see in the shape of a stone. Or, I have artist friends who use my findings sometimes in their artworks. So, they're little bits of inspiration, and we learn from that."

Popular culture also played a role in the lives of the Nones who talked with me. They mentioned a wide variety of films ranging from those with obvious attraction to subsets of the unaffiliated, the cult classic *Dogma*, and the blockbuster *I Am Legend*, in which the lead character (played by Will Smith) is an Atheist. Television programs such as the zombie drama *The Walking Dead*, the popular musical drama *Glee* (in which Chris Coffer's character Kurt Hummel tells his ailing father, "I don't believe in God, but I believe in you"), the comedy *The Big Bang Theory*, and, of course, *Star Trek*'s Mr. Spock were also mentioned with some regularity. Celebrity Atheists, Humanists, or Agnostics, such as George Carlin, Ricky Gervais, Kathy Griffin, Penn Jillette, Bill Maher, Keanu Reeves, Julia Sweeney, Uma Thurman, and Joss Whedon, also came up in conversation. But well-known non-believers were not the only influencers of the unaffiliated. Nones were also inspired by people seen as global moral exemplars, including those associated with institutional religious traditions, like the Buddha, the Dalai Lama, Jesus (though not usually "Jesus Christ"), Thich Nhat Hanh, Martin Luther King, Jr., Nelson Mandela (whom several identified as an Atheist), Adrienne Rich, Mother Teresa, Desmond Tutu, Alice Walker, and Walt Whitman. Their influences were wide ranging and often surprising—to me, at least. Apparently the cartoon character SpongeBob SquarePants in an Atheist (or maybe a Muslim).

While the resources cited as "important" or "influential" in the spiritual lives of the Nones who talked with me certainly said something about who they were in terms of spiritual identity, these identities were clearly mapped to more or less fluid spiritual communities where resources were engaged, shared, shaped, and entered into interwoven stories of the self. These resources neither constructed one-dimensional unaffiliated "types" nor made as much sense apart from the communities in which they circulated. The books, music, art, material objects, and popular culture more generally that appeal to Nones disclose the social networks within which their spiritual lives unfold. The value of such resources is largely determined by their roles in these social networks. As we will see in the chapters that follow, these networks of relationships are in fact a central resource—perhaps *the* central resource—for unaffiliated identity and practice.

4

Being None

Family, Friends, Fido & Food

> Food is a kind of conversation in my family. . . . I tell my mom I love her with food. My kids know they matter to me in part because of how we do food. We connect with neighbors and friends over food. You know, it's life, so we're sharing life when we share food. We're taking care of each other. That's just about the most spiritual thing I can think of.
> —Felicia Oliveria, *age 31, Alexandria, Virginia, "Humanist"*

> I've told things to these guys I couldn't to a pastor, and they're there for me through thick and thin. When we say we're "soul mates," it's because it goes that deep. These are the people who are always going to be there for me. It doesn't matter that our religious views are different here and there. That's about the last thing that counts at all.
> —Paolo Morelli, *age 23, Baltimore, Maryland, "None"*

> Dogs are evolved beings—they're completely spiritually open and available to others. If I believe in God at all, it's because of the loyalty and compassion I've seen in my dogs.
> —Frances Page, *age 28, Fort Collins, Colorado, "Agnostic"*

"If food is a code, where is the precoded message?" anthropologist Mary Douglas asked nearly half a century ago, at once poking at a linguistics cliché and setting the stage for a rich analysis of the "grammar" of everyday meals.[1] Food, feasting, and the relationships surrounding everything from cultivation to consumption are standard symbolic and metaphorical fare across religious traditions, crossing easily into popular media through films like *Babette's Feast, Like Water for Chocolate,* or *Big Night.* Even when meals are not specifically religious, it is hardly uncommon to understand practices of cultivating, preparing, and sharing food as having meaning and value far beyond simple physical utility. As Douglas put it, the "grammar" of food-sharing practices renders their messages decipherable within "the pattern of social relations." With what now reads as charmingly dated insight, Douglas lays out the social structure of high modern food sharing:

Drinks are for strangers, acquaintances, workmen, and family. Meals are for family, close friends, honored guests. The grand operator of the system is the line between intimacy and distance. Those we know at meals we also know at drinks. The meal expresses close friendship. Those we know at drinks we know less intimately.[2]

While the 1970s culinary-social boundaries described by Douglas have surely shifted today, as many meals are prepackaged, eaten alone, and taken outside the home, practices related to preparing and sharing food continue to be rich with social and often spiritual significance. Meals function as hubs for relational engagements as superficial as those between the server and a customer at a local bistro, or as richly hued as those that unfold among family members and friends at a Thanksgiving dinner. They enrich familial relationships in ways that have significant psychological and even scholastic implications.[3] Prepared or selected for snacks, meals, and gifts, food can likewise mark ethnicity, gender, social class, and economic status. And, as the anthropologist Claude Lévi-Strauss famously argued, prepared foodstuffs can mark boundaries between culture and nature, between what is understood as belonging within the "cooked," "civilized" world with its customs, traditions, and rules and the "raw," "savage" world of unbridled instinct and emotion.[4] Food is nature transformed; its effects are often experienced as transformative, and those who effect such transformations are often seen as having specialized powers. Indeed, as Michael Pollan explains, this seemingly magical quality is encoded in the language surrounding food preparation:

> In ancient Greece, the word for "cook," "butcher," and "priest" was the same—*mageiros*—and the word shares an etymological root with "magic." ... Even the most ordinary dish follows a satisfying arc of transformation, magically becoming more than the sum of its ordinary parts. And in almost every dish, you can find, besides the culinary ingredients, the ingredients of a story: a beginning, a middle, and an end.[5]

The flavors, smells, and textures of food, as well as the occasions at which it is served and the manner in which it is presented, form and shape memories and moods that become important parts of our life stories. Even among those who profess no religious belief or who engage in no regular institutional religious practice, cultivating or obtaining, preparing, and sharing food retain powerful spiritual resonances. The story of the self is filled with tales of family meals, food-centered gatherings with friends, the food-related exploits of children and often pets, and so on—many of these experiences highlighted as among the most spiritually significant in a life. It is no surprise, then, that Nones and Somes in my early test survey marked "preparing and sharing food" as among the top four "spiritually meaningful" practices in their lives (23% for both groups).[6] Although "enjoying time with family" (32% for Nones; 51% for Somes) and "enjoying time with friends" (24% for both groups) were ranked higher, among Nones who shared their stories with me—as with Paul Harland's "Lost Souls' Saturday Night Jam Band *and Potluck*"—food was often a feature of these relational experiences as well.

Clearly, one category of spiritual significance is very often implicated in the spiritual themes that may emerge from another. Wendy Patterson, Spiritual None from South Harbor, Maine, whom we met in the previous chapter, described the interwoven chords of her spirituality as they moved through various relationships and parts of her life in this way:

> A lot of the time, when I feel most "spiritual" is when I'm with my friends and we're all laughing together or when we're comforting someone who's going through something. Or maybe it'll be when I'm at the farmer's market and I see all this beautiful food people have tended with their own hands. I'm awed by that. Even when I'm working and the work is, you know, in that certain kind of place. I can't really describe it. You just feel it, right? There are moments in all of that—sometimes just a fleeting moment—when I know—you know, your body tingles or you see maybe a light around the scene—you're in it and out of it at the same time, just for an instance. Then I know I'm part of something big, something amazing. But whatever that is, [it] is also a part of my life. It's always there even if I'm not aware just then. It's not separate, it's not somewhere else.

This chapter explores the spirituality of Nones by way of the four, often overlapping categories of practice that Nones identified as most meaningful in their spiritual lives: *family* (enjoying time with family); *friends* (enjoying time with friends); *Fido* (enjoying pets and other animals); and *food* (preparing and sharing food). At least two of these "4Fs" came up for every person who talked with me when I asked them to describe the practices or activities that were particularly important to them spiritually. Nearly two-thirds (63%) hit on all four categories at some point during our conversation, with only a relatively small group (11%) leaving pets and other animals out of their spiritual narratives. By contrast, more than a quarter (26%) shared stories of spiritually meaningful practices that did not include children in any significant way.

Of course, as we have seen throughout our exploration of the spiritual lives of Nones, these categories hardly cover the waterfront in terms of spiritual practice and significance. Making and listening to music, creating and sharing art, jogging, meditating, and a number of other activities have already come up among the Nones we have met. We will also consider practices such as gardening, enjoying nature—each of these often closely connected to one or more of the Four Fs—and the more individual spiritual practice of journaling. Likewise, we will take a look at material objects and geographical spaces that featured in Nones' spiritual stories. ·

In general, a number of qualities tended to distinguish practices understood as "spiritual" or "spiritually meaningful" described by Nones:

- They are primarily relational, rather than either individualistic or institutional, highlighting interpersonal intimacy and connectedness.
- They are most often embedded in the experiences, locales, and temporalities of everyday life rather than separated in space and time.
- They are embodied, sensate, and social, more than cognitive, private, and interiorized.
- They are provisional and practical, changing on the basis of new experiences, resources, and life stages and drawing on diverse resources across religious, philosophical, and other wisdom traditions.
- They are dynamic over time while remaining coherent within identity narratives.
- They are often understood as transformational, highlighting personal growth and communal or social change.
- They tend to highlight experiences of authenticity and connectedness in the present moment, rather than future-oriented expectations traditionally associated with "salvation" or various other afterlife schemas.

Relational Unaffiliated Spiritualities

Previous studies of "lived religion" have tended to focus on highly individualized practices such as meditation, yoga (both of which are often practiced with others); versions of prayer; and often poorly articulated, apparently idiosyncratic systems of belief cobbled together from diverse religious and philosophical traditions. From the now infamous "Sheila" of *Habits of the Heart*[7] to more recent explorations of the Spiritual-But-Not-Religious, the focus of attention has been on autonomous agents engaged in individualized practices related to specific religious or spiritual belief sets. This work largely rests on the unexamined assumptions that spiritual and religious collectivity unfolds primarily in institutional settings, and that spiritual practice outside of these settings is primarily private or individualistic.[8]

Even commentators who acknowledge the social complexity of unaffiliated spiritual practice (and the extra-institutional practices of the religiously affiliated) tend to frame it in individualistic terms. Sociologist of religion Meredith B. McGuire instructs readers of her thoughtful and thorough study, *Lived Religion: Faith and Practice in Everyday Life*, which includes the stories of several people with no religious affiliation, that "*individual religion* is . . . fundamentally social. Its building blocks are shared meanings and experiences, learned practices, borrowed imagery, and imparted insights."[9] But McGuire nonetheless describes the practices of her subjects as constituting "individual religion," understood in contrast to the assumed communal nature of institutional religion.[10] The "building blocks" for extra-institutional spirituality may share genes with institutional religions, but once the door to the church is closed, "lived religion" is lived alone in the minds of many scholars and public commentators. Even when the practices described by her subjects intersect with those of others in their lives, McGuire tends to focus on individual action. This is the case with "Margaret," an unaffiliated former Lutheran whose spirituality centered on gardening. McGuire notes that Margaret valued the garden in part because it allowed her to prepare healthier meals for her family. She donated excess food from her garden to a local food bank, and participated in a weekly healing circle, which, along with "the healing effects of working the soil, connecting with nature," was important to her own well-being. Little in Margaret's spiritual life seemed unconnected to others, uninfluenced by her relationships with family, friends, and nature. Yet Margaret's spirituality is for McGuire an example of "individual religion," which does not lead to consideration of how social relationships inform spiritual experience and meaning.[11]

This is surely in no small part a function of the typically individualized focus of research—we talk with individual persons about their religion or spirituality, their practices or beliefs. "Tell me about your spiritual life," I would typically begin conversations with Nones, or, "How would you describe your spiritual life?" Yet, as emerged repeatedly in my research, even when people are asked about their *individual* spirituality or religiosity, their narratives consistently draw in many others. Contrary to the common assumption, it is not the institutional or extra-institutional locales within which spiritual practices take place that make them "individual" or "corporate." It is how people understand and describe these experiences. People who describe their spiritual lives as unfolding primarily in extra-institutional contexts understand their spirituality as profoundly social and relational, pressing against researchers' often individualizing queries (including my own). As we saw in Chapter 3, the spiritual resources that Nones draw upon connect them to many others, unaffiliated and affiliated alike, situating unaffiliated spirituality in networks of relationships and various communities no less than is the case for the religiously affiliated. This relational impulse is a part of everyday spirituality, even as it is practiced outside congregational settings. (We should also acknowledge the likelihood that individuals whose spiritual practices are centered in institutional contexts at least sometimes experience those practices in strongly individualistic terms.)

Felicia Oliveria, the 31-year-old Humanist quoted in the epigraph, offered a particularly dramatic example of unaffiliated insistence that I understand the relational nature of her spiritual life. I contacted Felicia before an East Coast trip to see if she would be available for an interview. She responded immediately, but suggested that I join her and her family for dinner rather than talking over coffee. "We can follow up after," she assured me, "but you'll want to see me and my tribe in our native habitat." Felicia was convinced that I could not begin to comprehend her spiritual life unless I saw and experienced it in the context of an extended network of family, friends, and neighbors who contributed to the spiritual significance she attributed to various practices.

Felicia's "natural habitat"—a generous townhouse near a regional park—was nothing if not vibrant. Fire engine red, to bright lemon, to apple green walls, each stenciled with various plants, flowers, and animals, were but a colorful backdrop to the livelier scene that awaited once I had made my way from the foyer through the living room to the kitchen. There, Felicia's partner, Denise, and their two boys, joined by a parade of neighbors, friends, cousins, aunts, and uncles whose names I never quite got, were singing and dancing (literally) through the preparation of several complicated, colorful, vegan dishes.

"What's the occasion?" I wondered, given the throng of people buzzing from kitchen to dining room to outdoor picnic table with plates and bowls of food.

"Wednesday," Felicia laughed. "This is how we do Wednesday. It's a High Holy Day."

Wednesday, it turned out, was the one night each week when neighbors in the townhouse community gathered for dinner at Felicia and Denise's house. "We wanted to get to know them," Felicia explained. "We wanted the boys to have the experience of knowing the people who live near them. And we wanted the neighbors to get to know us, too—you know, the friendly lesbian couple next door with the politely out-of-control boys. So, a few weeks after we moved in, we invited all of them over." From that initial desire for neighborly connection, the gathering eventually grew to include a wide network of friends and family. "Now pretty much everybody comes," Felicia said. "My sisters live not too far away, and Denise's brother comes over from DC pretty often. We put in a little community garden a couple years ago, so we're expecting Michele [Obama] to show up one of these nights!"

The Wednesday night neighborhood dinner, Felicia told me, "is pretty much the embodiment of my spirituality. If there turns out to be a god, *she* would be in this kind of midst." Felicia paused briefly. "Of course, I don't actually believe in that," she winked. Then she gestured to the open living room filled with people. "But I do believe in *this*."

"*This*" is a number of things for Felicia, who grew up "kind of Catholic" but whose spirituality was shaped less by experiences in church than by the spirituality of family life. Felicia reported being aware of the relational quality of spiritual life at an early age, as her extended Portuguese family gathered in her parents' home near Sacramento, California. This spiritual quality was only indirectly related to the family's sporadic attendance at a local Catholic church. Her spirituality was shaped instead by her family's collaborative preparation and sharing of food on Sundays, holidays, and special occasions. "For me, Sunday was about what a happened *after church*, whether we happened to go or not," Felicia told me. "That's when my mom and my aunts would be making Sunday dinner, gossiping and singing in the kitchen, kids running around everywhere, my dad and uncles out back playing cards or throwing horse shoes. That was the ritual. That was sacred." She continued,

> Food is a kind of conversation in my family. You know, you'll walk into my mom's kitchen, and before she says "hello" even, she'll be sticking a bite of something in your mouth. On my end, I try to get her to use more fresh vegetables instead of meat, but I don't lecture her about it— much. I come with a basket of organic tomatoes, or fresh kale, or something like that. I start making a salad and she tells me it needs seasoning. When she starts chopping up onions and peppers, I tell her she doesn't have to fry them. It goes like that. That's just how we connect.

Like other Humanists who talked with me, Felicia understood "spirituality" as the valuing and nurturing of the embodied human spirit. Experiences that heightened awareness of that spirit in herself and others, such as nudging her mother toward healthier foods with a basket of vegetables or the Wednesday neighborhood dinners, counted as "sacred" for Felicia. These sacred practices formed a tradition with moral resonances as well. "You want to pass that along to your kids," she said. "You want them to understand that way of being with people, with food you make for them. You want them to know where it comes from and to appreciate the work it takes to grow it and all that."

Sociologist Abby Day sees this relational spirituality as a mode of religious belief she describes as "believing in belonging." Day insists that modern religious belief is not a propositional phenomenon. It is not, that is, "pre-formed but a lived, embodied performance, brought into being through action where the object of worship is not an entity such as a god or a 'society,' but the experience of belonging itself."[12] Felicia's gesture to her houseful of family, friends, and neighbors and her claim "I believe in *this*" are expressions of the sort of belief that Day has identified as characteristic of the anthropocentric, as opposed to theocentric, orientation of modern life, for both the affiliated and the unaffiliated.[13] For those with a traditional theocentric orientation, spiritual or religious identity is formed extensively (though by no means exclusively) through belief in a supernatural being or force, while those with anthropocentric orientations form a sense of self-as-spiritual primarily through relationships, Day argues.[14] Belief remains a meaningful category to the extent that patterns of association embody and enact people's beliefs. To adapt the old adage, "Tell me who your friends are, and I'll tell you what you believe." Day found that Nones and Somes alike expressed strong belief in the idea of belonging in itself. Felicia's gesture highlighted her belief in the value of gathering people, as well as her faith in the network of social relationships, which was so important to her spiritual narrative that she felt certain I had to see and experience it myself to understand.

Phillip Norman, a 47-year-old None from Lakewood, Colorado, gave his unaffiliated spirituality, which moves across institutional and extra-institutional contexts in expressly relational terms, an interpretation that would be quite familiar to students of Émile Durkheim's classic definition of religion as a force for social cohesion:

> As far as I'm concerned, community *is* religion. Family *is* religion. All the rest of it—the doctrines and rituals—I think those came about to help create tribes, communities, families, and so on. You know, you need a few rules to make things work. You need some traditions that bind you. You need stories. That's why I've stayed connected to a Benedictine community even though I'm pretty much Agnostic. I don't believe what they believe in terms of doctrine. I don't believe in a personal god. But I respect how they live with each other and how they care about all the people who come through their doors. I try to bring those values into the rest of my life, with my family, my friends, and my employees.

In this quotidian, unaffiliated spirituality, while certain times and spaces may be opened ritualistically to "sacred" or "spiritual" experience, it is primarily the nature of relationships within these zones that marks their spiritual significance. It is the deepened quality of interpersonal relationships, rather than time, space, or physical and emotional sensations in themselves, that render an experience "fuller, richer, deeper, more worthwhile, more admirable, more what it should be," as the philosopher Charles Tayler puts it.[15] As Nones talked about how relationships with family, friends, and others factored into their spiritual lives, themes of intimacy, trust, authenticity, and the ability to be honest and vulnerable with others emerged as elements of this "fullness." Given the experience of spiritual intimacy, specific activities, times, places, or rituals were much less important to Nones than they traditionally are in institutional religions. A few of those who talked with me did highlight more formal occasions for spiritual practice, but even in instances such as Felicia's weekly neighborhood dinner, what was stressed as "significant" about these occasions was the value and enrichment of interpersonal relationships.

This was the case with Nathan Carmichael, the 54-year-old Agnostic from San Jose, California, who described a New Year's ritual practiced for many years with his wife and a small group of longtime friends:

> First we write down anything we regret or that we might want to let go of from the previous year. One at a time, we put the papers in the fire. Sometimes you'll say, like, "I'm letting go of . . . ," you know, "being impatient about this thing I'm working on" when you put your paper in the fire. But you don't have to say anything if you don't want. . . . Then, we write down a hope for the coming year, and we go around again. You know, it's setting a good intention.

"What makes this ritual seem 'spiritual' to you?" I asked Nathan. "Oh, it's not really in itself," he said. "I probably wouldn't do it on my own. But we've known these friends for more than a decade, you know, so it really matters that we do this *with them* every year. They're really important to us as friends, as people in our life. That's what makes it 'spiritual.'" [Emphasis added.] Nathan stressed that he would be unlikely to conduct the ritual if he and his wife were no longer connected to these close friends. In itself, the practice of writing down regrets and hopes was not particularly meaningful for him. The tradition was "spiritual" primarily because of its function within a particular cluster of close friends.

Unaffiliated Spirituality in Families

Many of the people who talked with me said that this spiritually intimate, relational emphasis, especially with regard to family, was missing from their experiences with institutional religion. This, we will recall, was what ultimately undermined the Roman Catholic affiliation of Frank, the Spiritual-But-Not-Religious man whose devout family had been treated insensitively by their parish priest during two family crises. So, too, former United Methodist Michael Clancy found that giving up church allowed for more family time. Ellen Sweet, a 44-year-old Spiritual None from South Bend, Indiana, likewise found that her involvement in a Roman Catholic parish got in the way of her family's relationships more than it enhanced them. She told me, "You know, the church goes on so much about families—especially about mothers and children—but it's more like the important thing is you being a mother who goes to church, you having kids you drag to church and Sunday school. There's not much interest in the quality of the relationship between parents and kids on a real practical level."

Such assessments were common among the Nones who talked with me, across religious and denominational backgrounds. But, once people got beyond reflections on prior religious experience, discussions of the spiritual significance of family life became less comparative and critical. Thomas Murray, an Atheist from Long Island, New York, talked about how he and his two sisters cared for their father through the final stages of terminal cancer. The experience, which lasted for most of a year, was for Thomas "the hardest, best thing I ever did." It was also an experience that pressed him to explore more fully what an "Atheist spirituality" might be. He said,

> I've been an Atheist since I was a teenager. We were raised UU [Unitarian Universalist], so that really was okay. I didn't feel any kind of pull to some kind of supernatural being. I mean, I wasn't going to start praying for a miracle or hope that dad would go to heaven when he died. But I also knew this was an important time. I knew it would change me—that it *should* change me—and I guess I thought that being attentive to what that meant and really being there for my dad and my sisters, too, through this . . . I guess I think that was probably what I would mean by "Atheist spirituality." You know, really being there for people, especially the people you learned how to be who you are from—your family.

Thomas and his sisters all lived near their father, but they had rarely visited with him together before the last year of his life. Their parents had divorced when Thomas was in college, after which "family gatherings" were centered in the home of their mother and her husband, who live in Florida. Each of the three children checked in on their father regularly and invited him to birthday parties and other family events at their homes. But, "he was more like a *part* of our families than he was *in* our families," Thomas said, stressing his father's more marginal relationship within the extended family. Until his father's diagnosis, he was not closely connected to the everyday lives of his children or grandchildren, but rather was invited periodically to events out of a sense of propriety or obligation. Indeed, even when their father was first diagnosed with cancer, the siblings divvied up responsibility for doctor appointments, treatments, and home visits, seldom coming together simply to spend unstructured time with him and with each other.

All that changed as his condition worsened, Thomas told me, and interacting with his father along with his sisters was an important element of what he understood as the spiritual significance of the experience. Thomas explained,

> We all wanted to be with him as much as we could, so even though we were still coordinating visits to make sure someone was always there with him, we'd just show up, too, outside of the planned time— sometimes two of us, sometimes all three. A lot of times my sisters' kids would come along. It's like we were taking care of each other at least as much as we were taking care of Dad, you know? Getting ready for what was going to happen—that he was going to die—but also having this experience together with him. You know, having it to remember together. But it was more than "making a memory" together. It was just going through it together and the way that changed us.

Thomas reported that he was surprised that the experience felt "religious" to him:

> You know, the experience is bigger than you. There really is a profound connection that makes you see how people accept religion. I mean, even when my dad was so sick—really in pain, and he could be really difficult—unkind sometimes—you could see how there was a kind of, I guess "grace" would be the religious word, in just being there with him and having my sisters there, too. It seemed impossible that you could endure it one more minute, but you did. All of us were together kind of *in* Dad's pain and wanting it to be over for him but not wanting to lose him. I mean, I really, honestly don't think I ever went to a place where I believed he'd somehow still be with us after, you know . . . I'm just not wired like that. But I could see more than I ever had how people could believe in a hereafter, I guess, and in how we're all connected in a religious way because we all go through these kinds of experiences. We all lose people we love. What was profound for me was that I felt that as a human spirit—the loss of it and what that feels like and also what it felt like to still have that connection with my sisters and their kids, with my mom, through my dad. I want to value that. To not take it for granted. Because, you know, like with my dad—poof—it's gone.

Stories of caring for ailing or dying family members, often parents or grandparents, were common among the Nones who talked with me about their spiritual lives. The birth of children, as with Benjamin Altos, the "Spiritual Agnostic" we met in Chapter 1, also featured regularly in spiritual narratives. Between his and his wife's panic the week before their twins were born, and their realization a few weeks later that they did not need to "do the whole religion thing," Benjamin described the birth of his daughters itself as "the thing that keeps me an Agnostic more than an Atheist. You have this experience that, on the one hand, is really ordinary—happening all over the world since the beginning of time, right?—and, on the other hand, is full-on miraculous. It's got all this crazy, handwringing stress in it, and yet it's perfect. Completely perfect. I don't know," he told me, shaking his head, "you think there has to be something more—something more even than a vague force or power. You know, something—maybe a being, maybe some other form of consciousness—that understands it all, who intended it all." He added, "I guess you're the most irrational about your kids, right? You'd invent a god for your kids."

More ordinary engagements with family were also important in the spiritual lives of Nones. Frances Page, a 28-year-old Agnostic from Fort Collins, Colorado, talked about the "spiritual connection" she shared with her two older sisters. The three sisters live in different parts of the country, so they meet online via Skype between periodic visits in person. Frances's sisters are both members of the United Church of Christ (UCC), the denomination in which they were all raised, but she felt no pressure either from them or her parents, who are also still active in the denomination, about her agnosticism. "UCCs are the not most hard core Christian of churches," Frances shrugged. "They're really tolerant." She did not think her sisters' religious affiliation or beliefs factored much into their relationship. "Our relationship is more on a personal, human level," she said, "which doesn't mean it isn't spiritual. We have shared experiences and memories that go deep. We have the kind of commitment to each other I think you only have with family. I'm just aware of them always in my life, and when we get together on Skype, it really is the most important time of the week for me."

Phan Hung, a 23-year-old None from San Jose, California, likewise saw everyday engagements with family as important spiritually. Phan told me he valued in particular time spent with his great-grandparents, who are in their nineties. "They're very wise people," he said. "Any minute I have with them, I am learning something about life. It can be practical things—how you make this kind of soup—or more their ideas about how to be a good person, to obtain success and happiness. It doesn't really matter what. You will always learn something from them. This is how I feel like I have their spirit in me, and this spirit will continue on." The relationship was, Phan told me, enriching in both directions, embedded in daily routines of mutual care and Vietnamese traditions of reverence and respect for the elderly. "It's a two-way street. They know I care for them," he said, "and I think that's very important for older people—to know they won't be neglected. . . .. I buy their groceries, but it's not just doing a chore. It's showing them I know what they prefer, that I have been paying attention to their life."

For married Nones (51% of those who talked with me) and those in domestic partnerships (11%), uninterrupted time with spouses and partners counted as especially important in their spiritual lives. Married and partnered Nones often highlighted the spiritual significance of sexual intimacy. Stories of regular "date nights" and weekend excursions to "recharge" and nurture relationships were often shared. When he was in his late twenties, Peter Kerry, a 49-year-old None from Seattle, Washington, joined his then girlfriend, now wife, on a "spiritual relationship pilgrimage" to the Esalen Institute in Big Sur, California, where they participated in a workshop on "openhearted intimacy" that "utterly transformed" their relationship. "My wife is much more overtly spiritual than me," Peter revealed, "but Esalen really tapped into that spiritual core in me, too, so we could be more authentically intimate." The couple continues the practices they learned with regular "stay-at-home retreats" that might involve one preparing a special dinner for the other or giving each other massages. And, Peter told me, they return to Big Sur every few years for "a spiritual refresher."

Other shared spiritual practices featured more often in the narratives of married Nones. Activities such as running, yoga, and meditation were highlighted as important in the spiritual lives of couples and families. For Carlos Valdez, a 33-year-old Agnostic from Fort Worth, Texas, who is currently completing a medical residency in Los Angeles, a run with his wife, Carly, a nurse at a different hospital, after long, demanding workdays, was "kind of sacred time." Carlos told me,

> It's usually a time when you're just too tired to talk, but too amped up to sleep. So, we don't really. You know, we try to avoid the impulse to immediately download the day to each other because you're really not paying attention then. We just grab the dog, and go out for a run. And, at first, you're just doing it yourself. We're like zombies, in our own worlds. But then I'll notice her breathing or how we're pacing each other. It's just a shift in awareness—oh, we're together now. We're taking care of each other. Carly will crack a joke about something. And, you know, we're home. I literally have a sense of awe about that every day.

Though time with family was marked as spiritually significant for most of the people who talked with me, some noted difficulties in seeing the spiritual in busy lives. "I'd like to think that making breakfast or doing the laundry had some sort of spiritual meaning," said Linda Olson, a 35-year-old Spiritual-But-Not-Religious None from Erie, Pennsylvania. "Wow, wouldn't that be great? But it hasn't seemed that way so far. I have to look for spiritual moments with my family. Really try to make them happen. It's just not on the radar for my kids and my husband—for me, for that matter—when we're trying to get to school, or soccer, or band, or whatever. You know, the schedule is our god, more or less."

For Linda and a number of other Nones, finding the spiritual in everyday family life required intentional action, and that didn't necessarily happen on a regular basis. Henry Nelson, a 59-year-old Secular None from Egan, Minnesota, was something of an exception. Harry made a point of scheduling what he called "close-ups" with his five grandchildren—whole days spent with just one of the grandchildren—throughout the year. Henry confessed, "Well, part of me feels like I got soft once I was a granddad." He continued,

> I feel like it's important that each of them knows me in their own way and that I know them as just them. I think it's the basis for a really deep, deep bond that means more to them and to me. You know, they're not just "one of the grandkids." They're specific. They're unique. I want to know them on that level. And, I want them to know me one-on-one, too. I mean, we're all making memories with this, but they'll carry it on, which is, I know, kind of selfish or like an egomaniac. It's true: I want them to remember me—to have stories of when we did this or talked about that. But there's something else that really is about a deeper relationship between us now, right now. That's what love is, really—that feeling of connection, of them being known as they are. You know, I'm a scientist, so I know there are powerful evolutionary reasons for this, but it sure does feel spiritual, I guess.

For most of the Nones who talked with me, however, the spirituality of family time was not a matter of searching intently for the spiritual within the everyday or constructing occasions within which it might emerge. Rather, it was about nurturing, acknowledging, and celebrating the spiritual as it revealed itself in the ordinary flow of family life. It is worth remembering, after all, that religious practices like the Jewish Passover Seder or the Christian Eucharist are modeled on everyday family meals, not the other way around. Such religious rituals elevate quotidian life practices into formal religious rituals—so much so, indeed, that their humble, household roots are often forgotten. But for many Nones, the spirituality of family life claims the sacred, the holy, the spiritual—whatever—as an essential element of close relationships among adult partners, parents and children, siblings, and extended family members.

It is important to note, too, that "family" had a fairly expansive definition for many of the people who talked with me. The majority of the participants in my study were married or in a long-term partnership with someone with whom they shared a home (62%). But a little more than a third (38%) of those who shared their stories were unmarried or were not in a domestic partnership, though a substantial portion of the people in this group (13%) did report that they were in serious relationships. Another subset of the group that would be traditionally tagged as "single" lived with one or more other adults (11%). Most of these were described as "friends" or "roommates," but a couple of people shared housing with adult relatives. Several were single parents of one or more children (8%). This left a scant 6% who lived without near-daily engagement with a significant other, though many in all of these clusters did report close relationships with siblings or friends that they counted as "family." (See Appendix B for additional detail.) The point here is that traditional groupings of those who are "married" or "partnered" and those who are "single" often obscure the significance of a wide range of close blood and non-blood relationships that have profound, sustained influence on narratives of the self and spiritual identity. The difficulty tracking configurations of committed, long-term relationships that don't fall within the traditional lines of "married" and "single," "family" and "friends" leave much out of the picture of what contemporary American life looks like in its fullest diversity. For example, Veronica Warner, a 44-year-old None from Columbia, South Carolina, has been in a committed relationship for the past 10 years with a man with whom she does not share a home and whom she does not expect to marry. "Neither one of us is the marrying kind," she told me. "We do well with a little space between us, but we love each other. We're 100% there for each other."

Spiritual Friendships and Spirituality among Friends

The line between who is counted as family or friend was thus often blurred in my conversations with Nones. Take Kirk Clark, a 20-year-old Atheist from Columbus, Ohio, who saw his friend Micah as a "brother from another mother." The two had known each other since junior high school, had gone through the process of coming out as gay men together, and attended the same college. "When you ask me about my family," Kirk said, "I really do think of Micah first. We're just close beyond what I am—what is possible—with either of my quote-unquote 'real' siblings or with my parents. We just care about each other like brothers. Sometimes we fight like brothers, too. But we know we always have each other's back." For Kirk, spending time with his closest friend was a deeply spiritual experience most significantly because Micah reinforced a sense of authenticity for Kirk. He told me,

> People think that because we're both gay, we have to be sleeping together. But they're missing a whole different kind of closeness that

is totally spiritual for me. It's not about we belong to the same group. I mean, this is a guy who really knows my spirit—my essence, the truth of who I am that, sure, includes being a proud gay man, but goes way beyond that. He knows what my goals are. He knows what I want to achieve in life, and he'll completely kick my ass to help me stay on track. He knows when a relationship is wrong—when it's keying into my fears more than my dreams, you know? I know him in the same way. We're, like, each other's filters and mirrors. There's just a complete trust that is rock solid. So, when we talk on the phone after a date, or text after class, or just hang out, it's just the most important thing. It's what really matters.

This spiritual significance in friendship was highlighted throughout my conversations with Nones. As with family life, people often drew comparisons between the richness, connection, authenticity, or other qualities they experienced as "spiritual" in relationships with friends and their experiences in institutional religious settings. Agnostic Paolo Morelli told me of a group of friends he had known since his early teens that he counted as "soul mates." The group had connected at a science camp they all attended throughout junior high and high school. They had remained in close contact through college and after. One of the young men was from a Catholic background, like Paolo, but three were from Mainline Protestant families and one was Jewish. None of the six is actively religious as an adult. "It doesn't matter," Paolo told me of the religious backgrounds of his friends and their spiritual connection. "I've told these guys things I couldn't to a priest, and they're there for me through thick and thin," he said. "When we say we're 'soul mates,' it's because it goes that deep. These are the people who are always going to be there for me. It doesn't matter that our religious views are different here or there. That's about the last thing that counts at all." What seemed important to Paolo's understanding of this network of friends as "spiritual" was that their relationship had continued through most of his life and that he could imagine it extending into the future. It was defined by a level of trust and honesty that he could not imagine as possible in a traditional religious community. The quality of his relationships with this group of "soul mates" formed a key narrative theme in his life that made it vital and meaningful.

Regular conversations with trusted friends, special insights offered by friends, the consolation and support of friends during difficult times, and other shared experiences with friends shaped a theme of spiritual intimacy among the Nones who talked with me. Particularly important in many spiritual narratives was the idea that friends often come into our lives in surprising ways, at what seems to be just the right moment or with the perfect gift of wisdom or compassion.

This happenstance often contributes to the designation of the relationship as "spiritual."

Angela Casper, a 19-year-old None from Hampton, Nebraska, described the origin of her relationship with her best friend, Dora, as "a total miracle." The two met when Dora "butted in" on an argument Angela and her then boyfriend were having in the food court of a local mall. Angela explained,

> He wasn't yelling or anything but he was being a total douche—picking on me and being really critical, which he did all the time. It went on for a while, till Dora turns around—I hadn't even seen her there—and she goes, "Stop talking to her like that. It's not cool." And then she turns and says to me, "You don't have to let him talk to you like that." And, I thought, no, I don't. I mean, I knew that, but hearing this total stranger say this, it was like, oh, this isn't just all in my head. He *is* a douche. And I got up and went and sat down with her at her table. We've been best friends since then. Isn't that just a miracle? I mean, we just had this special connection from the very beginning.

Something of the "miraculous" likewise figured into the story of how 62-year-old Trevor Swift, a None from Boston, met his closest friend nearly 40 years ago. The two men struck up a conversation while waiting in the DMV. "The time just flew by," Trevor said. "It was kind of crazy. When we get to the front of the line and we both go up to the window because we're, you know, walking and talking at the same time. Not really paying attention. The lady says to me, 'Your brother has to wait behind the line.' She calls him, 'my brother.' We both laughed, but it was true. Mike's been like a brother ever since. Turns out we lived not a mile from each other. Now we live on the same block. Raised our kids together. I can't really get over that when I think about it."

For Angela and Trevor, neither a wholly unbelieving None, the unexpected origin of their close friendships was an important element in what made it seem more "spiritual" than other friendships. In Angela's case, Dora's interjection into the argument with a boyfriend she describes four years after the encounter as "controlling" and "damaging to my self-esteem," was nothing less than "God sending me an angel." Angela said her relationship with Dora was different from other friendships because "we were put into each other's lives for a reason." She insisted, "You don't have to be a church person, which I'm really not, to see that there are things that are more than coincidence at work in the world. For me, that's kind of a God thing."

Trevor, too, saw the surprise of his meeting Mike and their immediate connection as "a very spiritual thing." In his late twenties, Trevor had stopped going to the Presbyterian Church he and his family had attended intermittently in the early years of his marriage. But, he said, "It's not like I entirely stopped believing in God. I just didn't need church for that." A veteran of the Vietnam War, Trevor said he often felt awkward and misunderstood in the fraught aftermath of the war. "It was a tough time then," Mike said. "There were a lot of strong feelings about the war. At church, people didn't know what to say to you, and I always felt a little out of step with all of it." When Trevor met Mike, he told me, "You just had the sense that God was looking out for me—that he sent this friend into my life. You know, we all need that one, true friend, and I didn't have that. So, it really was a gift for me. That makes it special."

Such serendipitous origin stories for friendships that counted as "spiritual" came up frequently among the Nones who talked with me, but the qualities of certain friendships over time were important regardless of how the friendship began. A particular depth and durability of the friendship—feeling valued by friends in one's own uniqueness, enjoyment of time spent together, sharing in suffering and loss, wanting the best for each other, having similar interests and goals, standing up against threats and offering support in adversity, and so on— were often identified as characteristic of "spiritual friends." Paolo Morelli's "soul mates" were "the people who are always going to be there for me." The spiritual quality of the friendship transforms the nature of the relationship, as with Trevor's sense of his friend Mike as a "brother," or Kirk Clark's insistence that his friend Micah was "family."

Such spiritual characterizations of friendship run throughout literary, philosophical, and religious traditions. Aristotle counted the true friend as the most perfect of relationships because it elevated the ethics of both (or all) parties in the friendship. A friend, Aristotle famously said, is "another self," who both reflects and calls out the best qualities of the other.[16] We love our friends for their own sakes—for the ways they are different from us, the ways they challenge us. But even this, Aristotle teaches, is a form of self-love that enriches each friend herself. In the virtuous person of good character, this self-love is not narcissism, for it involves a harmony between mind and soul that produces a self most fully realized in expressions of kindness, generosity, and love toward others. It is this harmony within the self that makes friendship a spiritual practice[17] and marks some friendships as "spiritual" in themselves. In the Middle Ages, Thomas Aquinas extended Aristotle's thinking on friendship into Christian teaching, seeing friends as mediators of moral virtue for one another, and virtuous friendships as analogies for the relationship between God and humans.[18] We saw this moral value in Kirk's discussion of his friendship with Micah, who helped Kirk to move toward achieving his goals by being there to "completely kick my ass to help me stay on track." For the contemporary feminist theologian Mary E. Hunt, friendship is "by nature a spiritual communion" when it is entered into on the basis of mutual love and respect.[19] Nones' understanding of friendships as "spiritual," then, recognizes the significance of relationships that, especially among women, as Hunt and others note, have often been ignored or minimized in religious traditions, in favor of family bonds and prayerful or mystical relationships with venerated divinities. Outside institutional religious contexts, friendships do not have to compete for meaningful roles against supernatural beings or forces, or, perhaps more important, against religious authorities.

Yet, Nones also found spirituality through shared experiences with others who were not thought of as particularly close friends. Megan Coleman, a 44-year-old Spiritual-But-Not-Religious None from Salem, Alabama, shared a story of getting lost on a hike with Sondra, a coworker who was a somewhat casual friend. The two had separated from a larger group of coworkers who were hiking together, to go in search of a restroom. "Neither one of us was 'wee in the woods' type people. We had that much in common," Megan laughed. They apparently also had in common not having a strong sense of direction or a keen ability to read maps, for Megan and Sondra took the wrong trail on their way back from the facilities and apparently continued in the wrong direction from there. "We meandered through the woods for something like two hours. The leader had asked us all to leave our cell phones behind—he had one, he said—so we wouldn't be distracted. And, damn, if we didn't both go for it." Megan continued,

> We kind of panicked for the first half hour or so, then Sondra just started laughing, and that kind of did it. We both just sort of relaxed into, you know, we're going to walk around this big, old nature preserve till we can find a sign or someone who can tell us how to get to the building where we came in. And, we just started talking about our lives. You know, really sharing. It was a truth-telling thing. I think we probably passed a sign or two just because we were just lost in conversation, too. But I think we both felt like we were getting found while we were being lost. I mean, we really just clicked together. All my walls just came down, and I could see who I was in a new way as I was telling Sondra my story. I had just never experienced anything like that—probably never will.

While the experience was spiritually transformative, it did not result in the two becoming "best friends," as happened with Angela and Dora and Trevor and Mike. To some extent, this was a matter of lifestyle logistics. Megan is the mother of three teenagers, with a demanding extracurricular schedule; Sondra is unmarried and has no children. They live in different parts of town and work in different departments of the same company. "We do hang out once in a while," Megan said, "if there's a work function. But, it's more like, we'll see each other at a meeting or in the cafeteria line, and it's like we *see* each other. Sometimes we'll give each other a little wink. It's enough."

There is an intimacy in experiences such as Megan had with Sondra that accrues to the spiritual. This quality often seemed to be enhanced when the experience took place with a casual friend or acquaintance. Patrick McCabe, a 51-year-old None from Santa Fe, New Mexico, talked about a conversation with two coworkers he didn't know well, David and Aaron, that "just happened to come up" over lunch. One of the three men, David, mentioned that he had to leave early for an important meeting at church. Patrick explained that he felt somewhat awkward as the conversation began:

> At first I thought, uh-oh, this is going in a bad direction. I mean, I really hardly knew these guys. I'd only been on the job maybe a month or two by then. I knew David is Catholic and real involved in his faith. He has crosses and religious stuff—nothing over the top, but you notice it—on his desk. Aaron is Jewish, and I'm, you know, not religious at all. So I hoped it would just move on.

Aaron, however, was more interested in what was going on for David at his church, which turned out to be a meeting with the bishop for parents of children who were being confirmed the following month. Patrick hung back as Aaron and David talked about the similarities of Catholic and Jewish rites for initiation of young adults into their faith traditions. But Aaron eventually asked Patrick about how his religion handled the transition to adulthood. Patrick continued,

> I'm sure he was just trying to be polite—to include the new guy in the conversation. But I didn't know how it would go with me being non-religious and not raising our kids in a church. For a second, I almost lied and said I was Presbyterian, which is how I was raised. But, you know, then I just went ahead and told them I wasn't religious and that we didn't take our kids to church or anything. I kind of expected that would shut down the conversation. What was kind of surprising was that they were both really interested in how we're raising our kids, you know, in terms of morals. They were really respectful, genuinely, I think. I talked to my wife about it all when I got home. It was a gift in a way. It really meant a lot to me that there were these guys I work with every day who I could have these kinds of discussions with—you know, the important stuff in your life—and we could bring our different perspectives on it.

When I asked Patrick what made this conversation "spiritual," he noted first that the three men were talking about religion, suggesting that when people talk about religion outside religious contexts and in terms of personal perspectives, it registers as "spirituality." But Patrick also saw his "surprise" at the group's ability to talk about religion from different viewpoints as an aspect of its spiritual significance. "A lot of times," Patrick said, "you keep to yourself on these things. But I think it's a real sign of spiritual progress in the world that, you know, 'a Catholic, a Jew, and a *whatever* walk into a bar . . .'—a cafeteria in our case—and we can carry on a perfectly civil, respectful discussion about religion. When I was a kid, you were your own thing, and that was it. The others were wrong. I don't think any of us thought that." As well, Patrick indicated that the conversation forged a connection among the three men that "went beyond work" and into the personal in ways that enhanced their professional relationship. "I just trust these guys a little more now," Patrick told me, "because I know them in a different way."

For both Patrick and Megan, there was what we might call a contained intimacy in these exchanges with coworkers—especially because they were unexpected and stood out from more ordinary experience—that registered as "spiritual." In general, the Nones who talked with me highlighted such interpersonal intimacies, whether with family, close friends, acquaintances, or strangers, as a fundamental element of what they understood as "spiritual experience." Here we see the anthropocentric and immanent spiritual orientation of contemporary life that has been highlighted by Charles Taylor, Abby Day, and others. For many Atheists and Humanists, this was expressed through stories that highlighted the importance of honoring, nurturing, and caring for "the human spirit" as the aim of the spiritual life. But even for Nones who professed belief in a supernatural being or force, the spiritual tended to focus on interpersonal intimacies, these often marked with words such as "connection," "closeness," or "bond," and with metaphors of presence—a friend was "always there for me" or "had my back"; a parent "stood behind me all the way."

For most of the Nones who talked with me, these intimate, immanent spiritual engagements carried something of a mystical or transcendent echo. "It was a God thing," Angela said of her encounter with her soon to be best friend, Dora—a "miracle." For many, the spirituality of relationships was in some way enchanted—enriched by the power of a divine presence—by their association with what might otherwise be seen as random, serendipitous, or coincidental experiences. There was very often "something more" that, coupled with the felt experience of interpersonal intimacy, created a frame for understanding an experience as "spiritual."

Even Atheists and Humanists frequently noted this enchanted dimension of spiritual experience, even if only by way of dismissing the reality of it. Thomas Murray, we will recall, saw the experience of caring for his dying father with his sisters as "religious" in some ways. It helped him to understand how people could be religious, even as he maintained that he himself wasn't "wired that way."

Jordan Cascade, a 30-year-old Humanist, likewise acknowledged the felt experience of a supernatural "something more" in his relationship with his fiancé, even as he discounted any transcendent reality in that experience. "I can see how people spiritualize all of these feelings," he said. "It really is uncanny sometimes how she seems to know me almost better than I know myself, and how we seem connected at just a very different level than with anyone else. You do think, there has to be something more than simply that I randomly met this smart, funny, beautiful woman and it turned out she was into me, too. You almost hate to think it's nothing but pheromones. But," he added, "it's easy to confuse a mystery with a miracle. There's a lot of beauty in the happenstance of life, too."

Some advocates of religion see such expressions as evidence of a yearning for a god or higher power. Research in cognitive biology and evolutionary psychology suggests that we are "wired" for religious feelings and beliefs, even when other intellectual commitments press against acceptance of the supernatural.[20] What seems important in the relational spiritualities of Nones, however, is not what religious or non-religious beliefs they might contain or the religious desires they might reveal or obscure. However these spiritualities might be theorized or theologized, the spiritual lives of Nones, as they themselves articulate their understandings of them, are oriented primarily around interpersonal relationships in which intimacy, trust, and personal authenticity are experienced to a heightened degree. They do not have to believe in a particular doctrine or theory to acknowledge the significance of relationships and the spiritual experiences that unfold within them, or to weave these relational experiences into narratives of the self-as-spiritual. Such experiences unfold outside the conventional structuring of religion as "believing, belonging, and behaving." They are centered, rather, simply in *being* in all its richness and its banality.

The spiritual significance of this interpersonal intimacy is not slight for the religiously unaffiliated. Its embodied reality is central to its spiritual value. Ellen Sweet, whom we met at the beginning of this chapter, reflected on the spirituality of her relationships after she stopped going to church:

> I think I felt lonely in church. I think I was really trying, but I missed a real sense of connection. I mean, not just the idea of it, the way we're brought up to think that God is always present even though you can't see him. I went to a class at church once where the priest said that we all have a "God-shaped void" in our hearts[21]—a hole that can only be filled through a relationship with God and Jesus. That felt true for me at the time—I mean, that there was truly some kind of spiritual hole. But I came to see that what was missing wasn't God. It was time with the people I love and care about, doing things we enjoy together or that we think are important. When I got reconnected to that, the hole in my

heart went away. It's filled with hugging my kids, or having coffee with my husband, or being with a friend when they're having a tough time. For me, there's just not anything more "real" or "present" than that.

Stanford University anthropologist Tanya M. Luhrmann has argued that the experientially vivid relationships with God or Jesus of which Evangelical Christians speak are the result of spiritual training that teaches them to interpret what others might experience as thoughts about what God *might* be saying as perceptions of God *actually* speaking into the mind from outside the self. Luhrmann says that Evangelicals "seem to learn to identify God's voice in their own mind the way we humans learn most abstract concepts, at least our everyday abstract concepts like 'time.' We give content to those abstract terms by, in effect, cognitively mapping that content out from everyday familiar experience."[22] The idea of a supernatural divinity who talks to us takes shape in the mind through analogies to other life experiences featuring trust, intimacy, and personal authenticity, such as with close family members, friends, or sometimes mere acquaintances or total strangers. The "connection" that Ellen tried to make in church depends, Luhrmann would say, on projecting lived experiences of intimacy with other humans onto the idea of God. But, for Ellen and other Nones who talked with me, the intimacy of relationships with others was counted as sufficiently spiritually meaningful in itself, without the need for institutional religious narratives or, we may assume, richly imagined conversations with a divine being. Indeed, in Ellen's case, churchgoing interrupted her spiritual intimacy with family and friends to the extent that she felt lonely in church. For her, religion took away from interpersonal, spiritual intimacy rather than contributing to it.

Dog Is My Copilot: Unaffiliated Spirituality with Pets and Other Animals

The intimacy at the center of relational spiritualities with family and friends often extends to pets and other animals. Slightly more than half (53%) of the people who shared their stories with me had pets at home—more than those who had children (27%). Further, more than three-quarters (77%) mentioned pets—their own, those of friends, the desire for pets—at some point in our conversation. Many also talked about their regard for and interest in non-domesticated or wild animals.

The bond between animals and humans is, of course, an ancient one. Domestic animals have been found in ancient Egyptian, Roman, and Greek burial sites, and the relationship between humans and animals has only grown stronger in the intervening millennia. Animals provide medical, therapeutic, and social support in a wide variety of clinical and domestic settings. They serve as expert trackers and identifiers of bodies, chemicals, and explosives for police departments, security agencies, and the military.[23] Some 80 million cats, dogs, birds, horses, fish, snakes, lizards, Guinea pigs, rats, pot-bellied pigs, and the like live as treasured companions and family members in American homes—some 60% of all households—and meeting the needs of these pets (and those of their human caregivers) contributed more than $55 billion to the economy in 2013.[24] Nearly all pet owners—91% according to a 2011 Harris poll—see their pets as "family members."[25] This makes pets and other animals important potential subjects for spiritual engagement and meaning. Pets were generally viewed by Nones as compassionate, non-judgmental companions to which their caregivers attributed remarkable degrees of intuition and empathy.[26] These qualities, as with family members and friends, invited pets into the narrative of the self-as-spiritual in a variety of ways. Further, the nonverbal nature of pets tended to amplify these qualities and in turn to elevate the connection many Nones felt with them.

Jack Bell, the 83-year-old strong Agnostic we met earlier, surprised me by describing a "spiritual connection" to his late wife through her cat, Gigi. Jack told me, with a bit of embarrassment,

> No one else really knew what it was like not to have Marilyn in the house any more besides Gigi. My daughter had said they'd take her—I never had anything to do with her when Marilyn was still with us—but I said, "no." I thought it would be wrong to put her out. And, if I'm honest, I needed the companionship in, oh, you know, the quiet times when everyone finally went home. I needed the discipline of getting up to feed her, putting her out, and so on. But, in a strange way, Gigi also keeps me connected to my wife—keeps her alive for me in a way—because she's not an object, a thing that just brings back memories. She's a living being I have to care for as well as Marilyn did—she loved that cat—which means I've had to pay attention to Gigi more like she did, to have a real relationship to her. It's silly, I know—an old guy like me with a fluffy cat—but I feel I guess what you could call a spiritual connection through her that I get the impression she feels, too. She just seems to know when to crawl up on my lap and distract me from too much brooding. That's exactly the kind of thing Marilyn would do when I was too caught up in anything—do something to take my mind off it for a little while. It's crazy, right?

I assured Jack that the connection he felt was not "crazy." Indeed, the role of pets in helping people to deal with loss and grief is well documented in both popular and academic literature.[27] But day-to-day interaction with pets also has more routine spiritual significance. For Isaac Jonas, a 49-year-old None living in Pasadena, California, early morning walks with his two Cairn terriers, Widget and Gadget, are "about as close to a spiritual discipline as I'm ever likely to get." Isaac told me the walks were not merely about exercise or spending time with his pets. They were occasions that shifted Isaac's human-centered view of things, briefly giving him a dog's-eye-view of life. "They get you out of yourself," he said. "You have to kind of see the world from their perspective while you're walking with them—you know, life from a foot above the ground. So, it really does give you a different perspective on things, quite literally, but also in the sense of just being open to the world and to people in different ways."

This expanded, enriched perspective came up frequently among pet-owning Nones. Linda Olson, a Spiritual-But-Not-Religious None, insisted that her "mutt" Sheamus was her most important "sensei," or spiritual teacher. "Sheamus is Mr. Present Moment," Linda said, "Mr. Loving Kindness. I mean, he just teaches me that every day—to pay attention to the present moment, to really be in it, and to approach everyone as though they're going to be awesome, wonderful friends. I don't think the Buddha could do much better than that." Sheamus is so integrated into Linda's spiritual life (or perhaps vice versa) that she has him sit with her while she does yoga every day. "He just makes me calmer, more focused, when he's around. So, yah, I do yoga with my dog. You can't really be hyper or perfectionistic when your dog's watching you."

The spiritual connection between many Nones and their pets often had to do with the assumed intuitiveness of their animal companions. Noelle Lamb, a Spiritual None we have met previously, talked about the uncanny ability of her Labradoodle, Zoë, to read and respond to her moods. "She just knows me," Noelle said, "whatever is going on. She'll come find me if I'm sitting around moping and put her head on my lap or do something funny with one of her toys to make me laugh. Or, she'll just bust into the room and bark if I've been working for too long without a break. It's really amazing how in tune she is." Noelle understood her experience with Zoë as having to do with more than the bond between her and her dog. It pointed, she said, to a widely integrated cosmology with moral implications:

> I think you see how we are all connected at a really basic, emotional level. But, I think humans shut that off. You know, we block each other out, and maybe even what we're feeling ourselves, personally. But animals don't do that. I don't think they can. So, we can really learn from them how it's probably supposed to be—how we can tune in a lot more

to how other people are feeling and how it really doesn't take a lot to show that we care about them. So, I think dogs are really important spiritually in that way. I think when you have a pet that you're really close to, it helps you to get in touch with more levels of yourself and others, and that makes you a better person.

In families with pets, this intuitiveness often played itself out within relationships between spouses or among children. Aaron Jacobson, a 43-year-old Agnostic, said he was convinced the family cat, Poppy, "was a family therapist in another life." Aaron reported that whenever he and his husband, Rob, argue, Poppy hops on countertops and tables and starts pushing or knocking things over until the couple is distracted from their argument. If the couple's four-year-old daughter and two-year-old son are bickering, Poppy jumps in between them repeatedly until they stop. "She always ends up getting us laughing," Aaron said, "which diffuses whatever tension there was. I mean, we kind of have an ideal life, so any of us is only ever arguing because we're tired or maybe if Rob or I are stressed about something at work. It's always stupid stuff. So, it's kind of like Poppy is saying, 'Hey, idiots, knock it off . . . before I knock this vase your Aunt Mildred got you off the table.'" Like Isaac and Noelle, Aaron saw Poppy's interventions as indicators of a more complex reality than is typically apparent to humans. Poppy made him aware of how, Aaron told me, "there's this current always running between all of us" that is forgotten in the course of daily life. "I think Poppy exists more in that current," he said, "and it means a lot to our family that she reminds us when we've gone too far away from it—when we've disconnected from each other and how good our life together really is."

Ellen Sweet also saw her family's two dogs as intimately connected to the spiritual life of her family. The family rescued Tosca and Mario, two Italian greyhounds. Rescuing the dogs was an important ethical practice for the family, Ellen said.

We wanted the kids to understand that you have to take care of other creatures, especially when, like with these dogs, they've been treated so horribly. We wanted them to take responsibility not just for the day-to-day stuff—walking them, feeding them, playing with them—but for understanding the kind of circumstances where people treat animals like just objects without feelings and souls. So, that was a big part of it. And, when you see these little sweeties, and how unconditionally loving they are, you understand better on an emotional level how important every part of creation is. Sometimes I'll just happen to hear one of the kids talking to one of the dogs, and I know they've really bonded. That's such a special thing.

For Frances Page, the emotional intuitiveness of animals and the spiritual connection that invites have similarly important ethical implications. Frances volunteers with a program that trains dogs and cats to be companions in hospitals, nursing homes, and with victims of disasters. She fosters several dogs at a time for up to a year as they are trained and assessed to serve as companions to hospitalized children, frail older adults, disabled people, and people coping with trauma. The experience has convinced her that dogs are "evolved beings—they're completely spiritually open and available to others. If I believe in God at all, it's because of the loyalty and compassion I've seen in my dogs. That makes me feel like I have a special responsibility to take care of them and to put them in situations, in relationships, where they're loved and honored. It makes me a more compassionate person, more empathetic, I think, to have responsibility for getting these guys ready to do such important work."

It was what she saw as the "nobility" of animals and their "soulfulness" that persuaded Lily Hampton, an Agnostic we met in Chapter 2, to become a vegan. A graduate student in Northern California, Lily does not currently have a pet of her own, but she grew up with dogs and cats, and she is an accomplished equestrian. "To ride well at all," she told me, "you have to connect with your horse. You have to have a deep, deep trust that comes from the soul. And I know I've had the same kind of soul connection with our family's pets. So, you can't just look into the eyes of these creatures with this incredible nobility and soulfulness, and then go eat a hamburger without realizing you're eating a ground-up, once living cow—a sentient being who spent its whole life eating grass, not harming anything. At least I can't."

Ethan Quinn, an Atheist, is also a vegan. His sensitivity to animals makes him feel "really, really conflicted" about having pets, which his children plead for on regular basis. "I know there are all these pets out there who need homes," he said, "but I also really feel like there's something wrong with having animals as kind of lifestyle accessories and all the commercialism that goes with that." Ethan lives in Washington, D.C., not far from the National Zoo, about which he also feels conflicted. But he and his family do often visit. "They're trying to protect animals ultimately," he explained to me, "so the animals being on display—which I really do think is wrong in itself—has a good purpose." And, he confessed, "I love looking into their eyes. You just see how they're really different from us. They're their own thing. But also, you have these instances when you feel like they do see you looking. They see that you care. I don't know, I guess it is important for humans to not be too far from animals so we don't forget that we're animals, too. I guess that's what I want my kids to get—that we're all in this together even if we're different species."

Creating Spiritual Abundance with Food

The intimacy, empathy, compassion, and connectedness that Nones described as marks of the spiritual in their relationships with family, friends, pets, and other animals came together perhaps most fully in conversations involving the fourth of the "Four Fs of Contemporary Spirituality," preparing and sharing food. The Wednesday night neighborhood dinner at the home of Felicia and her experience growing up with Sunday meals with her extended family highlight the spiritual significance of shared meal preparation and gathering with others for meals. The relationship between food and spirituality for those who talked with me also extended far beyond—both backward and forward—the kitchen and the dinner table. People were interested in the production of food, both by commercial farmers and in their own backyards, as well as with where and how they procured it. As with Felicia and her "tribe," the often very social magic of creating a meal frequently featured in spiritual narratives, but so too did the meditative qualities of solitary food cultivation and preparation. And, for many Nones, especially those who were not married, in domestic partnerships, and without children at home, dining with friends and acquaintances outside the home also sometimes had spiritual resonances.

Gretchen Drew, who describes herself as both Spiritual-But-Not-Religious and Agnostic, is unmarried and was not in a romantic relationship when we talked. When I asked her about how her spiritual life played out, she told me about a dinner group that meets once a month to explore different neighborhoods in Pittsburgh and try out new restaurants. "This wouldn't usually be my kind of thing," Gretchen told me, wrinkling her nose a bit. "It's a little more Yuppie than I tend to go in for. But a guy at work invited me, and, I don't know, I guess I was in a more open place, which turned out to be a good thing." The group has a few core members from different departments in the corporation where she works, and other people from within and outside the corporation—friends and spouses of the core group members—fill out the group each month. "Doesn't that just sound horrible?" Gretchen said with a mock grimace. "You wouldn't think anything spiritual would happen, right?" And, indeed, along with Megan and Patrick, Gretchen was one of very few Nones who mentioned work-related experiences in their spiritual narratives. In this case, the coordinating coworkers seemed to Gretchen to have a similar sensibility to hers: a desire to connect with one another, to understand the neighborhoods they visit in some depth, and to get to know the restaurants as more than simply commercial outlets for prepared food. The group meets late Saturday afternoons for a tour of the neighborhood, led by one or more of the group leaders who have done research on the area. They stop for drinks after the tour, before heading to the restaurant for dinner.

In between, they pop into shops, galleries, office buildings, and, in a city with an abundance of them, no few churches and other religious or spiritual sites.

Gretchen reported that a visit to a neighborhood the previous weekend had included stops at an ornate Byzantine Catholic Church, a Roman Catholic Church built by Polish workers, and a meditation lounge in a metaphysicalist book store. While the religious and spiritual locales visited by the group might have heightened the felt spirituality of the experience, Gretchen felt it was much more than this. She explained,

> Tom, the guy who invited me and was one of the tour leaders this time, is really great at making conversation with people. It always seems like he's known everybody forever even if he just met them ten minutes ago. So, wherever we went, whether it was a little Italian bakery or some hole-in-the-wall gallery, he'd get everybody talking to the people who worked there or even the customers. It was the same thing at the churches. We didn't just look at the architecture and the art. Tom would have us talking to a priest or an old lady who was just coming out from praying. It's like he really gets that to know the place, you have to know the people. And, it's the same thing wherever we end up eating. We'll get to know the wait staff and people in the kitchen. Lots of times the owner will come out and talk about how the restaurant got started—or the chef. And, you just hear these amazing stories that, I don't know, it kind of bonds us to have that experience together and to not do what I guess I kind of feared it would be like, which is everybody talking about work stuff and complaining about their bosses. And, we're not all there to be food critics either. We're having this really rich experience together. That's what the meal is: it's an experience. For me, and I know a lot of people who go, it really is very spiritual because we've made all these connections. I always have so much gratitude for that.

Experiences of connectedness and intimacy related to food did not always involve meals and other social gatherings. Cassie Anderson, a 27-year-old None from Kansas City, Kansas, is a prolific baker who experiences baking as "totally a contemplative practice." She told me she found the practice "therapeutic," adding, "But it's really more than that for me. It puts me into a kind of attentive silence that, I don't know, just feels really spiritual. When you're kneading bread, you're noticing without exactly thinking. It's a powerful experience." Another part of what makes regularly baking bread and other delights "more than that" is that Cassie shares what she bakes with friends and strangers (she brought me a loaf of to-die-for zucchini bread when we talked). "I just never go anywhere without a basket of something," she told me.

I really love making food. I love the process, you know, deciding what to make. Seeing what's fresh in the farmers market that week. I love how my kitchen smells while the bread is rising or a batch of muffins is baking. But that's really just for me. Other people don't get that part of it. So, I feel like it's a fair deal to give out most of the results. I mean, I can't possibly eat all this stuff. Also, it really matters to me that I'm sharing some of, you know, not just what I have, but something I took time to make. I'm nourishing people, and that nourishes me. I think that's really important.

Cassie gives loaves of bread and other baked goods to friends and family. "My dad will only eat my bread," she told me, "but I kind of think it's so he can check in on me every week." But she also drops off baskets of cookies and muffins at a nursing home a couple blocks from her apartment. If she happens to have something with her in the car, which is usually the case, she'll hand it out the window to homeless people she encounters at intersections. "There's something about food you made yourself," Cassie said, "giving it to people, that is just really the best thing. I mean, I wasn't raised religious or anything, and I'm not religious now, but this would be how I would do it if I were." She laughed, "If there's a church where they just cook and hand out food, sign me up for that!"

The front end of the meal—cultivating foodstuffs—has spiritual significance for Gary Shea, a 66-year-old Agnostic from Columbus, Ohio. "I'm not exactly a health nut," Gary told me, "but I do buy into this whole idea that it's better to know where your food came from than not." He grows much of what he, his wife, and his 36-year-old son (who moved back in with his parents when he lost his job) eat throughout the year. "We can't make it through the winter, of course, except for some potatoes," Gary said, "But we put up tomatoes and we freeze a lot." Growing food for the family made Gary feel that he was helping his wife, who shoulders most of the responsibility for cooking. "It's my little bit," Gary said, "and it keeps me out of her way!"

In addition to contributing to his relationship with his wife and to the sustenance of the family, gardening had other meanings for Gary that he counted as "more personally spiritual." Like many other home gardeners, Gary reported feeling more connected to nature and to the natural processes of life through his gardening. He explained,

You know, we're out in the suburbs, not too far from the city. Everything's paved and inhabited. You have to drive to the woods or even to the park. So, this gives me a chance to put my hands in the dirt and to reconnect a little with nature. I mean, know it's not exactly "nature" in the wilderness. But I am putting seeds in the ground. I'm watering things.

We compost, so I'm amending the soil with that. And then, you get to watch it grow, and harvest it, and pull out the dead plants in the fall, and start all over again in the spring. It's just a good feeling for me personally to be a part of that cycle.

Researchers have found that, particularly for people unaffiliated with institutional religions, gardening provides an important way to ground, as it were, their spirituality in everyday life through feelings of connectedness with nature, such as Gary described.[28] Gardening is also often experienced as an expression of the inner self—the self as creator, cultivator, nurturer. The Neopagan artist Corrie Milliman said her herb garden was "an artistic endeavor as much as any painting I've done. If you know me, you know that little plot is completely me. The way it's arranged, the colors, the way you see different things in different ways depending on where you're standing—it's no different than how I do a painting." For Corrie, participating in the "ritual of the seasons" was also an important part of the spirituality of her gardening. "I think you're never more aware of how time is a natural process, not a man-made control, than when you're working with a garden season after season, year after year," she told me.

Derek Chance, a 38-year-old Spiritual None from Stowe, Vermont, and his wife participate in a community garden near their home. For them, the garden is important as a place for social interaction, relaxation, and spiritual reflection. Derek described the couple's twice-weekly visits to their plot:

We go in the middle of the week—maybe on a Tuesday or Wednesday after work—and then we go again, usually on Sunday morning. It sort of has two different feels for us. The weekends have a lot more people, so they're more social, which is really great. We like talking to other gardeners about their gardens. It's a totally organic garden, so we're always trying to help each other with dealing with bugs. But people also share what they have extra, and we try to balance out what we're growing so it's diversified and there's not too much of any one thing. So one part of it is really the "community" part of the community garden—that you really are connecting with other people. But another big part—and this happens more during the week, when there aren't so many people around—is we'll just sit on one of the benches for a while after we're done weeding, or picking tomatoes, or whatever. There's a lady who seems to be there any day you come, and she hums a lot. So, you'll hear that. It's pretty. But otherwise, it's really tranquil and calm. You really relax in a deep way. I think that's the most spiritual part for me, just the quiet time after you've been digging in the dirt or watering the plants. You see that you're part of all this creation, that you're helping it to grow, but it's helping you, and the whole community. Literally, we're all feeding each other. It's kind of deep.

Nones with children at home often mentioned mealtimes as important occasions for bonding within the family, and sometimes with friends, even when meals were not as elaborate or ritualized as the Wednesday gathering that Felicia and her partner host. Noah Garrett, a 41-year-old Agnostic from Henderson, Nevada, and his fiancée, Pam, have four children from previous marriages between them. Pam's two daughters, ages 7 and 12, live with the couple full-time, and Noah's 13-year-old son and 15-year-old daughter stay with the family every other weekend, during breaks from school, and for two months in the summer. "It's a bit of a project to have everyone in the same place at the same time," Noah said, "but we make sure to have one, big, at-home family dinner every weekend we're all together where everybody is involved in some part of the meal." The kids take turns deciding on the menu, help with shopping and cooking, and periodically invite friends to the meal. "Pam and I make it a big priority," Noah told me. "We know that all of the kids coming together as a family when they all have other families, too, is a challenge. We want them to feel like this is *their family* whether they sleep here every day or not. Family dinner night helps to make those connections stronger." One of the features of the family dinner is that the meal begins with "an inspiration" selected and read by one of the kids. Noah explained,

> Both of our exes are religious. My ex-wife is just kind of normal Catholic, but Pam's kids' dad is way-out-there Evangelical. We're not raising them religious in our household, but my kids go to church with their mom and stepdad every week. Pam's kids see their dad less often, but when they do, he's thumping the Bible hard the whole time. So, they're all exposed to religion. We wanted to be respectful, on the one hand, but also faithful, if you will, to being Agnostic, more Humanist, rather than religious. So, instead of a prayer before dinner, the kids take turns finding an inspiration to read—just a short passage, maybe a poem, or sometimes with the bigger kids it's lyrics from a song. They'll throw in something religious once in a while—the Dalai Lama, or lately Pope Francis has been showing up with my daughter—but it's not heavy-duty religious. It's more about, you know, what helps you to be the best person you can be? What motivates you? What stirs your spirit? Once in a while, they'll write something themselves, which is just so amazing. And, when they have friends over to dinner, they really love it, too. Pam has been collecting all of them this year for a book that she's going to get printed up to give each of them for Christmas. It'll be like our Agnostic family bible.

The "family bible" crafted by Noah's fiancée for their children makes concrete the elements of an important ritual that informs the narrative of the self-as-spiritual for all of the members of the family. Its featured role in a family meal that also often extends to friends situates the spiritual at the heart of everyday family life, even if the logistics are somewhat complicated for Noah and Pam. The ritual likewise honors the religiosity and spirituality of all the participants and the families of which they are also members. In doing so, it highlights the various negotiations that play out within families and across other relationship clusters around religion and spirituality in a relationally complex and religiously plural world. The family dinner is the platform for working through these negotiations.

Once again, we see that the everyday spiritual lives of the Nones are seldom marked by the idiosyncratic, individualistic practices typically associated with extra-institutional spirituality or religion. Further, the stories I heard often had very little to do with the self-reflective, interiority that is characteristic of discussions of both traditional and emerging spiritualities. Those who shared their stories with me located their spirituality in everyday encounters with spouses, partners, children, siblings, friends, coworkers, and perfect strangers, these relationships taking homes, offices, parks, gardens, and other ordinary locales—even the lowly DMV—as sites in which the spiritual unfolded.

Journaling the Story of the Spiritual Self

Aside from prayer, which we will explore in the next chapter, one more private (mostly) individual practice that did often come up was journaling. More than a third of the people who talked with me mentioned journaling as an important spiritual practice, either currently or at some point in their lives. Journal writing has long been valued as a practice for self-development, creative insight, learning, and, with strong roots in early Protestantism, religious reflection, meditation, and prayer. The journals of traveling eighteenth- and nineteenth-century preachers and, especially, their wives, were popular reading for Americans during the Great Awakening, and stirred much emulation among literate Christians. Susanna Wesley's devotional journals helped to share the faith in England and the United States. Likewise, the journaling practice of Henry David Thoreau and other Transcendentalists etched not only their largely extra-institutional ideas but also their creative spiritual practices into the spiritual imaginations of generations of Americans. In late modern and postmodern American spirituality, Natalie Goldberg's tremendously popular 1986 book, *Writing Down the Bones: Freeing the Writer Within*, and Oprah's "gratitude journal" practice have continued a tradition that links spirituality to reflective writing for many.

Hanna Randall, a 48-year-old Spiritual-But-Not-Religious None from Flagstaff, Arizona, saw journaling as vital part of her spiritual vocation as a healer and holistic health educator. "It's a funny thing," Hanna said, "but I actually journal to get out of my head in a way." For Hanna, journaling is an embodied practice at least as much as a cognitive one. She explained, "We forget how physical writing is—I guess especially with computers. But, with a notebook and a pen, you're moving your thoughts through your body in a way that's different than talking about it with someone else or just thinking it through on your own. You come to parts of yourself you didn't know before. Your body takes you there as you write."

Hanna was perhaps the most disciplined of the journalers who talked with me, taking up her pen early every morning and at the end of each day. She has taken several workshops on journaling over the years, from time to time moving her private practice into a more social space. A couple of the workshops she attended focused specifically on journaling in relation to dreams. "Dreamwork,"[29] Hanna explained, was an important part of her spiritual life because it helps her to "balance out" the body work—Reiki, massage, reflexology—that is her "spiritual vocation" so that it "doesn't become the whole of me, the whole of my life. You have to leave space for the spirit to breathe, for the mind to open, or everything gets caught in the body." In the morning, she told me, "I try to capture my dreams. To see what I might have been learning as I slept. I try to move from there into a kind of wakefulness. I imagine my day. I meditate with words on the people I will encounter—clients, students." Sometimes, however, Hanna continued, "it doesn't feel all that insightful. I'm blank. I'll write about what my cat is doing. I'll look out the window and write about that." Even such seemingly banal notes can invite deeper reflection, these often pointing in relational directions. Hanna told me, "later on, I'll see connections I didn't realize were there. So, it's all important. You know, the whole earth and everyone in it—everyone who's ever been in it—are always teaching us. Journaling isn't the only way to connect to that, but I'm really verbal, so it works really well for me."

At night, journaling helps Hanna "to process the day. To put it to bed so I'm not blocked as much as possible when I go to sleep." Journaling is for Hanna a technology of the self—a way of representing to herself her own self-understanding as it is presented in her work, in her dreams, and in journaling itself.[30] The "balancing out" that Hanna experiences in her journal is, arguably, a way of regulating her understanding of her body, mind, and spirit across personal and professional domains of her life. It allows her to experience an interior self, or perhaps a private self, disconnected from the social, psychic, and physical demands of her bodywork practice. "I start writing, and I can feel the words on the page being pulled through my pen and onto the page. It just draws everything out of me that needs work or that I should let go of," she said. "Journaling is what takes me to a spiritual place so that I reconnect with myself. That keeps me from being just a drone when I'm working with people, which actually happens a lot to people who do bodywork."

This quite literal writing of the story of the spiritual self through journaling was not always directly a relationship between the inner or private self and an external, social, or public self. Charles Washington, a 26-year-old None from Marietta, Georgia, who described himself as a Jesus Follower, told me his journaling practice was an important part of his "walk with Jesus as a disciple. It's a way for me to share my thoughts with God and to reflect on what he's doing in my life." Charles has been keeping a journal since he attended a church camp in his early teens, writing "letters to Jesus or God" in which he shared reflections on his developing faith, his doubts, and his questions about how faith was playing out in his life. "It's also just a lot of ordinary, stupid things," Charles said. "But you hand it all over."

A few years ago, when he was an undergraduate at a Christian university in Oklahoma, Charles went on a "discernment weekend" during which his journaling became central in exploring his vocation—an exploration that helped him to understand his "deep dis-ease" with the church and to give up his identification with institutional Christianity. Charles explained:

> The leaders [of the retreat] were teaching us to pay close attention to how the Spirit was moving in us—they call it "discernment of spirits." You pay real close attention when you're praying or thinking through your day to when you feel good and when you feel upset or unhappy. Then you look for patterns—like, every time I do this thing, I feel really great, but when I do that, I feel awful. Or, I feel good at first, but later I have regrets. That's how the Spirit is showing you the way. And, for me, it was something I could do with my journal. I could look back over a few months or a year or more, and I could see that there were just so many times—especially as I got more involved—that when I was doing things in church, it wasn't making me happiest. It just wasn't fulfilling for me, whereas other things that I would previously have said were more of a hobby—like I do a lot of outdoors type activities—hunting, fishing, hiking—that was where I could see that I was really more aligned with God. And, it helped me to see that my way of following Jesus wasn't probably going to be in youth ministry, which I was planning to do, but just in living my life as a true disciple. I mean, I figured out that when you really do have relationship with Jesus Christ, your job is just to live from that in your ordinary life, not necessarily to get a job in a church or to be a "professional Christian," which is what I had almost been trying to do. And, I could see that all

with my own eyes in what I had written in my journal. So, it's really helped me out a lot.

All of the people who talked with me about journaling saw it as a practice that helped them to relax, to reflect on their lives, to develop insight on their deeper thoughts and feelings, to work through difficult decisions or solve problems, to encourage creative thinking, and to explore their relationships with others. Many Nones talked about journaling as a "meditative" or "prayerful" practice that helped them to get in touch with their inner self, soul, or spirit. A few also saw journaling as a way to connect with supernatural forces or beings, including God or gods. However, Tabitha Roberts, a 24-year-old Humanist from Lone Oak, Arkansas, had a more collaborative approach to journaling that involved writing regularly with an online community. She learned about the online journaling site in one of her college classes, where students reflected anonymously on readings for the course. Tabitha and some of her friends liked the practice, so they developed their own online journal to record and reflect on their experiences in college. The experience was "more spiritual than you would think" she told me:

> I do know some of the girls that were from the class, but not everybody. We use pseudonyms, though, and you kind of forget that, say, "Tammy Jammy" is someone you know. There's about twenty of us now, and most people write really regularly. You can tell when it's someone new, because they write a lot. I do less because I'm working full-time, and I just don't have as much time for it. But, still, I do share what's going on in my life now that I have graduated and I do have a job. It's a big transition, and I really was glad to be able to go, almost like, into a confessional and write what I was feeling and what was happening. And, I think it's really helpful for the other girls, because they'll go through this same sort of thing. It helps me, too, because someone will make a comment that is really encouraging or they'll post a picture that's funny or cheers me up. Also, lots of times someone will say something I wrote helped them, and I feel really good about that.

While journaling is generally a more private activity—even Tabitha's entries on the online journaling platform were not immediately interactive—it is worth noting that this individual practice is consistently relational in its effects. Hanna's journal helps her to avoid becoming "a drone" in her healing practice with others and to connect with other dimension of life. Charles's journaling enriches his relationship with Jesus outside a church context and has helped him to clarify vocational goals as a "true disciple" in everyday life. And, for Tabitha, journaling has a significant element of service to "the other girls" who contributed to the shared journaling platform. As we will see in the next chapter, journaling is often an important technology for prayer—this, too, typically extending in more relational than individualistic directions.

Spiritual Things and Places

With the exception of Tabitha, many of the people who talked with me about their journal writing practice also mentioned that the journal itself—the actual notebook and sometimes the writing instrument used—had a certain spiritual significance. "I know that's me in there," Olivia Merriman, a 47-year-old None from Durham, North Carolina, told me of a collection of journals she had kept since she was a teenager. "Years and years of me." Not unlike the "family bible" Derek's fiancée was crafting from their children's family dinner "inspirations," journals become for many people objects where evidence of the spirit (human or supernatural) is tracked and stored. Evan Raymond, a 46-year-old None from Blackfoot, Idaho, said of the journal he began during a tour in Iraq in the Army, "I hardly had time to write, and you couldn't say anything specific anyway. It's really just chicken scratch notes of the weather or it was a good day or a bad one. It's got little souvenirs—ticket stubs, receipts from this or that. I have labels from a kind of candy I got from a translator. But I know the feelings of that. When I pick it up, it has the spirit of that time in it."

Throughout my conversations with Nones, especially when I had the opportunity to meet with them in their homes, material objects came up as important within specific spiritual practices—recall Judith Leonard's photographs of her daughters and granddaughters—or as more general reminders of the spiritual in the course of everyday life, such as Karen Dade's "findings." Like several of the people who talked with me, Corrie Milliman keeps an altar on a small table in her studio on which she places objects that inspire her—an antique tin of buttons, a letter from her grandfather written the week he died, a Gaia figurine, some postcards from a friend who is traveling in South America, feathers, stones, shards of tree bark—as well as small paintings, quotations written on note cards, and a great abundance and variety of candles. Kenny Mahoe, a 28-year-old None from Makaweo, Hawaii, likewise has an altar—his, a mound in the backyard, comprising shells, fish bones, and, from time to time, he told me, fresh flowers. "I like them because they're what's left over, but they're becoming something else," Kenny said. "I don't worship them or anything, but I like having them there."

Felicia Oliveria and her family don't worship at their "altar" either. She showed me a collection on a sofa table of the sort you'd find in many homes—baby photos, family holiday and vacation photos, bronzed baby shoes, a framed copy of their domestic partnership declaration, figurines of lighthouses the family has visited along the East Coast, and a dish filled with brightly colored blown glass candies. "The family shrine!" she laughed at first, but she paused to reflect with more earnestness:

> Seriously, though, this really is a kind of an altar for us. It has something from every part of our life on it. Even that candy dish means something. My aunt gave it to me when Denise and I moved in together, which was a big deal in my family—I mean, that she was acknowledging us as a couple. Nobody else from my family got us anything. And, we got those candies in Vegas the first time we went on vacation together. So, I know it's just stuff, but it's important stuff. If the house were on fire—and the boys were outside already—I'd grab all that and run.

Most of the spiritual things mentioned, however, were less formally situated. Christopher Langer, a 55-year-old Humanist from Boston, Massachusetts, carries a photo of Frankie, the dog he had as boy, in his wallet. "He was the best dog ever," Christopher said wistfully. "Friendly as all get out, but he'd protect the family. You know, I know it's against the Humanist rules, but it makes me feel safe to have him with me, or, I guess to remember what that was like." Men's wallets turn out to be treasure troves of spiritual things. Lance Everett, None from Chicago, carries a silver coin his grandfather gave him. Frank Brunner, the Spiritual-But-Not-Religious None we met previously, has three fortune cookie papers in his wallet that form what he said was "my spirituality in a nutshell": "Always trust your heart;" "Everything has beauty, but not everyone sees it;" and "Make people smile, and you will live a joyous life."

Some objects were clearly spiritual or religious. Spiritual-But-Not-Religious None Glenda Storey, from Oak Creek, Arizona, surrounds herself with angels—jewelry, figurines, paintings, books, and so on. Natalie Darling, a former Catholic, Spiritual None, has a small collection of icons of traditional (Francis, Teresa) and non-traditional (Dorothy Day, Martin Luther King, Jr.) saints above her desk. Aaron Jacobson, an Agnostic Secular Jew, has a mezuzah—a small box that holds a scripture passage meant to remind Jews of God's presence in their homes—on his doorpost and he keeps a number of Jewish religious artifacts around the house. While he and his husband are not raising their children as religious Jews, Aaron told me he wants to give their kids "a little nudge to ask questions about their culture." But he also said these objects keep him connected to the tradition. "I swear, I touch that mezuzah every day," he told me somewhat sheepishly. "It's embarrassing. But it's also who we are. It's where we're from. And, it makes me feel good."

Mostly, however, the spiritual things in the stories of those who talked to me were "spiritual" because they connected with other parts of their lives—other people, mostly, and several pets—that form the center of their spiritual narratives. Nones told me about gifts from grandparents, parents, children, siblings, friends, spouses, and partners that had spiritual significance for them. People treasured found objects from their daily lives, their explorations of the natural world, and from vacation travel. Seldom were any of these expressly religious. Andy Elliot, a 41-one-year-old Atheist from Pittsburgh, Pennsylvania, told me his father gave him a hundred dollar bill when he was accepted into a master's program in fine arts to study photography. He keeps the bill in an envelope in his desk. "It just means so much to me," Andy said, "that this guy who worked all his life in a machine shop was saying, 'Sure, go to art school. Be an artist,' because I know it was a struggle for him to accept that the money he worked so hard to get me through college was going for *art*. I pull it out when my confidence is flagging. It's like a kind of talisman. As long as I don't have to spend it, I can tell myself I'm doing okay." Jessie Lansing, a 20-year-old Agnostic from St. Paul, Minnesota, has a pair of "special earrings" her favorite aunt gave her when she graduated from high school. "She got them at this friend of hers who is an artist. She made them just for me," Jessie said. "She had to tell her all about me. So, they have my story kind of *in them*, and also they have my aunt's story, too. I just love that."

Sacred objects are central to religious traditions, of course, making concrete the presence of divinities and other supernatural forces. But rabbi and spiritual writer Lawrence Kushner argues that they extend beyond these transcendent realities into the most intimate contours of everyday experience: "Places and things never forget what they have been witnesses to and vehicles of and entrances for."[31] These concretized memories, indeed, moved in the lives of the Nones who talked with me through objects and spaces embedded in their stories of family, friends, pets, strangers, and meals, with rich spiritual resonances. Very often, spiritual spaces were found in nature—the clichéd hikes in the woods or walks by the beach that fill most people with awe at some point. As we will see in the next chapter, many people found such spaces and activities in them particularly "prayerful." But it was not the case that natural vistas alone were highlighted as "spiritual." Often, the most mundane of places were noted as "sanctuary" or "sacred space." Robbie Smith, a 29-year-old Agnostic from Atlanta, Georgia, talked about a downtown office plaza near his office where he goes to people-watch and meditate:

It's a funny thing, how the buzz of that place—all the people hustling here and there—is so calming for me. I guess I see how we're all caught up in it—the craziness of careers and work things. And then, I'll just come down here, and get a coffee, and kind of step back from it and watch. It makes me see that we're all just people. We're all just trying. So, it gives me a little different perspective on what I'm doing in my life. I think it makes me more forgiving, going down there for twenty minutes to meditate a little, of myself probably mostly, but also of the people I work with. You know, it connects me to the humanness of even the kind of very abstract work I do with other people.

Many Nones described their homes, or spaces within them, as "sacred" or "spiritual" spaces. Julia Xavier, None from Los Altos, California, said of the small home she bought after an acrimonious divorce, "Every time I walk in the front door, I am just grateful. I really am. I could hardly afford to buy this place, but I did. And, I made it a place for me and my boys at probably the most difficult time of my life. I know there was something helping me through that. Every time I come home, I just feel whatever—whoever—that is closer to me." Julia told me she often walks through the house slowly, stopping to sit on one of her kids' beds or to adjust a painting on the wall, "and I just know that there is a spirit of goodness here that I wouldn't know anywhere else in quite the same way."

David Brown has argued that, in the ancient world, the city and home were "sacramental realities"—spaces in which there was a "mixing of power and piety [that] of course witnesses to the potential for corruption, but it also suggests with equal force that divine presence was seen."[32] For Robbie and Julia, very different spaces open them up to both the difficulties of their lives and the "goodness" that is present. Here again, the spiritual is a phenomenon that plays out in "spaces of encounter," marked by a deeper awareness of relationships and a felt intimacy with loved ones. But such encounters also appear, as in Robbie's case, with strangers who serve as reminders of humanness in the often dehumanized landscapes of commerce and corporate work.[33]

Obviously, Nones are not unique in finding and valuing spiritual significance in relationships with family, friends, and pets. They are not distinguished from the religiously affiliated by their reverence for nature, their love of gardening, or the spiritual connections they feel as they prepare or share food with others in the lives. And their family photos and other spiritual things are no more precious than such things are for those who center their spiritual identities in traditional, institutional religions. Everyday life and the relationships it holds are rich with spiritual nuances that would be recognizable to Nones and Somes alike. What may be different for Nones is that the nuances associated with encounters in everyday life are spiritually primary for them. Institutional religious frames— theologies and doctrines, corporate worship and personal piety, sacred objects and spaces—often serve for Nones as points of contrast for their own spiritual experiences, rather than as central characters and plotlines in the spiritual life. For those who identify and affiliate with traditional religions, the line between the secular and the sacred, even if increasingly porous, is functionally present. For Somes, as Nancy Ammerman has argued, "personal spiritual engagement is intimately tied, then, both to involvement in a religious community and to the *extension* of that spiritual tribe into the everyday life of the household."[34] The Nones, however, felt the spiritual moving more fluidly in various zones of life—household, workplace, marketplace—through networks of relationships that animated that spirit. This relational orientation in unaffiliated spirituality, which assumes what philosopher Michael Slote has identified as a receptiveness to others upon which empathy is grounded,[35] has important implications for other elements of life, including ethics and morals, especially as these are passed on to children. The suggestion here is not, of course, that the affiliated do not have this receptiveness as well, but rather that, as Ammerman suggests, the orienting center of spiritual and moral practice for Somes is the institutional religious community and its teaching. This shapes *responses* to others in daily life outside congregations. For Nones, receptiveness is largely unmediated by formal, institutional commitments, teachings, and practices.

We will consider the ethics of unaffiliated spirituality in Chapter 6. Before we do that, however, in Chapter 5 we take up one further practice that was prominent among Nones of all stripes who talked with me: prayer.

Praying between the Lines

Prayer among the Unaffiliated

I don't have to go to church to be a part of a religion—to pray. Prayer is really the one thing the church can't get its hands on.
>—George Brooks, *age 40, Tulsa, Oklahoma, "Jesus Follower"*

I wouldn't exactly say I pray in the sense of, you know, "Oh, Heavenly Father, could you help me pass this exam" or that kind of thing. If there is a god, you know, he's looking at me to do my own homework, to live my life right. But, sure, there are times when I'm running, and it's real, real calm . . . or I'll just stop on the bridge over the canal and look out at all of it. There aren't really any words, but you feel it deep inside yourself. . . . I would say that's prayer. At least for me.
>—Langston Green, *age 22, Trenton, New Jersey, "Agnostic"*

I almost don't mean to do it—praying. It's not like I expect anything to happen because of my words or what I want to happen. It's just, I don't know, better than doing nothing sometimes. It's better than just "thinking about" someone or "setting your intention."
>—Tabitha Roberts, *age 24, Lone Oak, Arkansas, "Humanist"*

The campus of Santa Clara University, an hour south of San Francisco, is a paradoxically religious locale in the heart of the famed Silicon Valley tech corridor. The university was the first in the state, founded in 1851 on the site of the Mission Santa Clara de Asís, one of the original Catholic missions along the historic El Camino Réal, during the nineteenth-century equivalent of the twenty-first-century tech boom—the California Gold Rush. Remnants of the mission still stand on the campus, surrounded by rose gardens and framed by wisteria-laden arbors that shade the path to the grand Mission Church. Classroom and administrative buildings echo the names of learned Jesuits who established the university, and the university's namesake is honored in an adaptation of a medieval enclosed garden meant to symbolize the Garden of Eden and to invite prayer and contemplation in the midst of hectic academic days. Still, I was surprised when 24-year-old Eddy Poston, a graduate of Santa Clara's engineering program and an Atheist, suggested we meet at Saint Clare's Garden to talk about his spiritual life. I was even more surprised when he told me he came to the garden often to "pray":

> People might think I'm hypocritical when I say I pray, but I don't think there's anything magical about that word. You don't have to pray to a god or a saint. You just pray. It's just you thinking or not thinking— clearing your head—so you're able to try to be a better person or help someone else out. I mean, I could say "meditation," I guess, but "prayer" is what feels more the right thing for me. It's what I grew up with. And, I had a class here where we would come out here to pray sometimes, and I got into the habit of coming here. . . . Just because I'm not Catholic now, because I'm an Atheist, doesn't mean I have to give up that word for what I'm doing. I mean, the Pope doesn't have a copyright on it.

Can an Atheist *really* pray? Does Eddie's appropriation of a terminology associated with traditional institutional religions disrespect those religions or honor them? Does it, as one Atheist insisted in an angry response to an article I wrote on Atheists at prayer, offend non-religious sensibilities as well?[1] Can prayer be non-theistic, as when the Dalai Lama, the exiled leader of Tibetan Buddhists (who don't believe in an ultimate deity) offers prayers of peace or holds prayer vigils?[2] And what of the many Nones—81% according to the "Nones on the Rise" report[3]—who do believe in a life force, higher power, or supernatural being that might be engaged through prayer but whose prayers are largely offered outside institutional religious contexts? How do these prayers fit into the spiritual narrative of the unaffiliated? How do they compare to the prayer practices of the affiliated?

The most recent data tell us that prayer is indeed a remarkably widespread and durable practice in the United States. Some 90% of the religiously affiliated in the US report that they pray on at least a monthly basis. Two-thirds (66%) say they pray every day, 88% at least monthly. That is a somewhat higher percentage than those in the general public who say they pray regularly (79%), the difference surely attributable to the comparatively small but nonetheless meaningful percentage of the unaffiliated (41%) who pray at least once a month.[4] Historically, prayer has taken place in sites maintained or identified by religious institutions or has been an activity encouraged by them. We would therefore not expect many Nones to participate in this practice, often seen by religious practitioners and scholars alike as "the religious phenomenon par excellence."[5] Still, the majority of Nones come from religious backgrounds where they would most likely have learned some kind of prayer practice. Though nearly 60% of Nones say they "seldom or never" pray, prayer is by no means foreign to the unaffiliated, including those who identify as Atheists, Agnostics, Humanists, Secular, and otherwise, without belief in a supernatural being or force.

Indeed, a strong plurality of those identified as Atheist/Agnostic in the Pew data—17%—reported praying on a monthly, weekly, or even daily basis.[6] Among the 37% of Nones who identify as Spiritual-But-Not-Religious, 65% reported praying regularly, 44% of these on a daily basis.[7] About half (51%) of the remainder—those who describe their religious affiliation as "nothing-in-particular"—pray regularly, 27% on a daily basis. Further, in my test survey on spiritual practices, 19% of Nones—a figure comparable to the portion of the religiously affiliated in the Pew data who reported praying fervently[8]—identified prayer as one of the top "spiritually significant" practices in their lives, along with the "Four Fs" we explored in the previous chapter. Prayer for Nones ranked lower in my survey than it did for Somes (23%), but it nonetheless came before practices like creating and sharing music (17%), enjoying time in nature (18%), creating and sharing art (18%), and enjoying physical activity (7%).

According to the late nineteenth-century French theologian Auguste Sabatier, "prayer distinguishes religious phenomena from everything like it or close to it, such as moral sense or aesthetic feeling." In Sabatier's view, prayer is thus *the* essence of religion.[9] Even if prayer is merely *an* essential practice in most religious traditions, it is reasonable to ask what kind of "religion" the prayer practices of Nones might be representing today. How do Nones pray? As importantly, what does prayer do for them? How does it function within what they understand as their spiritual lives and in life more generally? We take up these questions in this chapter. But first, because prayer means so many different things in different religious traditions and to different people within and outside those traditions, we briefly explore various understandings of prayer itself.

What Is Prayer?

What exactly do we mean by "prayer"? Neither history nor the wide range of contemporary practices, philosophies, and theologies of prayer allow for the development of a single, universal definition of prayer.[10] Prayer can be collective or individual, public or private, formal or extemporaneous. Prayer can be verbal or nonverbal, addressing a supernatural being in words or thoughts. It can be intended to move a divinity to act, or it can be motivated by the desire to connect spiritually with a god or with others in the world. In terms of its effects in everyday life, physical and emotional healing, psychological coping, and the attainment of material benefits are attributed to prayer.[11]

Prayer is often active and embodied in the form of ritualized movements, like Dorit Brauer's labyrinth prayer practice. As an embodied practice, the fourth-century Christian bishop Augustine of Hippo—a saint who sought vigorously to rid himself of carnal sins through prayer—believed, "prayer clarifies and purges our heart and makes it more capable of receiving the divine gifts that are poured out for us in the spirit."[12] This sense of prayer as a physical practice with psychological and spiritual benefits often resonates with Nones. But service to others has often been conceived as a kind of prayer as well; the truest expression of prayer is for many seen in moral action in the world God created.[13] Many Nones see acts of social transformation, as much or more than practices focused on personal enrichment, as prayer.

People are often surprised when they hear of prayer by Atheists, Agnostics, Humanists, and other non-believers. But these Nones are not entirely unlike practitioners in non-theistic traditions such as Buddhism, Jainism, Taoism, and forms of Unitarian Universalism, whose prayers would likewise not necessarily be directed to a supernatural being. Popularized in North America today by leaders and teachers such as the Dalai Lama and Pema Chödrön, both Tibetan Buddhists, and Zen Buddhists such as Thich Nhat Hanh and Cheri Huber, Buddhism generally is better known for meditative practices than for formal prayer. But Buddhist traditions include a number of utterances and ritual gestures, many of them addressed to deities, understood in modern Western Buddhism as "archetypes in the mind" rather than ontological realities.[14]

Buddhism scholar Rita M. Gross explains that Buddhist deities represent "obstacles to enlightenment [that] might be lessened or destroyed" through prayer as it transforms the mind of the one who prays. This thinking is behind the well-worn Buddhist teaching that if one encounters the Buddha on the road, the spiritually appropriate response is to "kill" him—to eliminate any false deity who blocks the road to personal enlightenment.[15] While there are elements of non-theistic practice that would likely be unacceptable to non-religious Nones—the institutionalization of a system of belief in any transcendent reality, hierarchical structures of religious authority and formation, or formal ritualized practice—prayer in non-theistic religions offers some insight into what such Nones may mean when they report that they pray. Indeed, many Atheists and Humanists see themselves as "more enlightened" than religious believers (affiliated or not) precisely because they understand prayer as a spiritually meaningful practice that does not involve a deity. They have "killed" all the buddhas, gods, and other spiritual beings or forces encountered along the road.

In the end, neither theistic nor non-theistic traditions fix a definition of prayer that applies to all those who pray—Nones or Somes alike. But they do point to the religious resources that are available for Nones to adopt and adapt in the prayer practices they described to me. My conversations about prayer with

Nones were guided by a fairly simple interview rubric[16] that invited interviewees to define prayer themselves:

- Do you pray? If, yes . . .
- Under what circumstances do you pray?
- How do you pray? (Where? When? In what manner?)
- To whom (or what) are your prayers addressed?
- What effects do you expect or hope for when you pray?
- What effects have you experienced when you pray?

I adapted these questions as seemed appropriate to the conversation with a particular interviewee and sometimes added other clarifying questions, such as

- How do you think prayer is different from meditation or contemplation?
- How do you think prayer is different from hoping, wishing, or desiring?
- Do you pray with others?
- How did you learn to pray in this way?

This approach ensured that practices I might not consider "prayer" were not excluded from consideration. It also stopped me from naming as "prayer" activities that those who talked with me would not have described as such simply because they fit within traditional categories of prayer, such as blessing, contrition, intercession, petition, praise, supplication, thanksgiving, lament, and so on, or because they involved actions I might associate with prayer as ritual, such as kneeling or folding hands. Further, the interview rubric allowed practices of non-theistic Nones—Atheists, Secular Humanists, and many Agnostics—to be counted when they themselves described them as prayer.

Nones at Prayer

When I asked the Nones who talked with me if they prayed, most of them said they did not. So, too, as in the "Nones on the Rise" survey, fewer than half (44%) of those who completed the "Nones Beyond the Numbers" survey reported praying,[17] some of them making their lack of interest in the practice quite clear:

- Not a chance!
- I see traditional prayer as begging.
- I pretend to pray at family gatherings, but I'm mostly thinking about how stupid praying is while I'm waiting to get to the buffet table.
- I have not prayed in more than 50 years.

- I don't pray. I don't think anyone is there to listen to prayers.
- Since I don't believe in any kind of "higher power" or the existence of a "soul" or "spirit," I don't pray.
- Prayer is a waste of time and energy. You could go do something—help someone, pick up trash. If I were god, I'd appreciate that a lot more.

For some Nones, setting their thoughts, intentions, concerns, and relationships within the construct of prayer seemed to undermine their own agency in and responsibility for effecting positive change. Likewise, as with Nones who resisted the language of "spirituality," the concept and practice of prayer carry all of the institutional religious meanings we have seen (and plenty more), which makes many Nones uncomfortable. Andy Elliott, an Atheist, told me:

> I do not pray. I think about family and friends who are sick or in need, and reach out to them, but I don't consider that prayer. I don't plea with a nonexistent being to grant my wishes; instead, I go about creating conditions that achieve my goals. If I want my friend to get healthier, or my aunt to recover from my uncle's death, I talk to them, send them cards, et cetera, rather than pray. If I want something for myself, say a job or some money, then I do things proactively that will help me obtain those goals. If I need encouragement, then I call my mom, or family, or friends and talk with them, listen to their advice, and start doing things that will help my situation. None of these things are prayer. None of them require prayer.

Andy's identification as an Atheist certainly correlates with his self-motivated and self-reliant understanding of care for others and self-care, but George Brooks, a 43-year-old "Jesus Follower" from Tulsa, Oklahoma, was not far from Andy in his thinking about prayer in relation to what Christians would traditionally call "good works." George was strongly critical of what he referred to as "church Christians," deploring practices of prayer that he saw as taking the place of concrete actions to address their needs and the needs of others. God, he said, requires faithful action *beyond* prayer. Indeed, for George, moving beyond prayer to action is a biblical mandate:

> Jesus is pretty clear about "pray in secret." I know there are other ways people read the Bible, but you have to look at how Jesus acted, too. He drew clear lines between the times he was off somewhere praying and the real work of, you know, healing people, feeding them, challenging corrupt power. He didn't tell the disciples to go forth and pray for people or pray with them. He sent them out to tell people the Kingdom of

God is at hand and to heal people.[18] I believe Jesus had real, practical work in mind setting up the Kingdom.

George's negative experiences in a number of churches—communities that he found irredeemably human in their penchant for gossip, pettiness, cliquishness, greed, and hypocrisy—prompted him to give up church membership. He saw personal prayer as "the one thing the church can't get its hands on," but he was critical of how some of the Christians he knew used prayer in light of the standard he believed Jesus had established in scripture:

> I don't really see church Christians pray as Jesus taught it. I see them using prayer as therapy and prayer as display of their faith. You know, a lady told me once that when she gardens it's prayer. I was like, "What?" That's not what prayer is—some hobby that makes you feel good. If you like to garden, or walk in the woods, or bake cookies, hey, that's great. But don't call it prayer. Even if you're helping others, that's really what that is: helping others. It's not prayer. Everything you do is not prayer. It drives me nuts how people say that. It cheapens what prayer really is. And I think it makes people are lazy disciples. "Oh, I prayed about that. It's all good now." That's not how it works. I mean, you're talking with Almighty God. Have a little reverence. If you want to ask for his help, ask him to help you get out of your own way. Ask him to bless your work in his name. Then go out in the world and do what God asks you to do.

Still, many of the Nones who talked with me did see prayer as an important part of their spiritual lives, some of them praying quite regularly. Unlike either George or Andy, many of the Nones who talked with me saw a considerable range in what could be considered prayer. For these Nones, prayer had several qualities that made it meaningful beyond ordinary experience. The experiences of Nones at prayer described in this chapter show us prayer as

- Discursively distinctive: The word "prayer" itself connotes a special kind of activity or experience that is qualitatively different from non-religious actions (such as "thinking about" someone in need) and other spiritual practices (such as meditation or contemplation).
- Experientially distinctive: Nones report that prayer *feels* different from other spiritual or non-spiritual activities. Likewise, experiences that seem spiritually rich are often described as "prayer" or "prayerful."
- Precarious and doubtful: A number of Nones reported that prayer offers a space to consider or challenge their belief in or experience of supernatural or transcendent others.

- Cognitive and verbal as well as sensate and embodied: Nones reported praying mentally, verbally, through various physical and creative activities, and in acts of service.
- Both an intentional practice and an unintentional (and sometimes unwanted) spiritual interruption in otherwise non-spiritual circumstances.
- Characteristically personal and private: Though Nones who talked with me reported praying about relationships, shared circumstances, or public concerns, only a few reported praying with others—this, generally within families—and only one person who talked with me reported praying at a public gathering.
- Both theistic and non-theistic: Many Nones reported praying to or experiencing the presence of a divine being or force in prayer, but both believing and unbelieving Nones also regularly described prayer practices that did not include any supernatural other.
- Oriented toward personal comfort, insight, or growth for the one praying and the one for prayed for: Nones frequently reported praying for specific benefits such as healing, almost always for others and in times of crisis. They also described prayer practices as oriented toward spiritual care or the enrichment of the self. No one talked with me about praying for more general or global concerns such as world peace, political concerns, or the environment.
- Relational and connective: Many Nones understood prayer as connecting them spiritually, emotionally, cognitively, and practically with others, both human and supernatural, both living and dead.
- Socially performative: Some Nones reported participating in common prayer practices for the sake of avoiding interpersonal conflicts or to offer comfort and support to someone to whom prayer was important.

These categories overlapped extensively in stories Nones shared with me. The "specialness" associated with the experience of praying, for instance, might be associated with the fact that the prayer seemed to come unbidden or that a prayer produced an important understanding of the self or of a significant relationship or situation. But among all of the characteristics of prayer, its discursive and experiential distinctiveness were most consistently noted.

Prayer as Discursively and Experientially Distinctive

Nearly all of the Nones who talked with me about prayer described the practice as distinct from other everyday activities, including those that they counted as "spiritual." For most praying Nones, the word "prayer" was remarkably capacious, tending to absorb not only other spiritual practices, but any other life practices involving personal reflection, concern for others, feelings of connectedness to other beings or the earth, or experiences marked by emotional, physical, or other intense feelings. Naming a practice as "prayer" tended to elevate it, mark it as special, and identify it as particular to the person praying. Prayer, we will hear, is "better" and "deeper" than other ways of expressing concern for others, coping with anxiety or loss, expressing hope, or exploring and enriching the self.

Cassie Anderson, the Spiritual baker we met in the previous chapter, grew up in a non-religious family. She told me of a regular practice of acknowledging gifts in her life by noting them in a "gratitude diary" that she only came to understand as prayer when a friend named it as such. The naming was significant for Cassie:

> I didn't actually know I was praying. I mean, I had seen people pray on TV or in movies. You know, all "Help me, Jesus! Help me, Jesus!" There were lots of Christian kids at school who would bow their heads or fold their hands before lunch or when we had tests. So, you know, I wasn't ignorant. I just wasn't doing it that way. . . . I was telling a friend about my gratitude diary, and she said, "Oh, you're praying." She told me about a prayer journal she learned how to do at a church group that was kind of like what I was doing. Honestly, I didn't know you could pray if you didn't really believe in god or Jesus. But, after she told me that, I really liked thinking of it as prayer, that I was praying. I don't know, it just made it seem more special. You know, not just a list of stuff I'm thankful about, but an actual prayer of gratitude. I mean, it just makes me feel good not just about the things that I list, but that I'm taking the time to acknowledge them even when I'm not having a good day—that I'm praying. I like that.

Calling the entries in her gratitude diary "prayer" made it special not because her daily list was addressed to a supernatural other. Rather, the act of naming gave Cassie a certain spiritual authority and her diary writing practice a spiritual power that derived at least in part from the fact that her practice was read by her religious friend as prayer-like. In this sense, the friend acts something like a priest who sanctifies Carrie's "prayer" practice both within and beyond the theological boundaries of traditional religion.

Nones who prayed tended to see prayer as happening in an experiential register that could not be captured by other words. For many Nones, the kinds of care for others and self-care that for both George, the Jesus Follower, and Andy, the Atheist, emphatically *did not* count as "prayer" were rendered more meaningful when named as such, whether or not such "prayers" were accompanied by belief in a supernatural being or force. Tabitha Roberts, the Humanist quoted at the beginning of the chapter, set prayer within this distinctive discursive regis-ter despite her non-theistic views. Prayer, she said, is "better than just 'thinking about' someone or 'setting your intention.'" She continued,

> You know, I don't actively pray or tell someone I'm praying for them. But sometimes someone will post something on Facebook where they're asking for prayer for something—maybe someone's sick or something. And I'll "like" that, which I think maybe makes people think I am pray-ing. Or, you know, my mom will say, "Send a prayer up for your Aunt Katie. She's having a tough time." And I'll say I will. And then I really will, like, say in my head something like, "Take care of Aunt Katie . . ." to no one in particular. I think that's okay because, like I said, it's more than just thinking about someone. I mean, I guess you're feeling about them, too. I don't know how else to say that. But when you tell someone you "prayed for" them, they understand that you care in a deeper way.

Even applied to activities that some Nones would describe as wholly "secu-lar," the word "prayer" carries strong traces of its relational, transactional, and psychological religious history. It can be seen as having a quality of enchantment or of encounter with the holy, even for people who would otherwise reject such terminology.

Prayer for Nones is also more than the word itself or words uttered in prayer-ful reflection. Echoing the traditions of Buddhist teachers and Christian figures from Thomas Aquinas to Ignatius of Loyola and beyond, prayer was also under-stood by Nones who talked with me as taking place in more fully embodied practices. These prayerful practices range from enjoying time in nature, to engag-ing in athletic activities, participating in volunteer work, and social or political activism. In these cases, rather than the word "prayer" amplifying the spiritual meaning of personal reflection, expressions of concern for others, or other prac-tices to which it applied, it is the specialness of certain actions that call them out as "prayer" or "prayerful."

Adam Noonan, a Spiritual None, counted as "prayer" the experience of surf-ing. When I asked him how he prayed, he told me:

> Every time I get out there on the board, floating in the water, I know there's God. There's something. It's big. I really never got that feeling in church. But, in the time that you're waiting and waiting, and you feel the swell of the water coming, you really know you're in the presence of something awesome. I mean, you really are literally *in* awe. Whether that's your wave or not, I don't know, just for me there's just this feeling

that you're connected with the highest power there is, the deepest power. It's like you're connected to the source of everything, which you really are in the ocean, right? "Mother Ocean," right? And when you do catch the right wave, and you have that sense, "yeah, this is so mine," you really do know you were on a wavelength—pun intended—with God. I think that's what prayer is, you know? That deep, deep connection, and you just ride it and that feeling will stay with you, like, all day.

Adam had only very limited experience of formal religion as a child, this in a nondenominational church, and his spirituality is obviously shaped by the New Age lexicon of Southern California surf culture. Nonetheless, as with Cassie, religious understandings of what prayer might feel like are a starting point for describing extra-religious prayer that moves well beyond these experiences, into embodied, sensate, and almost mystical registers.[19] Langston Green, a 24-year-old Agnostic from Trenton, New Jersey, had a similarly embodied understanding of prayer, which takes a caricature of Christian prayer as a departure point. Prayer for Langston emerges from his experience as a runner:[20]

I wouldn't exactly say I pray in the sense of, you know, "Oh, Heavenly Father, could you help me pass this exam" or that kind of thing. If there is a god, you know, he's looking at me to do my own homework, to live my life right. But, sure, there are times when I'm running, and it's real, real calm, and I feel a kind of peace that is different than just relaxation. It's like you're so—I don't know how to put it—*totally in your body* that you feel it before you know it. Sometimes I'll just stop on the bridge over the canal and kind of be overcome. There aren't really any words, but you feel it deep inside yourself and at the same time all around you. It's like the line between you and everything else just kind of goes away. You just know it's different. You feel it. I would say that's prayer. At least for me.

Other Nones experienced embodied prayer in service to others or the world— through acting in relation to the bodies of others. In these cases, prayer was not experienced as interiorized or sensate but as inherent in activities that expressed their ethical and political values. Joseph Carlson, a 34-year-old Humanist from Palo Alto, California, described his work as an emergency medical technician with a disaster recovery volunteer group, making a provisional claim on the language and definition of prayer:

For me, "praying" is doing your best to improve the lives of others. I mean, not just as an ideal, but in real, practical ways. On the ground.

As Humanists, we realize that without a god to pray to, we have to help each other out. That's what you could call my "spirituality" if you want to. We're it. Each of our lives can be a prayer, I guess you could say.

Joseph continued, linking the specialness of the word "prayer" to the experiential quality of activities that could count for him as "prayer":

> I mean, I probably wouldn't ordinarily call it that, but when you ask me if I pray, I would say that's what it is. And, I guess, when I think about it, it's important that, as a Humanist, I call it that, because I'm saying to religious people, more or less, "You know that special, spooky thing you do when you think you're talking to god, or Jesus, or whoever? We do that, too, except with real, living beings. We pray by caring actively. We pray by helping others." . . . When we're working to take care of people who have been, let's say, injured in a hurricane like in Haiti, you do that out of a sense of the highest regard for preserving human life and honoring the human spirit. You know every single life is important and you want it all to go as well is it can even in the worst conditions. I haven't prayed in a church or anything for a long time, but I think ultimately that's the point of any prayer—that things will get better for people. So, I'm not asking a god to do that. I'm saying I'll join with these other people and we'll do our part. We'll do our very best.

The spiritual lives of many Nones included other embodied practices that they considered prayer, often connected to very traditional religious practices. Here again, Dorit Brauer is illustrative. Brauer called on an understanding of prayer as a practice that facilitated personal enrichment, connection with natural and supernatural others, spiritual and emotional coping, and physical and mental healing. But she did not trouble much over technical distinctions between practices like prayer, meditation, and contemplation. "I don't think the Universe is so particular about what you call it," she told me. Still, she felt that her use of a traditional prayer ritual connected her to others, across history:

> People have been building labyrinths for centuries—millennia—you know. So when you are walking, or, for me, when I am building a labyrinth, I am aware on a certain level of that history. It's like you're walking with all of those people. You are praying with them. You know, all the spirits, or souls, or ghosts. You're in that same flow of energy across time. This is what prayer can connect you to. You know, where did all that energy from the past go? Nowhere! It's all still here in different

forms. You just have to connect to it, and praying by walking the labyrinth through time and space, you could say, is one way.

Although Brauer was clear about the prayerfulness of labyrinth walking, other embodied spiritual practices were often not initially described by Nones as prayer. Instead, when I asked about prayer, interviewees would return to practices such as yoga, meditation, massage, or Reiki, reframing them as prayer. For example, Bliss Winter, a Spiritual-But-Not-Religious None, practiced yoga several days a week in a group setting and most mornings on her own. In response to my question about practices important to her spiritual life, she mentioned her yoga practice, highlighting the benefits of personal enrichment, physical and emotional balance, and an overall sense of well-being, which she felt made her kinder, more patient, and open with others. She did not at first identity yoga as prayer. But when I asked about prayer, she responded, "I would say that, for me, yoga is prayer. I know it's not traditional prayer, like in church, but it does put me in touch with what's most important in my life and it helps me to be a better person. Isn't that what prayer is supposed to do anyway?"

It is possible that such responses point to a flaw in my methodology; my questions may have invited reinterpretation of other practices as prayer. (The majority of people who talked with me simply said that they did not pray and our conversations moved on from there without further consideration of prayer.) Still, even these research provocations speak to the suppleness of the discursive and experiential meanings of prayer in the culture at large. I never felt that the people who talked with me were struggling to fit what they saw as spiritually significant practices into a container I was calling "prayer" solely for my benefit. Rather, questions about prayer invited a different way of looking at their spiritualities—as with Cassie's appreciation of her friend's anointing of her gratitude journaling as "prayer"—that seemed to enrich their spiritual narratives. This again illustrates that the perception of extra-institutional spiritualities as "thin" or "vapid" is at least in part attributable to a proprietary quality in the language of religion, which many Nones automatically respect as not belonging to them unless they are invited to apply it to their own spiritualities. This leads me to suggest that the "whatever-ness" of unaffiliated spirituality may be equally due to a lack of language specific to extra-institutional practice. But when Nones feel they have permission to utilize this lexicon, the result extends the boundaries of the sacred well beyond religious locations, deep into the contours of everyday life, including non-religious life.

Thus, some Nones applied the label "prayer" to many of the quotidian spiritual practices described in the previous chapter—spending time with family and friends, enjoying pets, preparing and sharing food, enjoying time in nature.

Skinner Allan, a 31-year-old Agnostic from Kona, Hawaii, marked time he spent with his two young children as prayer. Skinner told me:

> When I spend time with my kids, that's prayer for me because it's about making that deep connection with them, really connecting with their hearts. You know, you're just sharing pure love, and I think that's what prayer is about. And it's also that you're grateful. It's about gratitude. I mean, I'm so glad I get to be the dad of these two little people, right? You know, they bring out the best in me, and I want to help them be their best. There's just nothing else like it, so every minute I spend with them my heart feels that kind of "Oh, thank you, thank you, thank you, for giving me these two beautiful kids and for letting me be their dad." I don't say that, but I feel it. I really do. I'm just grateful.

Karen Dade, a 32-year-old Spiritual None, insisted that "anything can be prayer if you do it with a prayerful intention." Indeed, she was a bit frustrated that I had categorized prayer as a spiritual practice. Karen argued,

> I think it gets everything wrong when you decide *this* is a religious thing, and *that* isn't. Prayer is religious, or spiritual, or holy, but doing the laundry isn't. Walking the dog isn't. I just think that's wrong. In fact, I think it's a lot of why the world is so messed up, because we don't acknowledge that everything is sacred. Everything has holiness. It's about how you approach it, you know, with reverence and a prayerful heart. When you do that, yes, doing laundry is a prayer because you're caring for the people who made the clothes and the people who will wear them. You're mindful of how much water you use and whether the detergent will harm the soil when it drains out in the water. The problem is that religion told us doing the laundry wasn't holy, that it couldn't be prayer. But I don't believe that.

There is a sense of prayer as incredibly expansive, on the one hand, potentially unfolding in any aspect of life without need of authorized discursive or ritual formulas. On the other hand, there are limits to what counts as "prayer," even for Karen, for whom mindfulness in any activity is a criterion. To call an activity "prayer" or "prayerful" is to make a number of claims on the cognitive, emotional, sensate, and moral state of the one who prays. The mind must be oriented in certain ways; the senses must be attuned to a presence of immanent or transcendent realities. Prayer, Nones told me, invites changes in consciousness—it "clears the mind," for example. But prayer moves beyond the strictly personal, too. It makes moral claims. It engenders gratitude. It makes one "a better person" by inviting reflection on the circumstances and needs of others. It enhances awareness of self, other, and world.

Overall, prayer showed itself as a practice with discursive distinctiveness for Nones. It was also distinctive in relational terms, carrying a sense of what we might think of as a contingent vulnerability between the one who prays and the one for whom she prays in light of the circumstances that invited (or, in some cases, as we will see shortly, unintentionally provoked) prayer. This is different from traditional prayer to a supernatural being, which ultimately aims to reduce or eliminate vulnerability both for the one who prays and for the persons or situations for which he prays. Prayer for Nones is often a spiritual technology of empathetic imagination, that is, drawing the person who prays into more deeply felt relationship with others, both human and nonhuman, natural and, less frequently among those who spoke with me, supernatural.

Precarious Prayer

The word "prayer" itself is an etymological cousin to the word "precarious," through a shared Latin root, *precārius*, meaning "given as a favor," "depending on the favor of another person," or "vulnerable to the will or decision of others."[21] While "prayer" tended to retain the idea of relying upon or petitioning another (God) for help, material benefits, and so on, the modern word "precarious" gave up the relational connotations of the root, focusing more on the experience of being in situations of physical vulnerability or risk.[22] Still, for some Nones, the word "prayer" calls on a more modern sense of precariousness, holding a space for feelings of uncertainty or risk in personal experience, human affairs, or the possibility of supernatural realities.

Prayer as a mediator of uncertainty was a feature of the practice highlighted by Samantha Nicholas, a 41-year-old Agnostic from San Diego, California. When I asked Samantha if she prayed, she answered, "Do I pray? Sure, you could call it that." She continued:

> I sit quietly every so often during the week. I try to calm my thinking. Sometimes I'm hoping for something for myself or someone else, but I don't have to be. I think that's what most people mean by "prayer." It's not so much about "talking to God" or "saving your soul." It's just about settling down for a few minutes and thinking about who or what you really care about. It doesn't have to be more than that.

"So why call it 'prayer' at all?" I asked her. "Well, because people just do," she began. "But," she continued,

> It's different than just sitting on a bench thinking, I guess. I mean, first of all, when you're praying, you know, you're trying to get to a different kind of mental or emotional state from the ordinary. Also, too, when you're "praying," I guess you are kind of saying there's maybe something else out there that, I don't know, gets what you're thinking— aligns with it or something. You're praying *to*, you're praying *for*, even if, like me, you're not sure there really is anything out there or what it might be.

Samantha emphasized the special character of the prayer experience. Her self-identification as Agnostic comes out in her understanding of what the act of praying connotes—"you are kind of saying there's *maybe* something else out there." Samantha's description also exemplifies a more general use of the word to name *any* practice of personal reflection. The Nones who talked with me tended not to distinguish between contemplation, meditation, and prayer. These practices can be named as "prayer" because the word is part of a cultural lexicon that can be deployed with or without specific religious meanings. This is possible, as Samantha put it, "because people just do"; prayer is understood, both in traditional and non-traditional usages, as an essentially private, subjective act. Unlike George Brooks, few people measure the motivations for and practices of prayer against a theological standard. If someone says she or he prayed, we tend to take that person at her or his word. Thus the word "prayer" marks a broad space for personal reflection that may include the processing of existential doubt, anxiety, and hope; a focused expression of concern for others; an exploration of personal concerns, questions, and values; and the opening or deepening of consciousness.

Prayer Unbidden

Clearly, what people believe prayer is will shape how they pray—how formally, how frequently, with what level of intentionality, and so on. Nones who reported that they pray more or less regularly, generally did so in ways that would hardly seem foreign or exotic to Somes. A possible exception is the kind of prayer that Tabitha Roberts, quoted at the beginning of the chapter, described as unintentional. "I almost don't mean to do it—praying," she said. Prayer, in this case, finds the one who prays, calling her to practice even against her own, sometimes quite strong, intentions.

The unbidden character of prayer was pronounced for Darnise France, a 37-year-old Atheist from Ashville, North Carolina. Unlike other unbelieving Nones, Darnise was somewhat uncomfortable with the acknowledgment that—"out of total desperation"—she sometimes prays. "It just sneaks up on me," she said. Raised in a conservative, African American Evangelical church, where her identity as a lesbian was strongly condemned and where she saw prayer deployed as a weapon against her and a wedge in her family, she had intensely negative feelings about most traditional religious practices. An episode with the pastor of her mother's church set prayer within a complex familial-religious trauma after Darnise came out to her family:

> You know, my mom asked me if I would talk with the preacher, and like a fool I said I would because I somehow thought I would be able to ask him to, you know, offer her some spiritual comfort so she could come to some peace with who I am even if she didn't agree. I mean, I assumed that they'd keep on praying for me—"pray away the gay"—but I thought I could make clear to him that, while that wasn't going to make a difference for me—it wasn't going to change me as a lesbian—I respected that her religion was important to her. I didn't think he'd be happy, certainly; but I thought he would get it. I don't know how I thought that, but I did. . . . When I get there to his office, he leads me to the sanctuary. And there's this whole group of people there who are supposed to be going to pray over me. I just could not get out of there. I think I was, you know, in shock for a while. And, they're, like, calling out the devil from me, and laying on hands, and "O, Lord Jesus, help her. . . ." Then he comes over—the pastor—and he starts some kind of prayer, and then he just slaps me across the face. . . . I still don't really know how I got out of there, because he almost knocked me clean out, but I did. I was done. Done and done again.

Like other former Evangelical Christians whose experience of religion provoked intense anger and rejection of religion in any form, Darnise worked to leave behind everything associated with her previous religious identity, including prayer. "I'm not saying I was a full on Angela Davis Atheist," she told me, "but I was pissed off. For a couple years, I was, like, deathly allergic to religion. If someone said, 'Let us pray,' I was, like, out of the room, out of the building, down the block." However, eventually, after her partner introduced her to yoga and mindfulness meditation, Darnise said, "I softened. I'm still an Atheist all right, but I've learned to work on my inner self in other ways that now I would say are 'spiritual'—just not, you know, in a Holy Spirit spiritual way. In a secular way." Still, Darnise—perhaps the only person I interviewed besides George

Brooks who was at pains to be very clear about the difference between prayer and meditation—was uncomfortable that prayer seemed to "sneak up" on her without her conscious intention. She explained that once the impulse to prayer has found her, it is impossible to resist. "I only pray in a crisis, out of total desperation," she said, shaking her head, "which is nonsense. Hypocritical. I know this, but I can't help myself." She worked out this "involuntary prayer impulse," as she put it, this way:

> I guess when I end up praying, it's me wanting there to be a higher power, wishing there were, even though I don't believe there is. So, as a last resort, my mind goes there. I guess you could say that prayer for me is a brief expression of hope in times of extreme fear. I hope it'll all be okay. I don't want to face that I don't really know if it will be. Maybe I want a second when I'm willing to believe there's some force that can make it all okay if I ask very sincerely. Maybe it's an evolutionary response. Maybe it's socially conditioned. Either way, there are times when it's the only way I can respond.

Darnise told me that prayer "snuck up" in this way, for instance, when a close friend was going through chemotherapy. "You know, I just kept saying, 'God, let him be okay. Let him be okay.' I mean, I know it was just anxiety, but it helped me. And, then it turned out that he *was* okay, so I felt like I had to give up a little, 'Thank you, dear Lord,' which I really did kind of mean at that moment." Darnise laughed, "Of course I never told him. He's AME [African Methodist Episcopal] down to the bone. I'd never hear the end of it."

It is clear that this kind of unbidden prayer functions as a coping mechanism engineered from deeply embodied memories and habits. But, for someone who was wounded within that same religious history, yielding to the impulse to pray also provokes painful memories and troubling self-assessments in the present. Thus, after a short pause in our conversation, Darnise confessed, "I'm too ashamed to tell anyone. I mean, it's embarrassing that I'd involuntarily go back to a thing that did me so much harm—that was meant to shame me and humiliate me like that. And that I'd be comforted by it." She shook her head and sighed. For Darnise, prayer unbidden was a kind of religious haunting that she could not exorcise even in a staunchly non-religious life, the immediate comfort it brought in times of stress ultimately undermined by the echo of religious trauma with which it was so powerfully associated.

Even Nones without dramatically difficult relationships with institutional religion or strong non-believing outlooks sometimes reported being surprised by prayer. Hanna Randall, a Spiritual-But-Not Religious None, told me she had a strong belief in higher powers, forces, and other beings like angels or the souls of people who have died. But, she said that prayer was not a regular part of her spiritual life, which, we will recall, focused on bodywork and journaling. When I asked Hanna if her journaling practice functioned as prayer, she said, "Oh, no. That's a completely different thing. That's about me exploring the presence of spiritual guides in my life—thinking about what I'm learning from that spiritually. It's more a thinking thing than a praying thing." Nonetheless, Hanna also reported that there were times when "prayer comes over me." For Hanna, this was not typically on high stress occasions, where it might function as a coping mechanism. Rather, she reported, "sometimes, just out of the blue, I'll feel a really strong need to just bow my head, or maybe I'll look up at the sky, and I'll be drawn into prayer. It's as though something—or someone—is calling me to prayer. Like the prayer finds me." "Do you offer a specific kind of prayer?" I asked. "It depends," Hanna said, continuing:

> I have a couple little books of prayers that my friend gave me. They're from every religion, you know, so it's not a particular thing in that way. But, I'll just kind of thumb through until I feel like I'm at the right one, and then I'll read it, maybe a couple times and think about what it says. Or, sometimes, I'll close my eyes and kind of talk to, you know, the spirit I feel was calling me. I'll say something like, "I heard you calling me, and I'm trying to listen to you now. I know you're reaching out to me, and I want to be open to you." Or, I'll say, "My heart and my mind are open to you," and then I'll just sit quietly for a little bit. Usually, I'll just go back to what I'm doing then, and hours later, or even days, I'll realize that the prayer was about something that I was trying to work out. Sometimes it happens when I'm really stuck and I don't quite know it yet. So, I don't think it's random that it happens. It just seems weird that it's a kind of thing that I really don't think of myself as doing, praying. But that's definitely what I think it is, these little prayers coming to me out of nowhere.

Unlike Darnise, who was raised in an intensely religious environment, Hanna's religious upbringing suggests few triggers for prayer. Both of her parents were Baptists, but after the family moved to Arizona, when Hanna was a toddler, they rarely attended church. "We did Christmas and Easter meals, and went to church once in a blue moon," she said. "It was nice when we did it, I guess, but other than that it really wasn't part of our family life. None of us kids is religious now in that way."

No matter how thin Hanna's religious upbringing might have been, however, the idea of prayer "finding her" mattered. "It's wonderful, I think, that this very vanilla sort of thing, bowing my head and praying, would come to me once in a while," she told me. "I guess I think maybe it's a kind of reminder that I've always had this spiritual leaning, even as a child. All of that is still part of who I am as a human [who is] being spiritual." It seems that for both Hanna and Darnise, different though their experiences with religion have been, prayer bridges past religious experience with their present-day spirituality.[23]

Performing Prayer

This role for prayer could be seen, as well, in the more consciously performative prayers of Atheists like Alicia Iyers-Marks, whom we met in Chapter 1. Here, developing a coherent spiritual life story is more important than religious belief or affiliation. Alicia was one of a few Nones who talked with me about "pretending to pray" for the sake of maintaining positive relationships or supporting others. After the death of her father, a strict, conservative Evangelical, Alicia had come to a certain peace with the religiousness of her mother, sister, and aunts. She said of calls to pray with her family, "It doesn't cost me anything to pray with them over a meal." When we came to discuss prayer in greater depth, I learned that Alicia found this "performance of prayer," as she described it, to be spiritually meaningful for her as well.

When I asked her if she prayed, Alicia laughed, "Oh, sometimes I think I pray more than the pope!" She explained that her job as a social services agency executive brought her into many situations involving prayer. "We're a secular agency," she explained, "but we work with a lot of religious organizations and, you know, social services people—they like to pray. Someone's always praying about something. I can go along with that. It's fine with me."

"But," I queried, "you don't initiate prayer yourself outside of family gatherings or work?"

"Oh, sure I do," she said. "I'll bust out a prayer in a second." Alicia explained her a/theology of prayer in colorful detail:

> I see it this way: there isn't a god. Let's just face it. There's not. So, if that's my starting point—and it kind of is—then nobody is ever praying to anybody but each other. Not my mother, not my auntie, not the nice nun who runs the food pantry, or the hipster pastor at the HIV/ AIDS clinic. They're performing prayer. They're doing something, for sure, but they're not talking to god. Why do they do that? They do it for comfort—it's nice to think there's someone out there looking out for you. They do it to handle anxiety. They do it to sort out their own thinking and feeling about complex things. They do it to let other people

know they believe in a god and have certain other sets of beliefs that tend to go with that. I don't need to do any of those things under the guise of praying.

Alicia explained, "When I pray, I'm communicating that I respect people's beliefs and honor their search for meaning—misguided though I may ultimately think it may be. That's what I'm doing when I pray at work [events] even though religious people may choose to interpret it otherwise." But her prayerful practice is more than this. She continued, articulating both how she defines prayer and what it means to her in practice:

> . . . people also pray to connect with the people they care about, to express love, and compassion, or gratitude. That's more what it's like when I'm praying with my family. And, sometimes when we have people over—friends, family—I want that feeling of, you know, "Look how much we love you all. Look at this wonderful food! Listen to all these great, smart, funny conversations we're having. Hey, let's all just squeeze each other's hands for a minute and notice all that." But, it would take forever to get all that out. The food would be cold. So, I just say, "Hey, why don't we pray," and people do. Me, my Atheist husband, our Evangelical family, my bizarrely Christian (if you ask me) lesbian and gay friends, the Unitarian minister from across the street—we just all hold hands and pray. We perform prayer. I mean, you know, maybe someone will come up with a different name for it sometime in the future, but "prayer" seems to be it for now. That works for me. It's spiritual for me. I would count it as "blessing." Just not in the way many of the believers around me might want to think. It's secular-spiritual.

The social function of prayer here is obvious. Alicia's prayer is not addressed to a supernatural other, but is meant to honor and bind a gathered group. Even in the ad hoc prayer session she described, prayer has a ritual function, calling upon elements of remembered and lived prayer practice among those gathered. Prayer also invites a shared mindfulness as family and friends appreciate the food they will eat in each other's warm presence. It aims, that is, to shift consciousness, even if only briefly. The prayer Alicia invites marks the occasion as special, elevating the event from the ordinary by calling attention to the bounty of good food, the importance of the people gathered, the delightfulness of their conversations, and so on. Both the word "prayer" and the practice itself give the experience a spiritual resonance that, as many other Nones noted, other words and practices do not seem to provide.

Alicia was also among the few Nones who talked about prayer in community. In some cases, practices that might have been counted as prayer in common were disallowed as such. The "inspirations" that Noah and his family shared, for instance, could easily be seen as a mode of common prayer; he made clear, however, that he did not understand them that way, although he knew that his children did. We will recall, too, that Natalie Darling, the former Roman Catholic None we've already met, attended Taizé services with some regularity, praying with others in this setting. But she didn't see it this way. She experienced herself as isolated from the worshipping community. "These are the people who rejected me," she told me. "They might pray *for* me—for me to change, for me to be like them. They might even pray for the church to change. Many of them sincerely do. But they're not praying *with me.*" Likewise, the Humanist Felicia Oliveria did not see prayer as spiritually meaningful, especially in the context of her gathered community. "When you've got all kinds of people coming together, with all kinds of religious beliefs or the lack thereof, saying, 'let us pray' is just asking for trouble." She added, "We teach our kids that prayers are just like wishes or dreams. They're not bad, and they make some people feel better. But they're not real. They don't make things happen."

The Nones who talked with me about prayer seemed to exemplify the idea of the early twentieth-century sociologist Marcel Mauss: prayer evolved from a collective, ritual practice with "social causes" to an individualized practice performed, perhaps with religious artifacts, largely beyond the boundaries of religious tradition.[24] But prayer among Nones retains substantial relational and social resonance. Stories of the self-as-spiritual draw on prayer as a way to amplify the spiritual significance of particular experiences. Calling an activity "prayer" makes it seem like "more than" just thinking about someone. Likewise, labeling an experience as "prayer" or "prayerful" highlights its often unexpected heightened spiritual resonances. Running, surfing, or even doing the laundry become "prayerful" activities when they shift people into different zones of consciousness, alignment with the natural world, or awareness of connection to others. And, prayer, even for the unreligious, can create or reinforce social bonds.

Nones Defining Prayer

It is striking that when Nones talked with me about prayer they generally offered—or assumed—a definition, either in relation to or as distinguished from what they believed to be a traditional religious definition. While theologians and scholars across the centuries have been unable to come up with a single, universal definition of prayer, many Nones were more than happy to do so. George Brooks's biblical understanding of prayer marked the practice as a private conversation with God or Jesus to "ask for help" or "bless your work." Samantha Nicholas contrasted what she assumed "most people mean by 'prayer' . . . hoping for something for myself or someone else"—with her own definition as "thinking about who or what you really care about." Samantha said that prayer was meant to "get [the one who prays] to a different kind of mental or emotional state." Alyssa Iyers-Marks, in a very different way, saw the "performance of prayer" as having the effect of "blessing" people and occasions when they gather. For Darnise France, prayer was a means of coping in stressful situations, but it also seemed to mark questions and doubts about her previous religious life as well as her current identity as an Atheist, which receive expression, if unintentionally and to some degree painfully, through prayer.

For Andy Elliott, prayer was a "plea" to "a nonexistent being" who "grants wishes." Cassie Andrews likewise had understood prayer as requiring a supernatural other and specific gestures (bowing your head, folding your hands), but her friend allowed her to see her intentional expression of gratitude as prayer. Adam Noonan highlighted feelings of connectedness to "the source of everything," while Langston Green saw prayer as a kind of embodied absorption into the natural world so that "the line between you and everything else goes away." For Atheist Eddie Poston, prayer was "you thinking or not thinking—clearing your head—so you're able to try to be a better person or help someone out." Joseph Carlson's practical, Humanist understanding of prayer likewise involved "improving the lives of others." So, too, in Andy Elliott's view, prayer is not "talking to God, or Jesus, or whoever," but rather acting in the world so that "things will get better for people." Spiritual None Karen Drake's insistence that anything that expresses caring for others counts as prayer seems consistent with the perspectives of many of these Nones.

All of these definitions are of course "true" in the lives of the people who offered them, functioning as ways of connecting the institutional religious echoes from their pasts and the religious language and symbols that circulate throughout American culture to Nones' mostly extra-institutional, sometimes non-theistic experience of the spiritual in everyday life. For most Nones, "prayer" is not generally defined by specific formulas (e.g., the so-called "Jesus Prayer" or the "Serenity Prayer" popularized through the 12-Step movement), theological meanings (e.g., prayer as "talking with God," offering thanksgiving, etc.), or any prescribed liturgical actions (e.g., kneeling, folding hands). Rather, prayer garners spiritual significance for Nones through the ability of the word "prayer" itself and actions that come to be named as "praying" to articulate experiences of awe, wonder, connectedness, doubt, emotional ambiguity, gratitude, physical intensity, sensate richness, ethical action, and so on, within the narrative of the self-as-spiritual. For Nones, calling something "prayer" distinguishes the spiritual from the ordinary, but it also can mark the emergence of the spiritual *within* the ordinary.

Recent work on prayer by Nancy Ammerman and Tanya Luhrmann invites comparison between the prayer practices of Nones and Somes. Ammerman's and Luhrmann's work suggests that those affiliated within a wide range of institutional religions—Catholic, Evangelical Protestant, Jewish, Mainline Protestant, Mormon, and Pagan, in Ammerman's population; Nondenominational Evangelical Protestant in Luhrmann's—prayer is understood in less fluid, more formalized terms as "reaching toward the divine," usually in imagined conversation, with more narrowly petitionary and spiritual self-cultivation intentions. Ammerman sees prayer among her subjects as "a primary way spirituality is carried from one place to another,"[25] from church to home, to work, to community. It is a mobile technology of scripture, doctrine, and ritual, but it seldom moves out of these institutionalized understandings, even when it's done in the home, at work, or in a hospital. Ammerman noted a wide array of settings for and practices of prayer, but they all assumed relationship with a supernatural other and, whether before a meal or at bedtime, focused on enhancing that relationship or appealing in some way to divine beneficence.

Yet Ammerman also found less conventional practices of prayer. For instance, as with most of the Nones who talked with me, for some of her subjects "meditation and praying were not mutually exclusive."[26] Still, the boundary was noted. Prayer might lead to meditation, or vice versa, but they are generally set as mutually exclusive categories of experience by her subjects.[27] Other practices— listening to music or dancing, for example—might have spiritual significance, but they did not appear to qualify for Ammerman's religiously affiliated subjects as "prayer." Likewise, gestures such as kneeling, bowing, or swaying during prayer were mentioned, but embodied activities like running, preparing food for loved ones, caring for a sick friend, and so on were not identified as prayer, though a subject might pray—a separate action—during these activities. Prayer could move religious belief and practice into everyday contexts, but for Ammerman's institutionally affiliated subjects it appears not to have moved beyond the theological boundaries of their religious traditions.

For Luhrmann's Evangelical subjects, prayer is a learned practice that has the effect of deepening the capacity of the one who prays to attend to thoughts, images, and bodily sensations as she prays, so that she experiences God as "immediately present" in prayer to the extent that "God talks back."[28] Prayer is a technology of religious self-cultivation in conformity with Evangelical theology. It institutionalizes individual practice. Even though prayer was meant to be deeply personal and unconstrained by the classic prayer formulas and rituals of Catholics and more liturgical Protestants that Evangelical Protestantism largely rejects as stilted and inauthentic, Luhrmann's Evangelicals did not understand prayer as taking place outside theologically prescribed guidelines. That is, even "spontaneous" prayer conformed to Evangelical doctrine, "authenticity" itself being determined by a prayer's adherence to doctrinal teachings. Such ways of thinking about prayer were important in developing proficiency in practice, authorizing the virtuosity of the one who prays, and reinforcing the religious meaning and significance of experiences of divine presence and engagement. Practices of discernment would disqualify theologically errant thought, feelings, or images that might come up in prayer, progressively conditioning the one who prays away from such notions and toward theologically normative imaginings and actions. Prayer for the Evangelicals in Luhrmann's study is perhaps religion's greatest "proof" of God's presence in human life—"*the* religious phenomenon par excellence."[29]

Most of the Nones who talked with me would not see their own "prayerful" experiences as "religious," but even non-religious Nones like Eddie Poston, Alicia Iyers-Marks, and Joseph Carlson were comfortable calling them "spiritual." Prayer for Nones facilitates spiritual being and becoming in relationship with other beings and the natural world, and—sometimes, just maybe—with a supernatural being or force. Prayer connects Nones to the concerns of others and connects them to their own religious past and to the religious contexts of the lives of people who are important to them. In this sense, prayer stands between the lines of traditional religion—"the one thing the church can't get its hands on," as George Brooks put it—and the "whatever" of contemporary spiritual-religiosity.[30]

6

Good Samaritan Nones

Religious Echoes & a Cosmopolitan Ethics of Care

But what will become of men then ... without God and immortal life?
All things are lawful then, they can do what they like?
—Dmitri Karamazov in Dostoevsky's *The Brothers Karamazov*

... I just don't need the promise of a dazzling afterlife or the threat of
horrible punishment to try to act on what I'm able to reason is the right
thing to do. If it turns out that there is a god, I think I'll be okay having
based my morality on reason and compassion.
—Gabrielle Manuel, *age 31, Arlington, Virginia, "Agnostic"*

I can see the value in religion in terms of encouraging morality generally, and, I guess, in teaching kids the basic moral rules. But it's obvious
that religion hasn't solved immorality. . . . I think that's a lot because
religion is so much focused on saving individual souls. I'm not interested in saving souls. I want to save the world—the real, actual world.
—Alex Woodard, *age 28, Endicott, New York, "Secular Humanist"*

"True story," Anna Solomon shook her head, "when I told my best friend—college educated, liberal, generally sophisticated, oh, and Catholic—that I had
come to the conclusion that I'm an Atheist, she actually said to me, 'So, now I
guess you get to live your life without any rules at all.'" Anna was surprised that
someone "so smart and not by any means a religious fanatic" would assume that
the rejection of a supernatural being or power was automatically a rejection of
commonly held ethical values and personal morals. I was less surprised, however. Throughout my research, whenever I talked with religious groups about the
spiritual lives of Nones, especially when I focused on non-religious Nones such
as Atheists, Agnostics, and Humanists, people did indeed often think that giving
up belief in God meant giving up the common ethical standards. It seems that
many of the religiously affiliated take the tortured musings of Dmitri Karamazov
as representative of their religiously unaffiliated family members, friends, neighbors, and colleagues.[1] They assume that morality derives primarily, if not exclusively, from religious teachings.

Regular churchgoers who expressed concern, sadness, and even shock about the moral lives of Nones often assumed that the religiously unaffiliated, especially non-theistic Nones, are nihilists—people who believe that ethical values are mere humanly constructed, culturally situated norms that change over time. Morality, in classic nihilistic philosophy, is neither universal nor eternal, and therefore there exists neither an inherent human moral disposition, nor moral laws imposed by a higher being, nor a moral purpose for life. For the nihilist, the reality of this moral relativism is demonstrated by changing ideas over time about the acceptability of practices such as slavery and the corporal punishment of women and children, the treatment of the physically and mentally disabled, or attitudes toward human exploitation of the environment.

Non-theistic Nones believe that there is no transcendent supernatural being behind the curtain handing down righteous rules. We will see, however, this does not mean that for them "it's an anything-goes world," as a woman at a denominational conference huffed. But for many Somes, that idea can be a hard sell.

Most Nones in fact *do* believe in God or a higher power, and most share the basic values of their religiously affiliated neighbors—including, very often, recognizably Christian values. Somes, however, often remain unconvinced that morality can effectively develop and be enacted outside institutional religion. How, they wonder, can the unaffiliated be confident in their moral compass without the benefit of a religious tradition handed down through the ages and a community of like-minded people to support their moral practice in light of this tradition? Absent a religious community, Somes also wonder, how do Nones validate or interrogate their moral choices? The religiously affiliated often worry about how the moral sensibilities of the children of Nones can be shaped. And, then there's one of the key questions with which we began our exploration: Does unaffiliation undermine the moral character of the nation overall?

Such concerns, while perhaps exaggerated at times, are not entirely unfair. After all, until the Enlightenment, no one in the Christian West seriously considered that it was possible for people to develop moral character and act morally without the benefit of institutional religious teaching, monitoring, and correction. The assumption that religious influences fully define moral practice in everyday life remains dominant in a country in which more than 80% of the population claim religious affiliation. In this light, it is understandable that Somes wonder about the moral lives of the religiously unaffiliated and their effect on the wider society. We will take up these concerns in this chapter. Before we talk in more detail about the moral practices of Nones, however, it is important to have some clarity about what we mean by terms like "ethics" and "morals" in the first place.

Ethics, Morals, and God (or Not)

The terms "ethics" and "morals" are more or less interchangeable in common usage, but in philosophy, "morals" describes the personal application of ethical principles in everyday life, as well as the character of the person making this application. People have morals (or not) and act morally (or do not). "Ethics"[2] refers to systems of moral rules—for example, "Aristotelian ethics," "Christian ethics," or "secular ethics." When Somes worry that unaffiliation might result in immorality, they are taking religious teachings as an ethical system upon which personal morality is grounded.

The study of ethics typically focuses on understanding how different systems of beliefs, values, and actions—religiously defined or not—contribute to "the good life" as well as what attitudes and behaviors are likely to undermine it. For ethicists, "the good life" refers not to an existence of worry-free luxury—the "champagne dreams and caviar wishes" that the "rich and famous" were assumed to have realized in the popular 1990s television series that celebrated their "lifestyles." Rather, for philosophers and ethicists, "the good life" is the life well lived, the life of value to the self and others, the life with a meaningful purpose. Throughout Western history, the goal of "the good life" has usually been assumed to depend on living virtuously,[3] striving for certain standards of excellence,[4] or, in Max Weber's famous formulation of modern Christian ethics, behaving as an idealized Protestant who works hard, provides for his dependents, and worships devoutly. [5]

Changing times have led to the development of other normative approaches to ethics. Much of this newer thinking focuses on the spheres of everyday life where unaffiliated spiritualities unfold. The "ethics of care" associated with Carol Gilligan, Nel Noddings, Virginia Held, and others, is perhaps the most influential normative ethical system developed in recent decades.[6] Care ethics situates "the good life" in the context of what is seen as the most fundamental of human relationships, that between parents and children.[7] Taking the home and its relationships as its starting point, care ethics attends to positive values as they are expressed by parents, siblings, extended family, neighbors, and others in the immediate and intimate relationships of the home.

Care ethics highlights attentiveness to others, compassion, cooperation, empathy, and interdependency. These qualities are valued not in themselves but as means to foster care *for* others, care *about* the circumstances of those living beyond immediate circles of concern, and *of* those who are caregivers to individuals and who work to improve the circumstances in which they live. When Felicia Oliveria described the gathered family, friends, and neighbors at her Wednesday night dinners as "my tribe," she was setting this extended, domestically centered network as the basis of moral practice for herself and her family. Their weekly dinners are a social and spiritual exercise, and they are profoundly moral as well, enacting Felicia's and her partner's Humanist values and, importantly, illustrating them to the couple's children and involving them in their practice.

An ethics of care extends moral action beyond the development of moral dispositions in an individual person, as in virtue ethics. It operates from what has been called an "immanent transcendent" perspective that reaches beyond the present moment or the whole lifetime of the moral person, without necessarily assuming a supernatural reality beyond what can be seen, felt, sensed, and otherwise known concretely.[8] It invites concern for the well-being of individuals, families, communities, and the earth today, and also for the flourishing of disadvantaged people and the planet in the future. An ethics of care is fundamentally a relational ethics. (Indeed, the terms are often used interchangeably.) The actions it suggests are undertaken always with receptivity to the needs, concerns, and desires of all of those within an immediate network of care and are extended beyond that to wider circles of concern.[9] I draw on the work of Gilligan, Noddings, and other care ethicists extensively in this chapter because a focus on sustaining and enriching relationships in the context of everyday life is characteristic of the Nones we have met and others we will encounter in the pages ahead.

Noddings describes this receptivity as "being attentive in a special way" to the interests, concerns, and needs of others. "Caring is not controlled entirely by the carer—it is a mode of shared control," writes Noddings.[10] Moral action, that is, is never based on individual virtues in themselves but rather on the quality of relational connections. Openness to another person, in the sense of being vulnerable ourselves and attentive to the vulnerability of the other, shapes character not by the acquisition of a set of virtues but by the lived experience of caring in relationship with others.[11]

Alex Woodard, the 28-year-old Secular Humanist quoted at the beginning of the chapter, evoked this lived expression of moral character when he voiced his appreciation of the South African concept of Ubuntu.[12] Alex encountered the concept in the youth group of the Episcopal church to which he belonged through high school, though he was quick to point out that Ubuntu is not a religious concept but a cultural one. Ubuntu refers to the inherent cosmic, social, and moral relatedness of human beings. This relatedness is suggested by a slogan of the 2009 General Convention of the Episcopal Church, which Alex attended as a youth representative: "I in you and you in me."

The philosophers Drucilla Cornell and Kenneth Panfilio explain the complexity of Ubuntu in this way:

In uBuntu [*sic*] human beings are intertwined in a world of ethical relations and obligations with all other people from the time they are born. The social bond, then, is not imagined as one of separate, atomistic, individuated livelihoods; instead, the ethical, political, and moral inscription on each of us by all other people is fundamentally drawn from the fact that we are born into a language, a kinship group, a tribe, and a nation. . . . We come into the world obligated to others and, in turn, these others are obligated to us. . . . It is only through the engagement and support of others that we are able to realize a true individuality and rise above our biological distinctiveness into a fully developed person whose uniqueness is inseparable from the journey to moral and ethical development.[13]

Alex put it somewhat more simply: "We are a system. We are plural. Each of us is everything. We only realize our full humanity when we understand that fact." For Alex, a graduate student in environmental engineering whom I met at a conference on socially conscious entrepreneurship and investing, this belief translated into a commitment to address environmental issues that undermine human thriving in communities in sub-Saharan Africa.[14] He and a group of student colleagues have been developing small, portable water purification systems that can be manufactured from local materials. Alex and his colleagues were at the conference in the hope of securing funding from an investment capital firm with a social entrepreneurship portfolio. He described his commitment to the project as moving beyond what he saw as a binary distinction between reason and religion:

Ubuntu is about living out who you are, which is an interconnected being. You reach out in every direction. This project is about me trying to do that—to make who we are be about living out the implications of that interconnectedness. So, we don't want to make something that we go over and give to people. You know, "Here you are, needy people! You're welcome." We want to work with them on developing something they can manufacture and distribute themselves.

Because I was at the conference as one of a group of religion writers, scholars, clergy, and lay ministers invited to explore the religious and spiritual implications of socially conscious investment, I asked Alex if his ideas were connected to his own religious experience. It was then that I learned that, although he had been raised Episcopalian, Alex no longer identifies as such. Indeed, like many of the people who shared their stories with me, Alex saw religion as something of an ethical barrier in the work he wanted to do.

He was particularly concerned by what he saw as an individualistic focus in Christian ethics:

> My experience with religion—and it wasn't a bad experience at all, really—is that there is so much emphasis on a relationship between you and God and maybe between you and your particular church, that there's no understanding of the dynamic that I think Ubuntu is about. So, people will give, you know, money or whatever to "them, over there" in a way that is completely disconnected. It's not about being in relationship with other people or other places. It's about doing good for the sake of yourself—to get a warm, fuzzy feeling. I mean, I think the people in the Episcopal Church who are promoting Ubuntu get it, but it doesn't permeate congregations.

Alex was like many Nones in seeing religions as playing a positive role in society. But he also saw moral limitations in traditional religion related to the idea of a "personal God":

> I can see the value in religion in terms of encouraging morality generally, and, I guess, in teaching kids the basic moral rules. But it's obvious that religion hasn't solved immorality, especially the kind of systemic immorality that you see in Africa, much of which developed through Western colonialism. And I think that's a lot because religion is so much focused on saving individual souls. I'm not interested in saving souls. I want to save the world—the real, actual world.

I wondered, then, if he thought non-religious people were less individualistic or more ethical. He continued, pointing to what he saw as similar limitations in much secularist thought:

> Not really. Not necessarily, I mean. I call myself a "Secular Humanist" intentionally, instead of, like, an Atheist or a Secularist, because I think it's important to emphasize the human part—that it's not all about reason or rationality, which I think is kind of the drumbeat of a lot of the Atheist-Secular movement. You have to *feel*—not just *know*—that we have a stake in each other's lives, in the life of the planet. And, you have to get that it's not about what any one individual thinks or feels, or about how a single, individual person is affected. You have to see the whole of it—the whole humanity, the whole environment—to really act in an ethical way. You know, being ethical sometimes requires sacrifice. It's not just about being nice or being generous. That can be

unreasonable at the level of an individual. When you're only focused on one person at a time, and when you're only interested in thinking it through as an abstract kind of puzzle—"How do I help this guy?" "What do I personally have to do to be a good person?"—you're not really going to get to, "Oh, we might have to give up something really meaningful, really big, to change the whole system."

Alex's perspective highlights many of the values of care ethics, which could be seen as a Western, academic version of the much older, culturally embedded Ubuntu ethic.[15] In both, even activities of self-care are not understood in individualistic terms. We tend to our own well-being because emotional, intellectual, physical, and spiritual strength and stability enable us to be more fully engaged in caring relationships with others. We saw this mode of self-care for the sake of others in the chanting practice of Wendy Patterson, the Spiritual None from Maine who chanted before and after her work as a massage therapist. The exercise helped her to free herself of their "issues and baggage" so she could be more present to her clients.

Alex's work also shows the way in which an ethics of care moves from personal morality to practices of justice. The interconnectedness emphasized in Ubuntu invites us to care more deeply not only for the people in our immediate surroundings, but also about the needs of people we encounter only indirectly as we absorb media reports, vote for political leaders and public policies, pay taxes that support community services more or less adequately, contribute to and volunteer in community service organizations, and so on. It is for this reason that Carol Gilligan also refers to care ethics as an "ethics of responsibility."[16]

While no one who talked with me specifically identified their approach to morality as influenced by care ethics (or, aside from Alex's discussion of Ubuntu, any other normative ethical system, for that matter), the relational character of unaffiliated spirituality we've seen throughout the book is clearly resonant with the norms of care ethics. This is certainly the case with the prayer as an expression of receptiveness to the needs of others and empathy for them among many of the Nones we met in the previous chapter. Perhaps especially for those who don't believe in a supernatural being or power, the contingent vulnerability—the sense that my experience of risk or safety depends on yours—as enacted in intentional, spontaneous, and even unbidden prayer marks the practice as profoundly receptive to the needs and concerns of those for whom one prays. Prayer evokes a sense of both hope and risk and, therefore, responsibility that makes spiritual and moral claims. The precariousness of the lives of people prayed for and those who pray, and the desire for positive change at the heart of prayer, situates it as a relational ethical practice.

When Tabitha Roberts, a Humanist, talked about prayer being "better than" simply "thinking about" someone, she was tapping into this moral dimension. More concrete actions that many Nones counted as prayer likewise express a practical receptivity that is characteristic of care ethics. For Skinner Alan, also a Humanist, praying was spending time with his kids—in the care of his dependents. Similarly, Joseph Carlson's sense of active prayer as "doing your best to improve the lives of others" in his work as an emergency medical technician clearly sets his Atheist prayer as a concrete moral practice. "We pray by caring actively. We pray by helping others," he insisted.

As Nones shared stories of spiritual lives centered on relationships with family, friends, pets, nature, and others in often overlapping extended networks, it seemed that they were speaking, to echo Gilligan, "in a different voice" morally than is commonly heard in the religious communities of my experience, acquaintance, and study. This is not to suggest that Nones are any more (or less) moral than Somes, but that the relational locus of their spirituality plays out somewhat differently in stories of the spiritual life. One of the most significant indicators of this difference—and this would perhaps surprise many Somes as much as it initially did me—was how often Nones of all stripes tended to describe Jesus as a moral exemplar by way of New Testament parables, especially the parable of the Good Samaritan (Luke 10:25–37). This stands in contrast to views of the "Golden Rule Christians" described by Nancy Ammerman.[17] I will return to this "Good Samaritan Ethics" later in the chapter. But, readers will likely have noticed that my discussion has not mentioned the source of morality assumed by most religiously affiliated people: God. So, before we move on I want briefly to address the common question of how all of this moral practice plays out in relation to belief in a supernatural being or power.

Can We Be Good without God?

Many Somes find it difficult to accept that anyone can be moral without believing in God. Many of the Atheists, Agnostics, Humanists, and other non-religious Nones, on the other hand, were quick to point out that this idea—that being a good person requires a god who will reward or punish—is not essential even in theistic belief systems. There are two parts to this argument. The first has to do with the sources of moral good—whether something is good only because God ordains it as such. The second focuses on what motivates good actions—whether we are moral only because God instructs us to be.[18]

First, non-theists argue, it is not necessarily the case that gods (if such beings exist) deem one activity "good" and another "evil." Indeed, across theistic traditions, gods are not always associated with purely good action. Consider the morally complex and contradictory gods of Egypt, Greece, Mesoamerica, Norse regions, Rome, and other ancient cultures. Both ancient and modern Buddhism and Hinduism recognize a range of deities with varied moral characters. In Jewish and Christian traditions, too, the actions of God cannot always be understood as unambiguously "good." Believers themselves often struggle over the morality of the binding of Isaac (Gen. 22:1–14), the testing of Job, or Jesus' initially dismissive reply to the Syrophoenician woman who seeks healing for her daughter (Mk. 7:25–30, Mt. 15:21–28).

Some ethicists argue that God's laws and commandments merely validate and codify what is already experienced and understood as naturally and reasonably good or evil. This argument is often buttressed with the claim that common sense tells us that divine fiat or example cannot render bad actions—killing, stealing, lying—"good."[19] We understand that when Zeus takes the form of a swan for the purpose of raping Leda, his divine action does not render rape a moral "good" any more than the sundry rounds of ethnic cleansing commanded by the God of the Hebrew Bible render such actions "virtuous."[20] "There are some things that are just right and some things that are wrong," 35-year-old Agnostic Leslie Powers insisted. "They're not right or wrong because God says they are. They're just right or wrong."

Non-theists point to non-religious sources of human morality beyond human culture, society, and even reason. Evolutionary psychology argues that humans and many other beings are wired for bonding, cooperation, generosity, altruism, and other qualities—the moral staples of an ethics of care, in fact—that enhance both the immediate flourishing and longer-term odds of survival for a species.[21] Frances Paige, an Agnostic, saw a "natural morality" at work in the dogs she fosters and trains, as well as in other animals. "When you're around groups of dogs for a while, you see how affectionate they are with one another, how much being kind and playful is a basic part of their nature," she said. "I'd like to think it remains a basic part of human nature, too." In the weeks after our conversation, Frances sent me links to videos and articles showing bonds of affection and loyalty among dolphins, elephants, whales, ants, bees, and other animals, and between animals and humans. She clued me in on research suggesting that even trees apparently communicate environmental threats among one another through airborne chemicals and their root systems.[22] These natural moral instincts are offered by many non-theists and other Nones as evidence of an innate conscience that functions without need of divine guidance, reward, or punishment. "Some level of morality is instinctive," Frances wrote to me. "It's a basic component of the survival of the species. The fittest have to be morally fit to some degree or everything would just devour everything else."

On this view, belief in God is not essential to living a moral life—even for theists—although belief in God may reinforce moral principles and practices that are both naturally and reasonably "good." Ethan Quinn, an Atheist, put it this way: "If being good people, trying to do the right thing, isn't somehow part of our DNA, I think we're kind of doomed as a species. Maybe your god will give you a gold star for helping poor people, but if you think helping poor people is only 'good' because your god told you it is, we're really in trouble in a world where everybody doesn't believe in your god." Further, Ethan observed, "Your god is incredibly inefficient."

Some Nones pointed out that people affiliated with theistic religions generally do not seem to worry about the morals of Buddhists. Since Buddhism is a non-theistic religion, they note, it cannot be the case that being good requires belief in a supernatural being. Deborah Moon, a 30-year-old Agnostic from Framingham, Massachusetts, described the contradictory thinking of an aunt about the morals of non-religious people:

> My aunt, who's very, very Christian, is convinced that because I don't believe in God as a being—an old man in the sky—I also must feel like I could rob someone or probably even commit murder without any moral qualms if I knew I wouldn't get caught. She completely thinks that if you're not religious and you don't entirely believe in God, you have absolutely no sense of right and wrong. That's on the one hand. On the other, I have a cousin who is a Buddhist. My aunt is certain my cousin is going to hell if he doesn't eventually "accept Jesus Christ as his lord and savior." But she also thinks Buddhism as a religion will keep my cousin from stealing cars, or whatever. She knows that Buddhists don't believe in God, but she said it didn't matter in the here-and-now. Religion itself, even the wrong religion, could help you to learn right from wrong and be good. But she just couldn't countenance that you could also learn about morals or really be a moral person outside of religion. I think that most religious people I know are like that. They don't worry much about an outbreak of Buddhist murderers. They equate morals with religion—any religion. And, when their religion includes a God, they equate religion with believing in God. They don't seem to get the logic that if Buddhists with no god or Hindus with hundreds of gods can be good people, so can Atheists, Agnostics, and other secular people.

The bottom line is that virtue is essentially "a-theistic." It may be enhanced by belief in a supernatural being or power—or not, if you subscribe to the belief that religions foment tribalism, prejudice, and violence—but what is good is so without need of a divine source. Thus, even for believers, it can be reasonably argued that believing in God is not essential to moral action.

What Motivates Moral Good?

Some non-theists go on to argue that any ethical system that depends on the threat of punishment or the promise of rewards is *less moral* than one that invites action based on moral instinct, human reasoning, and virtuous, compassionate choice. Neil Grosse, the Atheist limo driver we met earlier, asserted that reliance on a belief in eternal reward or punishment for moral motivation was evidence of "psychopathic ethical immaturity." His harsh assessment was reinforced by the trust he is able to bring to his work as a limousine driver. "I sit with my back to strangers pretty much every day of the week," he said. "If I thought some guy wasn't going to shoot me or rob me only because he was afraid of burning forever in the fiery pit of hell, I'd never unlock the doors. You have to trust that the vast majority of people have a natural moral instinct—that they behave right because they understand the impact on other people, themselves, and society if every-body behaves with no regard for others." He added, "That's the thing that gets me about religions—that they basically have no faith in the goodness of human nature. You know, they think you need a prize for not robbing a bank if you have a chance. I mean, even if God came up with a moral system—and I don't think that's the case—could you just be mature enough to put it into practice without promises and threats?"

As it happens, hell is less and less of a threat for believing Americans; and heaven is slowly losing a bit of its luster, too. Not surprisingly, as institutional religious affiliation and belief in God have declined in recent decades, so too has belief in heaven and hell. A Harris poll showed a significant drop between 2005 and 2013 in belief in heaven (down 7% to 68%) and hell (down 4% to 58%).[23] However, divine reward and punishment are not the only, or even the primary, elements of theistic ethics. Another feature is that God (or gods) gives rules such as the Ten Commandments to encourage people to do the right things and to avoid the wrong things in the here-and-now. Such a legal-istic approach concerned some of the Nones who talked with me no less than a reward- and punishment-based morality. Gabrielle Manuel, an Agnostic, summed up her ethical outlook, and its rejection of rule-based ethics, in this way:

> The questions that are important in most religions are important to me, too. What is "the good life"? What is our obligation to others, to ani-mals, to the planet? Why do some people sometimes do unimaginably

horrible things? Why do ordinary people do bad things? Why is there
suffering? What are we supposed to do about all that? I think the moral
challenge for each of us is to figure out how to respond to all that in our
own relationships and as a citizen of the planet. For me, that's not about
rules. It's about values. About thinking for yourself. For me, Bertrand
Russell had it right: "The good life is one inspired by love and guided
by reason." If it turns out that there is a god, I think I'll be okay having
based my morality on those values.[24]

Some non-theistic Nones called theistic ethics to account for offering
approaches to morality that defy human reason. Brittney Samuels, a Humanist,
laid out this argument as follows:

I think everyone, even religious people, questions whether there is a
god. You know, you can't get to believing in that through reasoning. It
takes, really, indoctrination. I'm not saying that's all bad, or that religion
is all bad. But it does seem, by the way people act, like, say, in the mort-
gage fraud crisis, that people give up their belief in God pretty easily
when it seems like they have something to gain. I just, part of me, thinks
that people hit these moments, and they think, "Now really, am I actually going to be tortured by devils for all eternity if I give these nice poor
people a loan I know but they don't know they can't afford? Probably
not." And, I think that's because what people are taught to believe about
God, and heaven, and hell as the basis of their morals, when you give it
even a little bit of thought, it just doesn't add up. And people just know
that, even if they say they're religious. So I think if religions had more
realistic teachings on morality—and some of that you do get through
the life of Jesus—maybe there would be less immoral behavior in the
churches themselves and in the rest of the world.

Brittney's statement suggests that theists secretly know that their own theistic morality is on shaky rational and scientific ground. Given this, their anxiety
about the morals of Nones is a projection based on their own moral insecurity.
Matthew Tyler, a 26-year-old Agnostic from Tiverton, Rhode Island, likewise
focused on the irrationality of religiously based ethical systems. But he saw value
in theistic theological concepts if they could be redeemed from what he saw as
their irrationality. The basic problem, he suggested, was in the religious retention
of theological cosmologies—the three-tiered universe of heaven above, earth in
between, and hell below—that have been disproved as geographical realities
by modern science. For Matthew, a junior high school science teacher, ideas
of "salvation" and "eternity" made sense when adapted to secular ethics within

a scientifically grounded cosmology rather than in the belief in an afterlife in heaven or hell:

> When you spend all this energy convincing people that heaven and hell are real places—you know, physical geographies in another dimension, or whatever—you actually ruin the value of concepts like "salvation" and "eternity" in ethical terms. I mean, even if we agree that the jury is out on the idea of a benevolent God, if you accept that where we are now—this earth, this city, the farms that grow our food, the towns where the workers come in from, the people we know, and the work we do, and all the other stuff—this is it. . . . If you accept that, then "salvation" is a whole other thing. It's not, "Save me, Jesus! Save me! Save me, personally!" It's about, "Hey, this is a good life. What do we have to do to sustain it?" And maybe, "How do we get other people in on that?" Then "eternity" isn't, like, the ultimate vacation. It's what you leave behind to whoever comes next because you were, in fact, an ethical person. . . . I just think religions—at least the religion I was raised in and that I've seen—are so individualistic and irrational, and that does make them immoral in some ways. Sure, go ahead, over-fish all the oceans! God made that for you! Pollute all the cities! Own a hundred guns to kill God's creatures! It doesn't matter. Say your confession and you're good to go into the next life. I mean, to me, that just seems crazy wrong. But when I say to kids, "Every day you are creating eternity with how you live your life," they're awed. They're like, "Wow! I am in charge of eternity!" You know, I tell them it's their job to save the world, and they're totally up for that.

In summary, non-theistic arguments for moral goodness independent of God or a belief in God rest on understanding morality as an inherent element of human nature. God may affirm good and condemn evil, but God does not create them. A non-theistic argument also asserts that morality motivated by the desire for reward or the fear of punishment is not morality at all. It is coerced behavior, not genuine good. Furthermore, rule-based theistic ethics are often seen by non-theists as discouraging mature critical reflection and obscuring larger life purposes with compulsively ritualized acts of micro-obedience. Finally, to the extent that the religious claims that ground theistic ethics can been seen as defying human reason and scientific knowledge, they may in fact contribute to immoral behavior when tempted theists find it easy to abandon them.

It is only fair to acknowledge that this argument is not entirely unproblematic from a theistic perspective. Many secularist writers who offer critiques of religious ethics, especially Christian varieties, often appear to have an unsophisticated sense of religious teachings and the more complex moral practices they spon-sor.[25] Many of those who talked with me were influenced by popular, often car-toonish, characterizations of fundamentalist religious ideologies (Christian and Muslim, in particular) that did not include, for example, humanistic notions of obedience as a function of enlightened free will. Theists may practice religiously grounded moral obedience out of a desire to be more fully in alignment and intimate relationship with God rather than from passive, unthinking forms of blind legalism or a craven desire for heavenly reward. The religiously affiliated may not, that is, display the degree of "ethical immaturity" assumed by Neil and many other non-theists.

Ethical Pluralism

Despite their confusions, questions, and criticisms about institutional reli-gions, for most of the Nones who talked with me unaffiliation did not mean wholesale rejection of religions and their moral teachings. Nones often saw unaffiliation as opening them to valuable moral insights from all kinds of reli-gions. Kenny Mahoe, a None from Makaweo, Hawaii, made exploring different religions and philosophies part of his spiritual and ethical practice. Kenny was raised as an Evangelical Christian, but he has relatives and friends from a wide range of religious and non-religious backgrounds—Atheist, Buddhist, Catholic, Episcopalian, Hindu, Mormon, native Hawaiian religions, and Taoist. "When I was growing up, all the other ones were just 'wrong,'" he told me. "You prayed for them. You invited them to church, especially suppers or when there was spe-cial music or a guest preacher. Hawaiians love to sing and we love to eat! But, really, you were hoping they'd 'be saved.' I don't know, I guess that just came to seem kind of mean spirited to me even though everything was set up to be really welcoming."

As a teenager, Kenny made a practice of studying each of the religious tradi-tions in his extended family, and he became an appreciative skeptic of a sort. "I really am fascinated by religions and philosophy," he said. "I like knowing how different religions or philosophies put it all together." He continued,

> But you could see at a certain point with all of them—even Atheism—that there's, like, a kind of trap—a set of unquestioned beliefs—that will ultimately close you off to other beliefs. And that's going to make you judgmental toward the other religions and toward people. I don't want that. So, the thing for me is, any time I feel myself getting too attached to one idea or another, to a certain way of doing it, I get rid of it. I challenge it for myself—try on something else. I don't want to get

too attached to any one thing, to have my thinking caught in one net.
I want to explore all the possibilities out there on any given day and to
be open to all of the people I meet.

Kevin Jacobs, a 63-year-old Agnostic from Dublin, Ohio, sees this appreciation of religious diversity as facilitated by being unaffiliated. "I learned so much
more about religion when I gave up believing in any one of them," he told me.

You stop arguing for and against them, and you're just able to see what
they offer in terms of their values. Do I disagree with things in some
religions? Yeah, sure. But that's almost irrelevant unless, you know, people are killing people because of their beliefs. I mean, when you step
back from it all—when you don't have anything at stake if someone
thinks differently or does things differently—then you see that there is
a lot of good in all of the religions, a lot of good in secular thinking, or
Humanism, or Atheism. You can bring that into your life.

Kevin talked about how his study of Confucianism had enriched his life and
contributed to his moral outlook. But he pointed out the limits of his embrace
of this tradition as well and how his unaffiliated status enables him to see both
positive values and problematic characteristics in religions:

I've learned so much from Confucianism about goodheartedness and
the Doctrine of the Mean. Am I Confucian? No. Would I have qualms
with their idea of social hierarchy? Yes. But, so what? I can learn from
Confucian teaching and respect people who follow that way without
having to either say it's a perfect system or reject it. When you're in a
religion, it's always midrash—you make up stories on top of stories to
try to smooth out the inconsistencies, fix up the out of date ideas, and
so on. Why? No religion is perfect. When you step outside the fold, you
can be a lot more generous about it. That's the real benefit of not being
religious.

Audrey Burns, an 18-year-old Wiccan from Porter, Indiana, likewise saw
her outsider perspective on more conventional religious traditions as a positive moral value. "I'm intrigued by differences," she said. "I have lots of different
friends who believe or don't believe lots of different things. I wouldn't want to
trade that for a world where we all think the same things, do the same things.
Who would get anything out of that? How would we really learn from each other
or help each other to grow in positive ways?"

Golden Rule Nones

Most Nones did rely to some extent on specific religious teachings in articulating their own moral outlooks. Regardless of where they stood with respect to religious belief or unbelief, the people I interviewed told me repeatedly how much they admired the Jesus of the Gospels, whom they saw as a radical defender of the poor and the outcast. Chief among their gleanings was certainly the Golden Rule, which was mentioned in nearly half of the interviews I conducted and was noted as an influence on moral practice more than a hundred times in the Nones Beyond the Numbers survey.

There are a number of ways to interpret this finding. The first is that Nones — like Buddhists, Hindus, Jews, Muslims, and others who do not identify as Christian — live in a culture saturated with Christian language, symbols, and rituals. Given this, and the Christian backgrounds of the majority of Nones, Jesus will likely factor into their spiritual narratives. Non-theistic Nones frequently cite the Golden Rule because versions of it exist across history, cultures, religions, and philosophical traditions. It can thus be seen as a universal moral principle that is not dependent on religious interpretations.[26] Non-theistic Nones often noted that the Christian version of the rule does not mention God, which they believed is a clear indication that Jesus himself thought it was possible to be a moral person without reference to a supernatural divinity.

On the face of it, the essence of Golden Rule ethics is simple enough: to treat each person as we would desire to be treated. The Rule "prescribes reciprocity as the foundational conceptual framework and context of consistency for shaping and evaluating our actions towards others."[27] That is, it assumes that we can make a better world if each of us takes our own preferences, needs, and concerns as a starting point and then applies these to our treatment of others in the world. As unobjectionable as that may sound, however, philosophers from Immanuel Kant to Ayn Rand have criticized ethical practice based on the Golden Rule. Some critics argue that the Rule is impractical in many situations. A police officer, for example, would likely not want to be arrested herself. A judge would not want to be sentenced to prison or death. Yet both are called to do unto others exactly as they would not have done unto them in the context of jobs that require that they take into consideration multiple and often conflicting needs.

Other critics note that the Rule takes the self as the basis for authentic knowledge of the needs of the other, ignoring the context in which the self and the other interact. I assume that the way I would want to be treated when I am ill, or sad, or otherwise in need is the same way you would want to be treated. I think, "Well, doesn't everyone just want a nice big hug when they're feeling blue? I know I do!" But your cultural background, social status, and personal preferences are actually quite likely to be different from mine, so it may embarrass, shame, or just annoy you when I come into your bodily personal space. "Doing as I would have" for you is not the same as "doing as *you* would have" for you. My genuine desire to care for you may, thus, result in more suffering.

The idea of reciprocity inherent in the Rule goes beyond disconnects in personal backgrounds and preferences. The overall ethic of the Golden Rule—the way it is meant to shape not just personal moral behavior but broader cultural practices of goodwill—assumes that the care I give to you (again, on the basis of my perspectives, wants, and experiences) will generally be reciprocated in my relationship with you, and in relationships with others who are "doing unto" me as they would like to be "done unto." The idea is that there is a consistency in how we care for one another, because we're all more or less the same. The trouble here is that, both at the level of personal relationships and general social circumstances, this sort of reciprocity may not be possible or, if it is, it may cause other harms. You may not, for instance, on the basis of cultural norms, material circumstances, or both, be able to reciprocate the caring gesture I offer to you— to "do as you would have" were the tables turned. Whether I expect such reciprocity directly or not, the imbalance can be hurtful to you. For my part, I might come to resent my caring not being acknowledged or returned in kind, whether from you or in a more general sense.

At its core, the Golden Rule is based on the idea of sameness. In small, relatively homogenous communities where it can fairly be assumed that everyone has the same background, values, and general preferences, taking one's own experience as a starting point for moral engagement can indeed foster an environment of social reciprocity that seems balanced and fair. But in more diverse, complex societies, this idea is more difficult to sustain in practice. What's more, the value placed on reciprocity over self-preservation, generosity, altruism, and, potentially, justice can also be seen as problematic. We help one another, a care ethicist would argue, because caring supports human flourishing and the enhancement of life in general, not as an investment in our own or others' care in the future.[28]

Sociologist of religion Nancy Ammerman has written extensively about what she called "Golden Rule Christians"—practicing believers across Christian denominations and ideological spectrums who take the scriptural teaching that one should "do unto others as you would have them do to you" (Mt. 7:12) as the core Christian value. Her extensive study of 27 Christian congregations suggests a profound paradox in congregational understandings of Christian teaching that center on the Golden Rule, which Ammerman found to be the normative distilling of Christian teaching among those she studied. This belief, on the one hand, reinforces congregational community on the basis of the idea sameness discussed earlier. On the other, it undermines the growth or revitalization of congregations because they can't readily engage with or integrate difference.[29] What Ammerman suggests is that one effect of internalizing a Golden Rule ethic is that it can flip the notion that we offer care for others because we assume they are basically like us into caring primarily for others who are like us, rather than for those who may seem different. Of the mostly suburban, middle-class Christians she studied, Ammerman writes:

> Most important to Golden Rule Christians is care for relationships, doing good deeds, and looking for opportunities to provide care and comfort for people in need. Their goal is neither changing another's beliefs nor changing the whole political system. They would like the world to be a bit better for their having inhabited it, but they harbor no dreams of grand revolutions. . . . The emphasis on relationships among Golden Rule Christians begins with care for friends, family, neighborhood, and congregation.[30]

Ammerman points out that Golden Rule ethics are largely detached from other coherent theological narratives or ideological perspectives, centering instead on virtuous practices among members of specific congregational communities.[31] She suggests that Golden Rule ethics practiced by congregationally affiliated Christians invites "a certain narrowing of the circle of care"[32] that can prevent serious or sustained engagement with larger, more distant or systematic problems in the world. When it is difficult to see people as "pretty much like me," that is, people tend to look for people who are more like them (or at least who aspire to be) as subjects of care. At the same time, this parochialism can also ensure a deeper level of care for the most vulnerable in a local community, such as the elderly, the sick, or children. Such practices, on the one hand, help to sustain existing congregational communities. On the other hand, they can limit congregational growth and engagement with the wider world—even in its local expressions—to the extent that Golden Rule Christians hesitate to reach out much beyond their narrow circles of care.

Among the Nones who talked with me, the Golden Rule played out as a moral guide in a somewhat different, less communitarian, but nonetheless relational, way. Take Gary Shea, a 66-year-old Agnostic from Columbus, Ohio, who was a member of a Lutheran church until his early forties. Gary acknowledged that religious principles were meaningful guides if, he stressed, "they aren't extremist." Gary cited the Golden Rule as a foundational principle of Christian ethics and moral practice that he carried into his life as an Agnostic. He also noted that versions of the Golden Rule are found in most world religions, and that in most of these traditions—including Christianity—the principle of reciprocity at the heart of this ethic does not rely on belief in a divine being. "The Golden Rule puts it on you," Gary said. "You're responsible for assessing every situation to determine what is the most fair, the most decent way to act toward someone. You can't use God as a crutch. You have to put yourself in the other guy's place—walk a mile in his shoes, so to speak."

A recovering alcoholic of some 15 years, Gary felt that one's moral capacity, ideally, develops over time on the basis of experience. This includes learning to practice the Golden Rule as an act of empathetic engagement rather than one of reciprocity per se. While this draws on the experience of the one offering care, Gary's extension of the Rule to include the idea of "walking a mile in another's shoes" balances the self-referential perspective that is often subject to criticism. He explained,

> Putting [the Golden Rule] into practice and really meaning it takes experience. You have to have some knocks, I guess, to know what it's like to not be treated fairly by others, to be treated like less. You know, when that happens to you a couple times, it sinks in. In my life, that's opened me up more to what people are experiencing when they feel disrespected, or manipulated, or taken advantage of. You know, even when you just need help and there is no one who will give you a hand. It's a painful thing. Some people just don't have that kind of experience, I guess. I had a boss once [who] would say, "Do unto others, before they do unto you!" And he'd laugh. I think he'd just never been on the other end of that stick. He'd never felt like what it was like to be "done unto" in that way, and he wasn't the type to give much thought to how other people feel.

Tim Lambert, a 21-year-old None from Newport News, Virginia, also saw the Golden Rule as central to his moral outlook, though his understanding of the Rule itself was somewhat idiosyncratic. He saw the Rule as grounded in the assumption of an exchange of kindness, support, caring, and the like in interactions between individuals—"do unto others and they'll do unto you, too." But his approach also had a more systemic perspective. This was illustrated in an anecdote he shared about a homeless woman he frequently encountered on his way home from his job as a server at a neighborhood restaurant. He began:

> I'm not sure where she is when I start my shift, but she's always right around the corner, inside the entrance to a parking garage where there's a little kind of alcove. I probably walked past her three or four times before I thought maybe I should try to help her, you know—"do unto others and they'll do unto you, too." I mean, I'm not a jerk for it taking a while

to register. I'm just tired after standing for eight hours, and I want to get home. But, then it just came into my head that she probably stands, or pushes her cart around most of the day, too. You know, I'm young, and it can wear me out. This lady's got to be, I don't know fifty-plus. She has to be just tired. I just never really thought about how exhausting it has to be just be homeless—as, like, your job. And, once you realize that, you just really can't not care.

Tim's application of the Golden Rule was based on a degree of sympathy that does not immediately rise to the kind of openness to the other *as* other that nurtures empathy. We cannot say that he sees the homeless woman on her own terms. He sees her though the lens of his own experience of being tired after a long day at work. And he takes his needs in this situation as a starting point for determining what hers might be. This made it difficult at first for him to determine how to help:

I wasn't sure what to do, because I don't really know any homeless people. But, I thought, "What would I want? What would help me?" Because, you think, "Oh, I'll toss them a couple bucks," but that's just more work. You have to go somewhere and get a burrito, or a burger, or something. I mean, when I get home, my girlfriend will want to go out, and I'm always, like, "Man, I just want to take a shower and get a couple hours of sleep." So, that's where I started: I tried to figure out how to help her freshen up and be a little more comfortable sleeping in that parking garage. The first time I brought her this airline blanket and pillow I had in a little pouch. And I brought her some of those wet naps we have in the restaurant. After that, I brought her a sandwich from work and a bottle of water. She really appreciated it. Then she told me her name—"Vivienne." I call her, "Viv," which she likes. She always says, "God bless you" and "You're such a good boy," which is corny, but it makes me feel good. I know I'm helping.

How, I wondered, did he see Viv "doing unto him, *too*"? Did he expect that his generosity would be reciprocated? Was it? "Yes," Tim told me, he did, and it was. He explained:

You think someone in that situation really wouldn't have anything to offer you or any way of, like, paying you back. But, in the first place, it just gave me a warm feeling to know I was helping someone that I didn't have to. You can't put a dollar value on that, but it's worth an airline blanket and pillow and some sandwiches. More than that. I mean, my

mom gets all . . . she calls me "my do-gooder" to her friends because
I help Viv out a little.

So far, Tim's story foregrounds his own experience of reward in terms of self-congratulation—the "warm, fuzzy feeling" Alex Woodard found so distasteful among the religiously affiliated, and the approval of Tim's mother and her friends. Still, Tim does move in a more ethically sophisticated direction in his assessment of his engagement with Vivienne. He continued,

> But also, now that Viv and I talk more, she's told me about how she has friends she shares things with when she has extra. Like, I brought her the toiletries from a hotel my girlfriend and I stayed at, and she said she gave some of them to her friend because there was three of everything. So, I think that starts what we talked about in one of my econ classes—a virtuous cycle. And, you don't know how exactly always, but that comes back to you. It's like practical karma, the professor said, and I agree with that. You know, I might not get a direct payback, but the world I live in gets a little bit better.

Tim can perhaps be criticized for comparing his experience of being tired after work to Viv's daily, 24/7 life on the streets. He takes it for granted that he knows what she needs, rather than simply asking her. But even this assumption leads him in the direction of relationship. The Golden Rule starts with the premise that there is something common to all humans that enables us to extrapolate from our own experience to at least approximate the experience of another. We may live very different lives, but there is sufficient overlap to encourage more than mere civility toward others. There is an invitation to receptivity, even if it begins with self-referential gestures of caring. And these gestures can extend outward, past the narrowly conceived circles of care that Ammerman saw among the religiously affiliated. Ammerman argues that "Golden Rule Christianity" is "the dominant form of religiosity among middle class, suburban Americans." What we see among Nones from similar backgrounds may reflect an adaptation of that style that reflects the affinity many expressed for engaging with people from different cultural, ethnic, and religious backgrounds.[33] That is, the "circle of concern" is imagined more widely than it would be in "Golden Rule" congregations. Tabitha Roberts tapped into this potential extension of "Golden Rule Christianity" to wider circles of concern when she talked about what frustrated her most in her previous church experience:

> When I went to church, there was just nobody like me, which is kind of ironic because everyone was so much alike—all white, all from the

same middle class suburb, all politically about right, smack in the middle. But I like being around all kinds of people, people who are really
different from me. At church, it was just same, same, same. I wanted
a whole other kind of thing where I could connect with people not so
much like me and then we could really learn from each other and, you
know, just appreciate each other's differences.

Just as prayer among Nones can be understood as a bridge between past affiliated religious experience and current unaffiliated identity and practice, so their
embrace of Golden Rule ethics may represent the reverberation of Christian
practices that themselves are rapidly changing. In my conversations with Nones,
Christian resources were often integrated into their perspectives and practices,
even by those who saw themselves as most distanced from religion in general
and Christianity in particular. Their frequent mention of the parable of the Good
Samaritan can certainly be attributed to the Christian background of the majority of Nones and the pervasiveness of Christianity in popular culture. But it is
also consistent with the relationality and appreciation for difference that are
characteristic of Nones.

Good Samaritan Nones

"I think of Jesus first and foremost as a healer," said Christopher Langer, a Secular
Humanist from Boston who had been educated by Jesuits. "He's such an icon
for reaching out to people most in need. That didn't end up making me believe
in a supernatural being who gives out miracle cures," he made clear, "but it's a
big social lesson. It's really the best side of Christianity." For half of the people
I interviewed, Jesus remained spiritually and ethically significant whether or not
they retained a belief in a supernatural being or power. In just over a hundred
interviews, the story of the Good Samaritan (Luke 10:25–37) came up nearly
20 times.

The parable is familiar in general terms to most of us, but the specifics perhaps
merit a brief review. The story is set within a debate Jesus has with a scholar of
Jewish law over how one earns eternal life. Jesus asks the lawyer what the law
teaches, and the man responds by offering the teachings from Deuteronomy
6:5 and Leviticus 19:18, "You shall love the Lord your God with all your heart,
and with all your soul, and with all your strength, and with all your mind; and
your neighbor as yourself." Jesus affirms that this is what the law commands,
and the matter seems to be settled. But the lawyer presses further, asking Jesus
to define what constitutes a "neighbor." It is here that the ethnic boundaries and
delineations of righteous behavior for different categories of people—priests

and laypeople—come into radical critique by Jesus, as he "shifts the debate from prior conceptions of the neighbor to defining the neighbor according to a prior conception of love" as is understood more expansively in scripture.[34]

Thus, Jesus offers a case study of a man left for dead by robbers along the side of the road. A priest happens to be traveling the same road. He sees the body, which he might reasonably assume is a corpse, and passes by, arguably because touching a dead body or attending to an outsider would, under Jewish law, be inappropriate for a priest. So, too, a Levite passes by. Again, he might well take the man on the road to be dead and a source of contamination, and he does not recognize him as a member of his tribe who would "a neighbor" according to the reigning interpretation of the law. Finally, a man from another tribe, a Samaritan, comes upon the body. Rather than adhering to the boundaries of who counts as a neighbor, he prioritizes the commandment to love and attends to the man. The mercy and compassion he offers the wounded man illustrate the radical degree to which love is meant to be offered to others, redefining whatever conception we might have of a "neighbor" according to his or her need. This is not a "do unto others" ethic whose starting point is "as *you* would have done unto *you*," but rather what radical love calls you to do *for others* in all of their otherness.

While most of the Nones who mentioned the parable did not parse its particulars in great detail, they consistently highlighted this focus on otherness. Win Nguyen, an Agnostic who was brought up as a Methodist, now sets an adaptation of Buddhist mindfulness meditation, Hatha yoga, and long mountain hikes at the center of her spiritual life. An understanding of Jesus as a social justice exemplar is also an important part of her ethical views. On a small home altar— among assorted crystals, Buddhist and Hindu figurines, feathers, seashells, small stones collected on nature walks, and photos of family and friends—leaned a contemporary Orthodox-style icon depicting Jesus as the Good Samaritan. When I asked her about it, she explained,

> I just was always inspired by that story ever since I was little. You know, that we could be that way toward each other. It's really the ideal for me of how people should behave. Not "do unto others," but more like "do what *they need* when you find them on the road." That still really matters to me even though I don't think of myself as a "Christian" in a religious sense anymore. Spiritually, though, I guess I still have that in my personal beliefs—that this was what Jesus stood for and expected us to emulate.

The unaffiliated may adopt a Golden Rule ethic with modifications that move it from a focus on reciprocity to relationality. "Good Samaritan Nones" like Win seem to up the ethical ante. For them, the ministry and character of Jesus call for more radical action requiring risk, challenge, and even conflict on behalf of the oppressed. Here, the other and her needs are the starting point for moral engagement, rather than a presumed likeness between the other and oneself. Indeed, in the parable of the Good Samaritan difference/otherness is the locus of moral action and the reason the Samaritan, himself an other among the Jews of the Christian gospel, is deemed "good."

This point was important to Jessie Lansing, an Agnostic who grew up in a Baptist family. "I'm not a Christian anymore," she said, "but I'm still impressed by the story of the Good Samaritan in the Bible, which was about seeing past ethnic or tribal categories. I wish Christians and other religions would learn that. We all just are who we are walking down the road. We want to be seen as no more and no less than that."

The parable of the Good Samaritan was an anchor for a more appreciative understanding of Christian scriptures for many Nones who talked with me, even when they no longer counted themselves as theists. "Being an Atheist doesn't mean I hate Jesus," said 30-year-old Jordan Cascade, who was raised in a conservative Presbyterian family in San Antonio, Texas. "You have to love the whole Good Samaritan story, or the way he stood up for the adultery woman [sic]. [John 8:1–11] You don't want to throw that away, because we need those stories." He paused, "It's just that my church experience didn't really focus on that. It was about no sinning, avoiding temptation. It was about helping yourself to get saved, not helping others so much."

Some Nones did routinely point out what they saw as hypocrisy in churches that do not exhibit this Jesus-like openness toward whomever their particular others might be. But many focused on what the gospel story continued to mean for them personally in terms of moral practice. Still, even those who did not criticize or condemn churches and their members for failing to live up to the Good Samaritan ethic seemed to feel that institutional religions were not up to the challenge of offering genuinely self-sacrificing service to others. Lily Hampton, an Agnostic, argued,

> The big church organizations—Habitat [for Humanity] or whatever— will do things like that. Or, maybe after a hurricane. But day to day, week to week, you don't really see [church members] where you live being involved—out on the streets with homeless people or protesting injustice. I think most of them are just trying to hold on to the members they have, to make them happy and comfortable. They take care of their own, in my experience.

Those active in churches will rightly argue that most local churches and many of their members are involved in all manner of social ministries. They donate to and staff food banks, homeless shelters, meal programs, after-school programs, environmental initiatives, anti-violence campaigns, and so on, tirelessly. But these activities are often almost invisible except to those most actively involved, even within the sponsoring church communities themselves. Good Samaritan practices do not read as being at the spiritual heart of most churches as they present themselves in worship services, websites, and other public platforms. They may even be in conflict with the narrower constructions of both community and service shaped by the more pervasive Golden Rule ethics described by Ammerman. For some of the Nones I interviewed, this ethos seemed morally thin.

Alex Woodard, for instance, talked warmly about annual trips with the youth group in the Episcopal church in which he was raised to Haiti, Mexico, New Orleans, and other "areas in need." He insisted that these trips had been incredibly important in his personal and spiritual development. But within the congregation, he said, "they were basically seen as extracurricular activities. You went on these trips, and did a presentation at church one week, then that was it. It was just a thing they did for the youth to develop Christian values of charity and compassion, I guess." Few churches, it seemed to Nones, expressed their identities in prophetic, radically other-oriented registers, even to their own members. For many, Jesus is the cute, swaddled infant of Christmas pageants; the kindly Good Shepherd who leads us beside still waters; the regal risen Christ who triumphs over sin and death. But, he is not often a dude who would leave the comfort of a cozy church coffee hour with folks of his own social milieu to part with cloak and coin for the benefit of the dazed Iraq war vet with two pit bulls at the highway underpass down the road from church.

Nones in and out of Ethical Community

It is possible to read the lingering significance of the Golden Rule and "Good Samaritan Jesus" among the religiously unaffiliated as a yearning for a more ethically engaged, prophetic Christianity or other institutionalized form of religion. Do these Nones hunger for participation in religious and/or spiritual communities that more boldly call for the sorts of ethical practices that "Good Samaritan Jesus" represents? Perhaps some do, but for the Nones who talked with me, the answer would mostly be, "not so much." Or, at least not in the ways religious organizations and religion researchers typically understand such participation, in terms of sustained, exclusive affiliation on the model of voluntary membership. We will recall that when Pew researchers asked Nones if they were "looking for a religion that would be right for you," a commanding majority—88%—said, "thanks, but no thanks."

My research, however, cautions me not to read this result as indicating that the unaffiliated are necessarily anti-institutional. Indeed, many were at least somewhat active in traditional religious communities. But the plural here— communities—is important. Many Nones reported participating on a regular basis in more than one community they identified as spiritual or religious. Some, like Natalie Darling, took in Taizé services at a local church on Saturday evening, despite feeling "cast out" of the Catholic Church, and also found a women's drumming circle to be "a sacred space for healing and encouragement." For Hugo Carmen, practicing yoga a few times a week, sitting in a quiet church from time to time for inspiration, lighting a candle or praying with elderly Latinas at the feet of a statue of the Virgin of Guadalupe were all parts of his regular spiritual practice. Yet the enduring attractiveness of "Good Samaritan Jesus" or other elements of institutional religious tradition does not translate for Nones into a desire for affiliation. Indeed, the appeal of "Good Samaritan Noneness" over "Golden Rule Christianity" may reflect the fact that the former is understood as a cosmopolitan ethic—an ethic for a pluralistic postmodernity defined by encounters with many varieties of ethnic, racial, national, gendered, and religious strangers of the sort the Samaritan found along the road.

In this cosmopolitan spiritual landscape, "Jesus is just alright" with Nones to the extent that he is seen as a particularly exemplary inhabitant of the "many dwelling places" (John 12:2–4) in a diverse cosmic household, rather than as the keeper of the "narrow gate" (Mt. 7:13–14). The appeal of Jesus to Nones has nothing to do with the institution developed by his followers, but rather with his willingness to walk across religious and other social boundaries, through the lives of ordinary people, attending to their suffering, healing their afflictions, welcoming them into conversation, and sharing stories of hope. For Nones, this stands in contrast to the doctrinal professions of faith of that have characterized the Christian tradition since the Reformation.

"I honestly couldn't tell you what it means to be 'saved in Jesus,' or 'baptized in the Holy Spirit,'" said Roger Davis, a Secular None from an Evangelical upbringing, in explaining his attachment to the parable of the Good Samaritan and his continuing non-theistic reverence for Jesus. "But I get what it is to help someone out, to really put yourself out there for someone going through something bad. I think that was what Jesus was all about. Was that Jesus truly God? At this point in my life, I'm pretty sure it doesn't matter. But I do believe it probably felt like that to the people he helped. I guess that's the point—that helping people is a sacred thing. Do that enough, people will see a god in you."

Here again, we see the relationality, receptivity, and compassion at the heart of care ethics. The Good Samaritan is "good" because he offers compassion to the man left for dead on the side of the road, rather than doing what is expected according to the law in such a situation, which in the cultural context of first-century Palestine would be to pass either a corpse or the body of someone not recognizable as being from his cultural group—as his "neighbor."[35] As Jessie Lansing noted earlier, this Samaritan approach looks past social categories such as tribe, clan, and nation, or, for that matter, religious affiliation and congregational community. It likewise presses beyond the self-referential starting point of Golden Rule ethics that, as philosopher Eva Kittay notes of many modern virtue- or character-based ethics, "begin with adult moral agents pursuing their own conception of the good" rather than determining what constitutes moral action out of an attentiveness to "the inevitable dependencies and interdependencies" of human encounters and the relationships—again—however fleeting they might be.[36]

It is easy to see that there is much virtue in this ethics-without-borders approach to achieving "the good life." Still, Somes often express concern that not having a formal spiritual community might undermine personal spiritual growth, moral accountability, and especially the moral formation of children. The value of institutional religious communitarianism is not entirely lost on Nones either. Julia Xavier, a None raised as a Jehovah's Witness, named plenty of ways in which her religious upbringing had disappointed her as she moved into adulthood. But when I asked if there was anything she missed about her prior religious life, she became taciturn. "Well," she said finally, looking down at her folded hands,

> I miss the community. I mean, there was so much that was just so restrictive, so completely not affirming, and so counter-rational. But I did always feel that I was part of something—that when we were going street to street, knocking on doors, we were doing something important together. Like we had this amazing truth. You know, we had it together. And we were sharing it. Even though we failed most of the time—got the door shut in our faces—it still felt like a special thing to be part of that. I guess I miss that feeling of common cause.

Julia told me she struggled with finding spiritual community for herself as an adult. "I float in and out of things. Maybe go to a class at a friend's church or a book group. But it's never *my community*." She also worried about how her son, raised with no significant exposure to religion, would come to understand the sense of community she had felt growing up. "I don't want him to be in a cult," she laughed. "Been there, did that, have the therapy sessions to show for it! But I do hope he finds a way to feel a part of a group of people who share a common purpose and spirit, who are committed to something together. I don't know where you do that besides a church or the military, which I wouldn't be in favor of either."

Such longings were also felt by Mario Perez, a 34-year-old None from Stanford, California, who hesitantly admitted that he missed the men's fellowship group he had been a part of for several years as a member of a nondenominational Evangelical church. He left the church after a leadership crisis, which he said prompted him to take more seriously doubts he had been having "for basically my whole life" about institutional religion and Evangelical Christian doctrines. He and his wife decided to take a break from church for a while, which happened to coincide with their move from a suburb of Chicago to Stanford, where she is a doctoral student and he works for a tech start-up. "That was six years ago," he said. "We sort of never got around to finding a church, and that seemed pretty okay to everyone."

In the hindsight of unaffiliation, Mario told me, he thought that the men's group was "a way to solidify your connection to the church, primarily so you would donate more in terms of volunteering for things and giving money." But he also felt that the men in the group did genuinely care about each other and helped each other to try to be better husbands and fathers. He described the social, spiritual, and moral support the group offered:

> That had a very specific definition—being a "good husband" or a "good dad." But, inside that box, they would really coach each other about being, you know, "a loving leader of the family." I didn't agree with all of it, but it was helpful to have this group of guys where you could come and say, you know, like, "We're having a hard time getting our kids to listen to us without yelling." And we would talk about it, and of course pray about it, and there would specific action steps that they would follow up on next time. I don't need it that structured, but I think it was the only time in my life I had a really consistent, committed group of male friends that you could just talk about stuff like that with. I think I did grow as a man, you know, morally, spiritually, because of that.

When I asked Mario if he had ever thought about creating a new community for himself, he hesitated. "You know, they always seem so ready-made when you have them in church," he said. "They're just there, and you go." I mentioned that there were a number of Humanist and Secular groups in the area, including the Sunday Assembly, where he might find community. "No," he said, "I'm not sure I'm spiritually that far down the road. I'm not exactly an unbeliever." He shook his head, "That's how they get you: you have to be one thing or the other. I'm in between."

It is impossible to say how the lack of a defined spiritual community affects Mario's morality or that of his family. He certainly felt that his 6-year-old son and 10-year-old daughter had a solid moral grounding that was reinforced both at home and at school. "They would get more activities at a church," he said, "I guess, but I don't think they'd be more moral. I think we're okay on that without being in church."

These longings notwithstanding, the Nones who shared their stories with me were hardly strangers to community, religious and otherwise. Paul Harland's spiritual-musical community is an enduring presence in his life and the lives of his family and friends. Felicia Oliveria seemed to create community throughout her life and to understand this practice as spiritual and ethical. Alex Woodard's work with his student colleagues drew on a strong Ubuntu ethic that carried through to his vision for a community-based water-filtration project for Africa. And Anna Solomon planned to raise her daughter in a Reform Jewish community in order to support her development of Jewish cultural identity. But within the community she also expected her family's views to help shape her daughter's values. "It's a delicate balance," she said. "We want her to understand that stories are stories—that they're not true in a factual sense. But they do teach important moral lessons. So, we'll focus on that." Gretchen Drew, the Spiritual-But-Not-Religious None who gathered with coworkers for neighborhood culture and dining adventures, likewise seems to have found a sense of community that she identifies as spiritual. Corrie Milliman saw the extended Neopagan community as a sustaining spiritual resource that encouraged her to grow spiritually and morally. "Caring for the earth is such a big thing for all of us," she told me. "I'm not an especially science-oriented person, but I have been able to learn a lot that has, year after year, changed how I think about the earth and how I respect it while I'm walking on it. I wouldn't have that outside of my community."

Some Nones do feel that it's worth attempting to develop the same benefits of community experienced by the religiously affiliated. In addition to organizations like Sunday Assembly, various Humanist societies, a growing number of Secular Alliances on college campuses, and even secular summer camps for kids, clusters of the religiously unaffiliated are beginning to develop intentional communities to explore shared interests and values, provide social support, and engage in service projects. Take Desmond Davis and his wife, Molly. The couple retired to Scottsdale, Arizona, from their home in Oregon several years ago. Both are in their late sixties and have been Secular Humanists, Desmond joked, "since secularism was invented." In Oregon, they had been a part of a secularist group that was the center of both their social and political lives. But when they got to Scottsdale, "we were in the desert," Desmond laughed, "secularly speaking. When you drive into town, you see it right away. It's church, church, church, synagogue, church, church, church, church, church, synagogue here. I don't know why we hadn't accounted for that, but it just didn't occur to us that we'd have no one really to talk with here who shared our views." After a few dry months, Desmond and Molly formed a Senior Seculars Meet-Up group that gets together once a month in the social hall of their retirement community. "Ooh, that raised some old lady eyebrows down at the Residents' Association," Desmond snorted. He continued,

> There's a good group of us now—sometimes a dozen, usually six or eight. We have a speaker each time or a topic we're covering, maybe a book we've all read, and we have a meal. We're getting to know each other more and more, which is really the goal. I mean, we're old. Our kids are all over the world. You have to have some friends to look out for each other. That's the nub of secular ethics: we have to take care of each other because God's not coming down from heaven to help you figure out your Medicare billing when it's messed up. And, you reach out, too. So, you know, we're working on a service plan so we can be part of meeting the needs of the community—instead of just being old Social Security leeches.

Few of the Nones who talked with me had the interest, enthusiasm, and time to develop an intentional community in this way. For Nones like Mario, who find themselves "in between" religious and non-religious perspectives, it might be difficult to define common spiritual interests and values around which such a group would be organized. But Nones who desire community can find it in other ways. From yoga classes, to meditation groups, to book clubs, dinner groups, running and cycling groups, and community service organizations, most of the Nones who talked with me were engaged with others who perhaps did not entirely share their interests and values, but with whom they felt affinities they experienced as spiritually supportive and, some noted, ethically reinforcing. In most cases, however, these affiliations were looser, more provisional, and ad hoc, and also more fleeting than those of the religiously affiliated or of Desmond and Molly.

I believe this reflects changes in practices of affiliation generally over the last half century, accelerated by the recent spread of digital social media, mobile technologies, and social networking practices. The idea of community as a contained, homogeneous, mutually reinforcing, and normative social configuration is increasingly giving way to modes of affiliation that thrive though engagement with difference, rather than reinforcement of commonality, and that prize situational compassion over sustained commitment. This growing global, digitally integrated cosmopolitanism poses ethical challenges for Somes no less than for Nones. Indeed, many people, regardless of religious affiliation, are concerned about the replacement of models of affiliation that emerged in the United States in the aftermath of World War II by ones that accommodate the more peripatetic lives of many Americans today.

But of course the ways people have gathered and engaged with each other have changed again and again throughout history. Early nomadic societies gave way to tribal groups, some more itinerant than others. The development of farming technologies allowed people to stay in one place for extended periods of time, fixing enduring communal norms that came to seem "natural." The emergence of exchange economies, commercial centers, roads, and shipping routes influenced the growth of villages, towns, cities, kingdoms, and eventually nations. For centuries, even as cities expanded and far-flung suburbs sprang up, community—a manageable cluster of people of reasonably similar backgrounds, some related, some not—has been held up as the ideal, indeed in many cases the *only*, way people could come together for the purpose of enriching life, including its ethical dimensions. Without community—the more formal the better, traditional thinking goes—human and planetary thriving will cease. This anxiety is at the root of Robert Putnam's *Bowling Alone*: that community is failing, devoured on the one end by the expansive appetites of globalization and fractured on the other by the isolating effects of broadcast media. The fear is that without community, including religious community, we cannot function as a democratic people. From this Durkheimian perspective, the abandonment of institutional religions by Nones has profound and pervasive ethical implications that go well beyond whether or not the unaffiliated believe in God. How can our virtues be marshaled in the care of one another, how can we avoid the harms of our baser natures, without the benefit of community?

The philosopher Kwame Anthony Appiah believes that life has largely moved beyond the traditional moral boundaries of community. Appiah suggests that we should embrace an ethic of cosmopolitanism that sees virtue, as do most of the Nones who talked with me, in accommodating difference and not insisting on commonality of interests, values, or practices. "People are different, the cosmopolitan knows, and there is much to learn from our differences," says Appiah. "Because there are so many human possibilities worth exploring, we neither expect nor desire that every person or every society should converge on a single mode of life. Whatever our obligations are to others (or theirs to us) they often have the right to go their own way."[37] Appiah argues that narrow communitarianism cannot shield us from global diversity and pluralism, which more homogeneous communities cannot possibly absorb. In this new reality, cosmopolitanism offers an ethical advantage; it assumes that we are all "citizens of the world" (*kosmopolitēs*) with common, human connections to every other person, despite profound differences in culture, politics, and religion.

Cosmopolitanism does not assume that voluntary community is passé or somehow flawed, but rather that it is simply not a practical possibility in many contemporary lives. This is not because people are isolating themselves in basement entertainment suites, but rather because everyday life for many people requires such a wide range of local and distributed interactions that sustained, geographically situated relational commitments, beyond families, small circles of friends, and other close associates, do not in fact enhance life, but draw vital energy away from it. At the same time, the appreciation of difference and curiosity about others in their very otherness makes a level of cosmopolitan connection attractive.

In the place of the kinds of communitarian relationships that might have been found in churches, bowling leagues, or Elk's lounges in the mid-twentieth century, we connect more and more through micro-engagements that count as significant experiences and sometimes aggregate over time into meaningful relationships. We bond though conversations, sharing stories, enjoying local and digitally distributed social experiences that may have very different meanings for participants, and through the belief that our differences need not prevent us, even when we disagree, from caring about one another. These cosmopolitan engagements and the relationships they often nurture carry with them ethical obligations regardless of geographical proximity or ideological similarity. Appiah explains that "there are two strands that intertwine in the notion of cosmopolitanism. One is the idea that we have obligations to others, obligations that stretch beyond those to whom we are related by the ties of kith and kind, or even the more formal ties of a shared citizenship. The other is that we take seriously the value not just of human life but of particular human lives, which means taking an interest in the practices and beliefs that lend them significance."[38]

Understanding "the good life" as interwoven by these two strands of cosmopolitanism, as many Nones we have met throughout this book at least implicitly do, both extends and strains traditional notions of community. Cosmopolitanism does not resolve contradictions among different ways of living or invite the conversion of those who practice their faith (or lack thereof). Appiah insists, "If we are to encourage cosmopolitan engagement, moral conversation between people across societies, we must expect such disagreements: after all, they occur within societies."[39] Difference and disagreement are facts of life in even the most culturally and religiously cohesive of communities. But they need not be sources of division. Indeed, they may, and in fact often do, contribute to human flourishing as our differences and disagreements invite us to develop tolerance, nurture capacities for negotiation, and open insights into our own beliefs and practices. Appiah suggests that cosmopolitanism is a way of knowing, a way of experiencing the complexity and contradiction of life, and of entering into conversation with diverse others, which reveals the always partial, always provisional, and often contested reality we share. "You will find parts of the truth (along with much error) everywhere and the whole truth nowhere," he writes. "The deepest mistake . . . is to think that your little shard of mirror can reflect the whole."[40]

This cosmopolitan ethos invites many Nones to claim as "community" relational configurations that would be unrecognizable as such to many Somes. When, for instance, I asked Lourdes Alvarez, a 19-year-old None from Jacksonville, Florida, who is currently a student at a university in California, if she had a spiritual community, she immediately said yes: her yoga class. This was not, I learned, a class that Lourdes had attended for an especially long time. It was a class she was taking through the university, three times a week, during a 14-week semester. How, I wondered, did this rise to the level of spiritual community? And what, if any, ethical obligations did Lourdes think her participation in this community entailed? She offered a characteristically cosmopolitan response:

> Well, first, I think of yoga as a spiritual practice, so that's the "spiritual" part for me, and I think for a lot of the people who take the class. But also because these are your peers, and this is an opportunity to do something different, not academic, with them, you're being with them in a different way. For me at least, that makes me notice people more— how they move, if they're in a down mood or maybe tense. And, I'll really feel bad about that. Usually, like after class, I'll ask them if they're okay. I just try to check in like that. And maybe we'll talk for a little bit. And I think that's helpful. . . . Also, I'll see some people in other settings, and I'll be, like, "Oh, I know you from yoga," and we kind of already have that connection. I mean, you have these moments with people, and over time they add up. You know, from one class to the next, one semester to the next, you start to get this kind of community going of people you just know from yoga, and you see them on campus. And you really do care about them. I mean, I may not even know someone's name exactly. But I would definitely help them out and vice versa. So, that's how I'd see my yoga class as a spiritual community because for me it's where the spirituality part gets triggered, and then I have to, you know, follow up on that when I see people.

It would be easy to read Lourdes's notion of spiritual community as superficial, especially in contrast to the idea of community as entailing abiding social and ethical obligations. But perhaps her idea of community can be redeemed by setting her micro-relationships with her yoga classmates in the larger context of the university. As Lourdes noted, students in the yoga class are members of her university peer group, with whom she might nurture more substantive relationships that could develop into something that would seem like "real community" to Somes. This is, in fact, the direction I initially took in my conversation with her.

"So, you're developing friendships with people in yoga that seem spiritual to you because you do yoga together?" I asked.

"Oh, not really friendships, necessarily," she said. "I have a lot of friends here. And my family back home, we're really close. And I have friends all around the country from my high school, who went to different colleges. I mean, sure, I might make friends with someone from yoga, but they're more like just people I see that I know. It's that level. I mean, we don't have to be best friends for me to hope you're having a good day, right?"

"And that feels like a spiritual community to you?" I asked, trying not to sound incredulous.

"Sure," Lourdes insisted. "They're 'the people from yoga'. We have that in common. We all take yoga, which, like I said, is spiritual for most people. But we're different, too. We have different majors, live in different dorms. I don't know—like, people come from all over the country, all over the world. It still feels like we have this one important connection, so we matter to each other."

Morally speaking, there is something both beautiful and worrisome in Lourdes's understanding of spiritual community. On the one hand, this young woman walks through her university life with what seems to be a genuine, if slight, spirit of connection and obligation to a diverse group of near strangers with whom she spends 50 minutes three times a week breathing deeply and stretching more or less gracefully. The idea that such brief encounters, which might seem quite trivial to those invested in more formal and durable communities, can nurture a sense of mutual care is really quite lovely, and its moral effects may not be insignificant. The afternoon I interviewed Lourdes, I had to stop off on the way home at a pharmacy to pick up a prescription refill. Mulling my conversation with Lourdes as I waited in line, I looked around at the various people in the pharmacy—my pharmacologically needy peer group—and wondered if I was actually able to care for them in even the arguably superficial way Lourdes claimed she did for her yoga classmates. What would it mean morally to cultivate even that thin notion of "spiritual community" in this place? In the grocery store? At the DMV?

Such exercises in intersubjective spiritual imagination will be familiar to many Christians, who are invited to "see the face of Jesus" in passing strangers—to acknowledge both their inherent divinity and their suffering. But my conversation with Lourdes awakened in me an appreciation for seeing the faces of my fellows of the pharmacy not as Jesus, but precisely as themselves—an elderly man unsteadily helping his frail wife to a chair; a harried mother wrangling a toddler while simultaneously trying to get an older child to cough into a tissue rather than all over the waiting area; a tall, fidgety young man in the bright uniform of a local fast food chain who checked his watch every 45 seconds or so. The exercise provoked in me a deep tenderness for each of them. "Bless you!" I chirped to the mother of the sneezing boy who was by now closer to me in the serpentine line. I worried somewhat uncharacteristically less about what germs I might have been exposed to than about the mother's obvious fatigue and anxiety. Sure,

I thought, yoga class could be a spiritual community—a cosmopolitan one in which relationships have spiritual and moral significance even when they seem superficial, random, and otherwise only tangentially connected to the more substantive elements of a person's life, which are shared most fully only with smaller circles of family, friends, and other intimates.

For Nones, functioning in a cosmopolitan world calls on ethical strategies grounded first in experiences of human goodness that are taken as a universal feature of life worth preserving and enhancing. Many Nones, as do Somes, believe that this goodness has its source in a divine being or cosmic force. Lourdes, who grew up in the Catholic Church, told me she was "pretty sure" she believed in God as well as in "cosmic spirits that kind of help to guide you and take care of you." Her identification as a None emerged from her belief in a catholicity turned universalist: "We're all united through God, I really do believe. God is a universal for everyone," she said. "But I don't believe that the spirit of God, if it is what I learned growing up, can be contained in just one kind of church or religion."

Fortunately, acting morally in the world does not require either that others believe what Lourdes believes—or what I believe, or you believe. Rather, the starting point for a cosmopolitan ethics of care is a very general sense of obligation to others, no matter how thin their connection might be or how slight a gesture of care might turn out to be. Certainly this is the case in Lourdes's insistence that her yoga classmates "matter to each other" and that this creates at least a vague moral obligation. For her, and for other Nones who shared their stories with me, this spiritual cosmopolitanism and the ethics of care that accompanied it were an antidote to the moral nihilism and relativism that so often concerns Somes about the morality of Nones. As a matter of lived moral practice, however, "you just really can't not care," as Tim Lambert put it, once you have an awareness of the diverse humanity of others. If activating that awareness takes believing in God—your particular god—then Ethan Quinn may be right: "Your god is incredibly inefficient."

Yet while the expansive sense of community and the general sense of moral obligation expressed by Lourdes was inspiring, it was also worrisome in that it seemed to identify no specific, practical obligation toward those whom one sees as being part of a spiritual community. When I asked Lourdes, for instance, if she had helped out or been helped by anyone in her yoga class, beyond the offers of concern or encouragement she mentioned, she said she had not offered care to members of the class—aside from thinking good thoughts on their behalf—and had not received concrete gestures of care from them. I followed up by asking what help she would be willing to offer them. She mulled the question briefly. "Um, well, probably not, like, donating a kidney," she said. "But, you don't know. I mean, maybe, in some cases, I would. But probably it would be more like I would lend someone money for lunch or give them a ride somewhere, because I have a car and a lot of kids don't at school. That sort of thing." It is hard to imagine a profound improvement in the flourishing of individual lives or a general enhancement of life on the basis of such limited gestures of care. As Alex Woodard insisted, "being ethical sometimes requires sacrifice." It might take a kidney.

Still, Lourdes herself suggested that she had not yet realized her moral potential. "I really think I'm going to do good things with my life," she mused. "I really want to help people. I don't know what that will look like yet, but that's a big part of why I'm in college and why I went out of state—so I could be exposed to more people and ideas. So, you know . . .," she shrugged, trailing off, the ellipsis in her reflection marking the path, I hoped, to a deeper consideration of what it means to act ethically out of the felt experience that all the people in your yoga class (in the pharmacy, in the grocery store, in the DMV) are members of your "spiritual community."

Some Nones would suggest that Lourdes has tapped into an innate moral sense that does not require the kind of systemization and training featured in institutional religions. All but the most fundamentalist of theists would likely also agree that morality is a basic part of human nature—whether this quality is the work of a divine hand or not—and that some of it is shaped by wider cultural norms. Many people across the spectrum of affiliation see religious constructions of community as the ideal form of social and spiritual configuration. But the realities of globalization and digital communication (both positive and negative) mean that few people, even in the most remote places, are likely to get through life without regular encounters with many very different others with very different beliefs and practices. For all people, the challenge of moral life in a diverse, complex, and widely networked world cannot be addressed on the basis of individual, independent perspectives on virtuous action that are applied to another. The idea behind many Nones' take on the parable of the Good Samaritan and other teachings of Jesus is that the Golden Rule doesn't quite get it right because it starts with the autonomous self who assesses the needs of the other, rather than with a relationship of care between one person and another. This reorientation in perspective opens the circle of concern for individuals and communities to a wider horizon of need and more complex expressions of compassion. Its moral function is ultimately connective rather than reciprocal, cosmopolitan rather than communitarian.

A big part of the moral challenge of life for Nones and Somes alike in the current global, digitally integrated age centers on the formation of conscience in children. Throughout the book we have seen Nones as parents responding to this challenge in a variety of ways from which, I would suggest, Somes might learn much. In the next chapter, we will explore how Nones are approaching the spiritual and moral formation of their unaffiliated children.

‖ 7 ‖

The Kids Are Alright

Raising the Next Generation of Nones

We want them to have the magic of being kids. And, we want them to figure out for themselves what they think about the God question. Is it possible there's a God? Sometimes it feels like that, so, you know, maybe. But, as far as religious beliefs, it's tough to find a middle ground.
—Benjamin Altos, *age 44, Danbury, Connecticut, "Spiritual Agnostic"*

We teach our kids to follow their hearts, to trust their feelings and intuitions about people. We tell them to think critically about complex issues. Those are the basic life skills you want them to have. If they can't apply that to moral issues, there's a problem with your parenting.
—Jennifer Leaks, *age 27, Silver Spring, Maryland, "None"*

On the one hand are all kinds of deep connections—through history, through traditions, through family—that bind us together as Jews even if we're secular now. We value that, and we want our daughter to value that. On the other, we also want her to be realistic about the wrongs done in the name of religion, and to understand how science gives us better ways to explain life's mysteries than people had in the past. We want her to be open to new ways of living with others that might make life a little better for everyone.
—Anna Solomon, *age 27, Jamestown, New York, "Atheist"*

Among Somes who buttonholed me at conferences and elsewhere during my research on Nones, the most frequent and most spirited questions and comments were about how unaffiliated parents raise their children to be morally grounded, socially responsible, and spirituality sensitive adults. No one came close to the stridency of arch-Atheist Richard Dawkins's now infamous claim that teaching children to believe in God, an afterlife, and other religious ideas constituted "child abuse" more grievous even than clergy sex abuse.[1] But Somes were often quick to damn the parenting of Nones. Their criticisms generally rested on three assumptions about unaffiliated parenting:

- Nones deprive children of clear moral guidelines normed in a like-minded community;
- Nones deprive children of spiritually comforting ways to make meaning of suffering and loss; and
- Nones deprive children of ways to understand their own creation as well as experiences of awe and wonder as "God-given" and, therefore, profoundly special.

We saw in the last chapter that the affiliated harbor some misunderstandings about the ethics and morals of the unaffiliated. But if they were confused about how the unaffiliated set their own moral compasses, the Somes who talked with me were often much more pointedly concerned about the moral formation of the children of Nones. "Maybe the Ten Commandments isn't perfect as a moral guide," a pastor friend argued, "but it gives you a moral starting point. There's a basic framework for talking about right and wrong in every religion. Maybe kids will push back, but they're pushing back *on something* that's been there for generations. It's life tested. What do Nones' kids have to go by? What do they push back on as they're finding their way? How can their parents even be helpful with that if they don't have anything to go on themselves?" Here again, Somes often assumed that being unaffiliated involves a kind of moral electroshock therapy that automatically erases all religious, philosophical, and experiential knowledge.

Comments and questions about how Nones prepare their children to contend with suffering and death likewise reflected the assumption that, absent a systematic religious approach to life's complex questions, Nones are left to make things up as they go along. This was a particular concern of grandparents. "How could someone do that to a child," asked a seventy-ish man at a denominational conference, "teach them that there's nothing to hope for after this life? When grandpa's gone, well, that's just it? He disappears and you never see him again? That's a horrifying idea for kids, that the people they love could just vanish forever."

A woman at a conference at a seminary in New York City was less censorious, but she worried that an upbringing without the benefit of religious traditions and the communities that sustain them would "rob children of the awe and wonder you only get through religion." She was one of many Somes who assumed that the glories of human experience were made all the more magnificent by the belief that a loving, supernatural being is behind them. I pointed out that people who don't believe in a god can appreciate the beauty of an ocean vista or the unbridled glee of a baby who's just discovered her ability to walk, but she insisted, "Yes, sure. But how much *more* it is to know that God made all that for us, that God wanted us to see that beauty, to know that child. *That's* how much

God loves us!" She frowned. "Do these kids of Nones just grow up not knowing how precious they are not just to their parents or their family, but to God? That just makes me sad."

How Nones can raise children to be happy, morally grounded adults who appreciate the wonder of the cosmos, have resources to draw on when faced with suffering and death, and understand their obligations to others and the planet, is not just a worry for the religiously affiliated. These are also important concerns for Nones themselves. "For religious parents—especially the strongly devout and heavily involved—it is a joy and duty to bring their children into the fold," writes sociologist Philip Zuckerman. Among unaffiliated parents, Zuckerman found, "there is much more self-doubt when it comes to raising their children." The challenge in unaffiliated parenting, he notes, is that Nones are often particularly scrupulous about avoiding anything that smacks of indoctrination or "brainwashing."[2] Moreover, many unaffiliated parents are questioned and criticized by their own parents, other family members, and friends about how their unaffiliation effects their children. Such criticisms can stir further doubt, but can also result in more clarity and creativity in parenting.

In this chapter, we'll look at how Nones approach the spiritual and moral development of children. We will see that many of the qualities that characterize Nones' spiritualities overall—relationality, an ethic of care, the value placed on diversity and difference, and a cosmopolitan ethos—are present in their approaches to the care of children. We will see, too, that the fluid, provisional, and experimental nature of Nones' own spiritual lives does often produce a discomfiting uncertainty about how to be "good parents." However, the unaffiliated parents who talked with me often felt that this uncertainty could also be a source of enrichment.

What to Expect When You're an Unaffiliated Parent

We will recall that Benjamin Altos and his wife Kate, having not given much thought to religion in the early years of their marriage, decided not to raise their twin daughters in a religious tradition—neither the Catholic Church in which Kate was raised and in which they were married, nor the United Methodist Church of Benjamin's family background. While the decision seemed organic to their relationship when the girls were newborns, it provoked considerable anxiety as the couple encountered unexpectedly negative reactions from family. Things didn't get easier when they announced that they didn't plan to baptize their daughters. Benjamin told me,

Neither of our families live near us, and religion hardly ever came up at all after we were married. And neither family, to be honest, are big churchgoers themselves. So, it was a surprise when it was such a big deal when we said we weren't baptizing the girls. My mom says to me, "So you don't believe in anything now?" Like, you say you're Agnostic, and now you don't believe in anything.

The response from Kate's family was also negative, often resulting in long, tearful telephone arguments between Kate, her mother, and her two sisters. "It was like they thought we were robbing the girls of some kind of family birthright because of this baptism thing," Benjamin said. "I mean, it wasn't even exactly a lot about religion, really. You know, there were family traditions, and heirlooms, and stuff. There was a lot of pressure on Kate especially. I know she felt a lot of times like they thought we were kind of not being good parents. We heard a lot that we were 'being selfish' for not getting the girls baptized."

The couple had a "welcoming party" for the babies, which Benjamin said provided something of a balm to the family. But they both still felt the weight of the judgments of their families and some friends. "You know, these are people who do love us," Benjamin said, "and of course we love them. So it hurt everyone for a while." The couple eventually came to see the conflict as having two parts, the first having to do with their families' own feelings of rejection and judgment of their religious parenting approaches:

> They raised us in more or less religious homes. So it occurred to us that they were maybe feeling the same way we were: that our saying we weren't going to raise the girls in a church was saying they had done it wrong. You know, Kate's mom would say things like, "We took you to church, and you didn't turn out so bad." So, we tried to be a lot more sensitive about how we talked about the decision. I guess, we started pretty harshly with, kind of, "We don't think we need this," which had to be hurtful to our parents who thought they needed their religions to raise us right. And, the truth is, it's not like we felt they did anything wrong, really. I mean, they weren't crazy religious like some people get. Like I said, neither one of us was raised fundamentalist or anything like that. We just believed different things as adults. So, then we'd try to say instead, "We learned the most important stuff from *you*," and we'd talk about the values they gave us. I think that helped a lot even though they really believe—still do, for the most part—that they got all those values entirely from the church. But I think they could understand we weren't saying they did it wrong. We were saying we wanted to try something different, but that we were still going to need their help with all of it.

I mean, I had probably the best talk of my life with my dad when he
told me how our pastor when I was growing up helped him during a
tough time in their marriage, which I never even knew about as a kid.
So, I could see why it mattered so much to him, and I could respect that.

The second part of the family turmoil, Benjamin and Kate discerned, had to
do with their own inability to describe how they were thinking about raising their
daughters. He recalled, "Kate's mom was fond of saying, 'They're not going to be
perfect, little angels every single day. What are you going to do about that?' And,
really, we didn't have a good answer. We had all this really abstract stuff about
'good values' and loving each other. We didn't know ourselves what it meant to
raise kids outside of a church," he recalled. "We'd read all these *What to Expect*
books and parenting books before the girls were born, but we didn't know anything about raising kids outside of a religion. Church was 'normal' for both of us,
even if we didn't go."

In the months after the girls were born, Kate went on a "secular parenting
reading jag," starting with frequent visits to the website atheistparents.com and
a discussion forum on the American Humanist Association website, where she
picked up a number of recommended books on non-religious parenting.[3] "Every
week she'd have a new book," Benjamin said. "It was kind of intense." The couple
learned much through these explorations, but it didn't entirely erase their confusion or doubt. "All the Atheist and Humanist stuff we'd read would assume you
want to teach your kids that there is absolutely not a possibility of there being
a God—no heaven, no hell, period. I mean, you read articles by Atheists saying
they tell their kids there's no Santa, no Tooth Fairy. We're not that strict about
it," he said, continuing,

> We want them to have the magic of being kids. And, we want them to
> figure out for themselves what they think about the God question. Is
> it possible there's a God? Sometimes it feels like that, so, you know,
> maybe. As far as religious beliefs, it's tough to find a middle ground. But
> in terms of raising the girls to be kind and thoughtful, to be good peo-
> ple who are caring towards others, we started to get on the right track
> because we just had a lot more information. That wasn't everything, but
> it was important to know that there were lots of people who were think-
> ing through all this, that we weren't entirely out there on our own.

Getting "on the right track" with regard to the spiritual and moral formation
of their daughters started with sorting through their own beliefs as Nones who,
like many former Mainline Protestants and younger Catholics, drifted away
from the churches of their childhood. The birth of their daughters, the dramatic

response of their families to their decisions not to baptize the girls or raise them religiously, and their own confusion about what that might mean in terms of parenting and family life invited reflection on their own beliefs and values. Benjamin explained:

> Like I said, neither one of us came from heavy-duty religious families, so not going to church for us before the girls wasn't a big deal. It wasn't dramatic. Honestly, we didn't really think about it at all. So, first we had to really figure out what we, personally, believe, which was kind of difficult. I mean, religions have it all laid out for you. Mostly, you don't think about it. You just go along with what they teach you. We had to figure out what we thought about that and what we thought *instead of that*. And we had to think about how we would teach the girls about it and how we'd talk to our families about that.

The couple started by making a list that included, "the Nicene Creed, heaven, hell, Santa Claus, the Easter Bunny, the Tooth Fairy, angels, devils, and evolution." The Nicene Creed contained the basics of the religious traditions in which both had been raised. The rest of the list was made up of things they assumed their daughters would encounter through their families and friends, from other kids at school, from media, and the culture in general. "It was basically things you would normally, if you are religious, believe your whole life, and then things you grow out of, and things, like evolution, where there's still some debate by some people."

Cultivating Curiosity, Conversation & Care

Benjamin and Kate also talked to other people about their beliefs. "I think we were really annoying for about a year," Benjamin laughed. "One of my friends called us, 'The Philosopher King and Queen.'" He continued,

> We'd go to brunch with friends, and we'd be, like, "So, where do you stand on the virgin birth and, uh, Santa Claus?" But it really did help us to sort out our own thinking. And that was the surprising part, because we'd both been pretty much raised in churches where you memorized things—the Ten Commandments, and prayers, and, in my church, Bible verses. It was kind of cool to be just going through all of it to figure out where we really did stand, and what our friends thought. I mean, we really learned a lot about people we'd known for years through those conversations, and that was kind of an amazing thing. And, it did help

us to be able to say to our families, "look, we're trying to figure this all out. Our minds aren't closed." We'd ask them why they believed what they believed. So, it got all of us talking more.

Their conversations with family and friends shaped the couple's perspectives on values. "Kate had been reading a lot about values-based parenting, but they were more abstract," Benjamin said.

You know, being honest, being kind, being thoughtful. We didn't disagree with that, but when we talked with people, we realized values could be different. We realized that what we valued—what we want the girls to value—is a kind of curiosity about this stuff—about everything—that we probably didn't have growing up. I mean, you just weren't encouraged to question the stuff you were taught at Sunday school. So, we didn't develop a kind of curiosity as kids about why people believe different things and what you can learn from other religions or people who aren't religious. But we did learn about helping other people and being fair, those sorts of things, from our families. Kate really felt that her parents taught her to take chances and be confident through sports in school. And I think my parents were really strong on being there for your siblings, because I have a younger brother and sister, you know, taking responsibility, and having your friends' backs. So, we came up with this list of values that is being kind to people, learning about other people, being curious about the world, and trying to make the world better because you were in it. In the end, it's not so much about what they specifically believe, but that they're interested in figuring it out, in talking to people about it. We just think if we help them with that, they'll believe what they believe, which might not be what we believe, but they'll be good people. They'll be happy. That's what we want for them. So, one of the main things we try to do is to try to encourage them to be thinking about things rather than giving them rules.

That "thinking about things" includes religious and spiritual things as well, which come up in the couple's extended family, as well as in school and other social settings in which the girls interact with children and adults from other religious backgrounds. It is also a part of Benjamin and Kate's own particular outlook as self-identified "Spiritual Agnostics." He told me,

Basically, the whole thing that got us going down this path was the feeling that we had of having given birth to these amazing girls. I mean, the beauty of that is overwhelming to most parents. We really sunk into that feeling, I think that's at the core of our spirituality—staying plugged into that feeling of how much we love each other, and our families, our friends. I do think in the religions we grew up in, that was the key thing on a certain level, but there were just all of these other rules around it. I mean, I think that's more why our families were so upset about the baptism—because it seemed like a rejection of *them*. They're not a hundred percent past that, but I think we've been able to explain it better because we've gone through this process. They know we didn't just give up everything we ever believed in or that we don't believe mostly in the same basic things they do. And, you know, we tell the girls how important it is to respect the different ways that people do their spirituality— sometimes in a church, sometimes not—and to focus on how much we love each other and how we care about people we don't even know.

With their emphasis on nurturing curiosity, Benjamin and Kate are cultivating in their daughters the kind of receptivity toward others that grounds the ethics of care we discussed in Chapter 6. They attempt to enact this ethic by exposing their daughters, who were age six when I interviewed Benjamin, to different people and cultures as much as they can. "That was a priority when we were looking for a school," he said, "that there were all kinds of kids and that they were encouraged to explore on their own. I mean, Danbury isn't the most diverse city, but it is a city, so you do have a lot of different cultures and religions. And, we take them into New York sometimes, which we'll do more as they get older." Through such practices, Benjamin and Kate are developing a degree of the "cosmopolitan curiosity" that Kwame Anthony Appiah suggests is essential for moral life in a pluralistic, globally networked world.

"One of the payoffs of cosmopolitan curiosity," writes Appiah, is that "we can learn from one another; or we can simply be intrigued by alternative ways of thinking, feeling, and acting."[4] This is the direction of Benjamin and Kate's approach to moral formation with their daughters, which seems to accommodate both their own uncertainty about the existence of God and whatever determinations their daughters will ultimately make on that score. But it does raise questions about the specifics of moral obligation toward others. "Making the world better because you were in it" can certainly be a meaningful life purpose, but for many religious groups, "better" often has reasonably concrete forms that draw from specific religious teachings: feeding the hungry, clothing the naked, housing the homeless. It may well be that the religiously affiliated are no more engaged in these tasks than are the unaffiliated, but they are at least consistently held up as ideals of moral action. Benjamin was less clear about what this might mean for his daughters. "I think you want them to develop to their fullest potential so that they will contribute to the world as they grow up," he said.

"We don't know what that will look like now, when they're so little. Maybe one of them will cure cancer. Maybe one will invent something that reverses global warming. Right now, it's the same as with the spiritual stuff: we don't want to push them in any one direction. We want them to explore as much as they can."

While for Benjamin, Kate, and their daughters, that exploration is mainly educational and cultural, other Nones focused on social practices as significant both morally and spiritually. Catherine Neville, a None from Belleview, Washington, was among the few people I interviewed who had been raised in an unaffiliated family. She said she had learned "a strong sense of justice" from her parents, which she aimed to pass along to her 12-year-old daughter. The two are active in environmental projects throughout the region, participating in regular beach cleanup days, volunteering at a community garden, and joining in protests against building an oil pipeline in the state and "fracking" for natural gas. "I want her to know that it matters not just that you think about these things, but that you're really involved—you're out there doing something," Catherine said. "And, she's really into it. She loves the earth, and she gets really inspired to see that there are so many different kinds of people who really do care. I think that's the most spiritually enriching thing, but it's also the values I want her to have."

Critique without Condemnation

For Stephen Rowan, a 55-year-old Agnostic from Albany, New York, the specifics of moral practice are particularly important, perhaps because the stakes for his family are very high. Stephen and his husband, Sean, have two teenaged boys, whom they have raised in what he described gently as "not the most liberal place in the world." He told me that he saw their whole family life as "a moral corrective" to the world in which he and Sean grew up. "The boys have always been the only kids in school with gay parents," he said. "So there have been some rough moments." Nonetheless, this focus on relational values seems to have been productive in a country where, among young people especially, opinions on homosexuality, gay people as parents, and marriage equality are rapidly changing.[5] "We've really worked on emphasizing patience and graciousness with the boys as people learn how to understand and accept others who aren't carbon copies of them," Stephen explained. "It's always been harder with parents and some of the teachers. But, on their own, the kids are like, 'Who cares?'"

Stephen felt that the approach to families in their neighborhood and at school, which focused on nurturing relationships, has had at least as much of an impact on the acceptance of lesbian and gay Americans as have political, legislative, and legal actions.

You can't say it was just one factor or another, but we've just seen it change so much since the boys were little. I mean, fifteen years later, there's this whole generation of kids who our kids helped to learn to be different in their thinking. When you have kids, you have some sense that you're creating the future, but, you know, you're just living your day-to-day life, really. It's not a campaign. When you stop to look back, you see that you have had an impact. Things have really changed. It's amazing to see a future Sean and I never could have envisioned and to know that it happened—it's happening—at least in part through our kids, through our family just going to Little League, and PTA, going to the grocery store, where anyone can see we're just an ordinary, decent, boring family.

Stephen's emphasis on relationships over rights (or, at least along with them) situates his family's approach to "the good life" squarely within the frame of care ethics. Even when activism or protest is called for, an ethics of care takes as a central *guideline* (rather than a fixed, universalized *rule*) the idea that moral actions should engender and express caring for and about others—including others with whom we disagree. Nel Noddings insists that in a normative care ethics, a moral person may "[subject] others to logical criticism but allows them to stand without condemnation" of the sort one might find in some (but by no means all) scripturally based, religious ethical systems.[6] When Felicia Oliveria talks about attempting to influence her mother's food preparation habits by bringing fresh vegetables and fruits to family dinners rather than by harping on her mother's less healthy ingredients, she is practicing this manner of criticism without condemnation. Stephen stressed that he and his husband teach their children to be respectful and attentive when faced with prejudices about their family, rather than engaging in what they see as unproductive arguments:

We always tell them, "Start with a question" or "Have a conversation, not an argument." Even when they're disagreeing with each other or with their dads, we want them to learn to be about understanding where the other guy is coming from. It's harder, I guess, but we didn't want them going through their lives arguing with people, defending themselves or, especially, us. That's not fair to kids, and it doesn't really help. It doesn't change anything. What changes things, we tell them, is when you try to make friends with someone you disagree with instead of trying to win an argument. That doesn't mean you don't share your beliefs, but you're not going to change anyone's thinking by acting in the same close-minded ways they do. The thing is that you want to try to be in conversation, even when that's hard.

Like other Nones, Stephen sees the dividends of this caring relational practice as more than moral or political, but also spiritual. "We know that one of the ways hate grows is by seeing people who live or believe different as having nothing to do with us, being not anything at all like us," he reflected, continuing:

> We never wanted to teach our boys that the people who oppose us are evil or somehow less than human. We want them to understand that we're all connected and we have to help each other be better people. So, it's really exciting when things do change—like when New York got marriage equality—because you know that didn't just happen because of gay people. It took a lot of straight people, lots of them who changed their minds and hearts. People being patient and gracious to other people made that happen. I would say that's really the spiritual dimension of it all. It's not just "do the right things," but really care about people, even people you don't like, and "the right things" are more likely to happen.

Unaffiliation as a Developmental Practice

Because the majority of Nones come from at least nominally religious backgrounds, most who talked with me had given much thought to what it meant to be a moral person without an institutional religious community. Many also expressed appreciation for the spiritual and moral grounding that their early religious experiences gave them. To decide that you no longer need to have a particular spiritual or moral teaching regularly reinforced in a religious setting, or that you need to learn to think about morality on your own, is not to reject religiously influenced ethics out of hand. Unaffiliation does not entail a 180-degree turn away from conventional moral teachings. As Jennifer Leaks, a 27-year-old None with two small children, explained, it can involve developing an independent moral and spiritual outlook, even if you still have connections with religious traditions. "I don't mind when they go to church with their grandparents," she said. "Sometimes we go, too. But they can't have that as a moral crutch. I mean, they have to learn at home and at school how to do right or they're not going to be able to make good, moral decisions as adults. The church thing is maybe a part of that . . . But, fortunately, church is not the whole deal."

The idea that unaffiliation can be a normal part of childhood development is focused especially on the maturation of moral decision-making. "You have to follow your conscience," said Olivia Merriman, a None from Durham, North

Carolina. That means thinking for yourself about moral questions, rather than relying on religious rules.

> That has to be something you can do on your own. I mean, I'm not against religion, but I do think that a lot of the religious people I know do a lot of things for show. They want to look like quote-unquote good people to their church. They do a little bit of charity. They're always saying they're praying for this person or that. But it's hard to see if that really goes very deep. When I stepped back from the church I was raised in . . . it's not just that I could see their moral problems better. I also had to think more about what it means to me to be a good person on my own. I think that's a good thing, really, for everyone to do. You know, to go out without a net, kind of. To be morally independent—not in the sense of making up your own rules, but in terms of finding out how your own conscience works.

This emphasis on the moral value of exercising your conscience independently, "without a net," may seem at odds with the relational register we have heard more consistently among Nones. But for Olivia, her moral and spiritual development also depended on networks of meaningful relationships. She described how this moral spirituality played out for her as a girl within a network of close relationships:

> Look, I think I was pretty much raised right. That included going to church, sure. But I really learned what it meant to be a good person—to be kind, to help other people as much as you can, to have a positive attitude as much as you can, and be a responsible person—from my mom and my grandma, and from my aunties—the ladies in the neighborhood who would come around to our porch in the afternoons. I think church was just for showing off what a good job they did of raising this nice, polite, respectful girl. Now, that's either in you by the time you're grown, or it's not. If it is, you can go to church if you want. Maybe that makes you feel better, feel closer to God. Maybe you like the people there or the music. Okay. But you're fine if you don't go. If you don't have a moral basis from how you were brought up, going to church isn't going to make much difference.

Morality is seen here as something that develops through childhood, primarily in the context of the home or other close relationships; church might be meaningful, but ultimately it is ancillary. Church might contribute to the developmental process, but in the eyes of many Nones, it is something one outgrows in young adulthood. More pointedly, unaffiliation is not something that just happens, according to some Nones. It is something that *should* happen as a normal part of growing up. In this view, continued religious affiliation into adulthood is an infantilizing practice.

As we have seen throughout this book, for many Nones the spiritual is a process of discovery that unfolds in the everyday contexts of relationships with family, friends, coworkers, strangers, and often pets. Because life changes over time across these relational contexts, spirituality also changes. Nones share this emphasis on spiritualities of "being" and "becoming" with their children. Andrew Morgan, a 36-year-old Agnostic from Dallas, Texas, has a 12-year-old son and a 9-year-old daughter. Before he and his wife divorced five years ago, he thought of himself as a "more or less lapsed Catholic," he told me. "The kids' mom and I were both Catholic when we got married. She still is. But I honestly was never down with all of it, and when we separated, I guess I just stopped pretending. For me the amazing thing was how much more spiritual I felt because I could spend time on things that were really spiritually nourishing to me—running, hiking. I do tai-chi now with my girlfriend, and it's so great." Explaining that to his children, while also trying to respect their mother's religious practice, was somewhat complicated, but Andrew saw it as "all part of the process of spiritual growth" for him and his kids:

> At one point, because I have them every other weekend, they asked me why we didn't go to church. That had been a little bit of a thing when we were negotiating custody. She wanted me to promise they'd go every Sunday. But, I couldn't do it, and, the truth is, now she's on the outside somewhat because of the divorce, which is sad because I know the Church really does mean a lot to her. She still goes, takes the kids, but I know she's hurting over it. For me, part of the divorce itself was not pretending any more about a whole lot of things, and I think ultimately, she could understand that. So, we give each other our space as parents as far as spirituality and religion goes. And that means the kids wondered why we don't go. So, I had to explain that I see things differently, but that it took me a while to come to that, which is how I think it goes for people. They know people change as they grow up, and I explained that for me it was like that—when I got older I just didn't feel the same way about the religion I was raised with. You know, they know they have to respect their mother's wishes the same way they do mine, but they know that as they get older they'll have different experiences, they'll learn about lots of other things, and they'll probably have a different take on God and all that. I think it's just a natural process. Even for people who don't go another way religiously, if they don't go deeper,

I think you really check out spiritually. So, it's always a process as you go from one point to another in your life. You're just not the same person you were at 12 as you are at 20 or 30, so, sure, you'll change spiritually.

The idea that unaffiliation would be factored into stage-based theories of development should not be unexpected. From Jean Piaget, to Erik Erikson, to Lawrence Kohlberg, Americans have been steeped—directly or indirectly—in various stage theories of human development.[7] We should note that stage theories are routinely criticized for assuming an idealized linear progression over time that is given the lie by the often messy complexities of life. We have seen that Nones from religious backgrounds move into unaffiliation for a variety of reasons and at different times in their lives. It also happens that many people move in and out of formal affiliation with institutional religions in the course of a lifetime. This spiritual and religious dynamic within a life is not an indicator of immaturity, but rather may reflect a more fully developed engagement with new spiritual outlooks and practices through changing life circumstances. Indeed, two of the people I interviewed contacted me some months after we talked to report that they no longer identified as Nones. One, who had identified as an Agnostic when we talked, had joined a Unitarian Universalist church. "I'm not any more settled on 'the God question' than I was," she said, "but I'm exploring it in a community now." The other, who had initially identified as a Spiritual-But-Not-Religious None, had become a member of the Lutheran congregation his fiancée attended. "It was a deal-breaker for her," he told me. "So I said I would try. But I'm really into it now, which surprises me a lot. It's so different from what I grew up with. It's just a really cool place to connect spiritually," he said. Throughout the writing of this book, various friends and colleagues reported their own moves into unaffiliation. "I haven't gone to church for four years unless it's a campus service or I'm asked to preach somewhere," a seminary professor told me. "It just stopped working for me spiritually." We would be hard pressed to determine whether any of these people are more or less spiritually or ethically mature.

Nonetheless, stage theories of moral development remain influential in popular and academic thought, and the unaffiliated are surely no less influenced by such theories than are the affiliated. A version of theistic unaffiliation factored into the evolutionary theory of religion suggested by Marcel Mauss. Even James Fowler's influential *Stages of Faith*,[8] adapted for a more popular readership in M. Scott Peck's bestseller *The Different Drum*, includes disillusionment with the faith of one's childhood as a normal part of spiritual maturation.[9] For Fowler and Peck, this disillusionment is, in fact, a step toward a more mature (and religiously affiliated) faith, characterized by independent reflection on the theological claims of faith against life experience. Fowler sees people who successfully move through this stage as open to paradox, mystery, and myth in ways that invite deeper, even mystical, engagement with God.

Religious disillusionment registers as positive moral value for many Nones. "Disillusionment is a good thing," said Peter Kerry, a None from Seattle, Washington. "It means you've given up on an illusion—an unreality. You're seeing things how they really are. You want to keep thinking it through, questioning, staying open, and following where your own thoughts and feelings are taking you rather than marching down someone else's path." For many of the unaffiliated, however, disillusionment is not a stage in a journey that leads to a new, more mature practice of faith. It is an accomplishment earned through reasoned reflection that opens whole new trails for mature engagement with life. There is often a greater openness of the sort that Fowler suggests, but it attends more to a diversity of perspectives and engages with pluralistic religious and non-religious traditions. Ethan Quinn, a 45-year-old Atheist with two teenaged daughters, put it this way:

> Look, for me it's always been about, are you asking questions? Or are you just gobbling up everything that gets shoveled your way without thinking? Both of them are going to have their moments of, you know, difficulty, because if you're a questioner, you're going to shake things up, upset some people. And if you're just swallowing whatever they give you, at some point, you're going to choke. The difference is that if you're a questioner, at some point, you're going to peel all the falseness away. Sure, you'll go down some wrong paths. You want to do that. You want to be willing to take risks and experiment with different ways of seeing it. But, you're eventually going to see things for what they are. In some religions, that counts as enlightenment, but it doesn't have to be all mystical. It's just following the evidence, sorting through the facts as best you can, and finding a functional truth. That's what I hope my kids will do. That's certainly what we try to teach them—that if you do your best to think it all through yourself, you're going to come to a kind of truth that really stands up. Then you have to test that some more.

There remains something of an individualistic orientation in these developmental narratives. Growing up, being morally mature, is associated with thinking and living independently. I think it is fair to assume that this would likely also be a part of most Somes' understanding of what it means to develop as a mature adult. A number of parents I interviewed at two Mainline Protestant churches insisted that their children attend church to get a moral grounding. But most allowed that their kids would make their own decisions about attending when they reached early adulthood. For some, that was at age 16; for others, it was when their children graduated high school or started college. These anecdotes suggest that for at least some of the religiously affiliated themselves, unaffiliation is understood as an uncontroversial (even if disappointing) option within the same developmental process.

Despite this focus on individual development and maturation, we also find in the networks of relationships that function as the context for Nones' spiritual lives an interdependence that grounds spiritual and moral development and practice. Linda Olsen, a Spiritual-But-Not-Religious None, described this relational interdependence as integral to her parenting. She and her husband, Tony, have four kids, ages 8, 9, 11, and 14, with a typically over-packed menu of activities through the week. Linda and Tony both work full-time, she as an obstetrician, he as a management consultant. It was Linda who said that "the schedule is our god" by way of describing how difficult it is to find time to nurture the family's spiritual lives. But Linda believes that this same over-scheduled complexity also contributes to the moral and spiritual development of her family.

> I know it's a cliché, but we really do have to work as a team just to get through the day. We have carpool twice a week with the younger kids, and we have to make sure the oldest gets on the bus on time. There's lunches, lunch money, gym clothes, permission slips, homework, breakfast, getting the dog out and fed—and that's just the morning. Tony was in the Marines for eight years, and he's really good at the logistics, but he always says that a plan is only as good as the people who execute it, so we really stress with the kids that they have to be reliable, they have to have each other's backs and help each other out if someone is struggling.

Linda continued, setting the coordinated cooperation of her family's morning routine as part of the moral formation of her children:

> There's a lot of moving parts just to get out the door. We call it "the swarm," because we all have to work together like bees. And they see Tony and I helping each other, too. I mean, we really do have a marriage partnership—I'm Mrs. Cliché today—but I think the kids learn from that, too. I mean, I guess all families have their version of this, but for us, the idea of helping each other, of being reliable, so everybody together is successful, that's something we really stress a lot. You know, it's not just you, whether it's in our family, or at soccer, or studying with their friends for a test. We want them to grow up understanding that you need other people, you need to be there for other people, to succeed in life.

Most Nones did emphasize independent, rational thinking about ethical questions as a marker of maturity. But this individual reflection was not generally at the expense of the relational practice that characterizes the spirituality of the unaffiliated overall. An emphasis on relationality in spiritual and ethical parenting was even more apparent in families with connections to more formal religious communities and their traditions.

Raising Unaffiliated Kids in Community

George Brooks, the unaffiliated Jesus Follower we met before, said that he and his wife Nicole are committed to raising their two children, ages 9 and 13, according to "biblical values." His daughter Leah had just turned three when the couple left the Evangelical emergent church of which they had been members, and their son Luke was born a year later. So the children have never had religious education in an institutional church community. "Not even Bible camp," George assured me. The family does, however, host agape gatherings—liturgies oriented around a shared meal meant to evoke the ethos of the first Christians—with a small group of fellow Jesus Followers, and they attend similar gatherings at the homes of these families.[10] The meals include readings from the Bible, spiritual music, periods of reflection on scripture and on "how God is working in our lives right now," and prayer. All of the kids participate in every part of the liturgical meal, from preparing food, to leading music and prayer, to offering reflections. "We want them to understand that our faith is just how we live every day. We gather on different nights, depending on people's schedules, or someone will ask to come together because they're discerning something important or going through something. It's not a special occasion. It's an everyday kind of thing."

George told me that two biblical teachings in particular guide his and Nicole's own moral life: The Great Commandment (Mt. 22:34–40) and the Beatitudes (Mt. 5:1–15). He and his wife have tried to instill the values of these teachings in their children. He explained,

> The first [Mt. 22:34–40] sets the basic framework for being a disciple: loving God and loving people. And the second [Mt. 5:1–15] shows you who those people are and how God values them. I know other people focus on the Great Commission [Mt. 28:8–20], which is about making disciples, or Matthew 3:2, which tells people to repent because the kingdom is at hand. But I really believe that these are the consequences of loving in the way Jesus shows us with his parables, in his miracles, and in the way he challenged corrupt authority and laid down

his life. My own take is that the church pretty much gets the order back-
wards: go round up a bunch of people—by force if you have to—tell
them they're miserable sinners, then—and only then—let them know
that God loves them.

Because the couple homeschools their children, as do a number of people
in their circle of Jesus Followers, they are able to integrate these teachings into
other elements of their education. Leah, their 13-year-old daughter, was focusing her English and literature lessons on poetry in the Bible. "She's way ahead of
her age." George boasted. "She's reading college level stuff about this. You know,
academic scholarship you would read, I guess, in graduate school or seminary,"
he said. "And then she teaches the other kids and us. See, that's how we do it
so we're all learning together. That's probably the most important thing about
it: that we all learn together that we need each other, we need other people."

Jesus Was a None

George insisted that I not portray him as "some kind of wacko, fundamentalist, Jesus freak who locks their kids in the house and makes them memorize
Bible verses," so I am obliged to note that he and his wife are politically progressive. His enormous pickup truck (he is a contractor by trade) sports a "Jesus is
a liberal" bumper sticker; another that reads, "Obama is not a brown-skinned,
anti-war socialist who gives away free healthcare. You're thinking of Jesus"; and
a third that promises, "I'm doing my part to piss off the religious right." I interviewed George in suburban Kansas City, Kansas, where I assumed such sen-
timents might raise eyebrows (or hackles). But he and his family actually live
slightly farther into the Bible Belt, outside Tulsa, Oklahoma. I wondered how
his progressive Christian billboard on wheels was received there. "Oh, I get lots
of looks," George acknowledged, "and a finger once in a while. A guy kicked me
off a job once because he said I was a 'hippy anarchist.' I don't even know exactly
what that means. But, we teach our kids you have to be who you are—a child of
God, every one of us—and you have to stand up for authentic biblical principles.
You have to act on them even when it might be hard or get you into trouble."

Acting on "authentic biblical principles" plays a central role in the spiritual
and moral formation of George and Nicole's children. The family volunteers
regularly at a homeless shelter and is involved in a mentoring program aimed
at helping poor families to access privileges that middle-class families take
for granted. Each of the kids has a particular area of service that they work on
through the year. Leah is involved in a racial reconciliation program and attends

an Interfaith Alliance group at a local community center. Luke does environmental projects through his Boy Scouts troop. "The thing that matters is that
we do these things in Jesus' name. That we're following him into the world as
people who love God and want to share that love with others," George said.
"That means you have to get to know people a little, hear their stories, and, when
it's time, to share your story, too. That's not about converting any one—getting
them to repent and come to your church. It's about loving others as God loves
you, which he did by sending his son as, first and foremost, someone who cared
for the sick, fed the hungry, and stood up for the poor." He added, "You know,
the Kingdom of God is a kingdom of friends. That means it can't just be about
doing for others. You have to get to know them, sit with them, hear their stories,
to make true friendships."

    After a long conversation with George, I was genuinely impressed and
inspired by his approach to his faith and how he, his wife, and their circle of
Jesus Followers were trying to shape the moral and spiritual outlooks and practices of their children. The family's focus on the practical moral implications of
biblical principles of radical love is certainly consistent with the basic contours
of an ethics of care exhibited by non-believing Nones. Still, I felt compelled to
ask George why he identified as a None. Was "Jesus Follower" really so different from "Christian" that it rendered him and his family truly "not religious?"
Wasn't refusing to call yourself "Christian" at least vaguely heretical for followers of Jesus? George's response anticipated some of the ideas that, we will recall,
Marcus Mumford would offer a few months later in *Rolling Stone*:[11]

> Look, I'm not trying to be dishonest about what I believe. I believe in
> God. I believe Jesus was his son, and that he was the promised messiah. I
> believe in the Holy Spirit, and all that creedal stuff that Christians mostly
> believe. And, as a family, we do lots of the kinds of things that Christians
> do—or at least they're supposed to—caring for the poor, and the envi-
> ronment, and trying to heal racial and religious divisions. But, you know,
> Jews do a lot of that work, too. Buddhists. Muslims. Atheists, even, I would
> guess. The way I do it—what inspires me, and motivates me, and gives
> me encouragement—is by trying to follow the Jesus I met in the Gospels.
> That guy specifically. And I just feel like that got lost in the church. It got
> smothered by Christian fundamentalists and twisted so much that it is
> no wonder that people think Christians are crazy, hate-filled, brain-dead,
> extremists. But, the thing is, Jesus wasn't a Christian. Jesus was—you
> think I'm going to say "a Jew" because that's the family and culture he
> was born into. But I really think Jesus was a None. He was walking away
> from that—tearing down the temple to build up the kingdom. That's not

an institution focused on getting members, keeping members, boosting tithes. That's a way of life based on genuine love. That's what we want our kids to understand—that they don't have to belong to a church or call themselves a particular thing to try to love people the way Jesus did. You break bread with people. You share stories. You help each other out.

"Jesus was a None," I said to George as we walked to the parking lot. "Now there's a bumper sticker for you."

The Moral Value of Spiritual Stories

If George Brooks had an unconventional relationship to traditional religion, Anna Solomon's relationship to the Reform Jewish synagogue to which she and her husband Nate belong was no less so—at least from my non-Jewish vantage point. But while George and his family practiced their faith in the Jesus Christ of the Christian gospels outside an institutional community, Anna and Nate practiced their *lack* of Jewish faith within an institutional community. We will recall that Anna is an Atheist who has a deep interest in Jewish history and culture. Nate is an Atheist as well. Living in rural Western New York, just north of the Pennsylvania border, the couple is surrounded by a dominant Christian culture. Participating in a synagogue community was important to them because it kept them plugged into Jewish culture. They felt strongly, Anna told me, that their soon-to-be-born daughter (Anna was eight months pregnant when we talked) would best develop culturally, spiritually, and morally through regular participation in a Jewish community.

Their situation and their approach to it contrast with those of Aaron Jacobson, an Agnostic we met in Chapter 2. For Aaron and his husband Michael, living in an urban area with a large Jewish population and maintaining close relationships with a large circle of Jewish relatives was sufficient to immerse their two children in Jewish culture. Glen Schmidt, also an Agnostic, was not connected to the Jewish community in Arizona where he and his wife, Erin, a non-practicing Christian, are raising two teenaged daughters. He did not feel that any religious community was necessary for the moral development of his children. "They're good girls," he said. "I think we've done all right in that department without confusing things with religious ideas. They study. They work hard. We've taught them to be respectful of people's religious views—especially in our families when we see them—but that we're just not a religious family. That's not how we do it."

Being in a rural area without a large Jewish population influenced Anna's thinking about how to raise her daughter, but it was not the most important motivation for her association with the synagogue. Anna told me,

> Frankly, if it was just about passing on Jewish culture as information, we could do that ourselves. It's what I studied in graduate school, and anything I might have missed is online or in a library. But, I think every person has to understand that they come from somewhere, that they have a history. For Jews, that's especially important because our past has been stolen from us so many times. Part of who you are is in that shared past, and we want her to have that as she's growing up. We want her not just to know, but to experience that she is part of a global community of Jews with this common history. That doesn't mean indoctrinating her theologically. People in the past rode in buggies. We tell kids that. They see it on TV and in movies. We're not worried they'll go back to that. Same thing: people in the past, and some people now, have this idea about God that makes them feel protected and special. That's okay. We just don't think that's factually true.

Distinguishing between the "factual truth" of God, which she and her husband rejected, and the story of God as it plays out in Jewish culture, was central to what a Jewish community would offer her daughter in terms of moral formation. She continued:

> The fact of the matter is that in every culture, the story of God is really more important than a belief in God. I know that will sound really controversial or even offensive to lots of religious people, but, the truth is, you know, that no one has ever seen God. Okay, Moses, according to the Bible. But no one anyone knows except for that story. So even if you believe, all you have is the stories—the Torah, the New Testament, the Koran. You see? Every religion, in every culture, has its stories, and the stories hold the values, right? In our culture, the story of God is the story of caring for the oppressed, of caring for the stranger, of working for liberation. I mean, people who are not Jewish think Judaism is primarily about a lot of rules for how to eat, and how to pray, and that sort of thing. You know, for Ultra-Orthodox and even some Conservative Jews, that's a big part of it. But it's really the stories that hold it all together, that do the teaching. I wouldn't want our child not to have exposure to that. We want her to know that, even if we don't think there is a god, we have this history and these stories, and they're hers. They'll show her who she is and how to live.

For Anna and Nate, spirituality took a back seat to cultural identity and morality in what they believed their daughter would gain through their involvement in a Jewish community. But it was not altogether absent. When I asked Anna how she hoped her daughter would develop spiritually as a secular Jew, she responded, "The stories and passing them along is really the crux of Jewish spirituality. I mean, in the Shoah, people knew that the God of Israel was nowhere to be found. All people had were the stories they could tell each other. That's what kept them alive not just individually, but as a people. That's what kept the tradition alive. So, whatever she ends up believing religiously or theologically, our daughter will have that spirit."

Anna and Nate's daughter was just shy of 18 months old as I was finishing this book, so the jury is still out on how successful her parents' involvement in a Jewish community will be in encouraging her positive self-identification as a secular Jew and guiding her moral development through the stories she finds in the tradition. Still, Anna's focus on stories over propositional beliefs illustrates the cosmopolitan moral and spiritual practice that Kwame Anthony Appiah has described as critical to life in a globalized, religiously plural world. Sharing and exploring stories, Appiah says, "is one of the central human ways of learning to align our responses to the world. And that alignment of responses is, in turn, one of the ways we maintain the social fabric, the texture of our relationships." Stories animate the imagined, interpretive, and face-to-face communities that are formed as we draw upon diverse resources to inform and inspire our everyday lives. Sharing stories is, thus, a gesture of care; listening to them is an embrace of that care. The alignment facilitated by the exchange, translation, and mutual interpretation of stories among families, communities, and strangers makes us citizens of each other's worlds. It shapes a cosmopolitan ethic of care that enhances our common life no matter how a supernatural being or force may or may not be a part of our stories.

The Wonder of It All

Raising well-adjusted, morally grounded children who understand their connection to others and the planet is not the sum of spiritual and ethical parenting. Nones and Somes alike also generally strive to nurture what Benjamin Altos described as "the magic of childhood"—a sense of curiosity and wonder about the world as its mysteries are revealed and explored. And while all parents hope to minimize experiences of disappointment, suffering, and loss, they also try to prepare kids for these inevitable experiences and to help them cope with them when they happen. For the religiously affiliated, the beliefs, stories, symbols, and rituals of faith traditions are important both as lenses through which joyful experiences are interpreted as "blessings" or "gifts" from God and as balms for life's sorrows. Many Nones draw upon the same resources. Nones regularly talked about encouraging children to value the "blessings" in their lives, both material and relational, and to appreciate the beauty, awe, and wonder encountered in the natural world as well as in art, science, and other human endeavors.

Hanna Randall, a Spiritual-But-Not-Religious None from Flagstaff, Arizona, whom we met earlier, has a daughter in college and another about to enter high school. She has been divorced from the girls' father, who is also unaffiliated, since they were small. Hanna felt she stressed their daughters' spiritual development more than their father did, but they both nurtured an appreciation of a "spiritual aesthetic" in life.

> I really wanted the girls to notice, and appreciate, and care for the natural world around us. You know we were always out hiking, or collecting little stones and bird feathers, gathering wildflowers. I mean, we live in such a remarkable landscape. You'd really have to work hard to not notice the magnificence of that and feel responsible for keeping it safe and healthy. And, we have such a mix of cultures here, too—Native, Hispanic, European—and they all have their own spiritualities, which I wanted my daughters to appreciate. So, they got a lot of that from me. But their dad—he's a scientist, a technician, which maybe you would read as not being spiritual. But, he gets really amped about finding what he calls "an elegant solution" to some complex problem, so they'd see the beauty of what the mind can do and how that's a really remarkable, special thing. I mean, I know my spiritual meanderings kind of drove him nuts, because I do believe that there are spiritual forces in the world that are real. He doesn't buy that, but he has his own way of doing it that I think has its own spiritual aesthetic. So, our kids got the idea that there's a spark in everything and you have to watch for it and tend it.

Noah Garrett, an Agnostic who is raising four kids in a blended family with his fiancée Pam, also felt strongly that good parenting required the development of a spiritual sensibility in kids. We will recall that family dinners at Noah and Pam's house begin with one of their children reading an "inspiration" that they've found in their reading or written themselves. Pam is collecting these into a "family bible," minus the religion. But the kids have had to deal with difficulties along the way to the more congenial experience they now appear to have with Noah and Pam.

"Look, there's no getting around that my ex and I had a pretty difficult divorce," Noah said. "Hard as that was for us, it was hell for the kids. And, you know, their mom did take them to church a lot during all that—she still does—and maybe that did help. But it also confused things because, like, my daughter, who was six when we separated, told me she prayed that we would get back together. And, I had to tell her that wasn't going to happen. You know, so now her dad's not there every day, and this all-powerful god her mom is telling her she can pray to can't do anything about it. It was a lot to sort out."

Noah tried to help his daughter sort it out, first, by explaining that he wasn't sure if there is a god, but that, if there is, he thought maybe god was more of a comforter than a problem-solver. He recalled,

> We had this talk where I explained that some people think there is a god, and some aren't sure, and some think there isn't at all. But I told her that even people who do think there is a god think that god is really about love more than about giving people what they ask for. He's more like a really good listener when you're sad, who really cares about you, and wants you to know that, even if it's hard now, it'll be okay. And, I said I'd want her to know that, too, and that, even if we don't all live in the same house all the time, I'm always loving her. That's something she could trust even when I'm not around. I told her she could still pray to god when she's sad, but she could also just remind herself, "My daddy and my mommy always love me no matter what, no matter where they are. So, I'll be fine." I wrote it down on a little note card for her, and she still has it. It became her little security prayer, but it was about trusting her parents and herself, not having faith in a god who might not be there or making wishes that can't be granted. And, later on, we made one together for her brother.

The experience of working through differences in their parents' religious outlooks with his kids, Noah told me, invited further reflection on the implications of being an Agnostic for his parenting more generally. "Probably it would have come up eventually if we hadn't gotten divorced," he said,

> But the kids needed a sort of clarity then that I really hadn't given any thought to before. I mean, when you're religious, it does seem like all the answers are there laid out for you. You can say you don't believe in that, but then you have to tell your kids what you *do* believe in because, you see in times of turmoil and stress, they have to have something to hold onto. You know, I always thought that I questioned believing in god because you couldn't really prove it. You know, like it was a science problem. But also, really, I didn't get much out of religion personally. I could see that my daughter was looking for some kind of bigger assurance, some superpower to lean on. So, it's tricky, especially because her

mom does believe in that. And it's also a thing that isn't about science or evidence. It's about feeling secure and loved. Ultimately, I want her to know she can rely on her parents, on her family, and on herself even when things are hard, even if we believe in different things. How much we love her, and our son, isn't different. They can always rely on that.

It should not be surprising that many Nones approached helping kids to cope with experiences of sadness, disappointment, and suffering by highlighting the loving connections of family and friends. As we saw in Chapter 4, such connections are at the center of the spiritual lives of Nones, and the ideal of relational closeness as a spiritual value would certainly make its impression on children. Indeed, a longitudinal study of families in Southern California found particularly "high levels of family solidarity and emotional closeness among . . . nonreligious youth" and their families.[12] Researchers found a strong likelihood that young people raised by even one non-religious parent would be unaffiliated as adults. This had less to do with personal rebellion against religion or differences in belief, they suggested, than with "the presence . . . of a warm, supportive relationship between parents and their children." Such relationships allow kids to feel loved and secure without recourse to a supernatural being or force, even in the face of challenging or painful life circumstances. For the majority of Nones who do believe in a transcendent "something else" that animates and cares for us, these relational connections in everyday life are no less central. Hanna Randall put it this way: "I've always told my girls that there are angels all around us and that they look out for us. But I've also made clear they're not our servants or pets. We have to be there for each other, and that's part of what the angels do—they guide us back to each other and toward people who will care for us and who we're supposed to care for."

Still, it's one thing to take comfort in those we love in times of trouble and another to wonder about the fate of loved ones after death. Certainly, many people have been traumatized by stories of hell and damnation, and many Americans have given up altogether on the idea of hell. We like our salvation universal, our heaven of the "big tent" variety. Yet many Nones do believe in an afterlife. The "Nones on the Rise" report showed that a quarter believe in reincarnation; a third have felt a connection to someone who died.[13] But many are less certain, and this uncertainty can be especially disturbing to unaffiliated children who experience the death of a loved one.

Brittney Samuels, a Humanist we've met previously, recalled talking with her sons, then aged 11 and 14, about the death in a car accident of a beloved uncle:

Well, it was awful because it's awful to lose anyone you love under any circumstances, but in Ryan's case, it was a death and a tragedy at the same time. You know, the boys just idolized him. And, they would hear people in our family, or the neighbors, you know, saying "he's in a better place," and they'd ask if that was true, and were they going to see him again. So, my husband and I talked about it, and we decided that it was really important for the boys to know that it hurts as much as it does because a terrible thing happened, and that's just going to take time to absorb. We lost someone we love very much. Saying he's somewhere else doesn't really make that any better. But we also wanted them to know that they still have a part of him in each of them. You know, we share the same genes, right? But also, he took them hiking all the time and they'd ride bikes together. So, they have all these memories and stories they'll have all their lives. We'll remind each other, and they'll tell their kids. And that's how he lives on in this place instead of some heavenly beyond. Part of that is really sad, and part of it is really good because it helps us to treasure every moment we have in our lives and every moment we have with the people we love. And, I can tell by the way they took that all in and the way they talk about Ryan now that they took real comfort in that, hard as it was to accept he was really gone.

Brittney and other Nones who talked with me were often critical of religious responses to loss, which they not only felt offered cold comfort to the grieving, but which they also saw as glossing over the reality of hardship and loss. "Look, I get none of us want our kids to suffer," said Atheist Neil Gross, who has four grown children and three grandchildren. "But the fact is that *there is* suffering, there is pain, and loss, and grief. I never wanted my kids to get through that by making up magical fairylands where people go when they die. I wanted them to respect life enough to honor its passing, to feel it in their hearts, and to live like it matters. When I go, I hope they'll remember that. I mean, jeez, they'll have plenty of good stories to tell."

Parenting in the In-Between

Stories, Anna Solomon believed, transmit moral values. For Brittney Samuels and Neil Gross, they carry into the future the memories of those we love and have lost. They soothe aching hearts. With Benjamin Altos, George Brooks, and Noah Garrett, close and caring relationships again appear at the center of unaffiliated spiritualities that may draw on the resources of institutional religions but do not rely upon them for spiritual and moral grounding. For all of these unaffiliated parents, life outside or on the margins of religious traditions demands a depth of reflection that has enabled them to fill in the gaps that appear when religious beliefs, practices, and communities no longer structure the spiritual life.

This raises another set of questions that emerged from unaffiliated parents who had less to say about the moral and spiritual formation of their children. Certainly, most of those I talked to were attentive to the moral and spiritual well-being of their children. Felicia Oliveria and Stephen Rowan both noted that, as same-sex parents, their life circumstances have forced them to reflect on parenting in ways that heterosexual parents do not. Stephen put it this way: "The world is set up for straight people, so as a gay person, you have to always be thinking about whether, when, and how to call attention to the fact that you're different. When you have kids, if you're going to be a decent parent, hiding out really isn't an option. And, the practicalities of having a child—adopting, using a surrogate, having a donor—mean that you've given *a lot* of thought to all of it before hand. You don't just get knocked up and figure it out as you go." Similarly, Linda Olsen and her husband have used the many moving parts in their family life as an opportunity for moral development among their kids. So, too, we saw that the complexities of Noah Garrett's and his fiancée's blended family have required an attentiveness to the spiritual lives of their children that would have obvious moral implications. Indeed, the spiritual premium placed on time with family, friends, and pets that we have seen throughout the book supports the idea of moral development that plays out in the context of caring relationships. This is the underlying argument of the book: unaffiliated spirituality is fundamentally relational; that relationality is expressed through the care of others; and this is a valuable ethical and spiritual orientation in an increasingly cosmopolitan, religiously diverse world.

Still, many of the 36 people I interviewed who have children at home (another 9 have adult children) had little to say when I asked about the moral and spiritual formation of their children. Many reported that it was not a significant concern. Some saw spirituality as something kids were meant to sort out on their own. Others displayed a consequentialist outlook on their children's moral life; no one had turned out to be a serial killer or a bank robber, so whatever moral guidance they had received had worked out. This may be all well and good. It is difficult to argue that morality is not to a large extent innate—we care for one another out of self-interest and an evolutionary drive to preserve the species. Other moral values are developed at the level of culture, often varying over time—competitiveness or career ambition in one era, solidarity and justice in another. But in a culture in which religions have been, for better and worse, the primary spiritual and ethical systems for generation upon generation, we can fairly ask whether increasing unaffiliation, along with the globalized cosmopolitanism that defines much of life on the planet today, contributes to a diversification of outlooks and practices that undermines any common moral purpose. I believe we have seen that Nones are no less moral than Somes. But "Noneness," by definition, does not connect one to any common philosophical, theological, spiritual, or ethical system that defines life purpose and shapes the formation of children—even if that system is eventually rejected or substantially adapted. The relational spirituality and ethics of cosmopolitan care that appear to characterize the unaffiliated were not identified specifically as such by any of those who shared their stories with me. I drew them out interpretively from patterns of practice that Nones described or that I observed. These bigger questions about what unaffiliation may mean for the ethical, spiritual, and religious character of the United States and the rest of the world remain open as unaffiliation and religious diversification continue to grow. In the conclusion, I consider what this "None-ing of America" may mean in terms of national identity, values, and engagement with the wider world. I also reflect on how the current affiliational shift impacts institutional religions and their members, who continue to dominate the religious landscape in the country. And finally, I look to changing definitions of "religion" and "affiliation" themselves as starting points for new conversations about spirituality in America among Nones and Somes.

Conclusion

The None-ing of American Religion & Spirituality

The spirit blows where it chooses, and you hear the sound of it, but you
do not know where it comes from or where it goes.

—John 3:8

Faith—is the Pierless Bridge
Supporting what We see
Unto the Scene that We do not . . .

—Emily Dickinson

The drive along Highway 1 in Northern California offers one of the most
breathtaking of vistas in America—arguably, in the world. Late in the winter, usually the green season in California, there is fierce competition along
the coastline between the abundant flora along the side of the road—fields of
bright yellow mustard flowers, yawning orange poppies, the surprise of purple
lupines, thick beds of pink and yellow ice flowers—and the brilliant blue upon
blue of ocean and sky on the horizon. It is certainly a privilege to live in such
a place, one which I try to take advantage of as often as I can, driving through
the rolling hills just north of my home in the Silicon Valley and then winding
south into Half Moon Bay, where I connect with Highway 1.

Typically, this is a Sunday drive that reveals what is often taken to be another
competition. Here, the surfers at Pilar Point, the hikers along the Coastside
Trail, the cyclists whizzing by as the road heads south toward the cliffs at
Miramontes Point at the opposite side of the bay, where golfers enjoy the lush
greens and endless ocean views of a luxury resort—all these spirited souls surrounded by the beauty of the natural world and the companionship of family,
friends, and, many, many dogs—seem to stand against the various churches—
Baptist, Catholic, Episcopalian, Evangelical, Lutheran, and Nondenominational
Christian—along the same stunning stretch of highway. The half-empty church
parking lots, apparently unnoticed by the cyclists, hikers, and Sunday drivers,

seem to testify to how the spirit—of God, of human life, of whatever—is moving across the religious and spiritual landscape of America today. If this is a competition, traditional institutional religion can hardly claim to be winning. The latest data that rolled out of the Pew Forum as I was completing this book makes that clear: the religiously unaffiliated percentage of the population continues to grow—and rapidly at that. The continuing decline in religious affiliation is tempered only slightly by an increasing religious pluralism that, though it means there are more religiously affiliated Hindus and Muslims in the United States, does not conceal the dramatic decreases in the percentage of Americans who identify as Christian, especially Mainline Protestant and Catholic.

But perhaps it need not be the case that institutional religion is in competition with extra-institutional religion and spirituality. After all, the religious landscape has never really been stable, neither the ground where dozens of cows graze on cliffs above the Pacific Ocean nor the complex geography that shapes and is shaped by the ebbs and flows of spiritual and religious experience in the United States. Californians, in particular, are ever aware that the earth beneath our feet is always shifting. Change is always happening, whether or not we are attending to it in a particular moment. Yet we know that we will all be subject to the effects of its tremors in one way or another. It turns out that this moment in American religious and spiritual history includes more of a seismic resettling back into older patterns of religious affiliation that were in place for generations before the affiliational blip of the 1950s than it is a dramatic tectonic rupture between "traditional religion" and "secular spiritualities." The so-called "rise of the Nones," that is, appears to be as much a demographic correction as it is either a failure of congregational leadership and community or a wholesale rejection of the sorts of activities, relationships, beliefs, symbols, values, ethics, and ideas that have long been associated with religions in general and, in the American story, Christianity in particular.

Surely, any unanticipated movement of the ground beneath our feet is unsettling and disorienting, but the various shifts on the religious landscape that have brought the spiritual lives of the religiously unaffiliated more clearly into view hardly mark out a soulless secularism emerging across the nation. Nones, as all of the reliable data tell us and as the narratives we have heard in these pages confirm, are neither more nor less spiritual people than are Somes. This becomes obvious when we look for the "spiritual" not in the narrow bands of activity and belief most congenial to demographic research (professing a belief in God, attending worship, praying, etc.) and most consistent with both academic and popular understandings of what constitutes "religion" and its narcissistic, nihilistic stepchild, "spirituality." Rather, when we consider the concrete practices that ordinary people identify within their everyday lives as contributing to their own human thriving, to the enhancement of life in general, and to the felt experience of connection to diverse others—human and animal, natural and supernatural—we see America as a robustly, if more complexly, spiritual nation. For some, that spirituality is centered on institutional religious locales, doctrines, liturgies, artifacts, and associated activities. For a growing plurality of others, however, such traditional religious sites and practices are variously starting points, resources, and counterpoints for continuing explorations and constructions of the "good life" as it unfolds in cosmopolitan networks of relationships. In every part of the nation, it seems, other religious and philosophical resources, and experiences of difference, diversity, and interpersonal connection, increasingly come to be named in stories of the self as "spiritual." That these "spiritual lives" are narrated through identifiably religious idioms by many who likewise identify as non-religious—Atheists, Agnostics, Humanists—gives the lie to any sharp boundaries between what is understood as "religious" and "secular" in the context of everyday lives.

For the majority of Nones who retain a belief in a supernatural being or power that acts within human life, the relational orientation of unaffiliated spirituality expresses a practical theology of immanent transcendence that sets any supernatural engagement primarily in the concrete reality of the here-and-now rather than in either a mystical bridging of divine and human worlds or a promised eternal hereafter. God's presence was felt, for example, in the lives of Angela Casper and Trevor Smith through their "miraculous" connection with friends who proved to be practically transformative and spiritually enriching in their everyday lives. For non-believing Nones, non-theistic practices of self-transcendence take place in an "immanent frame"[1] that allows that humans themselves can contribute to the healing of the world and the enhancement of life today through compassionate, ethical action that lays the groundwork for a worldly "eternity." This was the case for Andy Elliott, Joseph Carlson, Alex Wood, Matthew Tyler, and several other non-theistic Nones who saw their spiritual and ethical engagement with people in need as effecting "salvation" and creating "eternity."

The language often used by these non-religious Nones to make pointedly secular claims is undeniably religious, again confusing categories meant to sharply distinguish one mode of life from another. Routinely transgressing such boundaries, believing and non-believing Nones insist that affiliation and unaffiliation, religion and the secular, belief and unbelief need not be in competition, but instead constitute a wide variety of resources that can be deployed in the service of human thriving and in the enrichment of our common lives. Given the emergence of what we might think of as liminal religion—a spiritual religiosity that moves actively between traditional religion and Enlightenment-style secularism—the way forward for those affiliated with institutional religions who are committed to the continued vibrancy of religion and spirituality in America would seem to be in exploring how Nones make use of traditional religious resources in their spiritual lives—indeed, perhaps inviting them to do so—by way of generating conversation, sharing stories, and encouraging common action, rather than by pursuing their conversion to affiliated status. How, those affiliated with institutional religions and their leaders might productively ask, can we minister in a world that is neither reliably religious in conventional terms nor wholly unreligious, as is often suggested by both fundamentalist Atheists and their religious sparring partners? How do we practice religion in between these extremes—in a cosmopolitan spiritual space in which the embrace of difference and compassion toward diverse others are foundational values?

My travels with many religiously unaffiliated people across the United States over the past few years have made clear that the hand-wringing anxiety I have often observed among the religiously affiliated about the spiritual and moral health of the nation as more and more people choose their own religious paths is hardly merited. As I have noted throughout, Nones are neither more nor less spiritual or moral than are Somes. But they are, I have argued in this book, spiritual, religious, and moral in ways that are somewhat different from the religiously affiliated:

- Nones who talked with me tended to take relationships with family, friends, and, for many, pets or other animals as the starting point for experiencing and interpreting what constitutes the spiritual life.
- They were more spiritually and socially cosmopolitan in their embrace of all manner of difference, rather than narrowly communitarian or tribal.
- Their modes of social and spiritual organization and engagement were more networked and provisional than hierarchical and traditional.
- Nones were relational more than locational and socially compassionate more than ideologically or theologically passionate in their spiritual lives.

This general orientation in unaffiliated spirituality presses against conventional understandings of extra-institutional spiritual practice as inherently individualistic, interiorized, and private. And it in no way adheres to the stereotype of Nones as spiritually shallow, immature, and self-referential. Importantly, the vast majority of the unaffiliated become Nones out of at least nominally religious, usually Christian, backgrounds and within what remains a culture laden with religious discourses, symbols, and meanings that shape everyday life far beyond congregational settings. The lives of most Nones are often deeply intertwined with those of Somes in families, workplaces, neighborhoods, and the like. The entanglement of affiliated and unaffiliated spiritualities calls out for continued study, as well as for more intentional social and spiritual engagement between the Nones and Somes. Such explorations and engagements can create opportunities for Americans in general to enrich and expand their understandings of what it means to be "religious" or "spiritual" in America today and to consider the implications this will have for other aspects of our common life, including politics, education, medicine, and science. The continued "None-ing" of America also provides a profound opportunity to consider what it means for the United States to be an *ethical nation* on the basis of values that function with integrity within both religious and unreligious systems of thought and practice. Such consideration—by academics, religious leaders, journalists, and other contributors to the common narratives that make up American identity—will surely prove far more enlightening than the continued pitting of rabid religious fundamentalists against equally fanatical secularists.

The possibilities presented for creative, responsive ministries presented by the emergence of liminal religion in the United States mean that the None-ing of America is hardly bad news for institutional religion. Certainly, it challenges the notions of uninterrupted numerical and financial growth as indicators of congregational and denominational success that seem to have been hardwired into the minds of many religious leaders. But already we are seeing that the pressures on institutional religions provoked in large measure by unaffiliation are encouraging new, creative ministries within and well beyond traditional congregations. Churches, synagogues, and mosques are increasingly opening their doors to others while stepping beyond the thresholds of their affiliated communities to minister in parks, pubs, bowling alleys, pizza parlors, laundromats, and food trucks.[2]

The explorations, conversations, and shared actions encouraged by the changing winds of American religion and spirituality draw on gifts that the religiously affiliated have used to make common cause with those in their own demographic set, despite religious narratives and practices that are often far more different across religious traditions than they are between Somes and Nones. As in these ecumenical and inter-religious engagements among institutional religious groups, surely occasions for enrichment will arise in encounters between Nones and Somes, even from beliefs and practices that cannot be embraced or even countenanced by one or more parties to dialogue. This is not to suggest that either the affiliated or the unaffiliated ought to sanction overtly (or through what passes as polite "tolerance") practices that disadvantage, diminish, dehumanize, demean, or otherwise violate the human dignity of others. Rather, it is to suggest that the cosmopolitan ethics of care often illustrated, if seldom substantively articulated, by the Nones who spoke with me—an ethics that readily connects to religious ethics but which does not depend on shared theological and cosmological beliefs—is a more productive starting place for the development of universal moral standards and practices than are religious doctrines and dogmas on which there is seldom wholesale agreement within religious groups, let alone across or beyond them. The many Nones who called upon the Christian parable of the Good Samaritan and other scriptural references evoking other-oriented compassion and justice seemed very open to such ethical explorations. Where Somes have, by definition, long experience with practices of philosophical systemization that can assist in the articulation and sharing of common values, the spiritual lives of Nones have much to teach about a cosmopolitanism that responds humanely, compassionately, and with respectful curiosity to difference and to change itself.

Such efforts will not, I expect, produce a New Age of spiritual enlightenment, a new Awakening, an Emergence of one sort or another, or some other coherent, quasi-institutional religious or spiritual movement. Religion as we have known it, even when it attempts valiantly to adapt to changing cultural norms, seems not to be poised for a 1950s style comeback of any sort. Consider the incredible popularity of Pope Francis, which seems to grow daily, even as Catholic dioceses throughout the United States decommission parish churches and their Protestant neighbors do the same. New ways of engaging with religious others are not likely to tick up the percentage of the religiously affiliated. Indeed, to spend sustained time in conversation with diverse members of the fastest-growing religious demographic cohort in the United States is to understand that religious identity, like social-self identity more generally, is fluid rather than fixed. This fluidity is a feature of contemporary culture that influences the affiliated as well as their unaffiliated neighbors. Being a Catholic, an Evangelical Protestant, a Buddhist, or a Jew today is hardly the same as it was 10 years ago, let alone 50, and the meanings of these traditions and the identities of those who affiliate with them will continue to change. So, too, being None will continue to change. The earth is always moving beneath our feet. The only way to mark the trail ahead seems to be to stay in conversation with those around us, sharing our stories as we walk together into our religious and spiritual future.

In the end, the None-ing of America is not a turn away from religion, but rather the emergence of multiple, sometimes overlapping, sometimes diverging narratives of religious and spiritual experience that move through more diverse conceptions of what it means to be human and to be citizens of the nation and the world. Such cosmopolitan, relational religiosity and spirituality are challenging for a nation that has long thought of itself as "religious" in very narrow terms. But it hardly represents a loss of values, morals, or community across the nation. Rather, we are challenged to find new ways of articulating and sharing the changing story of the spirit as it emerges from the lives of Nones and Somes together. Elements of this shared story have long spun through the corridors of everyday life, but they have seldom been central in the broader religious narrative in the United States. Yet the shape of this narrative—the story of what it means to be religious and spiritual in America today—continues to matter, even as institutional religion wanes, because it has such a profound influence on how we see ourselves as a just and moral people and how we act toward others in the world. The energies of the majority of Americans who continue to affiliate with institutional religions, then, is best spent not in attempts to "recapture" Nones and draw them back into churches, synagogues, and mosques. It seems a far better spiritual investment to listen more deeply to their stories so that we can develop a richer, more complex story of the American spirit. Embracing this narrative challenge, it seems to me, is a fundamental practice of faith in America today, one which, as the great religious doubter Emily Dickinson put it, constructs the surest bridge to a world we cannot see.

Appendix A

ON METHODOLOGY

In the research and writing of this book, I brought to bear resources from anthropology, cultural studies, sociology, theology, and other academic fields. These helped me to interpret quantitative data, to shape engaging questions for interviews with Nones, to provide appropriate background information on historical and theoretical material related to religious affiliation, and to respond to questions from people I met at church-related events, conferences, and other public speaking engagements. Primary research for the book took multiple forms: focus groups, surveys, interviews, and participant observation. My hope is that scholars of religion, spirituality, and theology will also find the fruits of this work meaningful, though I expect some may wish I had traveled in a more central disciplinary path through the American religious landscape.

Survey 1: Spiritually Meaningful Practices

In 2010 and 2011, I conducted six focus groups in local and online settings to identify practices that people considered "spiritually meaningful." Participants for the focus groups were recruited through a flyer posted on public bulletin boards in various locations in San Jose, California (3 groups), and Pittsburgh, Pennsylvania (2 groups). The flyer read:

Spiritual? Religious? Both? Neither?
What does "spirituality" mean to you?
What activities or practices do you find spiritually meaningful?
Writer seeks participants in focus groups on spirituality today as research for book project.

One additional focus group was conducted through a Facebook survey and discussion. Participants in this focus group were recruited with a Facebook advertisement and through postings on my Facebook page, on Facebook group pages that seemed likely to draw relevant participants, and through Twitter. A total of 124 people participated in the focus groups (San Jose = 24; Pittsburgh = 18; Facebook = 82). I gathered input from students in two sections of a graduate seminar on contemporary spirituality ($n = 16$) and participants in a church forum on spirituality ($n = 11$).

I asked participants in all of the focus groups one question: "What practices or activities do you find most spiritually meaningful?" I gave participants five minutes to write down their responses individually, then asked them to share them with the group as I wrote them on a flip chart. After everyone had shared, I allowed additional responses. After a short break, I asked participants to rank the practices listed by putting dots on the 10 they found "most spiritually meaningful." Although it was not a planned part of the focus groups (as opposed to the classroom and church settings), in every case participants were interested in discussing their responses and rankings, as well as differences in the phrasings of practices. For instance, much discussion in one focus group centered on whether "spending time" or "enjoying time" with family was spiritually meaningful. Groups tended to feel that "spending time" was not always spiritually meaningful, but that "enjoying time" might have that possibility. Another group discussed whether "gardening" as a spiritually meaningful activity was the same as "enjoying nature." People debated whether "contemplation," "meditation," and "prayer" were the same things. There was much discussion about whether yoga is a physical activity, a spiritual one, or both. Likewise, hiking was considered both a physical activity and an opportunity to enjoy nature. Dance was, some focus group members argued, physical, artistic, and spiritual. And, in the groups conducted in Pennsylvania, more consideration was given to whether fishing and hunting are in the same category of potentially spiritually meaningful activity.

With some massaging, I adapted the top 20 most spiritually meaningful practices identified by all of the groups. To this list, I added activities commonly included in demographic studies of religiosity that had not come up in the focus groups (attending worship; reading/studying scripture). Based on conversations with colleagues, I added two other practices that focused on congregational practices outside worship (participating in congregational committees, meetings, and other activities; participating in congregationally sponsored service projects), and participating in volunteer or service activities generally. These 25 items (see Table A.1) became the basis for an online survey, which I intended to use both to better understand the range of contemporary spiritual practices beyond those marked in standard demographic surveys and to identify potential

Table A.1 **Spiritually Meaningful Practices for the Unaffiliated (Ranked According to Spiritual Practices Survey Results)**

1. Enjoying time with family
2. Enjoying time with friends
3. Enjoying time with pets or other animals
4. Preparing and/or sharing food/meals
5. Praying
6. Enjoying nature
7. Listening to/playing music
8. Enjoying/creating art
9. Physical activity/sports (cycling, running)
10. Yoga
11. Meditation
12. Hiking
13. Personal travel
14. Journaling/writing
15. Participating in a community group (non-religious)
16. Dance
17. Volunteering (non-religious)
18. Caring for the sick or dying
19. Service activities with a religious group
20. Political activities
21. Dreamwork/interpretation of dreams
22. Fishing/hunting
23. Reading/studying scripture
24. Attending worship
25. Attending a non-worship activity, event, or meeting at church, synagogue, or other religious group

interview subjects for the larger *Choosing Our Religion* project. The survey also included several open-ended questions on religious and spiritual background and a request for contact information if the respondent was interested in being interviewed for the book project.

As noted in the Introduction, because I am neither a sociologist nor a demographer, I began the survey with a test run. My plan was to revise the survey on the basis of the test survey responses. The test involved sending a draft of the survey to 20 personal and professional contacts, asking them not to complete the survey themselves, but to send it to 10 of their own contacts, preferably people I did not know. I also asked if they might take some additional care to send the survey to contacts they knew as being religiously unaffiliated. Over the course of the weekend on which the survey was distributed in March 2012, I received 1,166 responses from across the United States, along with slight representation from Canada, the United Kingdom, and Australia. Of the respondents, 22% identified as religiously unaffiliated, 78% affiliated.

The response was obviously much greater than I had anticipated or even had hoped for. Because the results provided insight into meaningful spiritual practices for what turned out to be a reasonably large cross-section of respondents and also generated a pool of potential interview subjects, I elected not to revise the survey or conduct it a second time.

Survey 2: Nones Beyond the Numbers

From the demographic information collected in the Spiritual Practices Survey, I identified 219 people who had selected "none/no religion" as a response to the question, "What is your religious identification or affiliation?" These respondents identified their primary residence as being in one of seven of the nine US Census divisions. In April 2012, I emailed each of these people a link to a second survey, the "Nones Beyond the Numbers Survey." In an attempt to deepen the pool of respondents and potential interviewees, I also posted a description of the survey and a link on my personal website, on my Facebook page, and on Twitter. In addition, I announced that a link to the survey was available on my website at speaking engagements throughout 2012 and 2013. In order to cultivate participants from the remaining US Census divisions, I also emailed the survey description and link to contacts in Florida and Georgia (Division 5) and in Texas and Louisiana (Division 7). I collected initial responses to the survey from May 2012 to December 2012. I revised the survey slightly and reopened it from January 2014 to December 2014. The second set of survey responses informed some of my analysis, but respondents were not included in the interview pool.

The "Nones Beyond the Numbers Survey" is an extensive, open-ended narrative survey that asks respondents about their religious and spiritual history, their spiritual and religious beliefs, the resources that enrich their spiritual lives, their spiritual practices, and their moral perspectives and practices. The survey also collected more detailed demographic information than had the "Spiritual Practices Survey." (Questions from the survey are shown in Table A.2.) A total of 233 people responded to the survey.

Table A.2 **Nones Beyond the Numbers Survey Questions**

Question	Question Format
1. I am over 18 years old.	Yes/No
2. I currently reside in the United States or a US territory.	Yes/No
3. Generally speaking, I identify as a "None." That is, I do not identify or affiliate with a particular religion or religious denomination.	Yes/No
4. I understand that the Nones Beyond the Numbers Survey is part of a research project conducted by Elizabeth Drescher, PhD, to explore the spiritual lives of people who selfidentify as religiously unaffiliated. I understand that demographic data from the survey and information from my narrative responses, including direct quotations, may be included in academic papers, general interest articles, books, other publications, and public talks by Dr. Drescher or colleagues. I understand that personally identifying information such as my name and other incidental personal details will be adapted in publications or public talks to maintain my privacy unless I specifically allow this information to be used in research and publication.	Yes/No
5. Reports on demographic surveys typically maintain the full confidentiality of participants. The Nones Beyond the Numbers survey, however, is primarily a narrative survey. In publications and other settings for sharing information from the survey, it can enhance the credibility of the results to share the name and other details of people who are described or quoted. Nonetheless, it is understood that some people who wish to share their perspectives would prefer to retain their privacy and anonymity. Please indicate whether you would like to be IDENTIFIED or ANONYMOUS in reporting from the survey.	Identified/Anonymous
6. To participate in the survey, you must provide your name and email address.	Fill-in blank
7. What is your primary occupation?	Fill-in blank
8. What is your gender?	Multiple Choice
9. What is your age?	Multiple Choice

(continued)

Table A.2 **Continued**

Question	Question Format
10. How would you describe your race or ethnicity?	Multiple Choice
11. How would you describe your sexual identity?	Multiple Choice
12. How would you describe your current primary relationship status?	Multiple Choice
13. Do you have children under the age of 18?	Yes/No
14. What is your educational background?	Multiple Choice
15. In what region of the United States do you currently reside?	Multiple Choice
16. What is your annual household income?	Multiple Choice
17. Nones sometimes also identify in other ways than "None" or "unaffiliated"—for example, "spiritual," "Spiritual but Not Religious," "Agnostic," "Humanist." In what other ways do you further describe your religious or nonreligious outlook or identification?	Open-ended
18. How would you describe your religious or spiritual upbringing?	Open-ended
19. How would you describe your approach to spirituality, religion, selfrealization, and meaningmaking today?	Open-ended
20. How did you come to develop your approach to spirituality, religion, selfrealization, and meaningmaking?	Open-ended
21. What activities do you find most "spiritual," "religious," or otherwise important in your spiritual life?	Open-ended
22. What religious, spiritual, or other leaders or thinkers have influenced your perspective on or practice of religion, spirituality, selfrealization, or meaningmaking in general? Are there particular books, movies, music, art, or other resources that have been useful to you?	Open-ended
23. What rituals, if any, are important to you religiously, spiritually, or in terms of selfrealization and meaningmaking generally?	Open-ended
24. How, if at all, do your religious, spiritual, or other meaningmaking perspectives influence your participation in community, volunteer, or other social action?	Open-ended

(continued)

Table A.2 **Continued**

Question	Question Format
25. If you pray on a regular basis (monthly, weekly, daily), could you describe your prayer practice? What specifically do you do when you pray? How do you think prayer works in your life?	Open-ended
26. If you have children, or if you are a significant adult in the life of a child or children to whom you are not a parent, how do you share your approach to meaningmaking, selfrealization, spirituality, or religion with them?	Open-ended
27. Do you share your religious, spiritual, or other meaningmaking outlook and practices in a community of any sort? If so, how does this community function?	Open-ended
28. How do you make sense of the presence of suffering or evil in the world?	Open-ended
29. What do you think happens when we die?	Open-ended
30. How do you tend to make ethical decisions or choices in your everyday life? What are the guidelines or standards that might guide those choices?	Open-ended
31. How do your religious, spiritual, or other meaningmaking perspectives influence your participation in the American political process?	Open-ended
32. What values or principles, if any, guide your approach to life?	Open-ended
33. How do your religious, spiritual, or other meaningmaking perspectives influence your participation in work or other professional activities?	Open-ended
34. Based on your own experience and observation, what would you say are some of the POSITIVE things that religion and spirituality contribute to the lives of people and the world in general?	Open-ended
35. Based on your own experience and observation, what would you say are some of the NEGATIVE things that religion and spirituality have caused in the lives of people and in the world in general?	Open-ended
36. Would you be willing to participate in a face-to-face or phone interview?	Yes/No

Interviewees and Interview Structure

From the "Nones Beyond the Numbers Survey," I was able to solicit 86 participants in face-to-face, phone, or video-chat interviews. An additional 21 interview subjects were identified through personal and professional contacts. I conducted two test interviews with personal contacts—one a personal friend, another a neighbor I do not know particularly well—in addition to Dorit Brauer, who is featured in the Introduction. My intention had been not to include materials from these interviews, but I found their responses to be sufficiently meaningful that I did include them, though not extensively. Other than these three subjects, I did not know any of the interviewees personally before we talked. All interviewees signed a standard release form, which included the options of being identified by their actual name or a pseudonym. As mentioned in the Introduction, Dorit Brauer was the only subject who asked not to use a pseudonym.

Five initial interview subjects were not included in the final interview population. Two interviewees asked not to be included in the research after the interview was completed. Two interviewees contacted me after the interviews to report that they no longer identified as unaffiliated. Their input influenced my analysis, but they are not counted in the total population for the study. One interviewee arrived at the interview site intoxicated and was, therefore, not included in the study. This left a total interview population of 103.

I mapped interviews to an extensive speaking and conference travel schedule from April 2012 to January 2014 and a personal trip in September 2012 that allowed me to conduct face-to-face interviews in seven of the nine US Census divisions. In addition, I conducted several interviews in the San Francisco Bay Area throughout the project. Interviews were conducted in the cities and states listed in Table A.3. Fourteen subjects outside my travel itinerary, in divisions 6 (East South Central) and 7 (West South Central), were interviewed by phone, Skype, or Google+.

Interviews were conducted as open-ended discussions, but I did use a structured guideline with questions to cover the areas of interest in the project (see Table A.3). Questions were regularly adapted in the course of conversations, and unanticipated questions did often arise. When participants had completed the "Nones Beyond the Numbers Survey," I often drew from their responses to initiate conversation. Interviews were generally conducted in public settings such as libraries, coffee shops, or hotel lounges, but several interviewees invited me to their homes. Where that seemed appropriate and safe, I agreed. For example, I met with Judith Leonard once in a coffee shop, then visited her apartment on a subsequent visit to New York. I met Felicia Oliveria first at her home and then interviewed her in the lounge at the hotel I was staying in later that week.

Table A.3 **Interview Locales and Dates**

Interview City	Month	Year
Chicago, IL	April	2012
Notre Dame, IN	April	2012
San Diego, CA	April	2012
Chicago, IL	June	2012
Champaign, IL	June	2012
Pittsburgh, PA	June	2012
Washington, DC	June	2012
New York, NY	June	2012
San Jose, CA	July	2012
San Francisco, CA	July	2012
Kansas City, KS	July	2012
Mission, KS	July	2012
Wailea, HI	August	2012
Kona, HI	September	2012
New York, NY	September	2012
Minneapolis, MN	November	2012
Chicago, IL	November	2012
Berkeley, CA	January	2013
San Jose, CA	January	2013
Pala Alto, CA	February	2013
Berkeley, CA	March	2013
Las Vegas, NV	March	2013
Philadelphia, PA	April	2013
Princeton, NJ	April	2013
New York, NY	May	2013
Chicago, IL	June	2013
Valparaiso, IN	July	2013
Phoenix, AZ	July	2013
Albuquerque, NM	July	2013
Boston, MA	August	2013
Bar Harbor, ME	August	2013
Augusta, ME	August	2013

(continued)

Table A.3 **Continued**

Interview City	Month	Year
New York, NY	October	2013
Durham, NC	October	2013
New York, NY	November	2013
San Jose, CA	November	2013
Cleveland, OH	January	2014
Boston, MA	January	2014

I visited Corrie Milliman's studio and Kenny Mahoe's backyard meditation space. Other interviews were conducted in the homes of mutual contacts. Not all of the interviews were conducted in the hometown or city of the interviewee.

Interview Process

In my work as a religion writer, I have frequently interviewed people, often extensively. However, journalistic interviews, especially when one is writing against a deadline, are generally rather narrowly focused, aimed at highlighting a topic, idea, or concern that the writer, rather than the interviewee, already has in mind. For the interviews for *Choosing Our Religion*, however, I hoped to encourage more open, free-flowing conversations that would invite the exploration of areas of Nones' spiritual lives that had been largely unexplored, often even by the interviewee. Because I am not an anthropologist, psychologist, or sociologist with extensive training in qualitative interviewing practices, in order to ensure that my conversations with Nones were as open to Nones' own understandings of what counted as "important" or "meaningful" topics or concerns, I began my research by reviewing qualitative research methodologies generally and approaches to narrative inquiry in particular. My research was guided in this regard extensively by John W. Creswell's *Qualitative Inquiry and Research Design: Choosing among Five Approaches* (2012) and the essays in D. Jean Clandinin's *Handbook of Narrative Inquiry: Mapping a Methodology* (2007), especially "Talking to Learn: The Critical Role of Conversation in Narrative Inquiry" by Sandra Hollingsworth and Mary Dybdhal. This research enabled me to situate my project methodologically at the intersection of narrative inquiry and ethnography, setting my conversations with Nones as individual biographical stories that, collectively, could illustrate important religious, spiritual, and ethical themes in the context of the wider American religious and spiritual landscape. This narrative-ethnographic approach also allowed me to make the best use of my experience with literary-critical and social-historical analyses of narrative texts. The question guide I developed for the interviews is shown in Table A.4.

As a starting point for conversation with participants in the project, I attempted to establish something of a rapport with interviewees via email, and in many cases also through phone calls, during which I described the work I was doing and discussed the type of conversation I hoped we might have. In addition, I asked interviewees how they had found the "Spiritual Practices Survey" or the "Nones Beyond the Numbers Survey." Here, my initial use of my own personal and professional networks to test the first survey proved particularly helpful because it was very often the case that the survey had been shared by someone one or two removes from me. For instance, almost all of the college-aged people who participated in the project had been directed to one or another of the surveys by parents or family friends who knew (and sometimes were concerned about) the person's unaffiliated status. Likewise, because I had reached out early in the process to several African American and Latina/o friends and

Table A.4 **Narrative Interview Guiding Questions**

Category	Conversation Prompts
A. Spiritual Identity	A1. Tell me about yourself a little. How would you describe yourself spiritually?
	A2. You indicated in the survey that you are a [None, Agnostic, Atheist, SBNR, etc.]. What does that mean to you? How does that play out for you spiritually?
	A3. How would you respond to someone who asked you what your religion is?
	A4. How important is your spirituality as a part of your life overall?
	A5. What impact does it have to you to think of yourself as a [None, Agnostic, Atheist, SBNR, etc.]? How does that make a difference in your life?
B. Religious Background	B1. You said in the survey responses that you grew up as a [religious group]. What was that like for you? Were you active in that religion?
	B2. Are both of your parents from the same religion?
	B3. Are your siblings religious or spiritual?
	B4. How does that background figure into your spiritual life now?

(continued)

Table A.4 **Continued**

Category	Conversation Prompts
C. Becoming None	C1. How did you come to approach your spirituality in the way you do now?
	C2. What were some of milestones on your spiritual journey? Were there particular experiences that influenced your development as a [None, Agnostic, Atheist, SBNR, etc.]?
	C3. Are there particular people in your life who influenced your development as a [None, Agnostic, Atheist, SBNR, etc.]?
	C4. Are there particular books, movies, classes, that influenced your development as a [None, Agnostic, Atheist, SBNR, etc.]?
D. Spiritual Practices	D1. Are there particular activities or routines that are important in your spiritual life? Do you do these things alone or with others?
	D2. Are there particular places that are important in your spiritual life? How do you engage in these places spiritually? Do you go there on your own or with others?
	D3. Are there particular objects—icons, jewelry, clothing, etc.—that are important in your spiritual life? Why are these important?
	D4. Are there particular rituals that are important in your spiritual life? Do you do these things alone or with others?
E. People	E1. Is your family a part of your spirituality? How so? What impact does this have on your spiritual life?
	E2. Do you share your spirituality with friends? How so? What impact does this have on your spiritual life?
	E3. Do you share your spirituality at work? How so? What impact does this have on your spiritual life?
	E4. Are you part of what you would describe as a spiritual community of any sort?
	E5. What other people are important in your spiritual life? How so?
F. Prayer	F1. Do you pray?
	F2. What are the times or circumstances when you pray? What prompts you to pray?
	F3. How do you pray? What do you do? Where?
	F4. Do you expect any particular effect or result when you pray?
	F5. Have you experienced any particular effect or result when you pray?
	F6. Do you pray with others?

(continued)

Table A.4 **Continued**

Category	Conversation Prompts
G. Ethics and Morals	G1. How do you think your approach to spirituality factors into your morality?
	G2. What would you say are the most important moral or ethical values you hold?
	G3. Is there anything in particular that guides your ethical decision-making or choices?
	G4. How does your spirituality influence things like your political views, how you vote in elections, or participate in political activities?
	G5. How does your spirituality influence the way you conduct yourself professionally in your work?
	G5. How does your spiritual outlook help you to teach your children about morals?
H. Other	H1. Is there anything about your spirituality that you think it's difficult to explain or for others to understand?
	H2. Do you ever experience interpersonal tension or conflict because of your approach to spirituality and religion? How do you deal with that?
	H3. Is there anything else that you think is important in your spiritual life that you would want to share with me?
	H4. Is there anything you would like to ask me about the *Choosing Our Religion* project?

colleagues, the project has greater ethnic diversity than is often the case in such studies. As importantly, however, for the conversations I hoped would emerge, these initial connections often gave the subject a friend, colleague, or acquaintance in common, which warmed our interaction beyond what more clinical approaches might allow.

To further reduce what might be perceived as a clinical nature in the interviews, which I believed would result in more stilted, less richly narrative responses, I did not conduct extensive personal histories in the interviews themselves. Rather, I collected personal history information from participants' survey responses, asked clarifying questions via email, and drew on this background in the conversations that followed. For example, one of the questions I regularly drew from was a survey question about religious upbringing ("What was your religious identification or affiliation growing up?") in order to explore this background further and develop a fuller family history. Drawing upon this survey information, I would ask, "You indicated in the survey that you grew up as a Catholic. What was that like?" Such questions would very often invite responses that identified family configurations (traditional two-parent household, divorced parents, number of siblings, etc.), allowing nuancing of what "growing up Catholic" meant for a particular person (e.g., whether the family was particularly devoted and involved in the church or more nominally Catholic), and identifying important personal and spiritual themes that might be revisited later in the conversation. This approach generally allowed for the interviews to take the shape of conversations between friends, acquaintances more than academic inquiries in which the interviewee is subject to the researcher's interests and questions.

The length of the interviews varied, lasting generally between two and four hours. Interviews were recorded, and I took notes throughout the interview process that generally focused on themes that emerged from the conversation, specific quotes that seemed important, and other areas for exploration later in the interview or in a follow-up email. After each interview, it was my practice to set aside my notes and write a reflection on what I had heard and observed, including what stood out generally, questions the conversation raised about the spiritualities of Nones, what themes seemed important, and any other elements of the conversation that struck me as significant. I sent each participant a follow-up email thanking them for their time, asking them if I might email them with follow-up questions, and inviting them to email me if they felt there was anything else they thought I should know about their spiritual lives. All but nine of the participants emailed me, many several times, with additional reflections, information on resources that inform and enrich their spirituality, invitations to spiritual events they were planning to attend or programs from events they had attended, contact information on other Nones they thought I might want to interview, and personal notes such as birth and graduation announcements. Though I had not initially planned to do so, I met face to face additionally with 18 of the participants and had extensive follow-up phone conversations with three.

Limitations

No study is perfect, of course, and this one is not without limitations. For instance, although I knew only three of the interviewees before the interviews, as noted, the majority of them did come to me via my personal and professional networks. While this had certain relational advantages that enriched the quality of our conversations, it nonetheless meant that the participants were less diverse than would likely have been the case with a more randomized study, especially with regard to educational attainment and socioeconomic background. The group as a whole was, for instance, more white (73%) than is the US population (66%), and all of the participants were middle class or upper-middle class.

Because the interviews were conducted in cities, fewer Nones from smaller towns and rural areas were included in the study. Some of the participants from smaller towns did travel to cities in which I was interviewing for our conversations. And, I conducted a phone and a video chat interview with participants from rural areas. But the population remains primarily urban or suburban. My hope is that future studies will explore rural religiosity and spirituality, among both the affiliated and the unaffiliated. The lives of non-white, rural, and economically disadvantaged people certainly deserve much more attention than they have been afforded by either academic or mass market researchers and writers, no less in the study of religion and spirituality than in other fields.

In terms of religious and spiritual outlooks, because the project began with questions about the *spiritual lives* of the religiously unaffiliated, the pool of participants naturally included only people who felt such questions were relevant to them. A portion of Nones is not just religiously unaffiliated but also religiously indifferent. Many Nones who talked with me in other contexts of my life—at dinner parties, on Twitter, in airports—simply had no interest in spirituality or religion and would not have found my project worthwhile. As a non-religious man sitting next to me on a plane put it when he found out what I was researching, "I don't mean to sound rude, but, that sounds like a waste of a perfectly good PhD. Maybe if we stopped studying religion it would just dry up and go away. Then smart people like you could get to work on ending world hunger or saving the environment." Ouch. Obviously, such perspectives are not reflected in the book, but they do seem worth further study.

Likewise, with regard to the interviews themselves, the project has the limitation of directing participants' stories specifically toward spiritual and religious activities, beliefs, themes, and questions. Rather that asking people to tell me about their lives and then looking for evidence of the spiritual in those narratives (the approach taken, for example, by Nancy Ammerman in *Sacred Stories, Spiritual Tribes*), I asked questions like "How would you describe yourself spiritually?" and "Can you describe some of the things you do that you think of as 'spiritual'?" While my more pointed questions did focus the responses of participants, it is certainly the case—as we saw in the Chapter 5, on prayer—that my questions often prompted participants to consider as spiritual activities that they might not initially have thought of as such. I would suggest that such invitations to spiritual reflection have the benefit, first, that a researcher does not read an activity as spiritual when the person doing it would not think so herself. For example, many people do yoga or meditation without consideration of the spiritual and religious histories and meanings of these practices. Second, it is valuable to understand what parts of a life are marked by people as "spiritual," "religious," or "moral" when they do have the opportunity to reflect. This was certainly part of the elevation of relationships and practices of everyday life that would not often be marked by researchers as "spiritual" that we saw in Chapter 4. Such questions empower people not merely to report their own spiritual perspectives, but to approach sharing the story of the self as a spiritual practice in itself. In the end, I see such thematically directed approaches as important counterparts to more generalized qualitative research.

Appendix B

CHARACTERISTICS OF INTERVIEW SUBJECTS

Table B.1 **Age Distribution of Unaffiliated by Percentage**

	18–29	30–49	50–64	65+
US Population[1]	22%	35%	26%	18%
Pew Population[2]	35%	37%	21%	8%
Study Population[3]	36%	44%	13%	8%
$n = 103$	$n = 37$	$n = 45$	$n = 13$	$n = 8$

1. Source: US Census Bureau, Current Population Survey, 2012, available online at http://factfinder2.census.gov.
2. Source: Pew Forum on Religion & Public Life, "America's Changing Religious Landscape: Christians Decline Sharply as Share of Population: Unaffiliated and Other Faiths Continue to Grow," May 12, 2015.
3. Percentages may not add to 100 due to rounding.

Table B.2 **Gender Distribution of Unaffiliated by Percentage**

	Female	Male
US Population	52%	48%
Pew Population	44%	56%
Study Population	42%	58%
$n = 103$	$n = 44$	$n = 59$

Table B.3 **Racial and Ethnic Distribution of Unaffiliated by Percentage**

	White	Black	Hispanic	Asian	Mixed/ Other[4]
US Population	66%	11%	15%	5%	2%
Pew Population	71%	9%	11%	4%	4%
Study Population	73%	8%	9%	7%	3%
n = 103	n = 76	n = 8	n = 9	n = 7	n = 3

4. Pew tracks only "other." US Census tracks "mixed." Study data tracked "mixed" or "other."

B.4 Household Configuration

Table B.4 **Household Configuration**

	Single	Domestic Partner	Married	Children at Home	Children Not at Home	Pets at Home[5]
US Population	37.1%	5.4%	49.6%	27.3%	NA	61%
Study Population n = 103	38%	11%	51%	35%	22%	53%

5. Source: The Humane Society of the United States, "Pets by the Numbers" (January 30, 2014), available online at www.humanesociety.org/issues/pet_overpopulation/facts/pet_ownership_statistics.html.

B.5 Geographic Distribution of Unaffiliated by Percentage

Interviewees were solicited in each of the nine US Census divisions within each of the regions noted here. The finer geographical detail at the division levels reveals variations in the regional data that are worth noting. For example, the bulk of the interview participants in the South were from Division 5 (South Atlantic) and Division 7 (West South Central). In the former case, more than a third of the subjects were from the Washington, D.C. metropolitan area. In the latter case, all but two interviewees were from Texas. Only one interviewee was from Division 6 (East South Central). Likewise, three-quarters of those

Table B.5 **Geographic Distribution**

	Northeast	*Midwest*	*South*	*West*
US Population	18%	22%	37%	23%
Pew Population	20%	22%	28%	30%
Study Population	22%	21%	25%	30%
n = 103	*n* = 24	*n* = 22	*n* = 26	*n* = 31

interviewed from the West were from Division 9 (Pacific). Though there was variation across Mountain and Pacific states, a third of the interviewees from the West reside in California.

As explained in Appendix A, interviews were generally conducted face to face in the context of travel for speaking engagements or professional meetings in seven of the nine US Census divisions. However, in order to ensure representation across all nine US Census divisions, 14 subjects outside my travel itinerary, who lived in the remaining two divisions, were interviewed by phone, Skype, or Google+.

B.6.1 Religious/Spiritual Self-Identification of Interview Subjects

Table B.6.1 shows the primary religious identifications for the subjects of the *Choosing Our Religion* project. Subjects were invited in the course of interviews to describe their own religious or spiritual identity category, which invited a much wider range of self-descriptions than those shown here. During our conversations, interviewees were asked a version of one or more of the following questions in an attempt to focus religious identification without closing down other possibilities:

When someone asks "what is your religion?" what are you most likely to say?

You indicated in the "Nones Beyond the Numbers Survey" that you would describe yourself as [None, Agnostic, Spiritual-But-Not-Religious, etc.]. Does that still seem to be the best description?

To the extent that your religious or spiritual outlook can be labeled, would that description be the most accurate one?

Table B.6.1 **Religious/Spiritual Self-Identification**

Self-Description	Percentage n = 103
Agnostic	29.1%
	n = 30
Atheist	6.8%
	n = 7
Humanist	8.7%
	n = 9
Jesus Follower	3.9%
	n = 4
Neopagan	0.97%
	n = 1
None	22.3%
	n = 23
Secular	2.9%
	n = 3
Secular Humanist	1.9%
	n = 2
Spiritual-But-Not-Religious	7.8%
	n = 8
Spiritual	11.7%
	n = 13
Spiritual Humanist	0.97%
	n = 1
Strong Agnostic	0.97%
	n = 1
Wiccan	0.97%
	n = 1

B.6.2 Primary Religious Upbringing of Interview Subjects Compared to US Population

Because the majority of the people interviewed for *Choosing Our Religion* were raised with parents from different religious backgrounds (72%), and a large plurality likewise were raised in families that changed religious affiliation during the subjects' childhood (43%), it is difficult to define "religious upbringing" of the interviewees with precision. However, in attempt to focus the data, interview subjects were often asked versions of the following questions about their religious upbringing:

Were your parents members of a particular religious group? If so, what religion(s)?

Would you say that one of these traditions was more influential in your family?

Were you raised in any particular religious tradition? If so, which one?

What would you describe as the primary religious tradition in which you and your family participated when you were growing up?

As appropriate, participants were also asked the following:

You mentioned that your parents were members of [religious group] and that you attended services at [religious group] most often. Would it be accurate to say that your religious upbringing was *primarily* in the [religious group] tradition?

Based on these questions, Table B.6.2 reflects the range of primary religious affiliations of interviewees before age 18. The percentage of interviewees in each religious grouping is compared to the percentage in that group nationally. It is important to note that the national percentages are for 2012. Because the ages of the interviewees ranged from 18 to 82, however, appropriate comparative data would have been for the period when each interviewee was under age 18. For interviewees over age 40, it can fairly be assumed that participation in the religious group in which they were raised was greater than it is today.

Table B.6.2 **Primary Religious Upbringing**

Religious Group	Percentage n = 103	General US Population Percentage[6]
American Baptist	4.9% n = 5	1.2%
Atheist	0.97% n = 1	1.6%
Buddhist	0.97% n = 1	0.7%
Catholic	14.6% n = 15	22%
Christian Science	0.97% n = 1	N/A
Episcopalian	11.7% n = 12	1.0%

(continued)

Table B.6.2 **Continued**

Religious Group	Percentage *n = 103*	General US Population Percentage[6]
Evangelical Protestant[7]	18.4% *n = 19*	30.5%
Free Methodist	0.97% *n = 1*	0.3%
Jehovah's Witness	1.9% *n = 2*	0.7%
Jewish	4.9% *n = 5*	1.7%
Lutheran (ELCA)	6.8% *n = 7*	4.6%
Mar Thoma	0.97% *n = 1*	N/A
Methodist (UMC)	7.8% *n = 8*	5.1%
Mormon (LDS)	1.9% *n = 2*	2.0%
None / No Religion	2.9% *n = 3*	19.6%
Pentecostal	1.9% *n = 2*	4.4%
Presbyterian (PCUSA)	4.9% *n = 5*	1.1%
Quaker	0.97% *n = 1*	<0.3%
Seventh-Day Adventist	0.97% *n = 1*	0.5%
Southern Baptist	0.97% *n = 1*	6.7%
Unitarian Universalist	1.9% *n = 2*	0.5%
United Church of Christ	7.8% *n = 8*	0.8%

6. Sources: Pew Forum on Religion in Public Life, "2008 U.S. Religious Landscape Survey" (Washington, DC: February 2008); Pew, "Nones on the Rise;" and Barry A. Kosmin and Ariela Keysar, "American Religious Identification Survey [ARIS 2008]" (Hartford, CT: Trinity College, March 2009).

7. Includes Nondenominational Protestant.

NOTES

Introduction

1. An extensive literature on the spirituality of labyrinths has developed, much of it taking the form of spiritual pilgrimage memoirs not unlike that written by Brauer. See, for example, Gernot Candolini, *Labyrinths: Walking Toward the Center* (New York: Crossroad Publishing, 2003). Likewise, many guides to prayer and walking meditation on labyrinths and on facilitating labyrinth-centered spiritual and healing practices have also been produced. See, for example, Lauren Artress, *Walking the Sacred Path: Rediscovering the Labyrinth as a Spiritual Tool* (New York: Penguin, 1995, 2006), and Melissa Gayle West, *Exploring the Labyrinth: A Guide for Healing and Spiritual Growth* (New York: Broadway Books, 2000). Information on training in labyrinth construction and facilitation, as well as a database of labyrinths across the world, can be found through the Veriditas nonprofit founded by modern American labyrinth spirituality pioneer Lauren Artress at http://www.veriditas.org.

2. Dorit Brauer, *Girls Don't Ride Motorbikes: A Spiritual Adventure into Life's Labyrinth* (2012).

3. As a matter both of clarity and respect, I capitalize the words "None" and "Nones" throughout. Likewise, when they appear as personal spiritual or philosophical descriptions of subjects of my study, I capitalize words such as "Agnostic," "Atheist," "Humanist," "Pagan," and so on.

4. Reflexology is a pressure point therapy focused on the feet. See Beryl Crane, *The Complete Illustrated Guide to Reflexology: Massage Your Way to Health and Well-being* (London: HarperCollins, 2010).

5. Brauer is certified in "family constellations therapy," a family therapy developed by German psychotherapist Bert Hellinger to treat transgenerational traumas. See Hunter Beaumont, *Toward a Spiritual Psychotherapy: Soul as a Dimension of Experience* (Berkeley, CA: North Atlantic Books, 2008).

6. In his study of Baby Boomer spirituality, *A Generation of Seekers: The Spiritual Journeys of the Baby Boom Generation* (San Francisco: HarperSanFrancisco, 1993), Wade Clark Roof described "seekers" as those adults who "do more than just drop out of churches and synagogues; they turn to serious metaphysical quests on their own in hopes of finding a more fulfilling way of believing and living" (79).

7. Famously, Robert Bellah et al. described, in *Habits of the Heart: Individualism and Commitment in American Life* (Los Angeles: University of California Press, [1985] 1996), "Sheilaism," the apparently self-referential, self-authorized "radically individualistic religion" of a young nurse, Sheila Larson (235). The demeaning interpretation by Bellah and colleagues of Sheila's spiritual experience and self-understanding has been critiqued by a number of scholars since it first appeared, but the idea of those not affiliated with traditional religions as having constructed a narcissistic, non-committal, largely therapeutic religiosity persists in the popular culture, religious institutions, and academe. For a recent critique see Meredith B. McGuire,

Lived Religion: Faith and Practice in Everyday Life (New York: Oxford University Press, 2008), 151–154.

8. Courtney Bender, in *The New Metaphysicals: Spirituality and the American Religious Imagination* (Chicago: University of Chicago Press, 2010), discusses the ways in which practitioners of "alternative spiritualities" in Cambridge, Massachusetts claim historical lineage and authority through recourse to both conventional religious and medical traditions, including locating practices in sites (churches, clinics) associated with these fields.

9. Dorit Brauer, Facebook page, accessed March 1, 2013.

10. Scholarship on this historical sweep is noted throughout the book. A selection of prominent works include: Catherine L. Albanese, *A Republic of Mind and Spirit: A Cultural History of American Metaphysical Religion* (New Haven, CT: Yale University Press, 2007); Jon Butler, *Awash in a Sea of Faith: The Christianizing of the American People* (Cambridge, MA: Harvard University Press, 1990); Robert C. Fuller, *Spiritual But Not Religious: Understanding Unchurched America* (New York: Oxford University Press, 2001); Lee Gilmore, *Theater in a Crowded Fire: Ritual and Spirituality at Burning Man* (Berkeley: University of California Press, 2010); David A. Hollinger, "After Cloven Tongues of Fire: Ecumenical Protestantism and the Modern American Encounter with Diversity," *The Journal of American History* (June 2011): 21–48; Susan Jacoby, *Freethinkers: A History of American Secularism* (New York: Metropolitan Books, 2005); Jeffrey J. Kripal, *Esalen: America and the Religion of No Religion* (Chicago: University of Chicago Press, 2007); Katherine Lofton, *Oprah: The Gospel of an Icon* (Berkeley: University of California Press, 2011); Leigh Eric Schmidt, *Restless Souls: The Making of American Spirituality* (Berkeley and Los Angeles: University of California Press [2005] 2012); and Robert Wuthnow, *After the Baby Boomers: How Twenty- and Thirty-Somethings Are Shaping the Future of American Religion* (Princeton, NJ: Princeton University Press, 2007).

11. On the historical development and representation of the "spiritual-but-not-religious" label in the American news media, see Elizabeth Drescher, "News Coverage of the Spiritual-But-Not-Religious," *Oxford Handbook of Religion and the News Media*, edited by Diane Winston (New York: Oxford University Press, 2014).

12. The tradition of demeaning the religiously unaffiliated, and those who self-identify as Spiritual-But-Not-Religious in particular, has moved vibrantly into present-day popular and academic commentary. For a recent example in popular media, see Lillian Daniel, "Spiritual But Not Religious? Please Stop Boring Me," *Huffington Post* (September 13, 2011), available online at http://www.huffingtonpost.com/lillian-daniel/spiritual-but-not-religio_b_959216.html. For a more nuanced, but nonetheless negative, academic treatment, see Linda A. Mercadante, *Belief Without Borders: Inside the Minds of the Spiritual But Not Religious* (New York: Oxford University Press, 2014), chapter 9.

13. Vernon, Glenn M. 1968. "The Religious 'Nones': A Neglected Category," *Journal for the Scientific Study of Religion* 7, no. 2, cited in Pew Forum on Religion & Public Life, "Nones on the Rise: One-in-Five Adults Have No Religious Affiliation," available online at http://www.pewforum.org/files/2012/10/NonesOnTheRise-full.pdf.

14. On this, see Elizabeth Drescher, "Nones in the News: Mass Media Explorations of the Religiously Unaffiliated," in *The Oxford Handbook of Religion and the American News Media*, edited by Diane Winston (Oxford and New York: Oxford University Press, 2014).

15. Pew Forum on Religion & Public Life, "2008 U.S. Religious Landscape Survey" (Washington, DC: February 2008), and Barry A. Kosmin and Ariela Keysar, "American Religious Identification Survey [ARIS 2008]" (Hartford, CT: Trinity College, March 2009).

16. Pew Forum on Religion & Public Life, "Nones on the Rise."

17. Pew Research Center, "America's Changing Religious Landscape: Christians Decline Sharply as Share of Population; Unaffiliated and Other Faiths Continue to Grow" (Washington, DC: May 12, 2015), 4.

18. Ibid., 70.

19. Pew Research Center, "The Future of World Religions: Population Growth Projections, 2010–2050: Why Muslims Are Rising Fastest and the Unaffiliated Are Shrinking as a Share of the World's Population" (Washington, DC: April 2, 2015), 158. The initial release of this data occurred as I was completing the book. It did not include data on religious outlooks and other

elements of religious and spiritual practice that were part of the 2012 "Nones on the Rise" report. I have integrated the data from the 2015 report to the extent possible throughout, but I rely on the 2012 report data extensively throughout for more nuanced factors in religion and spirituality among the unaffiliated and affiliated.

20. The often ill-defined concept of a social "tribe" was popularized by Ethan Watters in *Urban Tribes: Are Friends the New Family?* (New York: Bloomsbury, 2003). Watters associated the term with young, never-married adults who form networks of friends, some of whom may live together, who provide companionship and some level of mutual caretaking. (The television shows *Friends* and *Sex in the City* modeled this for a generation.) In Watters's usage, tribes break up, or are at least significantly reconfigured, by marriage and geographical career changes. The paradox of the intimacy of the young adult tribes and their malleable or ultimately expendable nature are missed in many appropriations of the term (as with Nancy Ammerman's undefined use in *Spiritual Stories, Sacred Tribes*, where a tribe as a less formal affiliational cluster is presented as self-evident). Generally, however, "tribe" is applied to a variety of youth and young adult subcultures characterized by a certain hybridity of identities and relationships, the fluidity of social networks, and a nomadic quality associated with frequent career changes in contemporary culture, especially, but not exclusively, among young people. On this, see Rupert Weinzierl and David Muggleton, "Chapter 1: What Is 'Post-Subcultural Studies' Anyway?" in *The Post-Subcultures Reader*, ed. David Muggleton and Rupert Weinzierl (Oxford: Berg, 2003). For a cogent discussion of Christian ministry to young adult "tribes," see Carol Howard Merritt, *Tribal Church: Ministering to the Mission Generation* (Herdon, VA: Alban Institute, 2007).

21. My research methodology, including the "Nones Beyond the Numbers" online narrative survey, focus groups, and an earlier test survey on spiritually meaningful practices, is discussed in Appendix A. Appendix B provides a demographic summary of subjects of extended interviews.

22. Courtney Bender, *Heaven's Kitchen: Lived Religion at God's Love We Deliver* (Chicago and London: University of Chicago Press, 2003), 91, 108–112, discusses how "double-voiced religious talk" allows individuals to express religious and spiritual ideas while also acting on "good manners," allowing participants in a conversation to test whether "faith talk [is] possible and imagine ways to proceed toward such discussion," or, by extension, not to.

23. Pew, "Nones on the Rise," 16, and Pew, "2008 U.S. Religious Landscape Survey," 29. The extent to which Nones emerge from Christian backgrounds also counts for the more extensive focus in the book on unaffiliated practice in relation to institutional Christian practice.

24. See, for example, David Kinnaman and Gabe Lyons, *UnChristian: What a New Generation Really Thinks about Christianity . . . And Why It Matters* (Grand Rapids, MI: Bakers Books, 2007); Robin R. Meyers, *Saving Jesus from the Church: How to Stop Worshiping Christ and Start Following Jesus* (New York: HarperCollins, 2009); Drew Dyke, *Generation Ex-Christian: Why Young Adults are Leaving the Faith . . . And How to Bring Them Back* (Chicago, IL: Moody Publishers, 2010); David Kinnaman, *You Lost Me: Why Young Christians Are Leaving Church, and Rethinking Faith* (Grand Rapids, MI: Baker Books, 2011); Diana Butler Bass, *Christianity after Religion: The End of the Church and the Birth of a New Spiritual Awakening* (San Francisco: HarperOne, 2012); and Francis Spufford, *Unapologetic: Why, Despite Everything, Christianity Can Still Make Surprising Emotional Sense* (New York: HarperCollins, 2013).

25. See also, Pew Forum on Religion & Public Life, "Many Americans Mix Multiple Faiths: Eastern, New Age Beliefs Widespread" (Washington, DC: December 2009), available online at http://www.pewforum.org/files/2009/12/multiplefaiths.pdf.

26. Other than Dorit Brauer, who preferred her full name, all interview participants are identified by a pseudonym. Other details, aside from those that might specifically identify the subject, are generally accurate, though they may have been adapted slightly to preserve anonymity. The first reference to a particular subject will include her or his pseudonym, age, home location, and self-described religious or spiritual designation. Anonymous subjects will be referred to by their first name in order to distinguish between subjects for whom a pseudonym is used and others named in the book. Other details, such as ethnicity and sociocultural background, are woven through the discussion of particular subjects. A table of subject characteristics (age, gender, race, location, religious or spiritual self-identification) is found in Appendix B.

27. Barbara Calamari and Sandra DiPasqua, *Holy Cards* (New York: Abrams, 2004, 2012).
28. Robert A. Orsi, *Between Heaven and Earth: The Religious Worlds People Make and the Scholars Who Study Them* (Princeton, NJ: Princeton University Press, 2007), 73.
29. Donald D. Hall, "Introduction" to *Lived Religion in America: Toward a History of Practice*, edited by Donald D. Hall (Princeton, NJ: Princeton University Press, 1997), vii–xiii, describes the emergence of the term "lived religion" in the American academic lexicon from the French field of sociology of religion. Nancy Ammerman, ed., *Everyday Religion: Observing Modern Religion Lives* (Oxford and New York: Oxford University Press, 2007), prefers the term "everyday religion," while Meredith B. McGuire, *Lived Religion*, adds the more awkward "religion-as-lived" to the lexicon. I discuss this terminology in relation to "spirituality" in the Chapter 1.
30. On this, see Pew Research Center, "Religion and Electronic Media: One-in-Five Americans Share Their Faith Online" (Washington, DC: November 6, 2014).
31. Elizabeth Drescher, "Five Must-Reads on Nones: A Tipping Point in American Spirituality and Religion," *Religion Dispatches* (December 24, 2012), available online at http://www.religiondispatches.org/ archive/atheologies/6657/five_must_reads_on_the__nones__a_tipping_point_in_american_religion_and_spirituality/.
32. Elizabeth Drescher, "Quitting Religion But Not the Practice of Prayer," *Religion Dispatches* (March 17, 2013), available online at http://www.religiondispatches.org/archive/atheologies/6973/quitting_religion__but_not_the_ practice_of_prayer/, and Elizabeth Drescher, "What Do the Religiously Unaffiliated Pray For?" *Washington Post* (May 2, 2013), available online at http://www.faithstreet.com/onfaith/2013/05/02/what-the-nones-teach-us-on-the-national-day-of-prayer. For one example of an angry response to this perspective, see my blog post "I Am a Disgrace to Journalism (Or Maybe Not)," *The In Between Blog* (June 21, 2013), http://elizabethdrescher.com/2013/06/.
33. On this, see also Courtney Bender and Omar McRoberts, "Mapping a Field: Why and How to Study Spirituality," Working Group on Spirituality, Political Engagement, and Public Life (New York: Social Science Research Council, October 2012), 5–6.
34. Grace Davie, *Religion in Britain since 1945: Believing without Belonging* (Malden, MA: Blackwell, 1997), has been particularly influential in the development of theories that separate believing, belonging, and behaving. This so-called "separation theory" has shaped much of the discussion of churchgoing and the lack thereof in the United States. See, for example, Stuart Murray, "Church after Christendom: Believing/Belonging/Behaving," chapter 1 of *Church after Christendom* (Waynesboro, GA: Paternoster Press, 2004) and the adaptation in Diana Butler Bass, *Christianity after Religion*.
35. Here, I draw most directly from the language of Nones themselves, but I have also heard their descriptions to a certain extent through the work of Courtney Bender in *The New Metaphysicals*, which focuses on "*institutions* (fields of production), *language* (discourse), and the practices of *bodies, times, and spaces*" as well as the role of "shamans" and "mystics" in the spiritual lives of metaphysical practitioners in Cambridge, Massachusetts (19; emphasis in the original).

Chapter 1

1. Pew, "2008 U.S. Religious Landscape Survey," 31; Pew, "Nones on the Rise," 16.
2. The term "Evangelical Protestant" is somewhat difficult to define precisely, but it is generally applied to those Christian denominations with more conservative ideologies, including "fundamentalist" beliefs in (1) biblical literalism and inerrancy, (2) the birth of Jesus by the Virgin Mary, (3) the crucifixion of Jesus Christ as atonement for the sins of humankind, (4) the literal, bodily resurrection of Jesus, and (5) the historical reality of the miracles performed by Jesus as described in the Christian gospels. This includes many nondenominational Protestant groups as well as conservative Assemblies of God, African Methodist Episcopal, Free Methodist, Holiness, Presbyterian Church in America, Missouri Synod Lutheran, Southern Baptist, and a number of other denominations. Together, people exiting churches in the wider Evangelical tradition account for the majority of Nones. For a more nuanced discussion of

the strains of Evangelical Protestantism in America, see Randall Balmer and Lauren Winner, *Protestantism in America* (New York: Columbia University Press, 2002), 70–83.

3. Pew, "America's Changing Religious Landscape," 3. Data on Nones from the General Social Survey are reported in Michael Hout et al., "More Americans Have No Religious Preference: Key Findings from the 2012 General Social Survey," Institute for the Study of Societal Issues, University of California, Berkeley (March 7, 2013), available online at http://issi.berkeley.edu/sites/default/files/ shared/docs/Hout%20et%20al_No%20Relig%20 Pref%202012_Release%20Mar%202013.pdf. Information about the General Social Survey itself is available online at http://www3.norc.org/GSS+Website/About+GSS/. It is worth noting that 2013 polling from Gallup, considered somewhat less reliable, shows a slightly smaller percentage of Nones in the US population, 15% against the 20% found by Pew and the GSS in 2012. Gallup reporting on religious affiliation since 1948 is available online at http://www.gallup.com/poll/1690/religion.aspx.

4. See Patricia O'Connell Killen and Mark Silk, eds., *Religion and Public Life in the Pacific Northwest: The None Zone* (Lanham, MD: Rowan & Littlefield, 2004).

5. Hout et al., "More Americans Have No Religious Preference," 11. GSS uses five geographic regions (Northeastern, Midwestern, Southern, Mountain, and Pacific), whereas Pew uses four (Northeast, Midwest, South, and West) so the data sets are not entirely comparable with regard to regional changes.

6. "America's Changing Religious Landscape," Appendix D, "Race by Religious Tradition."

7. Ibid. and Pew, "Nones on the Rise," 21. However, the Pew report, which compares 2007 and 2012 data, shows no growth among Hispanics. The GSS data categorizes race differently, showing "Whites," "African Americans," and "Mexican Americans." In the latter category, which may or may not include other Latina/o Americans, there was an a nearly 10% increase in unaffiliation between 1990 and 2012.

8. Pew, "Nones on the Rise," 58. The most recent Pew data became available too late in my research to allow exploration with the Nones I interviewed or in-depth analysis. However, the increase in unaffiliation among lower income groups certainly merits attention. This is especially the case given the nearly 20% increase in Nones earning less than $30,000 a year who indicated that religion is "important"—from 40% in 2007 to 47% in 2014. I cannot help but wonder to what extent turbulent economic conditions in the same period, often requiring multiple jobs with hours that extend through traditional churchgoing times and wage depression that might limit financial giving, may have forced unaffiliation on low-income workers who would otherwise have participated in a religious community.

9. See, for example, Religion & Ethics Newsweekly, "None of the Above: The Rise of the Religiously Unaffiliated" (October 9, 2012), available online at http://video.pbs.org/video/2288849147/; Heidi Glenn, "Losing Our Religion: The Growth of the 'Nones,'" *The Two-Way*, National Public Radio (January 13, 2013), http://www.npr.org/blogs/thetwo-way/2013/01/14/169164840/losing-our-religion-the-growth-of-the-nones, accessed January 23, 2013; Jesse J. Holland, "Many Millennials are Skipping Church, Marriage and Political Affiliations, Study Finds," PBS Newshour (March 17, 2014), http://www.pbs.org/newshour/rundown/millennials-skipping-church-marriage-political-affilliations-study-finds/, accessed March 18, 2014; Trent Crabtree, "Survey Finds Millennials Are Less Religious Than Previous Generations," *USA Today* (May 29, 2015), http://college.usatoday.com/2015/05/29/survey-finds-millennials-are-less-religious-than-previous-generations/, accessed May 30, 2015; Katherine Foley, "Millennials Are Losing Their Religion—and Social Media Might Explain Why," *Quartz* (June 2, 2015), http://qz.com/416973/social-media-may-be-helping-millennials-lose-their-religion/, accessed June 2, 2015.

10. The Pew, "Nones on the Rise" report (p. 18) showed rates of unaffiliation by age cluster as follows: age 18–29: 32%; age 30–49: 21%; age 50–64: 15%; age 65+: 9%.

11. US Census Bureau, Current Population Survey (CPS) Database, http://www.census.gov/cps/, accessed February 6, 2014. For a discussion of this data in relation to religious affiliation, see Elizabeth Drescher, "True or False: Less Religion Means More Diversity," *Religion Dispatches*, February 7, 2014.

12. General Social Survey, 1972–2012 Cumulative Datafile.

13. Susan Jacoby, "The Blessing of Atheism," *New York Times* (January 5, 2013), and Kimberley Winston, "Meet the Nones: Unbelief Is Now the World's Third-Largest 'Religion,'" *Sojourners* (December 19, 2012), available online at http://sojo.net/blogs/2012/12/19/unbelief-now-world's-third-largest-'religion'.

14. On Nones as Spiritual-But-Not-Religious, see Linda A. Mercadante, in *Belief Without Borders: Inside the Minds of the Spiritual But Not Religious* (New York: Oxford University Press, 2014), e.g., pp. 7, 11–12, 32–34, and passim.

15. David Kinnaman, *You Lost Me: Why Young Christians Are Leaving Church . . . And Rethinking Faith* (Grand Rapids, MI: Baker Books, 2011), and Vern L. Bengtson, *Families and Faith: How Religion Is Passed Down across Generations* (New York: Oxford University Press, 2013).

16. Pew, "Nones on the Rise," 22.

17. Nancy Tatom Ammerman, *Sacred Stories, Spiritual Tribes: Finding Religion in Everyday Life* (New York: Oxford University Press, 2014), 42.

18. Ammerman's study included a small number of subjects (11 out of 95) who were unaffiliated. Within this sample, she found that the unaffiliated were less likely to use theistic language to describe their own spirituality (see pp. 31–44). While I did not apply the discourse analysis methodology used by Ammerman and colleagues, my analysis of narrative survey responses of more than 200 Nones and interviews with more than 100 suggests that Ammerman has over-characterized the spirituality of Nones based on the responses of a very small sample. Especially among Nones who retain some degree of identification with traditional religion, theistic language was used often and traditional practices were quite commonly reported.

19. Anthony Giddens et al., *Essentials of Sociology*, 3rd edition (New York: Norton, 2008, 2011), 119.

20. Often, this classification is related to generational categories—Millennials, GenXers, Baby Boomers, Silents, Greatest. Critiques of generational cohort theory, however, highlight limits in its applicability among female, non-white, and recent immigrant populations, as well as its limited ability to account for changing social, cultural, and psychological factors in the formation of core identity. On this, see for example Mary Elizabeth Hughes and Angela M. O'Rand, "The Lives and Times of the Baby Boomers," in *The American People: Census 2000*, ed. Reynolds Farley and John Haaga (New York: Sage, 2005), 224–238; and Jill Quandagno, W. Andrew Achenbaum, and Vern L. Bengtson, "Setting the Agenda for Research on Cohorts and Generations: Theoretical, Political, and Policy Implications," chapter 13 of *The Changing Contract Across Generations*, ed. Vern L. Bengtson and W. Andrew Achenbaum (Hawthorne, NY: Aldine De Gruyter, 1993). Those studying the religiously unaffiliated also have a penchant for developing typologies related to patterns of belief or behavior. For example, Wade Clark Roof, in *A Generation of Seekers: The Spiritual Journeys of the Baby Boomers* (San Francisco: Harper San Francisco, 1993), 76–82, distinguished "highly active seekers" from other religious and non-religious Americans. Robert C. Fuller, in *Spiritual but Not Religious: Understanding Unchurched America* (New York: Oxford, 2001), 2–5, described the "unchurched" according to three types: (1) those who are indifferent to religion; (2) those with an ambiguous relationship to religion; and (3) those who are spiritual but not religious in the sense of being "concerned with spiritual issues but [choosing] to pursue them outside of a formal religious organization." Linda A. Mercadante, in *Belief without Borders: Inside the Minds of the Spiritual but Not Religious* (New York: Oxford University Press, 2014), 71–85, offers a mix of generational categories and an ideological-behavioral typology, defining those in her mostly over-age-50 spiritual-but-not-religious cohort as "Dissenters," "Casuals," "Explorers," "Seekers," and "Immigrants."

21. Pew, "Nones on the Rise," 11. Comparable data were not yet available from the 2015 Pew report as this chapter was finalized.

22. Jaweed Kaleem, "'No Religion' Is Increasingly Popular Choice for Americans: Pew Report," *Huffington Post* (October 9, 2013), available online at http://www.huffingtonpost.com/2012/10/09/no-religion-pew-report_n_1949598.html.

23. Wade Roof Clark, *A Generation of Seekers: The Spiritual Journeys of the Baby Boom Generation* (San Francisco: HarperSanFrancisco, 1994).

24. Pew Forum on Religion & Public Life, "Many Americans Mix Multiple Faiths" (Washington, DC: December 2009), 6.

25. Ibid., 3.

26. On rates of religious affiliation in eighteenth- and nineteenth-century America, see Roger Finke and Rodney Stark, *The Churching of America: Winners and Losers in Our Religious Economy* (New Brunswick, NJ: Rutgers University Press, 2002), 24. Jon Butler argues that the narrative of religious revival in the Great Awakening significantly exaggerates its impact on both secular and religious culture, including sustained increases in religious participation. See Jon Butler, "Enthusiasm Described and Decried: The Great Awakening as Interpretative Fiction," *The Journal of American History* 69, no. 2 (September 1982): 305–325. Likewise, in *The Spiritual Unrest* (New York: Frederick A. Stokes, 1910), journalist Ray Stannard Baker describes a pervasive religious "indifferentism" throughout twentieth-century America. Overall, however, it was not until the 1950s—in the aftermath of World War II and in the shadow of the Cold War and reactionary McCarthyism—that religious affiliation began to be more stridently pursued as a national value. On this, see Robert S. Ellwood, *The Fifties Spiritual Marketplace: American Religion in a Decade of Conflict* (New Brunswick, NJ: Rutgers University Press, 1997).

27. Julian Baggini, *Atheism: A Very Short Introduction* (Oxford: Oxford University Press, 2003), 2.

28. Adapted from Robin LePoidevan, *Agnosticism: A Very Short Introduction* (Oxford: Oxford University Press, 2010), Kindle Edition, loc. 397.

29. Ibid. Only one interview subject specifically claimed an identity as a specific type of Agnostic. Most shown in Appendix B as Agnostics moved between soft and hard positions through their lives, but the majority tended in their spiritual practice to maintain what could fairly be described as a "Soft Agnostic" position.

30. Charles Taylor, *A Secular Age* (London and New York: Oxford University Press, 2007), 5.

31. Brian Zinnabauer et al., "Religion and Spirituality: Unfuzzying the Fuzzy," *Journal for the Scientific Study of Religion* 36 (December 1997): 549–564. For an important discussion of the roots of the spiritual-but-not-religious label in the Baby Boomer 12-step culture of the 1980s, see Wade Roof Clark, *A Generation of Seekers: The Spiritual Journeys of the Baby Boom Generation* (San Francisco: HarperSanFrancisco, 1994), 69–70. See also Robert C. Fuller, *Spiritual, but Not Religious: Understanding Unchurched America* (New York: Oxford University Press, 2001).

32. On Neopagans and Wiccans, see Sarah M. Pike, *New Age and Neopagan Religions in America* (New York: Columbia University Press, 2004). Some readers might be surprised to find these more defined religious or spiritual identifications listed among types of Nones. However, in regular national surveys, such groups are routinely categorized as "None." In addition, unlike other, smaller religious or spiritual sects, Neopagans and Wiccans do not have a single institutional center around which they are organized. Thus, while their religious or spiritual identities may be more formalized than are those of other Nones, they function outside the institutional religious mainstream. Outside specific studies of their practices, communities, and beliefs, their voices are most fully heard in studies of American religion that move beyond such spheres. An important recent exception is Nancy Ammerman's *Sacred Stories, Spiritual Tribes*, which does aggregate and distinguish a small cohort of Pagans.

33. Roland Barthes, "Textual Analysis: Poe's 'Valdemar,'" trans. Geoff Bennington, *Untying the Text: A Post-Structuralist Reader*, ed. Robert Young (Boston: Routledge & Kegan Paul, 1991), 139.

34. Mandy Ross, *Naming Ceremonies* (Chicago: Heinemann Library), 2004.

35. On this, see the discussion focusing on John Lardas Modern and Andrew Perrin's insights in Courtney Bender and Omar McRoberts, "Mapping a Field: Why and How to Study Spirituality," SSRC Working Paper (October 2012), 5–6. Though the authors are focusing here on the uses of the terms "spiritual" and "spirituality" in social resistance, disciplining, and institution, the discussion readily extends to the related terms like "None."

36. I am grateful to Robert Orsi for suggesting this line of thinking in a productive conversation on the prayer practices of Nones.

37. Zachary is referring to Matthew 25:31–46, in which Jesus teaches that those who did not help the hungry, the stranger, the sick, the naked, and the prisoner were in fact turning away Christ himself. These, at the final judgment, will be thrown into "the eternal fire prepared for the devil and his angels" for "eternal punishment."

38. On emerging church evangelicalism, see James S. Bielo, *Emerging Evangelicals: Faith, Modernity, and the Desire for Authenticity* (New York and London: New York University Press, 2011).

39. Brian Hiatt, "Mumford & Sons: Rattle and Strum: How Four Brits Turned Old-timey Roots Music into the Future of Rock," *Rolling Stone* (March 28, 2013). As I was finishing the book, a new classification emerged for people who retain Christian beliefs but who have left the church over various frustrations: "Dones." See Tom Schultz, "The Rise of the Dones," Holy Soup blog (November 12, 2014), available online at http://holysoup.com/2014/11/12/the-rise-of-the-dones/.

40. Erik H. Erikson, *Life History and the Historical Moment* (New York: W. W. Norton, 1975), 19. Emphasis added.

41. On changing popular and scholarly notions of identity, see Richard Jenkins, *Social Identity*, 2nd edition (London: Routledge, 2004). Jenkins argues that "individual and collective identity are as much an interactional product of 'external' identification by others, as they are of 'internal' identification; and [that] identity is produced and reproduced both in discourse—narrative, rhetoric and representation—and in the practical, often very material, consequences of identification" (176).

42. Paul Ricoeur, *Time and Narrative*, volume 3, trans. Kathleen Blamey and David Pellauer (Chicago: University of Chicago Press, 1988), 248–249.

43. Ibid., 246.

44. Anthony Giddens, *Modernity and Self-Identity: Self and Society in the Late Modern Age* (Stanford, CA: Stanford University Press, 1991), 53, 54. Emphasis in the original.

45. On the debates around open communion, see James Farwell, "Baptism, Eucharist, and the Hospitality of Jesus: On the Practice of 'Open Communion,'" *Anglican Theological Review* 86, no. 2 (Spring 2004): 215–238, and Kathryn Tanner, "In Praise of Open Communion: A Rejoinder to James Farwell," *Anglican Theological Review* 86, no. 3 (Summer 2004): 473–485.

46. Details on the spiritual practice survey are found in Appendix B.

47. See B. Zinnbauer et al., "Religion and Spirituality: Unfuzzying the Fuzzy."

48. On "lived religion," see Robert A. Orsi, "Everyday Miracles: The Study of Lived Religion," in *Lived Religion in America: Toward a History of Practice*, ed. David D. Hall (Princeton, NJ: Princeton University Press, 1997), 3–21; "Is the Study of Lived Religion Irrelevant to the World We Live In?" *Journal for the Scientific Study of Religion* 42, no. 2 (June 2003): 169–174; *Between Heaven and Earth: The Religious Worlds People Make and the Scholars Who Study Them* (Princeton, NJ: Princeton University Press, 2004), 187–188. On "everyday religion," see Nancy Ammerman, "Introduction" to *Everyday Religion: Observing Modern Lives*, ed. Nancy Ammerman (New York: Oxford University Press, 2007), 5. On "religion as lived," see Meredith McGuire, *Lived Religion: Faith and Practice in Everyday Life* (New York: Oxford University Press, 2008), 15–16.

49. Orsi, "Everyday Miracles," 7.

50. To be fair, scholars in the comparatively new academic field of spirituality, and Christian spirituality in particular, have likewise attempted their own claim on what are traditionally seen as the more substantive qualities of "religion." See, for example, Sandra M. Schneiders, "Spirituality in the Academy," *Theological Studies* 50 (December 1989): 676–697.

51. It is, however, worth noting that, while Ammerman and McGuire do include the religiously unaffiliated in their studies and consider their practices under the "lived" or "everyday religion," Orsi's work focuses primarily on Roman Catholics who would generally consider themselves as practicing within a religious tradition. In this sense, Orsi's use of the term "lived religion" is in distinction from other kinds of Catholic religion specifically ("official religion," e.g., or "institutional religion"). It is within this religious frame that he claims "lived religion" as a more suitable descriptor than "spirituality." Ammerman and McGuire (more so), however, do consider the practices that the religiously unaffiliated have themselves identified as "not religious" within a religious frame by labeling as "lived" or "everyday religion" actions, attitudes, and so on, that practitioners themselves would name as "spiritual." Where Orsi may be distinguishing among different kinds of Catholic religious practice, that is, it seems that

Ammerman and McGuire are categorizing as "religious" practices that may not be experienced as such by practitioners.

52. Bender and McRoberts, "Mapping a Field," 4.
53. On discursive genealogies, Gayatri Chakravorty Spivak, "Preface" to Jacques Derrida, *Of Grammatology*, trans. Gayatri Chakravorty Spivak (Baltimore, MD: Johns Hopkins University Press, [1974, 1976] 1997), xxxix.
54. Here, see Talal Assad's important "Reading a Modern Classic: W. C. Smith's *The Meaning and End of Religion*," *History of Religion* 40, no. 3 (2001): 205–222.
55. Pew, "Nones on the Rise," 58–63.
56. Talal Asad, *Genealogies of Religion: Disciplines and Reasons of Power in Christianity and Islam* (Baltimore, MD: The Johns-Hopkins Press, 1993).
57. Walter Principe, "Toward Defining Spirituality," *Studies in Religion/Sciences religieuses* 12, no. 2 (1983): 128–129.
58. Margery Kempe, *The Book of Margery Kempe*, ed. Sanford Brown Meech, vol. 1 (London: Oxford University Press; H. Milford, 1940), 121. See also Elizabeth Drescher, "'Friends in the Spirituality': Alternative Modes of Spiritual Guidance in The Book of Margery Kempe" (paper presented at the Annual Meeting of the American Academy of Religion, Philadelphia, PA, November 19, 2005).
59. On Kempe's unconventional spirituality, see Carolyn Dinshaw, *Getting Medieval: Sexualities and Communities, Pre- and Postmodern* (Durham, NC: Duke University Press, 1999).
60. On the influence of Guyon in contemporary America, see Patricia A. Ward, *Experimental Theology in America: Madame Guyon, Fénelon, and Their Readers* (Waco, TX: Baylor University Press, 2009).
61. Schneiders, "Spirituality in the Academy," 679.
62. This construction likewise came up in discussions of a supernatural being or force; e.g., "god, a higher power, or whatever." I discuss this usage in Chapter 2.
63. Barbara A. Fox, in *Fillers, Pauses and Placeholders*, ed. Nino Amiridze et al. (Amsterdam: John Benjamins, 2010), 2.
64. Andreas Jucker et al., "Interactive Aspects of Vagueness in Conversation," *Journal of Pragmatics* 35, no. 12 (2003): 1731–1769. Cited in Vera I. Podlesskaya, "Parameters for Typological Variation of Placeholders," in *Fillers, Pauses and Placeholders*, ed. Nino Amiridze et al. (Amsterdam: John Benjamins, 2010), 28.
65. This is largely the interpretation found in "God, Religion, Whatever: On Moralistic Therapeutic Deism," chapter 4 of Christian Smith with Melissa Lundquist Denton, *Soul-Searching: The Religious and Spiritual Lives of American Teenagers* (New York: Oxford University Press, 2005), and "Worshipping at the Church of Benign Whatever-Ism," Part I of Kenda Creasy Dean, *Almost Christian: What the Faith of Our Teenagers Is Telling the American Church* (New York: Oxford University Press, 2010).
66. Abby Day and Gordon Lynch, "Introduction: Belief as Cultural Performance," *Journal of Contemporary Religion* 28, no. 2 (2013): 205. My appreciation to Fenella Cannell for pointing me to this research.
67. Talal Asad, "Thinking about Religion, Belief, and Politics," in *The Cambridge Companion to Religious Studies*, ed. Robert A. Orsi (Cambridge: Cambridge University Press, 2012), 51 (emphasis in the original).
68. Manuel Manga, "Design Your Own Secular Spirituality" (forum, Humanists in Silicon Valley, Palo Alto, CA, January 27, 2013).
69. Sunday Assembly Silicon Valley (Sunday assembly, San Jose, CA, February 9, 2014). Sunday Assembly description from http://sundayassembly.com/about/, accessed November 11, 2013.
70. Jonathan Z. Smith, *Imagining Religion: From Babylon to Jonestown* (Chicago: University of Chicago Press, 1982), xi.

Chapter 2

1. Lewis R. Rambo, *Understanding Religious Conversion* (New Haven, CT: Yale University Press, 1993), 5. Rambo distinguishes conversion to a religious group from conversion away from

religion. The latter phenomenon he defines as "deconversion," which he relates to "apostasy or defection" as "the repudiation of a religious tradition or its beliefs by previous members" (13). With most of the people I interviewed, I would tend not to use the language of "conversion" or "deconversion" to describe the process of becoming None.

2. The conversion of Paul, originally named Saul, appears in Acts 22:6–8: "While I was on my way and approaching Damascus, about noon a great light from heaven suddenly shone about me. I fell to the ground and heard a voice saying to me, 'Saul, Saul, why are you persecuting me?' I answered, 'Who are you, Lord?' Then he said to me, 'I am Jesus of Nazareth whom you are persecuting.'"

3. Augustine, *The Confessions*, translated with an introduction and notes by Henry Chadwick (Oxford and New York: Oxford University Press, 1991).

4. On the enlightenment of the Buddha, see Donald S. Lopez, Jr., *The Story of Buddhism: A Concise Guide to Its History and Teachings* (New York: HarperCollins, 2001).

5. Memoirs of this New Atheist trinity are Richard Dawkins, *An Appetite for Wonder: The Making of a Scientist* (New York: HarperCollins, 2013); Sam Harris, *Waking Up: A Guide to Spirituality without Religion* (New York: Simon & Schuster, 2014); and Christopher Hitchens, *Hitch 22: A Memoir* (New York: Hachette, 2010).

6. "What did we do wrong?" and "why don't they like us anymore?" narratives of unaffiliation are typified by David Kinnaman and Gabe Lyons, *UnChristian: What a New Generation Thinks about Christianity . . . and Why It Matters* (Grand Rapids, MI: Baker Books, 2007), and Kinnaman, *You Lost Me: Why Young Christians Are Leaving Church . . . and Rethinking Faith* (Grand Rapids, MI: Baker Books, 2011). The biblical prodigal parable (Luke 15:11–32) is reworked to address religious skeptics in Timothy Keller, *The Prodigal God: Recovering the Heart of the Christian Faith* (New York: Penguin, 2008).

7. Outside this more controversial New Atheist cohort, recent memoirs of unaffiliation include Dan Barker, *Godless: How an Evangelical Preacher Became One of America's Leading Atheists* (Berkeley: Ulysses Press, 2008); C. M. Blakeson, *Spiritual Confessions of an Agnostic* (Bloomington, IL: Abbot Press, 2013); William Lobdell, *Losing My Religion: How I Lost My Faith Reporting on Religion in America—and Found Unexpected Peace* (New York: HarperCollins, 2009); Hemant Mehta, *I Sold My Soul on eBay: Viewing Faith through an Atheist's Eyes* (Colorado Springs: WaterBrook Press, 2007); Sarah Sentilles, *Breaking Up with God: A Love Story* (New York: HarperCollins, 2011); and Chris Stedman, *Faitheist: How an Atheist Found Common Ground with the Religious* (Boston: Beacon, 2012).

8. The literature on religious conversion is extensive, and in no way congeals into a unified field of study. In addition to Rambo, *Understanding Religious Conversion*, which offers a seven-stage model for religious conversion, a number of helpful studies of conversion influenced by a range of academic fields and methodological approaches are Chana Ullman, *The Transformed Self: The Psychology of Religious Conversion* (New York: Plenum, 1989); Walter Conn, *Christian Conversion: A Developmental Interpretation of Autonomy and Surrender* (New York: Paulist, 1986); Diane Austin-Broos, "The Anthropology of Conversion: An Introduction," in *The Anthropology of Religious Conversion*, ed. Andrew Buckser and Stephen D. Glazer (Lanham, MD: Rowman & Littlefield, 2003), 1–11; Ines W. Jindra, "How Religious Content Matters in Conversion Narratives to Various Religious Groups," *Sociology of Religion* 72, no. 3 (2011): 275–302; Lee. A. Kirkpatrick and Phillip R. Shaver, "Attachment Theory and Religion: Childhood Attachments, Religious Beliefs, and Conversion," *Journal for the Scientific Study of Religion* 29, no. 3 (1990), 315–334; Massimo Leone, *Religious Conversion and Identity: The Semiotic Analysis of Texts* (New York: Routledge, 2003); and Raymond F. Paloutzian, "Religious Conversion and Spiritual Transformation: A Meaning-Systems Analysis," in *Handbook of the Psychology of Religion and Spirituality*, ed. R. F. Paloutzian and C. L. Park (New York: Guilford, 2005), 331–347. Raymond F. Paloutzian defines "religious conversion" as a subset of wider category of "spiritual transformation [that] constitutes a change in the person's meaning system" in "Religious Conversion and Spiritual Transformation: A Meaning-Systems Analysis," 334. My thanks to Steven C. Bauman for sharing with me a more nuanced understanding of this literature.

9. Only eight of the people I interviewed were from non-Christian backgrounds. Five were raised as Jews; three were raised in nonreligious families. Though the experiences of some of

these Nones will be discussed in what follows, it is difficult to discern overall patterns from so small a subsample.

10. See, for example, Mark C. Taylor, *After God* (Chicago: University of Chicago Press, 2007), 43–84, and Charles Taylor, *A Secular Age* (Cambridge, MA: Harvard University Press, 2007).

11. The idea of the religious marketplace was development most prominently by Roger Finke and Rodney Stark, *The Churching of America, 1776–1992: Winners and Losers in Our Religious Economy* (New Brunswick, NJ: Rutgers University Press, 1992; updated 2nd edition, 2005). Finke and Stark offer a "supply-side" theory of religious affiliation that shows more conservative, other-worldly oriented churches as "winners" in an unregulated religious marketplace.

12. Thomas Luckman, *The Invisible Religion: The Problem of Religion in Modern Society* (New York: Macmillan, 1967), 99, cited in Meredith B. McGuire, *Religion: The Social Context*, 5th edition (Longrove, IL: Waveland Press, 2002), 371.

13. See, for example, Catherine L. Albanese, "Introduction," *American Spiritualities: A Reader* (Bloomington: Indiana University Press, 2001).

14. Leigh Eric Schmidt, *Restless Souls: The Making of American Spirituality*. Second Edition with a New Preface (Berkeley and Los Angeles: University of California Press, 2005, 2012), 286–287.

15. Courtney Bender, *The New Metaphysicals: Spirituality and the American Religious Imagination* (Chicago: University of Chicago Press, 2010), 182–183.

16. Matthew S. Hedstrom, *The Rise of Liberal Religion: Book Culture and American Spirituality in the Twentieth Century* (New York: Oxford University Press, 2013), 6.

17. Ibid., 71.

18. Ibid., 7.

19. David A. Hollinger, "After Cloven Tongues of Fire: Ecumenical Protestantism and the Modern America Encounter with Diversity," *The Journal of American History* (June 2011): 21–48.

20. A particularly sharp critique of the modern commercialization of spirituality is offered in Jeremy Carrette and Richard King, *Selling Spirituality: The Silent Takeover of Religion* (New York: Taylor & Francis, 2005). The authors argue that " 'spirituality' has become a new cultural addiction and a claimed panacea for the angst of modern living" (1).

21. Kathryn Lofton, *Oprah: The Gospel of an Icon* (Berkeley and Los Angeles: University of California Press, 2011).

22. Ibid., epigraph.

23. Ibid., 15.

24. Tom Beaudoin, *Consuming Faith: Integrating Who We Are with What We Buy* (Lanham, MD: Sheed & Ward, 2003), 7.

25. Lofton, *Oprah: The Gospel of an Icon*, 58.

26. As would be expected, the terms "pluralism" and, especially, "secularism" (with variations, "secularity" and "the secular") are the subject of much scholarly discussion and debate. It is beyond the scope of the chapter to rehearse this discussion, but a very helpful overview of the debate and its stakes is provided in Courtney Bender, "Pluralism and Secularism," ch. 6 of *Religion on the Edge: De-centering and Re-centering the Sociology of Religion*, ed. Courtney Bender, Wendy Cadge, Peggy Levitt, and David Smilde (New York: Oxford University Press), 137–158.

27. Roof, *A Generation of Seekers*, 60.

28. Michael Hout and Claude S. Fisher, "More Americans Have No Religious Preference: Politics and Generations," *American Sociological Review* 67: 165–190. Cited in Pew, "Nones on the Rise," 29. See also, Robert D. Putnam and Claude S. Fisher, *American Grace: How Religion Divides and Unites Us* (New York: Simon & Schuster, 2010), 121–132.

29. Robert D. Putnam, *Bowling Alone: The Collapse and Revival of American Community* (New York: Simon & Schuster, 2008).

30. Pew Research Center, "Millennials in Adulthood: Detached from Institutions, Networked with Friends" (Washington, DC: March 7, 2014), 4, available online at http://www.pewsocialtrends.org/files/2014/03/2014-03-07_generations-report-version-for-web.pdf.

31. Will Herberg, *Protestant, Catholic, Jew: An Essay in American Religious Sociology* (New York: Doubleday, 1995).

32. On this, see Elizabeth Drescher, "Habitus by the Book: From Medieval Obedience to Digital Improvisation," chapter 2 of *Tweet If You [♥] Jesus: Practicing Church in the Digital Reformation* (Harrisburg, PA: Morehouse, 2011), 34–53.

33. Grzegorz Brzozowski, "Spatiality and the Performance of Belief: The Public Square and Collective Mourning for John Paul II," *Journal of Contemporary Religion* 28, no. 2 (2013): 254.

34. Enzo Pace, "Religion as Communication: The Changing Shape of Catholicism in Europe," chapter 2 of *Everyday Religion: Observing Modern Religious Lives*, ed. Nancy T. Ammerman (New York: Oxford University Press, 2007), 38–40.

35. Abby Day, "Varieties of Belief over Time: Reflections from a Longitudinal Study of Youth and Belief," *Journal of Contemporary Religion* 28, no. 2 (2013): 290.

36. "Katie," comment on Elizabeth Drescher, "Poll: Americans A-Okay with Prayer at Public Meetings," *Religion Dispatches* (April 23, 2014), available online at http://www.religiondispatches.org/dispatches/elizabethdrescher/7812/ poll__americans_a_okay_with_prayer_at_public_meetings/. A discussion of contemporary meanings of prayer as they are shaped by the unaffiliated is presented in Chapter 5 of this volume.

37. Kevin D. Dougherty, Byron R. Johnson, and Edward C. Polson, "Recovering the Lost: Remeasuring U.S. Religious Affiliation," *Journal for the Scientific Study of Religion* 46, no. 4 (December 2007): 483–499, and Steve Bruce, *God Is Dead: Secularization in the West* (Oxford: Oxford University Press, 2002).

38. Charles Taylor, *A Secular Age* (Cambridge, MA: Belknap Press, 2007), 22.

39. Fenella Cannell, "The Anthropology of Secularism," *Annual Review of Anthropology* 39, no. 85 (2010): 93.

40. The highlighting of commonalities across religions, rather than the toleration or exploration of differences, is the gist of much of the work of Eboo Patel. See his *Acts of Faith: The Story of an American Muslim, the Struggle for the Soul of a Generation* (Boston: Beacon Press, 2007). Patel's approach is cogently critiqued by Stephen Prothero, *God Is Not One: Eight Rival Religions That Run the World—and Why Their Differences Matter* (New York: Harper Collins, 2010).

41. See Elizabeth Drescher, "The Internet Is Not Killing Religion, Religion Is Killing Religion," *Religion Dispatches* (April 11, 2014), available online at http://www.religiondispatches.org/archive/culture /7777/the_internet_is_not_ killing_religion__religion_is_killing_religion/; and Allen B. Downey, "Religious Affiliation, Education, and Internet Use," self-published report (March 2014), available online at http://arxiv.org/pdf/ 1403.5534v1.pdf.

42. National Vital Statistics Report, volume 62: 7 (January 6, 2014), 3, available online at http://www.cdc.gov/ nchs/data/nvsr/nvsr62/nvsr62_07.pdf.

43. Ibid., 46.

44. James C. Riley, *Rising Life Expectancy: A Global History* (New York: Cambridge University Press, 2001), 7.

45. Indeed, Erik Erikson's famous—and controversial—eight-stage model was expanded to include a ninth life stage describing the characteristics of late adulthood that the psychologist did not consider in his earlier schema. See Erik H. Erikson and Joan M. Erikson, *The Life Cycle Completed* (New York: W. W. Norton, 1997).

46. Whereas (other than during the Great Depression) Americans employed outside the home seldom changed careers through the mid-1960s, US Bureau of Labor Statistics reports that the average American worker changes jobs every 4.4 years in 2012. See Bureau of Labor Statistics, "Number of Jobs Held, Labor Market Activity, and Growth among the Youngest Baby Boomers: Results from a Longitudinal Study" (Wednesday, July 25, 2012), available online at http://www.bls.gov/news.release/pdf/nlsoy.pdf.

47. While Americans appear to be relocating less than in the 1970s, see Raven Malloy et al., "Declining Migration within the US: The Role of the Labor Market," Finance and Economics Discussion Series Divisions of Research & Statistics and Monetary Affairs (Federal Reserve Board, Washington, DC, April 2103), some 24% have moved in the past five years. See Gallup, "381 Million Adults Worldwide Migrate Within Countries: U.S. One of the Most Mobile Countries in the World" (May 15, 2013). Accessed online at http://www.gallup.com/poll/162488/381-million-adults-worldwide-migrate-within-countries.aspx?utm_source=alert&utm_medium=email&utm_campaign=syndication&utm_content=morelink&utm_term=All%20Gallup%20Headlines.

48. Giddens, *Modernity and Self-Identity*, 53.
49. Neopaganism includes many sub-classifications, including Druidism, which draws on ancient tree-worshipping traditions from the British Isles, and Wicca, which tends to have more feminist orientations, reclaiming magic, healing, and nature goddess traditions often associated with witchcraft. See Sarah M. Pike, *New Age and Neopagan Religions in America* (New York: Columbia University Press, 2004), and Lee Gilmore, *Theater in a Crowded Fire: Ritual and Spirituality at Burning Man* (Berkeley: University of California Press, 2010).
50. John Shelby Spong, *Why Christianity Must Change or Die: A Bishop Speaks to Believers in Exile: A New Reformation of the Church's Faith and Practice* (San Francisco: HarperSanFrancisco, 1998), xix.
51. On Christian weight-loss programs, see Lynne Gerber, *Seeking the Straight and Narrow: Weight Loss and Sexual Reorientation in Evangelical America* (Chicago: University of Chicago Press, 2011). Glenda could not recall the name of the program in which she participated, but some of the details she shared suggest that it was not unlike the First Place program Gerber describes.
52. Melody Beattie, *Codependent No More* (Center City, MN: Hazelton, 1986) and John Bradshaw, *Healing the Shame That Binds You* (Deerfield Beach, FL: Health Communications, 1988) were mainstays of the Twelve-Step and wider recovery and self-help movements of the 1980s and 1990s. For a comprehensive history of this movement as it emerges from nineteenth-century New Thought mysticism and Protestant Oxford evangelicalism and expands largely through print media and, in the age of Oprah, "a hybrid discourse of spiritual seeking and self-love" (p. 228), see Trysh Travis, *The Language of the Heart: A Cultural History of the Recovery Movement from Alcoholics Anonymous to Oprah Winfrey* (Chapel Hill: University of North Carolina Press, 2009). I discuss the teachers, gurus, and other companions who factor into the spiritual lives of Nones in the next chapter.
53. Reiki is a healing technique based on the principle that the practitioner can channel energy into the patient by means of touch, to activate the natural healing processes of the patient's body and restore physical and emotional balance. See Pamela Miles, *Reiki: A Comprehensive Guide* (New York, Penguin, 2008).
54. Details of the survey of 300 non-church-going Catholics in the Diocese of Trenton, NJ, which was commissioned by Bishop David M. O'Connell and conducted through the Villanova University Center for the Study of Church Management, are reported in William J. Byron and Charles Zech, "Why They Left: Exit Interviews Shed Light on Empty Pews," *America* (April 30, 2012), available online at http://americamagazine.org/issue/5138/article/why-they-left.
55. See Michael Lipka, "Majority of U.S. Catholics' Opinions Run Counter to Church on Contraception, Homosexuality," Pew Research Center Fact Tank (September 19, 2013), http://www.pewresearch.org/fact-tank/2013/09/19/majority-of-u-s-catholics-opinions-run-counter-to-church-on-contraception-homosexuality/.
56. See, however, Alexander W. Astin, Helen S. Astin, and Jennifer A. Lindholm, *Cultivating the Spirit: How College Can Enhance Students' Inner Lives* (San Francisco: Jossey-Bass, 2010), which explores the implications of longitudinal studies of the spiritualities of college students showing that, while religious engagement declines during college, spiritual interests grow substantially.
57. Student reflection on religious identity, The Christian Tradition, Santa Clara University (April 9, 2013). Used by permission.
58. H. Richard Niebuhr, *Church and Culture* (New York: Harper, 1951), chapter 3.
59. Erica Engstrom and Beth Semic, "Portrayal of Religion in Reality TV Programming: Hegemony and the Contemporary American Wedding," *Journal of Media and Religion* 2 (2003): 145–163.
60. Christian Smith with Melissa Lundquist Denton, *Soul-Searching: The Religious and Spiritual Lives of American Teenagers* (New York: Oxford University Press, 2005), 162–163.
61. On Hedstrom and Hollinger, see p. 57. On Lofton, see p. 58.
62. Kenda Creasy Dean, *Almost Christian: What the Faith of Our Teenagers Is Telling the American Church* (New York: Oxford University Press, 2010), 4.
63. Ibid., 3.

64. Smith and Denton's characterization of young people's religious outlook as "moral therapeutic deism" and Dean's insistence that this outlook is developed primarily in Christian families and churches are supported by Nancy Ammerman's study of what she terms "Golden Rule Christians," who reduce their ethical assessment of Christian teaching to the biblical adage "do unto others as you would have them do to you." See Nancy T. Ammerman, "Golden Rule Christianity: Lived Religion in the American Mainstream," Chapter 9 of *Lived Religion in America: Toward a History of Practice,* ed. David D. Hall (Princeton, NJ: Princeton University Press, 1997), 196–217. I discuss this ethical disposition in Chapter 6.

65. Pew Religion & Public Life Project, "The Shifting Religious Identity of Latinos in America" (Washington, DC, May 7, 2014), 5, available online at http://www.pewforum.org/2014/05/07/the-shifting-religious-identity-of-latinos-in-the-united-states/.

66. Pew Religion & Public Life Project, "A Portrait of Jewish Americans: Findings from a Pew Research Center Survey of U.S. Jews" (Washington, DC, October 1, 2013), 8, available online at http://www.pewforum.org/files /2013/10/jewish-american-full-report-for-web.pdf.

Chapter 3

1. See Charlotte Ward and David Voas, "The Emergence of Conspirituality," *Journal of Contemporary Religion* 28, no. 1 (January 2011): 103–121.

2. Distinguishing social relationships as "groups," "networks," "communities," and so on, is far beyond the scope of the present work. Here, although I will use these words somewhat interchangeably, I generally understand a "network" as a system of relationships, connections, and interactions largely oriented around the exchange of information, while I see a "community" as a social network oriented around shared interests, values, concerns, and imagined actions within which members have at least notional moral commitments to one another. On this, see Thomas A. Lewis, "Heterogeneous Community—Beyond New Traditionalism," in *Critical Studies, Returning (to) Communities. Theory, Culture and Political Practice of the Communal,* edited by Stefan Herbrechter and Michael Higgins (Amsterdam and New York: Editions Rodopi, 2006), 55–72; and Lou Caton, "Stanley Fish Meet Jean-Paul Sartre—Community, Difference and Multicultural Theory," in *Returning (to) Communities: Theory, Culture and Political Practice of the Communal,* ed. Stefan Herbrechter and Michael Higgins (Amsterdam: Rodopi, 2006), 73–88.

3. Eckhart Tolle, *The Power of Now: A Guide to Spiritual Enlightenment* (Novato, CA: New World Library, 1999), 28.

4. Deepak Chopra, like Tolle, was established as a spiritual guru largely through his association with Oprah Winfrey. He has written some 75 books, many of them bestsellers. His *Perfect Health: The Complete Mind/Body Guide* (New York: Bantam, [1990, 2000] 2007) launched him as a spiritual celebrity. Carolyn Myss, author of *Anatomy of the Spirit: The Seven Stages of Power and Healing* (New York: Random House, 1996) was, likewise, promoted by Winfrey. Brené Brown, who recently made her way to Winfrey's "Super Soul Sunday" sofa, was launched through a viral TED Talk in 2012 that drew from her book *The Gifts of Imperfection: Let Go of Who You Think You're Supposed to Be and Embrace Who You Are* (Center City, MN: Hazelden, 2010).

5. Centers for Spiritual Living website, "Centers and Services," http://csl.org/centers-and-services.html, accessed January 29, 2014. The organization is an entwined incarnation of the United Church of Religious Science and Religious Science International, the renaming apparently meant to distinguish the organization from the Church of Christ, Scientist (Christian Science), founded by Mary Baker Eddy, and to shed the lingering Christian implications of the designation "church" (though CSL ordains "ministers" and holds Sunday "services").

6. Mitch Horowitz, *Occult America: The Secret History of How Mysticism Shaped Our Nation* (New York: Bantam, 2009), 99–100.

7. On this extra-institutional history, see for example, Catherine L. Albanese, *A Republic of Mind and Spirit: A Cultural History of American Metaphysical Religion* (New Haven, CT: Yale University Press, 2007); Courtney Bender, *The New Metaphysicals: Spirituality and the American Religious Imagination* (Chicago; London: University of Chicago Press, 2010);

Kathryn Lofton, *Oprah: The Gospel of an Icon* (Berkeley: University of California Press, 2011); Glenn Mosley, *New Thought, Ancient Wisdom: The History and Future of the New Thought Movement* (Conshohocken, PA: Templeton Foundation Press, 2006); and Leigh Eric Schmidt, *Restless Souls: The Making of American Spirituality* (Berkeley: University of California Press, 2012).

8. New Vision Center for Spiritual Living website, "What Practitioners 'Do,'" http://www.newvisionaz.org/pages/practitionersdo.html, accessed July 21, 2013. The New Vision Center website was subsequently updated, and the URL is no longer active. An archived version is available from the author.

9. The "Real Love" group is based on the teachings of author and speaker Greg Baer, M.D. See, New Vision Center for Spiritual Living (Phoenix, AZ) website, "Real Love Groups," http://www.newvisionaz.org/classes, accessed July 23, 2013. The New Vision Center website was subsequently updated, and the URL is no longer active. An archived version is available from the author.

10. On the development of such interpretive communities, see Stanley Fish, "Interpreting the Variorum," *Critical Inquiry* 2, no. 3 (Spring 1976): 465–485.

11. Danielle Fuller and DeNel Rehberg Sedo, "'And Then We Went to the Brewery': Reading as a Social Activity in a Digital Era," *WorldLiteratureToday.org* (May–August 2014), available online at http://www.worldliteraturetoday.org/2014/may-august/and-then-we-went-brewery-reading-social-activity-digital-era#.U-_x4FbWY3c.

12. Courtney Bender, *Heaven's Kitchen: Living Religion at God's Love We Deliver* (Chicago: University of Chicago Press, 2003), 91.

13. Ibid., 93.

14. Pierre Bourdieu, *Distinction: A Social Critique of the Judgment of Taste* (Cambridge, MA: Harvard University Press, 1987), 124–125.

15. Pierre Bourdieu, "The Social Space and the Genesis of Groups," *Social Science Information* 24 (1985b): 204. On "habitus," see Pierre Bourdieu, *Outline of a Theory of Practice* (Cambridge: Cambridge University Press, [1977] 2000), 78–79.

16. On such "imagined communities," see Benedict Anderson, *Imagined Communities: Reflections on the Origin and Spread of Nationalism*, 2nd edition (London and New York: Verso, 1983, 1991).

17. Dan Merica, "'None' Leaders to Chart Path for More Political, Cultural Power for Religiously Unaffiliated," CNN Religion Blog (January 25, 2013), available online at http://religion.blogs.cnn.com/2013/01/25/none-leaders-to-chart-path-for-more-political-cultural-power-for-religiously-unaffiliated/.

18. The term derives from the writing of Diarmuid O'Murchu, particularly *Quantum Theology: Spiritual Implications of the New Physics* (New York: Crossroad Classic, 1997, 2004).

19. Ramamurti Shankar, *Principles of Quantum Mechanics*, 2nd edition (New York and London, 1994), 112–113.

20. Nancy Ammerman, "Religious Identities and Religious Institutions, in *Handbook for the Sociology of Religion*, ed. Michele Dillon (Cambridge: Cambridge University Press), 209, cited in Lichterman, "Studying Public Religion," 119.

21. David Chidester and Edward Tabor Linental, *American Sacred Space* (Bloomington: Indiana University Press, 1995).

22. Available online at http://www.atheistnexus.org.

23. Available online at http://www.thinkatheist.com.

24. Available online at http://www.centerforinquiry.net.

25. Available online at http://humanist-society.org.

26. Neil is referring here to Hemant Mehta, one of the contributors to the "Friendly Atheist" blog on the Patheos platform, available online at http://www.patheos.com/blogs/friendlyatheist/about-the-contributors/.

27. Matthew O. Jackson, *Social and Economic Networks* (Princeton, NJ: Princeton University Press, 2008), 24–25.

28. On the spirituality of Burning Man, see Lee Gilmore, *Theater in a Crowded Fire: Ritual and Spirituality at Burning Man* (Berkeley and Los Angeles: University of California Press, 2010).

29. A recent South-by-Southwest gathering included a full schedule of offerings in the "Art, Science, and Inspiration" segment on topics such as "Spirituality through Interactive Technology" and "spiritual odysseys" as well as a wide variety of gospel, hip-hop, and folk music performances with spiritual themes, and events at churches throughout the Austin area.

30. Olivia Solon, "'Atheist Church' Seeks £500,000 in Crowdfunding to Build Online Platform," *Wired* (October 20, 2013), available online at http://www.wired.co.uk/news/archive/2013-10/20/sunday-assembly-expansion.

31. Sunday Assembly website, "Our Story," available online at http://sundayassembly.com/story/, accessed January 6, 2014.

32. John McDermott, "The Church of No Religion," *Financial Times* (August 23, 2013), available online at http://www.ft.com/intl/cms/s/2/9229a7b8-0abd-11e3-aeab-00144feabdc0.html.

33. Pew, "Nones on the Rise," 10.

34. Shayne Lee and Phillip Luke Sinitiere, *Holy Mavericks: Evangelical Innovators and the Spiritual Marketplace* (New York and London: New York University Press, 2009), 135.

35. Rick Warren, *The Purpose Driven Life Journal: Reflections on What on Earth Am I Here For?* (Grand Rapids, MI: Zondervan, 2003). Cited in *Holy Mavericks*, 138.

36. J. D. Payne, *Kingdom Expressions: Trends in Influencing the Advancement of the Gospel* (Lawrence, MA: Thomas Nelson, 2012), defines ' "seeker-sensitive" or "seeker-driven" churches as those concerned to "accommodate . . . non-believers" who "often had to overcome significant cultural and social barriers in order to be present. . . ." Services in seeker-driven churches "would be entertaining but with little expectation for the participants, with the entire focus on the unbeliever. Secular music was common, as was the use of drama and messages that were evangelistic and apologetic in nature" (112–113). For a strong critique of this approach, see Dorothy Littell Greco, "How the Seeker-Sensitive Church Is Failing a Generation," *Christianity Today* (August 2013), available online at http://www.christianitytoday.com/women/2013/august/how-seeker-sensitive-consumer-church-is-failing-generation.html?paging=off.

37. Greco, "How the Seeker-Sensitive Church Is Failing a Generation," 144.

38. Ibid., 21.

39. Becky Garrison, "Atheism Is Boring," *OnFaith* (November 13, 2013), available online at http://www.faithstreet.com/onfaith/2013/11/25/atheism-is-boring/30013.

40. "Atheist Church Split: Sunday Assembly and Godless Revival's 'Denominational Chasm,'" *Huffington Post* (January 6, 2014), available online at http://www.huffingtonpost.com/2014/01/06/atheist-church-split_n_4550456.html.

41. "About the Cosmic Mass," Matthew Fox website, http://www.matthewfox.org/about-matthew-fox/the-cosmic-mass/.

42. "Monday Nights: Teachings Based on *A Course in Miracles*," Marianne Williams website, http://www.marianne.com/events.htm.

43. Neil Postman, *Entertaining Ourselves to Death* (New York: Viking, [1985] 2005).

44. Luther H. Martin, *Hellenistic Religions: An Introduction* (New York: Oxford University Press, 1987), 91–93.

45. Peter Stallybrass and Allon White, *The Politics and Poetics of Transgression* (Ithaca, NY: Cornell University Press, 1986), 27.

46. Tom Beaudoin, *Consuming Faith: Integrating Who We Are with What We Buy* (Lanham, MD: Sheed & Ward, 2003), 7.

47. Immortal Technique, "Dance with the Devil," *Revolutionary, Vol. 1*, musical recording (Viper Records, 2001).

48. Wuthnow, *All in Sync*, 92.

49. Ibid., 238. Emphasis in the original.

50. See Chapter 1, p. 42.

51. In addition to Lofton, *Oprah*, and Beaudoin, *Consuming Faith*, op. cit., on the particular case of the spiritual commercialization of music, see Simon Firth, *Sound Effects: Youth, Leisure, and the Politics of Rock 'n' Roll* (New York: Pantheon, 1981).

52. Alasdair MacIntyre, *After Virtue: A Study in Moral Theory*, 2nd edition (Notre Dame, IN: University of Notre Dame Press, 1984), p. 194 in Wuthnow, *All in Sync*, 28–31.

53. Horace Clarence Boyer, ed., *Lift Every Voice and Sing II: An African American Hymnal* (New York: Church Publishing, 1993).

54. "Bio," Peter Mayer website, http://www.petermayer.net/bio/.

55. "About," Quiet Company website, http://www.quietcompanymusic.com/about.

56. John Burnett, "For an Ex-Christian Rocker, Faith Lost Is a Following Gained," *All Things Considered* (National Public Radio), audio broadcast (December 5, 2013). Available online at http://www.npr.org/2013/12/05/247338182/for-an-ex-christian-rocker-faith-lost-is-a-following-gained.

57. Tia De Nora, *Music in Everyday Life* (Cambridge: Cambridge University Press, 2000), 139. On "emotional work," DeNora cites Arlie Hochschild, "Emotion Work, Feeling Rules and Social Structure," *American Journal of Sociology* 85 (1979): 551–575.

58. Gordon Lynch, "The Role of Popular Music in the Construction of Alternative Spiritual Identities and Ideologies," *Journal for the Scientific Study of Religion* 45, no. 4 (2006): 486.

59. De Nora, *Music in Everyday Life*, 47. The term "technologies of the self" originates in Michel Foucault, *Technologies of the Self: A Seminar with Michel Foucault*, ed. Luther H. Martin, Buck Gutman, and Patrick H. Hutton (Amherst: University of Massachusetts Press, 1988).

60. Ibid., 63.

Chapter 4

1. Mary Douglas, "Deciphering a Meal," *Dædalus* 101, no. 1 (Winter 1972): 61.

2. Ibid., 61, 66.

3. Cody Delistraty, "The Importance of Eating Together," *The Atlantic* (July 18, 2014), citing the Organisation for Economic Co-operation and Development (OECD), "Who Are the School Truants?" (January 2014), available online at http://www.theatlantic.com/health/archive/2014/07/the-importance-of-eating-together/374256/.

4. Claude Lévi-Strauss, *The Raw and the Cooked*, trans. John and Doreen Weightman, vol. 1 of *Mythologies* (Chicago: University of Chicago Press, [1969] 1983).

5. Michael Pollan, *Cooked* (New York: Penguin, 2013), 4.

6. See p. 43. The survey did not ask about cultivating food, but a number of survey respondents and interview subjects did mention gardening as spiritually significant. See Appendix A, *On Methodology*, for details on the spiritual practices survey.

7. Robert Bellah, et al., *Habits of the Heart: Individualism and Commitment in American Life : With a New Preface* (Berkeley: University of California Press, 2008). On the dismissiveness of Bellah and colleagues' treatment of Sheila's spirituality, see pp. 275–276, n. 7.

8. See, e.g., Lillian Daniel, "Spiritual But Not Religious? Please Stop Boring Me," *Huffington Post* (September 13, 2011), available online at http://www.huffingtonpost.com/lillian-daniel/spiritual-but-not-religio_b_959216.html, and Linda A. Mercadante, *Belief without Borders: Inside the Minds of the Spiritual but Not Religious* (New York: Oxford University Press, 2014). By way of contrast, Ammerman, *Sacred Stories, Spiritual*, pays particular attention to communal settings of spiritual practice, even among subjects not affiliated with traditional religious groups, including a number of Pagans who participated in her study.

9. McGuire, *Lived Religion*, 13. Emphasis added.

10. Ibid., 11 and passim.

11. Ibid., 7–8.

12. Abby Day, *Believing in Belonging: Belief and Social Identity in the Modern World* (Oxford: Oxford University Press, 2011), 194.

13. On this see Taylor, *A Secular Age*, 221–225.

14. Ibid., 156–157.

15. Taylor, *A Secular Age*, 5.

16. Aristotle, *Nicomachean Ethics*, Book 9.4.

17. Lorraine Smith Pangle, *Aristotle and the Philosophy of Friendship* (Cambridge: Cambridge University Press, 2003), 142, 146.

18. See Daniel Schwartz, *Aquinas on Friendship* (New York: Oxford University Press, 2007).

19. Mary E. Hunt, *A Fierce Tenderness: A Feminist Theology of Friendship* (New York: Continuum, 1991), 81.

20. On this see Pascal Boyer, "Religion: Bound to Believe?" *Nature* 455, no. 23 (October 2008): 1038–1039.

21. The quote is from seventeenth-century French philosopher Blaise Pascal.

22. Luhrmann, *When God Talks Back*, 46.

23. Reina Remigo, "Best Friends: A Look at the Human-Animal Bond and Spirituality Using a Mixed-Methods Approach," PhD dissertation, Sophia University (2014).

24. American Pet Products Association (APPA), *2013–2014 National Pet Owners Survey* (Greenwich, CT, 2014).

25. Harris Interactive, "Pets Are Really Members of the Family—Three in Five Americans are Pet Owners" (June 10, 2011), available online at http://www.harrisinteractive.com/ NewsRoom/HarrisPolls/tabid/447/ctl/ReadCustom%20Default/mid/1508/ArticleId/ 814/Default.aspx.

26. Anecdotal claims of animal intuition and empathy are increasingly borne out by clinical research. See, for example, Anaïs Racca et al., "Reading Faces: Differential Lateral Gaze Bias in Processing Canine and Human Facial Expressions in Dogs and 4-Year-Old Children," *PLoS ONE* 7, no. 4 (2012): e36076. doi: 10.1371/journal.pone.0036076, cited in Juliane Kaminski, Sarah Marshall-Pescini, eds., *The Social Dog: Behavior and Cognition* (San Diego, CA: Academic Press, 2014), 223.

27. Froma Walsh, "Human-Animal Bonds I: The Relational Significance of Companion Animals," *Family Process* 48, no 4 (December 2009): 462–480, and "Human-Animal Bonds II: The Role of Pets in Family Systems and Family Therapy," *Family Process* 48, no. 4 (December 2009): 481–499.

28. Anita Unruh and Susan Hutchinson, "Embedded Spirituality: Gardening in Daily Life and Stressful Life Experiences," *Scandinavian Journal of Caring Sciences* 23, no. 3 (September 2011): 567–574.

29. See Montague Ullman and Claire Limmer, eds., *The Variety of Dream Experience*, 2nd edition (Albany: State University of New York Press, 1999), and Jeremy Taylor, *Dream Work: Techniques for Discovering the Creative Power in Dreams* (Mahwah, NJ: Paulist Press, 1983).

30. James W. Bernauer and Michael Mahon, "Michel Foucault's Ethical Imagination," in *The Cambridge Companion to Foucault*, 2nd edition, ed. Gary Gutting (Cambridge: Cambridge University Press, 2005), 159–160.

31. Lawrence Kushner, *Honey from the Rock: Ten Gates of Jewish Mysticism* (New York: Harper & Row, 1977), 54, cited in Belden C. Lane, *The Solace of Fierce Landscapes: Exploring Desert and Mountain Spirituality* (New York: Oxford University Press, 1998), 37.

32. David Brown, "4: Placement and Pilgrimage," in *God and Enchantment of Place: Reclaiming Human Experience*, by David Brown (New York: Oxford University Press, 2004), 171.

33. Ibid., 177.

34. Ammerman, *Sacred Stories, Spiritual Tribes*, 169.

35. Michael Slote, *From Enlightenment to Receptivity: Rethinking Our Values* (New York: Oxford University Press, 2013).

Chapter 5

1. See Introduction to this volume, 11–12.

2. See, "Words of Truth, A Prayer Composed by: His Holiness Tenzin Gyatso The Fourteenth Dalai Lama of Tibet," available online at http://www.dalailama.com/teachings/words-of-truth, and Alys Francis, "In Pictures: Dalai Lama Leads Peace Prayers," Al Jazeera (July 7, 2014), available online at http://www.aljazeera.com/indepth/inpictures/2014/07/pictures-dalai-lama-leads-peace--20147782825501175.html.

3. Pew, "Nones on the Rise," 42.

4. Ibid., 22.

5. Jean-Louis Chrétien, "7: The Wounded Word—The Phenomenology of Prayer," in *Phenomenology and the "Theological Turn": The French Debate*, ed. Dominique Janicaud, Jean-François Courtine, Jean-Louis Chretien, Michel Henry, Jean-Luc Marion, and Paul Ricoeur, *Perspectives in Continental Philosophy* (New York: Fordham University Press, 2000), 147.

6. Pew, "Nones on the Rise," 52.

7. Ibid., 65.

8. Ibid., 52.

9. "C'est la prière qui distingue le phénomène religieux de tous ce qui lui ressemblent ou l'avoisinent, tels que le sentiment moral ou le sentiment esthétique." Auguste Sabatier, *Esquisse d'une philosophie de la religion d'après la psychologie et l'histoire* (Paris: Fischbacher, 1897). Quoted in W. S. E. Pickering, "Introduction to an Unfinished Work," in Marcel Mauss, *On Prayer*, trans. Susan Leslie, ed. W. S. F. Pickering (New York: Berghahn Books, [1909] 2003), 7.

10. The vast literature on prayer, which moves across religious traditions in academic, religious, and popular treatments, makes the impossibility of definition clear. Beyond resources identified in the notes and bibliography, a not particularly representative selection of resources that informed my work here includes Samuel E. Balentine, *Prayer in the Hebrew Bible: The Drama of Divine-Human Dialogue*, Overtures to Biblical Theology (Minneapolis: Fortress Press, 1993); Hans Urs von Balthasar, *Prayer*, trans. Graham Harrison (San Francisco: Ignatian Press, [1955] 1986); Laurence Binet Brown, *The Human Side of Prayer: The Psychology of Praying* (Birmingham, AL: Religious Education Press, 1994); Richard J. Foster, *Prayer: Finding the Heart's True Home* (New York: Harper Collins, 1992); Thomas A. Hand, O.S.A., *Augustine on Prayer* (Westminster: Newman Press, 1963); Friedrich Heiler, *Prayer: A Study in the History and Psychology of Religion* (London and New York: Oxford University Press, 1932; Rockport, MA: OneWorld Publications, 1997); F. S. Naiden, *Ancient Supplication* (New York: Oxford University Press, 2006); Rick Ostrander, *The Life of Prayer in a World of Science: Protestants, Prayer, and American Culture, 1870–1930* (New York: Oxford University Press, 2000); Stefan C. Reif, *Judaism and Hebrew Prayer: New Perspectives on Jewish Liturgical History* (Cambridge and New York: Cambridge University Press, 1995); Philip Zaleski and Carol Zaleski, *Prayer: A History* (New York: Houghton Mifflin, 2005).

11. For a review of prayer types posited by a wide sample of researchers and commentators, see Kevin L. Ladd and Bernard Spilka, "Inward, Outward, and Upward: Cognitive Aspects of Prayer," *Journal for the Scientific Study of Religion* 41, no. 3 (2002): 475–476. On religion, including prayer, as a discursive practice, see Paul Ricoeur, "Philosophy and Religious Language," *Journal of Religion* 54 (1974): 71–85. On prayer as a coping practice, see for example Christopher G. Ellison and Robert Joseph Taylor, "Turning to Prayer: Social and Situational Antecedents of Religious Coping among African Americans," *Review of Religious Research* 38, no. 2 (December 1996): 111–131. On prayer and religious identity, see for example John Paul McKinney, Kathleen G. McKinney, "Prayer in the Lives of Late Adolescents," *Journal of Adolescence* 22, no. 2 (1999): 279–290. On prayer and self-disclosure, see for example Larry VandeCreek, Mark-David Janus, James W. Pennebaker, and Bradley Binau, "Praying about Difficult Experiences as Self-Disclosure to God," *The International Journal for the Psychology of Religion* 12, no. 1 (2002): 29–39.

12. Augustine, *On the Lord's Sermon on the Mount* 2.3.14, quoted in Roy Hammerling, *A History of Prayer: The First to the Fifteenth Century* (Leiden and Boston: Brill, 2008), v.

13. This is a central feature of prayer in the rabbinic Jewish tradition. See Abraham E. Millgram, *Jewish Worship* (Philadelphia: Jewish Publication Society of America, 1971), 14–16.

14. David L. McMahan, *The Making of Buddhist Modernism* (New York: Oxford University Press, 2008), 192.

15. Rita M. Gross, "Meditation and Prayer: A Comparative Inquiry," *Buddhist-Christian Studies* 22 (2002): 80.

16. I adapted this rubric from Jacques Jansse, Joep DeHard, and Christine Den Draak, "A Content Analysis of the Praying Practices of Dutch Youth," *Journal for the Scientific Study of Religion* 29, no. 1 (1990): 100.

17. In the "Nones Beyond the Numbers" survey, 56 percent of participants responded "no" to the question, "Do you pray?" 41 percent answered "yes," and 3 percent did not answer. Of the 103 interview subjects, 53 percent ($n = 55$) said they did not pray, and 41 percent ($n = 42$) said they did. Another 6 interviewees equivocated during the interview, suggesting again that closed questioning may not reveal the complexity of Nones' thinking or self-understanding on matters of spirituality and religion.

18. George was most likely referring here to Luke 9:1–2: "Then Jesus called the twelve together and gave them power and authority over all demons and to cure diseases, and he sent them out to proclaim the kingdom of God and to heal." [NSRV] But see also Matthew 9:35, Matthew 10:7, Luke 10:9.

19. There is an extensive literature on the spirituality of surfing that explores this mystical dimension, as well as meditative or prayerful qualities of the sport. A representative collection of popular and academic works includes Jaimal Yogis, *Saltwater Buddha: A Surfer's Quest to Find Zen on the Sea* (Somerville, MA: Wisdom Publications, 2009); Andrew Francis and Sylvie Shaw, *Deep Blue: Critical Reflections on Nature, Religion and Water* (London: Equinox, 2008); Peter Kreeft, *I Surf, Therefore I Am: A Philosophy of Surfing* (South Bend: St. Augustine's Press, 2008); Michael A. Allen, *Tao of Surfing: Finding Depth at Low Tide* (Lincoln, NE: IUniverse, 2007); and Bron Taylor, "Suring into Spirituality, and a New Aquatic Nature Religion," *Journal of the American Academy of Religion* 75, no. 4 (2007): 923–951.

20. On the spirituality of running, see Robert R. Sands and Linda Sands, "Running Deep: Speculations on the Evolution of Running and Spirituality in the Genus Homo," *Journal for the Study of Religion, Nature, and Culture* 3, no. 4 (2009): 522–577.

21. *OED*, s.v., "prayer."

22. See, Peter Gilliver, "Precarious," *Oxford English Dictionary* (2013), available online at http://public.oed.com/aspects-of-english/word-stories/precarious/. My appreciation to Cynthia Read for pointing me to this resource.

23. Giddens, *Modernity and Self-Identity*, 53.

24. Marcel Mauss, *On Prayer*, trans. Susan Leslie, ed. W. S. F. Pickering (New York: Berghahn Books, [1909] 2003), 24.

25. Ammerman, *Sacred Stories, Spiritual Tribes*, 63.

26. Ibid., 74.

27. Ibid., 73.

28. Ibid., 158.

29. Jean-Louis Chrétien, "7: The Wounded Word—The Phenomenology of Prayer," 147. Emphasis added.

30. My appreciation to Keith Anderson for comments and questions that helped me to develop the conclusion to this chapter.

Chapter 6

1. Fyodor Dostoevsky, *The Brothers Karamazov*, translated by Constance Garnett (New York: The Modern Library, [1880] 1996), 672.

2. The term is usual pluralized ("ethics") and used as a collective noun when it refers to the multiple approaches to morality that can be developed within a broad category. There are, that is, many versions of virtue ethics, but only one Protestant ethic as described by Max Weber (see n. 9).

3. See, for example, Alasdair MacIntyre, *After Virtue* (New York: Bloomsbury Academic, [1981] 2013).

4. See, for example, Ron Berger, *An Ethic of Excellence: Building a Culture of Craftsmanship with Students* (Portsmouth, NH: Heinemann, 2003).

5. Max Weber, *The Protestant Ethic and the Spirit of Capitalism*, translated with an introduction by Stephen Kalberg (Chicago: Roxbury Publishing, [1905] 2001). Weber was not, of course, proposing a normative ethical system, but rather describing a de facto ethics that he believed developed at the intersection of Calvinist Protestantism and modern industrialization.

6. Foundational texts in care ethics include Carol Gilligan, *In a Different Voice: Psychological Theory and Women's Development* (Cambridge, MA: Harvard University Press, [1982] 2009); Nel Noddings, *Caring: A Feminine Approach to Ethics and Moral Education* (Berkeley and Los Angeles: University of California Press, 1984); Virginia Held, *Ethics of Care: Personal, Political, and Global* (New York: Oxford University Press, 2006).

7. Early articulations of care ethics, starting with the groundbreaking work of Gilligan, focused more specifically on the relationship between women and children. Gilligan's interest is in correcting gender bias in masculinist ethical systems that often marked women as "ethically

immature" compared to men. Though Gillian was clear in *In a Different Voice*, and subsequently, in allowing that care ethics was not restricted to women, her focus on gender has invited the criticism that care ethics is essentialist. On this, see Barbara Houston, "Rescuing Womanly Virtues," in *Science, Morality and Feminist Theory*, ed. Marsha P. Hanen and Kai Nielsen (Calgary: University of Calgary Press), 237–262; and Joan Tronto, *Moral Boundaries: A Political Argument for an Ethic of Care* (New York: Routledge, 1994).

8. This is the perspective of many contemporary materialist approaches to meta-ethics as well. See, for example, Patrice Haynes, *Immanent Transcendence: Reconfiguring Materialism in Continental Philosophy* (London: Bloomsbury, 2012); Mark C. Taylor, *After God* (Chicago: University of Chicago Press, 2007); and Donna Haraway, *How Like a Leaf: An Interview with Thyrza Nichols Goodeve* (New York: Routledge, 2000).

9. Nel Noddings, *Caring: A Feminist Approach to Ethics and Moral Education* (Berkeley: University of California Press, 1984), 13–15.

10. Nel Noddings, *Starting at Home: Caring and Social Policy* (Berkeley and Los Angeles: University of California Press, 2002), 14.

11. Ethicists often argue that care ethics is a subset of virtue ethics in that caring and receptivity are particular virtues. See, for example, Raja Halwani, "Care Ethics and Virtue Ethics," *Hypatia* 18, no. 3 (Autumn 2003): 161–192. However, others argue that, though the systems are compatible, virtue ethics retains an emphasis on the individual (even if that individual is virtuous in relationships) rather than on the dynamic relational field. Further, virtue ethics tends to highlight qualities of "excellence" that motivate an individual to achieve virtuous ends. (See Daniel Star, "Do Confucians Really Care? A Defense of the Distinctiveness of Care Ethics: A Reply to Chenyang Li," *Hypatia* 17, no. 1 (Winter 2002): 77–106; and Noddings, *Caring*, 96–97.)

12. See Michael Battle, *Ubuntu: I in You and You in Me* (New York: Seabury, 2009); and Michael Battle, *Reconciliation: The Ubuntu Theology of Desmond Tutu* (Cleveland: Pilgrim Press, 1997).

13. Drucilla Cornell and Kenneth Michael Panfilio, *Symbolic Forms for a New Humanity: Cultural and Racial Reconfigurations of Critical Theory* (New York: Fordham University Press, 2010), 164–165.

14. My thanks to The Reverend Rosa Lee Harden and Kevin Jones for the opportunity to attend SOCAP12, San Francisco, CA, September 2012.

15. Christian N. B. Gade, "What Is *Ubuntu*? Different Interpretations among South Africans of African Descent," *Journal of South African Philosophy* 31, no. 3 (2012): 484–503.

16. Carol Gilligan, "Reply to Critics," in *An Ethic of Care: Feminist and Interdisciplinary Perspectives*, ed. Mary Jeanne Larrabee (New York London: Routledge, 1993), 208.

17. Nancy T. Ammerman, "Golden Rule Christianity: Lived Religion in the American Mainstream," in *Lived Religion in America: Toward a History of Practice*, ed. David D. Hall (Princeton, NJ: Princeton University Press, 1997), 196–216.

18. A fuller version of this argument is developed in Julian Baggini, *Atheism: A Very Short Introduction* (New York and London: Oxford University Press, 2003), 37–57. My discussion relies to some extent on Baggini's summary, as well as His Holiness the Dalai Lama, *Beyond Religion: Ethics for a Whole World* (New York: Houghton Mifflin, 2011), 13–18; and David Baggett and Jerry L. Walls, *Good God: The Theistic Foundations of Morality* (New York: Oxford University Press, 2011), especially chapter 5.

19. See, for example, Louise M. Antony, "Good Minus God," *New York Times* (December 18, 2011), available online at http://opinionator.blogs.nytimes.com/2011/12/18/good-minus-god/.

20. See, for example, Ex. 23:23–24; Deut. 7:1–11; 20:16–18; Joshua 10:28–39. Likewise, though the Binding of Isaac (Gen. 22) ends with God sending a messenger to pull Abraham's blade from his son's throat, many scholars see the narrative as further evidence that violence— domestic, political, and otherwise—is often presented as a virtue in Abrahamic religions. On this, see Yvonne Sherwood, "Binding–Unbinding: Divided Responses of Judaism, Christianity, and Islam to the 'Sacrifice' of Abraham's Beloved Son," *Journal of the American Academy of Religion* 72, no. 4 (2004): 821–861.

21. There is an extensive, expanding literature on the evolutionary roots of ethics for both academic and popular readerships. See, for example, Elliott Sober, *Unto Others: The Evolution*

and *Psychology of Unselfish Behavior* (Cambridge, MA: Harvard University Press, 1988); Jeffrey R. Stevens and Marc C. Hauser, "Why Be Nice: Psychological Constraints on the Evolution of Cooperation," *Trends in Cognitive Sciences* 8, no. 2 (February 2004): 60–65; Philip Clayton and Jeffrey Schloss, *Evolution and Ethics: Human Morality in Biological and Religious Perspective* (Cambridge: Eerdmans, 2004); Richard Joyce, *The Evolution of Morality* (Cambridge, MA: MIT Press, 2006); Mariana Lozada, Paola D'Adamo, and Miguel Angel Fuentes, "Punishment and Cooperation in Nature," *Journal of Theoretical Biology* 289, no. 21 (November 2011): 12–16; Christopher Boehm, *Moral Origins: The Evolution of Virtue, Altruism, and Shame* (New York: Basic Books, 2012); Lance Workman and Will Reader, *Evolutionary Psychology*, 3rd edition (Cambridge: Cambridge University Press, 2014), 222–247. It is worth noting that evolutionary psychology has attracted no small measure of criticism. Critiques center on what is sometimes seen as a rush among evolutionary psychologists to see genetic adaptation for specific psychological purposes that may have multiple, and often uncertain, adaptive roots; what can appear as genetic determinism in some evolutionary psychology; and a tendency toward reductive explanations for complex behaviors such as religious belief and practice. On this, see Workman and Reader, *Evolutionary Psychology*, 29–33.

22. Ralph Kzarian, "Some Evidence That Trees 'Communicate' When in Trouble," *Environmental Conservation* 10, no. 2 (Summer 1983): 173.

23. Harris Interactive, "Americans' Belief in God, Miracles, and Heaven Declines: Belief in Darwin's Theory of Evolution Rises" (December 16, 2013), available online at http://www. harrisinteractive.com/NewsRoom/HarrisPolls/tabid/447/ctl/ReadCustom%20Default/ mid/1508/ArticleId/1353/Default.aspx.

24. Gabrielle slightly misquoted Russell here. The quote comes from Russell's 1925 essay "What I Believe" (New York: Routledge, [1925] 2013), in which he writes, "The good life is inspired by love and guided by knowledge" (10).

25. A full discussion of this theological and philosophical lacuna is well beyond the scope of this book. It is laid out with particular insight and wit by Terry Eagleton in *Reason, Faith, and Revolution: Reflections on the God Debate* (New Haven, CT: Yale University Press, 2009).

26. On this, see Jacob Neusner and Bruce D. Chilton, eds., *The Golden Rule: The Ethics of Reciprocity in World Religions* (New York: Continuum, 2008), and Jeffrey Wattles, *The Golden Rule* (New York: Oxford University Press, 1996).

27. William Scott Green, "Parsing Reciprocity: Questions for the Golden Rule," chapter 1 of *The Golden Rule: The Ethics of Reciprocity in World Religions*, ed. Jacob Neusner and Bruce D. Chilton (London and New York: Continuum, 2008), 1–8.

28. For other assessment of Golden Rule ethics, see Wattles, *The Golden Rule*, 77–89.

29. See Ammerman, *Sacred Stories, Spiritual Tribes*, 207–218; Nancy Tatom Ammerman, *Congregation and Community* (New Brunswick, NJ: Rutgers University Press, 1997), 368; and Nancy T. Ammerman, "Golden Rule Christianity: Lived Religion in the American Mainstream," in *Lived Religion in America: Toward a History of Practice*, ed. David D. Hall (Princeton, NJ: Princeton University Press, 1997), 196–216.

30. Ammerman, "Golden Rule Christianity," 203.

31. Ibid., 199, 201–203.

32. Ibid., 205.

33. Ammerman, "Golden Rule Christianity," 199.

34. Patrick M. Clark, "Reversing the Ethical Perspective: What the Allegorical Interpretation of the Good Samaritan Parable Can Still Teach Us," *Theology Today* 71, no. 3 (2014): 303.

35. Richard Bauckham, "The Scrupulous Priest and the Good Samaritan: Jesus' Parabolic Interpretation of the Law of Moses," *New Testament Studies* 44, no. 4 (October 1998): 475–489.

36. Eva Kittay, "Dependency, Difference & Global Ethic of Longterm Care," *The Journal of Political Philosophy* 13, no. 4 (2005): 453; cited in Clark, "Reversing the Ethical Perspective," 306.

37. Kwame Anthony Appiah, *Cosmopolitanism: Ethics in a World of Strangers* (New York: W. W. Norton, 2010). Kindle Edition, locations 140–143.

38. Ibid., Kindle locations 138–140.

39. Ibid., Kindle locations 852–854.

40. Ibid., Kindle locations 346–347.

Chapter 7

1. Richard Dawkins, *The God Delusion* (New York: Houghton-Mifflin, 2006), 358.
2. Philip Zuckerman, *Faith No More: Why People Reject Religion* (Oxford University Press, 2011), 202.
3. Kate emailed me an extensive bibliography that included a number of titles on parenting and moral formation, including Dale McGowan, *Parenting beyond Belief: On Raising Ethical, Caring Kids without Religion* (New York: AMACOM, 2007); Dale McGowan, Molleen Matsumura, Amanda Metskas, and Jan Devor, *Raising Freethinkers: A Practical Guide for Parenting beyond Belief* (New York, AMACOM, 2009); and Sam Harris, *Waking Up: A Guide to Spirituality Without Religion* (New York: Simon & Schuster, 2014); as well as humanist books for children, including Lisa Westberg Peters, *Our Family Tree: An Evolution Story* (Orlando: Harcourt Books, 2003); and Helen Bennett, *Humanism, What's That? A Book for Curious Kids* (Amherst, NY: Prometheus Books, 2005).
4. Appiah, *Cosmopolitanism*, Kindle Locations 1574–1577.
5. See Gallup, "On Social Ideology, the Left Catches Up to the Right" (May 22, 2015), available online at http://www.gallup.com/poll/183386/social-ideology-left-catches-right.aspx?, which tracks the increasing alignment of political liberals and conservatives on social issues such as marriage equality, abortion rights, and extra-marital sexual relations.
6. Nel Noddings, *Starting at Home: Caring and Social Policy* (Berkeley: University of California Press, 2002), 4.
7. Jean Piaget, *The Moral Judgment of the Child* (New York: Routledge, [1932] 2007); Erik Erikson, *Child and Society* (New York: Norton, 1950); and Lawrence Kohlberg, *The Psychology of Moral Development: The Nature and Validity of Moral Stage* (New York: Harper & Row, 1984).
8. Kohlberg's stage theory is adapted by way of explaining Christian moral formation by Fowler in *Stages of Faith: The Psychology of Human Development* (New York: Harper & Row, 1981).
9. M. Scott Peck, *The Different Drum: Community and PeaceMaking* (New York: Touchstone, 1987).
10. See Michael Symons, "From Agape to Eucharist: Jesus Meals in the Early Church," *Food and Foodways: Explorations in the History and Culture of Human Nourishment* 8, no. 1 (1999): 33–54.
11. See Chapter 1, p. 29.
12. Vern L. Bengtson, with Norella Putney and Susan C. Harris, *Families and Faith: How Religion Is Passed Down across Generations* (Oxford and New York: Oxford University Press, 2013), 164.
13. Pew, "Nones on the Rise," 53–54.

Conclusion

1. Taylor, *A Secular Age*, 542.
2. On this, see Lisa Napoli, "A Growing Movement To Spread Faith, Love—And Clean Laundry," National Public Radio (July 27, 2014), available online at http://www.npr.org/2014/07/27/335290086/a-growing-movement-to-spread-faith-love-and-clean-laundry; *Lancashire Telegraph*, "Eid in the Park: Special Weekend to Host a Series of Celebrations as Fasting Ends" (July 10, 2015); Keith Anderson, *The Digital Cathedral: Networked Ministry in a Wireless World* (New York: Morehouse, 2015).

BIBLIOGRAPHY

Albanese, Catherine L. *A Republic of Mind and Spirit: A Cultural History of American Metaphysical Religion*. New Haven, CT: Yale University Press, 2007.

Albanese, Catherine L., ed. *American Spiritualities: A Reader*. Bloomington: Indiana University Press, 2001.

Allen, Michael A. *Tao of Surfing: Finding Depth at Low Tide*. New York: iUniverse, 1997.

American Pet Products Association. *2013–2014 National Pet Owners Survey*. Greenwich, CT: American Pet Products Association, 2014.

Amiridze, Nino, Boyd H. Davis, and Margaret MacLagan, eds. *Fillers, Pauses and Placeholders*. Typological Studies in Language, v. 93. Amsterdam; Philadelphia: John Benjamins, 2010.

Ammerman, Nancy Tatom. "Religious Identities and Religious Institutions." In *Handbook for the Sociology of Religion*, edited by Michele Dillon, 207–225. Cambridge; New York: Cambridge University Press, 2003.

Ammerman, Nancy Tatom. *Sacred Stories, Spiritual Tribes: Finding Religion in Everyday Life*. Oxford; New York: Oxford University Press, 2014.

Ammerman, Nancy Tatom, ed. *Everyday Religion: Observing Modern Religious Lives*. Oxford; New York: Oxford University Press, 2007.

Ammerman, Nancy Tatom, and David D. Hall. "Golden Rule Christianity: Lived Religion in the American Mainstream." In *Lived Religion in America: Toward a History of Practice*, edited by David D. Hall, 196–217. Princeton, NJ: Princeton University Press, 1997.

Anderson, Benedict R. *Imagined Communities: Reflections on the Origin and Spread of Nationalism*. Rev. and extended ed. London; New York: Verso, 1991.

Anderson, T. R., and T. A. Slotkin. "Maturation of the Adrenal Medulla—IV. Effects of Morphine." *Biochemical Pharmacology* 24, no. 16 (August 15, 1975): 1469–1474.

Antony, Louise M. "Good Minus God." *New York Times*. December 18, 2011, http://opinionator. blogs.nytimes.com/2011/12/18/good-minus-god/ (accessed June 19, 2013).

Arias, Elizabeth. *United States Life Tables, 2009*. National Vital Statistics Report. Washington, DC: US Department of Health and Human Services, http://www.cdc.gov/nchs/data/nvsr/ nvsr62/nvsr62_07.pdf (accessed January 26, 2014).

Artress, Lauren. *Walking a Sacred Path: Rediscovering the Labyrinth as a Spiritual Practice*. New York: Riverhead Books, 2006.

Asad, Talal. *Formations of the Secular: Christianity, Islam, Modernity*. Cultural Memory in the Present. Stanford, CA: Stanford University Press, 2003.

Asad, Talal. *Genealogies of Religion: Discipline and Reasons of Power in Christianity and Islam*. Baltimore, MD: Johns Hopkins University Press, 1993.

Asad, Talal. "Reading a Modern Classic: W. C. Smith's 'The Meaning and End of Religion.'" *History of Religions* 40, no. 3 (February 2001): 205–222.

Asad, Talal. "Thinking about Religion, Belief, and Politics." In *The Cambridge Companion to Religious Studies*, edited by Robert A. Orsi, 36–57. Cambridge; New York: Cambridge University Press, 2012.

Astin, Alexander W. *Cultivating the Spirit: How College Can Enhance Students' Inner Lives*. San Francisco: Jossey-Bass, 2010.

Augustine. *Confessions*. Oxford World's Classics. Oxford: Oxford University Press, 2008.

Baggett, David. *Good God: The Theistic Foundations of Morality*. New York: Oxford University Press, 2011.

Baggini, Julian. *Atheism: A Very Short Introduction*. Very Short Introductions 99. Oxford; New York: Oxford University Press, 2003.

Baker, Ray Stannard. *The Spiritual Unrest*. New York: Frederick A. Stokes, 1910.

Balentine, Samuel E. *Prayer in the Hebrew Bible: The Drama of Divine-Human Dialogue*. Overtures to Biblical Theology. Minneapolis: Fortress Press, 1993.

Balmer, Randall Herbert. *Protestantism in America*. The Columbia Contemporary American Religion Series. New York: Columbia University Press, 2002.

Balthasar, Hans Urs von. *Prayer*. San Francisco: Ignatius Press, 1986.

Barker, Dan, and Richard Dawkins. *Godless: How an Evangelical Preacher Became One of America's Leading Atheists*. Berkeley, CA: Ulysses Press, 2008.

Barthes, Roland. "Textual Analysis: Poe's 'Valdemar.'" Trans. Geoff Bennington. In *Untying the Text: A Post-Structuralist Reader*, edited by Robert C. J. Young. London: Routledge, 1990.

Bass, Diana Butler. *Christianity after Religion: The End of Church and the Birth of a New Spiritual Awakening*. New York: HarperOne, 2012.

Battle, Michael. *Reconciliation: The Ubuntu Theology of Desmond Tutu*. Revised & updated ed. Cleveland, OH: Pilgrim Press, 2009.

Battle, Michael. *Ubuntu: I in You and You in Me*. New York: Seabury Books, 2009.

Beattie, Melody. *Codependent No More*. Center City, MN: Hazelden, 1987.

Beaudoin, Tom. *Consuming Faith: Integrating Who We Are with What We Buy*. Lanham, MD: Sheed & Ward, 2007.

Beaumont, Hunter. *Toward a Spiritual Psychotherapy: Soul as a Dimension of Experience*. Berkeley, CA: North Atlantic Books, 2012.

Bellah, Robert N. *Habits of the Heart: Individualism and Commitment in American Life : With a New Preface*. Berkeley: University of California Press, 2008.

Bender, Courtney. "Pluralism and Secularism." In *Religion on the Edge: De-centering and Re-centering the Sociology of Religion*, edited by Courtney Bender, Wendy Cadge, Peggy Levitt, and David Smilde, 137–158. New York: Oxford University Press.

Bender, Courtney. "Practicing Religions." In *The Cambridge Companion to Religious Studies*, edited by Robert A. Orsi, 273–295. Cambridge: Cambridge University Press, 2012.

Bender, Courtney. *The New Metaphysicals: Spirituality and the American Religious Imagination*. Chicago; London: University of Chicago Press, 2010.

Bender, Courtney, ed. *Religion on the Edge: De-Centering and Re-Centering the Sociology of Religion*. Oxford; New York: Oxford University Press, 2013.

Bender, Courtney, and Omar McRoberts. "Mapping a Field: Why and How to Study Spirituality." New York: Social Science Research Council, October 2012, 5–6. Working paper. Social Science Research Council Working Group on Spirituality, Political Engagement, and Public Life, October 2012, http://blogs.ssrc.org/tif/wp-content/uploads/2010/05/Why-and-How-to-Study-Spirtuality.pdf.

Bender, Courtney, and Ann Taves, eds. *What Matters? Ethnographies of Value in a Not So Secular Age*. New York: Columbia University Press, 2012.

Bengtson, Vern L. *Families and Faith: How Religion Is Passed Down across Generations*. New York: Oxford University Press, 2013.

Bennett, Helen. *Humanism, What's That? A Book for Curious Kids*. Amherst, NY: Prometheus Books, 2005.

Berger, Ron. *An Ethic of Excellence: Building a Culture of Craftsmanship with Students*. Portsmouth, NH: Heinemann, 2003.

Berlinerblau, Jacques. *How to Be Secular: A Call to Arms for Religious Freedom*. Boston, MA: Mariner Books, 2013.

Bernauer, James W., and Michael Mahon. "Michel Foucault's Ethical Imagination." In *The Cambridge Companion to Foucault*, edited by Gary Gutting, 2nd edition, 159–160. Cambridge: Cambridge University Press, 2005.

Bielo, James S. *Emerging Evangelicals: Faith, Modernity, and the Desire for Authenticity*. New York: New York University Press, 2011.

Blakeson, C. M. *Spiritual Confessions of an Agnostic*. Bloomington, IN: Abbot Press, 2013.

Boehm, Christopher. *Moral Origins: The Evolution of Virtue, Altruism, and Shame*. New York: Basic Books, 2012.

Bourdieu, Pierre. *Distinction: A Social Critique of the Judgment of Taste*. Cambridge, MA: Harvard University Press, 1984.

Bourdieu, Pierre. *Outline of a Theory of Practice*. Cambridge; New York: Cambridge University Press, 1977.

Bourdieu, Pierre. "The Social Space and the Genesis of Groups." *Social Science Information* 24, no. 2 (1985): 195–220.

Boyer, Horace Clarence, ed. *Lift Every Voice and Sing II: An African American Hymnal*. New York: Church Publishing, 1993.

Boyer, Pascal. "Religious Thought and Behaviour as By-Products of Brain Function." *Trends in Cognitive Sciences* 7, no. 3 (March 2003): 119–124.

Brauer, Dorit. *Girls Don't Ride Motorbikes: A Spiritual Adventure into Life's Labyrinth*. Pittsburgh, PA: CreateSpace Independent Publishing Platform, 2012.

Brown, C. Brené. *The Gifts of Imperfection: Let Go of Who You Think You're Supposed to Be and Embrace Who You Are*. Center City, MN: Hazelden, 2010.

Brown, David. *God and Enchantment of Place: Reclaiming Human Experience*. Oxford; New York: Oxford University Press, 2006.

Brown, David. "Placement and Pilgrimage." In *God and Enchantment of Place: Reclaiming Human Experience*, edited by David Brown, 153–244. New York: Oxford University Press, 2004.

Brown, Laurence Binet. *The Human Side of Prayer: The Psychology of Praying*. Birmingham, AL: Religious Education Press, 1994.

Bruce, Steve. *God Is Dead: Secularization in the West*. Religion in the Modern World. Malden, MA: Blackwell, 2002.

Brzozowski, Grzegorz. "Spatiality and the Performance of Belief: The Public Square and Collective Mourning for John Paul II." *Journal of Contemporary Religion* 28, no. 2 (May 2013): 241–257.

Bstan-'dzin-rgya-mtsho (His Holiness the Dalai Lama). *Beyond Religion: Ethics for a Whole World*. Boston, MA: Mariner Books/Houghton Mifflin Harcourt, 2012.

Bstan-'dzin-rgya-mtsho (His Holiness the Dalai Lama). "Words of Truth, A Prayer Composed by: His Holiness Tenzin Gyatso The Fourteenth Dalai Lama of Tibet," n.d., http://www.dalailama.com/teachings/words-of-truth.

Buckser, Andrew, and Stephen D. Glazier, eds. *The Anthropology of Religious Conversion*. Lanham, MD: Rowman & Littlefield Publishers, 2003.

Burnett, John. "For an Ex-Christian Rocker, Faith Lost Is a Following Gained." *All Things Considered*. Washington, DC: National Public Radio, December 5, 2013, http://www.npr.org/2013/12/05/247338182/for-an-ex-christian-rocker-faith-lost-is-a-following-gained (accessed December 6, 2013).

Butler, Jon. *Awash in a Sea of Faith Christianizing the American People*. Cambridge, MA: Harvard University Press, 1992.

Byron, William J., and Charles Zech. "Why They Left: Exit Interviews Shed Light on Empty Pews." *America*, April 30, 2012, http://americamagazine.org/issue/5138/article/why-they-left (accessed March 11, 2013).

Calamari, Barbara, and Sandra DiPasqua. *Holy Cards*. New York; London: Abrams, 2012.

Candolini, G. *Labyrinths: Walking towards the Center*. New York: Crossroad Publishing, 2003.

Cannell, Fenella. "The Anthropology of Secularism." *Annual Review of Anthropology* 39, no. 1 (October 21, 2010): 85–100.

Carrette, Jeremy R. *Selling Spirituality: The Silent Takeover of Religion*. London; New York: Routledge, 2005.

Casanova, José. *Public Religions in the Modern World*. Chicago: University of Chicago Press, 1994.

Caton, Lou. "Stanley Fish Meet Jean-Paul Sartre—Community, Difference and Multicultural Theory." In *Returning (to) Communities: Theory, Culture and Political Practice of the Communal*, edited by Stefan Herbrechter and Michael Higgans, 73–88. Amsterdam: Rodopi, 2006.

Center for Inquiry. Website, http://www.centerforinquiry.net (accessed August 9, 2014).

Chaves, Mark. *American Religion: Contemporary Trends*. Princeton, NJ: Princeton University Press, 2011.

Chidester, David, and Edward Tabor Linenthal. *American Sacred Space*. Bloomington: Indiana University Press, 1995.

Chopra, Deepak. *Perfect Health: The Complete Mind Body Guide*. Revised edition. New York: Three Rivers Press, 2000.

Chrétien, Jean–Louis. "The Wounded Word—The Phenomenology of Prayer." In *Phenomenology and the "Theological Turn": The French Debate*, edited by Jean–Louis Chrétien, Dominique Janicaud, Michael Henry, Jean-Luc Marion, and Paul Ricoeur, 147–175. Perspectives in Continental Philosophy. New York: Fordham University Press, 2000.

Chryssavgis, John, and Bruce V. Foltz, eds. *Toward an Ecology of Transfiguration: Orthodox Christian Perspectives on Environment, Nature, and Creation*. Orthodox Christianity and Contemporary Thought. New York: Fordham University Press, 2013.

Clark, Kelly James, ed. *Readings in the Philosophy of Religion*. 2nd edition. Broadview Readings in Philosophy. Peterborough, ON; Buffalo, NY: Broadview Press, 2008.

Clayton, Philip, and Jeffrey Schloss, eds. *Evolution and Ethics: Human Morality in Biological and Religious Perspective*. Grand Rapids, MI: W. B. Eerdmans, 2004.

Cornell, Drucilla. *Symbolic Forms for a New Humanity: Cultural and Racial Reconfigurations of Critical Theory*. Just Ideas. New York: Fordham University Press, 2010.

Coronel, Felipe Andres (Immortal Technique). *Dance with the Devil*. Vol. 1. Revolutionary. Viper Records, 2001.

Critchley, Simon. *The Faith of the Faithless: Experiments in Political Theology*. London; New York: Verso, 2014.

Curry, Thomas J. "Babette's Feast and the Goodness of God." *Journal of Religion and Film* 16, no. 2 (October 2012), http://digitalcommons.unomaha.edu/jrf/vol16/iss2/10 (accessed December 4, 2011).

Daniel, Lillian. "Spiritual but Not Religious? Please Stop Boring Me." *Huffington Post*, September 13, 2011, http://www.huffingtonpost.com/lillian-daniel/spiritual-but-not-religio_b_959216.html (accessed September 13, 2011).

Daniel, Lillian. *When "Spiritual but Not Religious" Is Not Enough: Seeing God in Surprising Places, Even the Church*. New York: Jericho Books, 2014.

Davie, Grace. *Religion in Britain since 1945: Believing without Belonging*. Making Contemporary Britain. Oxford; Cambridge, MA: Blackwell, 1994.

Davies, Brian. *Thomas Aquinas's Summa Theologiae: A Guide and Commentary*. London; New York: Oxford University Press, 2014.

Dawkins, Richard. *Appetite for Wonder: The Making of a Scientist*. New York: Ecco Press, 2014.

Dawkins, Richard. *The God Delusion*. Boston, MA: Houghton Mifflin, 2008.

Day, Abby. *Believing in Belonging: Belief and Social Identity in the Modern World*. Oxford; New York: Oxford University Press, 2011.

Day, Abby. "Varieties of Belief over Time: Reflections from a Longitudinal Study of Youth and Belief." *Journal of Contemporary Religion* 28, no. 2 (May 2013): 277–293.

Day, Abby, and Gordon Lynch. "Introduction: Belief as Cultural Performance." *Journal of Contemporary Religion* 28, no. 2 (May 2013): 199–206.

De Botton, Alain. *Religion for Atheists: A Non-Believer's Guide to the Uses of Religion*. New York: Vintage International, 2013.

Dean, Kenda Creasy. *Almost Christian: What the Faith of Our Teenagers Is Telling the American Church*. Oxford; New York: Oxford University Press, 2010.

Delistraty, Cody. "The Importance of Eating Together." *The Atlantic Monthly*, July 18, 2014, http://www.theatlantic.com/health/archive/2014/07/the-importance-of-eating-together/374256/ (accessed September 16, 2014).

DeNora, Tia. *Music in Everyday Life*. Cambridge; New York: Cambridge University Press, 2000.

Derrida, Jacques. *Of Grammatology*. Baltimore, MD: Johns Hopkins University Press, 1976.

Doe, Norman. *Canon Law in the Anglican Communion: A Worldwide Perspective*. Oxford; New York: Oxford University Press, 1998.

Dostoyevsky, Fyodor. *The Brothers Karamazov: A Novel in Four Parts with Epilogue*. New York: Farrar, Straus and Giroux, [1880] 2002.

Dougherty, Kevin D., Byron R. Johnson, and Edward C. Polson. "Recovering the Lost: Remeasuring U.S. Religious Affiliation." *Journal for the Scientific Study of Religion* 46, no. 4 (December 7, 2007): 483–499.

Douglas, Mary. "Deciphering a Meal." *Dædalus* 101, no. 1 (Winter 1972): 61–81.

Drescher, Elizabeth. "Poll: Americans A-Okay with Prayer at Public Meetings." *Religion Dispatches*, April 23, 2014, http://www.religiondispatches.org/dispatches/elizabethdrescher/7812/poll__americans_a_okay_with_prayer_at_public_meetings/.

Drescher, Elizabeth. "Practicing Church: Vernacular Ecclesiologies in Late Medieval England." PhD dissertation, Graduate Theological Union, 2008.

Drescher, Elizabeth. "Quitting Religion but Not the Practice of Prayer." *Religion Dispatches*, March 7, 2013, http://www.religiondispatches.org/archive/atheologies/6973/quitting_religion__but_not_the_practice_of_prayer/.

Drescher, Elizabeth. "The Internet Is Not Killing Religion, Religion Is Killing Religion." *Religion Dispatches*, April 11, 2014, http://www.religiondispatches.org/archive/culture/7777/the_internet_is_not_killing_religion__religion_is_killing_religion/.

Drescher, Elizabeth. "True or False: Less Religion Means Greater Diversity? When a Graphic Makes Info Harder to Parse." *Religion Dispatches*, February 7, 2014, http://www.religion-dispatches.org/archive/atheologies/7572/true_or_false__less_religion__means_greater_diversity/.

Drescher, Elizabeth. *Tweet If You [♥] Jesus: Practicing Church in the Digital Reformation*. Harrisburg, PA: Morehouse, 2011.

Drescher, Elizabeth. "What Do the Religiously Unaffiliated Pray For?" *Washington Post*. May 2, 2013, http://www.faithstreet.com/onfaith/2013/05/02/what-the-nones-teach-us-on-the-national-day-of-prayer.

Drescher, Elizabeth. "Where Are the Blessed Peacemakers: Why It's So Hard for Christians to Understand the Rhetoric of Nonviolence in Their Own Traditions." *Religion Dispatches*, April 17, 2012, http://www.religiondispatches.org/archive/atheologies/6391/ where_are_the_blessed_peacemakers/.

Drescher, Elizabeth. "Forget Right or Wrong: Why the National Day of Prayer Is Obsolete." *Religion Dispatches*, May 6, 2010, http://www.religiondispatches.org/archive/politics/2530/ forget_right_or_wrong/.

Drescher, Elizabeth. "Friends in the Spirituality': Alternative Modes of Spiritual Guidance in The Book of Margery Kempe." Paper presented at the Annual Meeting of the American Academy of Religion, Philadelphia, November 19, 2005.

Drescher, Elizabeth. "I Am a Disgrace to Journalism (or Maybe Not)." *The In Between*, June 21, 2013, http://elizabethdrescher.com/2013/06/.

Dworkin, Ronald. *Religion without God*. Cambridge, MA: Harvard University Press, 2013.

Dyck, Drew. *Generation Ex-Christian: Why Young Adults Are Leaving the Faith—and How to Bring Them Back*. Chicago: Moody Publishers, 2010.

Eagleton, Terry. *Reason, Faith, and Revolution: Reflections on the God Debate*. New Haven, CT: Yale University Press, 2009.

Edwards, Diane Tolomeo. "Babette's Feast, Sacramental Grace, and the Saga of Redemption." *Christianity and Literature* 42, no. 3 (Spring 1993): 420–432.

Edwords, Fred. "What Is Secular Humanism." American Humanist Association, http://american-humanist.org/Humanism/ What_is_Humanism (accessed May 19, 2012).

Eisenstein, Elizabeth L. *The Printing Press as an Agent of Change: Communications and Cultural Transformation in Early-Modern Europe. Vol. I, II*. New York; Oakleigh: Cambridge University Press, 1994.

Eliade, Mircea. *The Sacred and the Profane; The Nature of Religion*. New York: Harcourt, Brace, 1959.

Ellison, Christopher G., and Robert Joseph Taylor. "Turning to Prayer: Social and Situational Antecedents of Religious Coping among African Americans." *Review of Religious Research* 38, no. 2 (December 1996): 111–131.

Ellwood, Robert S. *The Fifties Spiritual Marketplace: American Religion in a Decade of Conflict.* New Brunswick, NJ: Rutgers University Press, 1997.

Engstrom, Erika, and Beth Semic. "Portrayal of Religion in Reality TV Programming: Hegemony and the Contemporary American Wedding." *Journal of Media and Religion* 2, no. 3 (August 2003): 145–163.

Erikson, Erik H. *Childhood and Society.* New York: W.W. Norton, 1993.

Erikson, Erik H., and Joan M. Erikson. *The Life Cycle Completed.* New York: W. W. Norton, 1998.

Feldman, Noah. "Cosmopolitan Law?" *The Yale Law Journal* 116, no. 5 (March 1, 2007): 882–1169.

Finke, Roger, and Rodney Stark. *The Churching of America, 1776–1990: Winners and Losers in Our Religious Economy.* New Brunswick, NJ: Rutgers University Press, 2002.

Fish, Stanley. "Interpreting the Variorum." *Critical Inquiry* 2, no. 3 (Spring 1976): 264–487.

Flory, Richard W., and Donald E Miller. *Finding Faith the Spiritual Quest of the Post-Boomer Generation.* New Brunswick, NJ: Rutgers University Press, 2008.

Foster, Richard J. *Prayer: Finding the Heart's True Home.* San Francisco: HarperSanFrancisco, 1992.

Foucault, Michel. *Discipline and Punish: The Birth of the Prison.* 2nd Vintage Books edition. New York: Vintage Books, 1995.

Foucault, Michel, Luther H. Martin, Huck Gutman, and Patrick H. Hutton, eds. *Technologies of the Self: A Seminar with Michel Foucault.* Amherst: University of Massachusetts Press, 1988.

Foucault, Michel, and Paul Rabinow. *The Essential Works of Michel Foucault, 1954–1984.* Edited by James D Faubion. New York: New Press, 1997.

Fowler, James W. *Stages of Faith: The Psychology of Human Development and the Quest for Meaning.* San Francisco: Harper & Row, 1981.

Fox, Barbara A. "Introduction." In *Fillers, Pauses and Placeholders*, edited by Nino Amiridze and Boyd H. Davis, 93:1–10. Typological Studies in Language. Amsterdam; Philadelphia: John Benjamins, 2010.

Fox, Matthew. "About the Cosmic Mass," http://www.matthewfox.org/about-matthew-fox/the-cosmic-mass/ (accessed February 18, 2014).

Francis, Alys. "In Pictures: Dalai Lama Leads Peace Prayers." *Al Jazeera*, July 7, 2014, http://www.aljazeera.com/indepth/inpictures/2014/07/pictures-dalai-lama-leads-peace--20147782825501175.html (accessed July 10, 2014).

Freitas, Donna. *Sex and the Soul: Juggling Sexuality, Spirituality, Romance, and Religion on America's College Campuses.* Oxford; New York: Oxford University Press, 2010.

Frith, Simon. *Sound Effects: Youth, Leisure, and the Politics of Rock 'n' Roll.* New York: Pantheon Books, 1981.

Fulkerson, Mary McClintock. "Practice." In *Handbook of Postmodern Biblical Interpretation*, edited by A. K. M. Adam, 189–198. St. Louis, MO: Chalice Press, 2000.

Fuller, Robert C. *Spiritual, but Not Religious: Understanding Unchurched America.* Oxford; New York: Oxford University Press, 2001.

Galloway, Andrew. "Marriage Sermons, Polemical Sermons, and The Wife of Bath's Prologue: A Generic Excursus." *Studies in the Age of Chaucer* 14 (1992): 3–30.

Gallup. "381 Million Adults Worldwide Migrate Within Countries: U.S. One of the Most Mobile Countries in the World," June 15, 2013, http://www.gallup.com/poll/162488/381-million-adults-worldwide-migrate-within-countries.aspx?utm_source=alert&%20utm_medium=email&utm_campaign=syndication&utm_content=morelink&utm_term=All%20Gallup%20Headlines (accessed April 17, 2014).

Gallup. "381 Million Adults Worldwide Migrate Within Countries: U.S. One of the Most Mobile Countries in the World" (May 15, 2013), http://www.gallup.com/poll/162488/381-million-adults-worldwide-migrate-within-countries.aspx?utm_source=alert&utm_medium=email&utm_campaign=syndication&utm_content=morelink&utm_term=All%20Gallup%20Headlines (accessed June 13, 2013).

Garrison, Becky. "'Atheism Is Boring.'" Blog. *FaithStreet*, November 13, 2013, http://www.faith-street.com/onfaith/2013/11/25/atheism-is-boring/30013 (accessed November 15, 2013).

Gerber, Lynne. *Seeking the Straight and Narrow: Weight Loss and Sexual Reorientation in Evangelical America*. Chicago; London: University of Chicago Press, 2011.

Giddens, Anthony. *Modernity and Self-Identity: Self and Society in the Late Modern Age*. Stanford, CA: Stanford University Press, 1991.

Giddens, Anthony. *The Consequences of Modernity*. Stanford, CA: Stanford University Press, 1990.

Giddens, Anthony. *The Constitution of Society: Outline of the Theory of Structuration*. Berkeley: University of California Press, 1986.

Giddens, Anthony, ed. *Essentials of Sociology*. 3rd edition. New York: W. W. Norton, 2011.

Gilligan, Carol. *In a Different Voice: Psychological Theory and Women's Development*. Cambridge, MA: Harvard University Press, 1993.

Gilligan, Carol. "Reply to Critics." In *An Ethic Of Care: Feminist and Interdisciplinary Perspectives*, edited by Mary Jeanne Larrabee, 207–214. Thinking Gender. New York; London: Routledge, 1993.

Gilmore, Lee. *Theater in a Crowded Fire: Ritual and Spirituality at Burning Man*. Berkeley: University of California Press, 2010.

Glenn, Heidi. "Loosing Our Religion: The Growth of the 'Nones.'" *The Two-Way*. PBS, January 15, 2013, http://www.npr.org/blogs/thetwo-way/2013/01/14/169164840/losing-our-religion-the-growth-of-the-nones (accessed January 15, 2013).

Goffman, Erving. *The Presentation of Self in Everyday Life*. New York: Doubleday, 1990.

Goldman, Marion S. *The American Soul Rush: Esalen and the Rise of Spiritual Privilege*. Qualitative Studies in Religion. New York: New York University Press, 2012.

Gorski, Philip S., ed. *The Post-Secular in Question: Religion in Contemporary Society*. Brooklyn, NY: Social Science Research Council; New York University Press, 2012.

Greco, Dorothy Littell. "How the Seeker-Sensitive Church Is Failing a Generation." *Christianity Today*, August 2013, http://www.christianitytoday.com/women/2013/august/how-seeker-sensitive-consumer-church-is-failing-generation.html?paging=off (accessed February 21, 2014).

Greenfeld, Liah. *Nationalism: Five Roads to Modernity*. Cambridge, MA: Harvard University Press, 1992.

Gross, Rita M. "Meditation and Prayer: A Comparative Inquiry." *Buddhist-Christian Studies* 22, no. 1 (2002): 77–86.

Hadaway, C. Kirk, Penny Long Marler, and Mark Chaves. "What the Polls Don't Show: A Closer Look at U.S. Church Attendance." *American Sociological Review* 58, no. 6 (December 1993): 741–752.

Hall, David D., ed. *Lived Religion in America: Toward a History of Practice*. Princeton, NJ: Princeton University Press, 1997.

Halwani, Raja. "Care Ethics and Virtue Ethics." *Hypatia* 18, no. 3 (August 2003): 161–192.

Hammerling, Roy, ed. *A History of Prayer: The First to the Fifteenth Century*. Brill's Companions to the Christian Tradition, vol. 13. Leiden; Boston, MA: Brill, 2008.

Hand, Thomas A. *Augustine on Prayer*. New York: Catholic Book, 1986.

Haraway, Donna Jeanne. *How Like a Leaf: An Interview with Thyrza Nichols Goodeve*. New York: Routledge, 2000.

Harris Interactive. "Americans' Belief in God, Miracles, and Heaven Declines: Belief in Darwin's Theory of Evolution Rises," December 16, 2013, http://www.harrisinteractive.com/NewsRoom/HarrisPolls/tabid/447/ctl/ReadCustom%20Default/mid/1508/ArticleId/1353/Default.aspx (accessed January 21, 20140.

Harris Interactive. *Pets Are Really Members of the Family—Three in Five Americans Are Pet Owners*. Harris Interactive, June 10, 2011, http://www.harrisinteractive.com/NewsRoom/HarrisPolls/tabid/447/ctl/ReadCustom%20Default/mid/1508/ArticleId/814/Default.aspx (accessed March 18, 2014).

Harris, Sam. *Letter to a Christian Nation*. New York: Vintage Books, 2008.

Harris, Sam. *Waking up: A Guide to Spirituality without Religion*. New York: Simon & Schuster, 2014.

Haynes, Patrice. *Immanent Transcendence: Reconfiguring Materialism in Continental Philosophy*. London; New York: Bloomsbury Academic, 2014.

Haynes, Richard. Atheist Nexus website, http://www.atheistnexus.org (accessed August 9, 2014).

Hedstrom, Matthew S. *Rise of Liberal Religion: Book Culture and American Spirituality in the Twentieth Century*. Oxford; New York: Oxford University Press, 2015.

Heiler, Friedrich. *Prayer: A Study in the History and Psychology of Religion*. Oxford; Rockport, MA: Oneworld, 1997.

Held, Virginia. *The Ethics of Care: Personal, Political, and Global*. Oxford; New York: Oxford University Press, 2006.

Henry, Patrick. "'And I Don't Care What It Is': The Tradition-History of a Civil Religion Proof-Text." *Journal of the American Academy of Religion* XLIX, no. 1 (1981): 35–49.

Herberg, Will. *Protestant, Catholic, Jew: An Essay in American Religious Sociology*. Garden City, NY: Anchor Books, 1960.

Hervieu-Léger, Danièle. *Le Pélerin et le converti: la religion en mouvement*. Paris: Flammarion, 1999.

Hiatt, Brian. "Mumford & Sons: Rattle and Strum: How Four Brits Turned Old-Timey Roots Music into the Future of Rock." *Rolling Stone*, March 10, 2013, http://www.rollingstone.com/music/news/mumford-sons-rattle-and-strum-20130328 (accessed March 11, 2013).

Hitchens, Christopher. *God Is Not Great: How Religion Poisons Everything*. New York: Twelve Hachette Book Group, 2009.

Hitchens, Christopher. *Hitch-22: A Memoir*. New York: Twelve, 2011.

Hollinger, D. A. "After Cloven Tongues of Fire: Ecumenical Protestantism and the Modern American Encounter with Diversity." *Journal of American History* 98, no. 1 (June 1, 2011): 21–48.

Hoover, J. Edgar. "Analysis of the New Left: A Gospel of Nihilism." *Christianity Today*, August 22, 1967.

Hoover, J. Edgar. "Christianity Encounters Communism." *Christianity Today*, December 21, 1962.

Hoover, J. Edgar. "Communist Menace." *Christianity Today*, May 19, 1962.

Hoover, J. Edgar. "Guidelines for a Civilization in Peril." *Christianity Today*, October 10, 1960.

Hoover, J. Edgar. "Morality for Violence." *Christianity Today*, April 28, 1972.

Hoover, J. Edgar. "Unmasking the Communist Masquerader." *The Educational Forum* 14, no. 4 (May 1950): 399–401.

Horowitz, Mitch. *Occult America: White House Séances, Ouija Circles, Masons, and the Secret Mystic History of Our Nation*. New York: Bantam Books Trade Paperbacks, 2010.

Housden, Roger. *Keeping the Faith without a Religion*. Louisville, CO: Sounds True, 2014.

Hout, Michael, and Claude S. Fisher. "More Americans Have No Religious Preference: Politics and Generations." *American Sociological Review* 67 (April 2002): 165–190.

Hughes, Mary Elizabeth, and Angela O'Rand. "The Lives and Times of the Baby Boomers." Washington, DC: Population Reference Bureau and Russell Sage Foundation, 2004.

Huffington Post. "Atheist Church Split: Sunday Assembly and Godless Revival's 'Denominational Chasm.'" January 6, 2014, http://www.huffingtonpost.com/2014/01/06/atheist-church-split_n_4550456.html (accessed January 8, 2014).

Humanist Society. Website, http://humanist-society.org (accessed August 10, 2014).

Hunt, Mary E. *Fierce Tenderness: A Feminist Theology of Friendship*. Minneapolis: Fortress Press, 2009.

Jackson, Matthew O. *Social and Economic Networks*. Princeton, NJ: Princeton University Press, 2008.

Jacoby, Susan. "The Blessings of Atheism." *New York Times*, January 5, 2013, http://www.nytimes.com/2013/01/06/opinion/sunday/the-blessings-of-atheism.html?_r=0 (accessed January 5, 2013).

Jacoby, Susan. *Freethinkers a History of American Secularism*. New York: Holt, 2005.

Janssen, Jacques, De Hart Joep, and Christine Den Draak. "A Content Analysis of the Praying Practices of Dutch Youth." *Journal for the Scientific Study of Religion*, 29, no. 1 (1990): 99–107.

Jindra, I. W. "How Religious Content Matters in Conversion Narratives to Various Religious Groups." *Sociology of Religion* 72, no. 3 (September 1, 2011): 275–302.

Jucker, Andreas H., Sara W. Smith, and Tanja Lüdge. "Interactive Aspects of Vagueness in Conversation." *Journal of Pragmatics* 35, no. 12 (December 2003): 1737–1769.

Kaleem, Jaweed. "'No Religion' Is Increasingly Popular Choice for Americans: Pew Report." *Huffington Post*, October 9, 2013, http://www.huffingtonpost.com/2012/10/09/no-religion-pew-report_n_1949598.html (accessed October 9, 2013).

Kazarian, Ralph. "Some Evidence That Trees 'Communicate When in Trouble.'" *Environmental Conservation* 10, no. 2 (June 1983): 173.

Keller, Timothy J. *The Prodigal God: Recovering the Heart of the Christian Faith.* New York: Riverhead Books, 2011.

Kempe, Margery. *The Book of Margery Kempe.* Edited by Stanford Brown Meech with notes by Hope Emily Allen. London: H. Milford, 1940.

Kilde, Jeanne Halgren. *When Church Became Theatre: The Transformation of Evangelical Architecture and Worship in Nineteenth-Century America.* Oxford; New York: Oxford University Press, 2002.

Killen, Patricia O'Connell, and Mark Silk, eds. *Religion and Public Life in the Pacific Northwest: The None Zone.* Religion by Region 1. Walnut Creek, CA: AltaMira Press, 2004.

Kinnaman, David. *Unchristian: What a New Generation Really Thinks about Christianity—and Why It Matters.* Grand Rapids, MI: Baker Books, 2007.

Kinnaman, David. *You Lost Me: Why Young Christians Are Leaving Church—and Rethinking Faith.* Grand Rapids, MI: BakerBooks, 2011.

Kirkpatrick, Lee A., and Phillip R. Shaver. "Attachment Theory and Religion: Childhood Attachments, Religious Beliefs, and Conversion." *Journal for the Scientific Study of Religion* 29, no. 3 (September 1990): 315–334.

Kohlberg, Lawrence. *The Psychology of Moral Development: The Nature and Validity of Moral Stages.* 1st edition. Essays on Moral Development, vol. 2. San Francisco: Harper & Row, 1984.

Kosmin, Barry A., and Ariela Keysar. American Religious Identification Survey [ARIS 2008]." Hartford, CT: Trinity College (March 2009), http://commons.trincoll.edu/aris/files/2011/08/ARIS_Report_2008.pdf.

Kreeft, Peter. *I Surf, Therefore I Am: A Philosophy of Surfing.* South Bend, IN: St. Augustine's Press, 2008.

Kripal, Jeffrey J. *Esalen: America and the Religion of No Religion.* Chicago: University of Chicago Press, 2008.

Kripal, Jeffrey J., and Glenn W. Shuck, eds. *On the Edge of the Future: Esalen and the Evolution of American Culture.* Religion in North America. Bloomington: Indiana University Press, 2005.

Kushner, Lawrence. *Honey from the Rock: Ten Gates of Jewish Mysticism.* San Francisco: Harper & Row, 1983.

Ladd, Kevin L., and Bernard Spilka. "Inward, Outward, and Upward: Cognitive Aspects of Prayer." *Journal for the Scientific Study of Religion* 41, no. 3 (September 2002): 475–484.

Lane, Belden C. *The Solace of Fierce Landscapes: Exploring Desert and Mountain Spirituality.* Oxford; New York: Oxford University Press, 2007.

Larrabee, Mary Jeanne, ed. *An Ethic of Care: Feminist and Interdisciplinary Perspectives.* Thinking Gender Series. New York: Routledge, 1993.

Le Poidevin, Robin. *Agnosticism: A Very Short Introduction.* Oxford; New York: Oxford University Press, 2010.

Lee, Shayne. *Holy Mavericks: Evangelical Innovators and the Spiritual Marketplace.* New York: New York University Press, 2009.

Leone, Massimo. *Religious Conversion and Identity: The Semiotic Analysis of Texts.* Routledge Studies in Religion. London: Routledge, 2003.

Lewis, Thomas A. "Heterogeneous Community—Beyond New Traditionalism." In *Returning (to) Communities: Theory, Culture and Political Practice of the Communal,* edited by Stefan Herbrechter and Michael Higgans, 55–72. Amsterdam: Rodopi, 2006.

Lichterman, Paul. "Studying Public Religion: Beyond the Beliefs-Driven Actor." In *Religion on the Edge: De-Centering and Re-Centering the Sociology of Religion,* edited by Courtney Bender, Wendy Cadge, and David Smilde, 115–136. New York: Oxford University Press, 2013.

Lipka, Michael. *Majority of U.S. Catholics' Opinions Run Counter to Church on Contraception, Homosexuality.* Washington, DC: Pew Research Center, September 19, 2013, http://www.pewresearch.org/fact-tank/2013/09/19/majority-of-u-s-catholics-opinions-run-counter-to-church-on-contraception-homosexuality/.

Lobdell, William. *Losing My Religion: How I Lost My Faith Reporting on Religion in America—and Found Unexpected Peace.* New York: Collins, 2009.

Lofton, Kathryn. *Oprah: The Gospel of an Icon.* Berkeley: University of California Press, 2011.

Lopez, Donald S. *The Story of Buddhism: A Concise Guide to Its History and Teachings.* San Francisco: HarperSanFrancisco, 2001.

Lozada, Mariana, Paola D'Adamo, and Miguel Angel Fuentes. "Punishment and Cooperation in Nature." *Journal of Theoretical Biology* 289, no. 21 (November 2011): 12–16.

Luckman, Thomas. *The Invisible Religion: The Problem of Religion in Modern Society.* New York: MacMillan, 1967.

Luhrmann, T. M. *When God Talks Back: Understanding the American Evangelical Relationship with God.* New York: Vintage Books, 2012.

Lynch, Gordon. "The Role of Popular Music in the Construction of Alternative Spiritual Identities and Ideologies." *Journal for the Scientific Study of Religion* 45, no. 4 (December 2006): 481–488.

Lévi-Strauss, Claude. *The Raw and the Cooked.* Introduction to *A Science of Mythology,* Claude Lévi-Strauss, vol. 1. Chicago: University of Chicago Press, 1983.

MacIntyre, Alasdair C. *After Virtue: A Study in Moral Theory.* 2nd edition. Notre Dame, IN: University of Notre Dame Press, 1984.

Malloy, Raven, Christopher L. Smith, and Abigail Wozniak. *Declining Migration within the US: The Role of the Labor Market.* Finance and Economics Discussion Series. Washington, DC: Divisions of Research & Statistics and Monetary Affairs Federal Reserve Board, April 4–14, 2014.

Manga, Manuel. "Design Your Own Secular Spirituality." Forum presented at the Humanists in Silicon Valley, Palo Alto, CA, January 27, 2014.

Martin, Luther H. *Hellenistic Religions: An Introduction.* New York: Oxford University Press, 1987.

Martin, Michael, ed. *The Cambridge Companion to Atheism.* Cambridge Companions to Philosophy. New York: Cambridge University Press, 2007.

Masuzawa, Tomoko. *The Invention of World Religions, Or, How European Universalism Was Preserved in the Language of Pluralism.* Chicago: University of Chicago Press, 2005.

Mauss, Marcel. *On Prayer.* New York: Durkheim Press/Berghahn Books, 2003.

Mayer, Peter. "Bio," http://www.petermayer.net/bio/ (accessed November 20, 2013).

McDermott, John. "The Church of No Religion." *Financial Times,* August 23, 2013, http://www.ft.com/intl/cms/s/2/9229a7b8-0abd-11e3-aeab-00144feabdc0.html (accessed August 27, 2013).

McFadden, Margaret H. "Gendering the Feast: Women, Spirituality, and Grace in Three Food Films." In *Reel Food: Essays on Food and Film,* edited by Anne L. Bower, 117–128. New York: Routledge, 2004.

McGowan, Dale, ed. *Parenting beyond Belief: On Raising Ethical, Caring Kids without Religion.* New York: American Management Association, 2007.

McGowan, Dale, ed. *Raising Freethinkers: A Practical Guide for Parenting beyond Belief.* New York: American Management Association, 2009.

McGuire, Meredith B. *Lived Religion: Faith and Practice in Everyday Life.* Oxford; New York: Oxford University Press, 2008.

McGuire, Meredith B. *The Social Context.* 5th edition. Longrove, IL: Waveland Press, 2002.

McKinney, John Paul, and Kathleen G. McKinney. "Prayer in the Lives of Late Adolescents." *Journal of Adolescence* 22, no. 2 (1999): 279–290.

McMahan, David L. *The Making of Buddhist Modernism.* Oxford; New York: Oxford University Press, 2008.

Mehta, Hemant. *I Sold My Soul on eBay: Viewing Faith through an Atheist's Eyes.* Colorado Springs, CO: Waterbrook Press, 2007.

Mehta, Hemant. "The Friendly Atheist," blog, http://www.patheos.com/blogs/friendlyatheist/about-the-contributors/ (accessed August 10, 2014).

Mercadante, Linda A. *Belief without Borders: Inside the Minds of the Spiritual but Not Religious.* New York: Oxford University Press, 2014.

Merica, Dan. "'None' Leaders to Chart Path for More Political, Cultural Power for Religiously Unaffiliated." *CNN Belief Blog* (January 25, 2013), http://religion.blogs.cnn.com/2013/01/25/none-leaders-to-chart-path-for-more-political-cultural-power-for-religiously-unaffiliated/ (accessed January 25, 2013).

Merritt, Carol Howard. *Tribal Church: Ministering to the Missing Generation.* Herndon, VA: Alban Institute, 2007.

Meyers, Robin R. *Saving Jesus from the Church: How to Stop Worshiping Christ and Start Following Jesus.* New York: HarperOne, 2009.

Millgram, Abraham Ezra. *Jewish Worship*. Philadelphia: Jewish Publication Society of America, 1971.

Modern, John Lardas. *Secularism in Antebellum America: With Reference to Ghosts, Protestant Subcultures, Machines, and Their Metaphors: Featuring Discussions of Mass Media, Moby-Dick, Spirituality, Phrenology, Anthropology, Sing Sing State Penitentiary, and Sex with the New Motive Power*. Religion and Postmodernism. Chicago: University of Chicago Press, 2011.

Mosley, Glenn. *New Thought, Ancient Wisdom: The History and Future of the New Thought Movement*. Philadelphia: Templeton Foundation Press, 2006.

Muggleton, David, and Rupert Weinzierl. *The Post-Subcultures Reader*. Oxford; New York: Berg, 2003.

Murray, Stuart. *Church after Christendom*. Milton Keynes, UK: Paternoster, 2004.

Myss, Caroline. *Anatomy of the Spirit: The Seven Stages of Power and Healing*. New York: MJF Books, 2011.

Naiden, F. S. *Ancient Supplication*. Oxford; New York: Oxford University Press, 2009.

Neusner, Jacob, and Bruce Chilton, eds. *The Golden Rule: The Ethics of Reciprocity in World Religions*. New York: Continuum, 2008.

New Vision Center for Spiritual Living. "What Practitioners 'Do,'" http://www.newvisionaz.org/ (accessed July 21, 2013).

New Vision Center for Spiritual Living. "Real Love Groups," http://www.newvisionaz.org/pages/real.html (accessed July 23, 2013).

Nickell, S. Alyssa Ninan. "The Limits of Embodiment: The Implications of Written and Artistic Portrayals of Mary at the Foot of the Cross for Late Medieval Affective Spirituality." PhD dissertation, Graduate Theological Union, 2011.

Niebuhr, H. Richard. *Christ and Culture*. San Francisco: HarperSanFrancisco, 2001.

Niose, David. *Nonbeliever Nation: The Rise of Secular Americans*. New York: St. Martin's Press, 2013.

Noddings, Nel. *Caring: A Feminine Approach to Ethics and Moral Education*. 2nd edition. Berkeley: University of California Press, 2003.

Ó Murchú, Diarmuid. *Quantum Theology: Spiritual Implications of the New Physics*. Revised and updated. New York: Crossroad, 2004.

Orsi, Robert A. *Between Heaven and Earth: The Religious Worlds People Make and the Scholars Who Study Them*. Princeton, NJ: Princeton University Press, 2005.

Orsi, Robert A. "Everyday Miracles: The Study of Lived Religion." In *Lived Religion in America: Toward a History of Practice*, edited by David D. Hall, 3–21. Princeton, NJ: Princeton University Press, 1997.

Orsi, Robert A. "Is the Study of Lived Religion Irrelevant to the World We Live in? Special Presidential Plenary Address, Society for the Scientific Study of Religion, Salt Lake City, November 2, 2002." *Journal for the Scientific Study of Religion* 42, no. 2 (June 2003): 169–174.

Orsi, Robert A. *The Madonna of 115th Street: Faith and Community in Italian Harlem, 1880–1950*. 3rd edition. New Haven, CT: Yale University Press, 2010.

Orsi, Robert A., ed. *The Cambridge Companion to Religious Studies*. Cambridge Companions to Religion. Cambridge; New York: Cambridge University Press, 2011.

Ortner, Sherry B. "Theory in Anthropology since the Sixties." *Comparative Studies in Society and History* 26, no. 01 (January 1984): 126–166.

Pace, Enzo. "Religion as Communication: The Changing Shape of Catholicism in Europe." In *Everyday Religion: Observing Modern Religious Lives*, edited by Nancy Tatom Ammerman, 37–51. Oxford; New York: Oxford University Press, 2006.

Paloutzian, Raymond F, and Crystal L Park. *Handbook of the Psychology of Religion and Spirituality*. New York: Guilford Press, 2015.

Pangle, Lorraine Smith. *Aristotle and the Philosophy of Friendship*. Cambridge; New York: Cambridge University Press, 2008.

Patel, Eboo. *Acts of Faith: The Story of an American Muslim, the Struggle for the Soul of a Generation*. Boston, MA: Beacon Press, 2010.

Payne, Jervis David. *Kingdom Expressions: Trends Influencing the Advancement of the Gospel*. Nelson's Quick Guides. Nashville, TN: Thomas Nelson, 2012.

Peck, M. Scott. *The Different Drum: Community Making and Peace*. New York: Simon & Schuster, 1998.

Peters, Lisa Westberg. *Our Family Tree: An Evolution Story*. San Diego, CA: Harcourt, 2003.

Pew Forum on Religion & Public Life. "2008 U.S. Religious Landscape Survey: Religious Affiliation: Diverse and Dynamic." Washington, DC, February 2008, http://religions.pewforum.org/pdf/report-religious-landscape-full.pdf (accessed March 19, 2008).

Pew Forum on Religion & Public Life. "A Portrait of Jewish Americans: Findings from a Pew Research Center Survey of U.S. Jews." Washington, DC: Pew Research Center, October 1, 2013, http://www.pewforum.org/files/2013/10/jewish-american-full-report-for-web.pdf (accessed January 12, 2014).

Pew Forum on Religion & Public Life. "Many Americans Mix Multiple Faiths: Eastern, New Age Beliefs Widespread." Washington, DC: Pew Research Center, December 2009, http://www.pewforum.org/files/2009/12/multiplefaiths.pdf (accessed January 4, 2009).

Pew Forum on Religion & Public Life. "Millennials in Adulthood: Detached from Institutions, Networked with Friends." Pew Research Center, March 7, 2014, http://www.pewsocial-trends.org/files/2014/03/2014-03-07_generations-report-version-for-web.pdf.

Pew Forum on Religion & Public Life. "Nones on the Rise: One-in-Five Adults Have No Religious Affiliation." Washington, DC: Pew Research Center, October 9, 2103, http://www.pewforum.org/files/2012/10/ NonesOnTheRise-full.pdf (accessed October 10, 2013).

Pew Forum on Religion & Public Life. "The Shifting Religious Identity of Latinos in the United States: Nearly One-in-Four Latinos Are Former Catholics." Washington, DC: Pew Research Center, May 7, 2014, http://www.pewforum.org/files/2014/05/Latinos-Religion-07-22-full-report.pdf.

Piaget, Jean. *The Moral Judgment of the Child*. New York: Free Press Paperbacks, 1997.

Pike, Sarah M. *New Age and Neopagan Religions in America*. New York: Columbia University Press, 2006.

Podles, Mary Elizabeth. "Babette's Feast: Feasting with Lutherans." *The Antioch Review* 50, no. 3 (1992): 551–565.

Podlesskaya, Vera I. "Parameters for Typological Variation of Placeholders." In *Fillers, Pauses and Placeholders*, 11–33. Typological Studies in Language. Amsterdam ; Philadelphia: John Benjamins, 2010.

Pollan, Michael. *Cooked: A Natural History of Transformation*. New York: Penguin, 2014.

Postman, Neil. *Amusing Ourselves to Death: Public Discourse in the Age of Show Business*. New York: Penguin, 1985.

Principe, Walter. "Toward Defining Spirituality." *Studies in Religion/Sciences Religieuses* 12, no. 2 (1983): 128–129.

Prothero, Stephen R. *God Is Not One: The Eight Rival Religions That Run the World*. New York: Harper Collins, 2011.

Pulleyn, Simon. *Prayer in Greek Religion*. Oxford Classical Monographs. Oxford; New York: Clarendon Press; Oxford University Press, 1997.

Putnam, Robert D. *American Grace: How Religion Divides and Unites Us*. New York: Simon & Schuster, 2012.

Putnam, Robert D. *Bowling Alone: The Collapse and Revival of American Community*. New York: Simon & Schuster, 2000.

Quiet Company. "About," http://www.quietcompanymusic.com/about (accessed June 2, 2013).

Racca, Anais, Kun Guo, KerstinMeints, and Daniel S. Mills. "Reading Faces: Differential Lateral Gaze Bias in Processing Canine and Human Facial Expressions in Dogs and 4-Year-Old Children." *PLoS One* 7, no. 4 (April 27, 2012), http://journals.plos.org/plosone/article?id=10.1371/journal.pone.0036076.

Rambo, Lewis R. *Understanding Religious Conversion*. New Haven, CT: Yale University Press, 1993.

Reif, Stefan C. *Judaism and Hebrew Prayer: New Perspectives on Jewish Liturgical History*. Cambridge; New York: Cambridge University Press, 1993.

Religion & Ethics Newsweekly. "None of the Above: The Rise of the Religiously Unaffiliated." October 9, 2012, http://video.pbs.org/video/2288849147/.

Remigo, Reina. "Best Friends: A Look at the Human-Animal Bond and Spirituality Using a Mixed-Methods Approach." PhD dissertation, Sophia University, 2014.

Ricoeur, Paul. "Philosophy and Religious Language." *Journal of Religion* 54, no. 1 (January 1974): 71–85.

Ricœur, Paul. *Time and Narrative*. Chicago: University of Chicago Press, 1984.

Riley, James C. *Rising Life Expectancy: A Global History*. Cambridge; New York: Cambridge University Press, 2001.

Roof, Wade Clark. *A Generation of Seekers: The Spiritual Journeys of the Baby Boom Generation*. San Francisco: HarperSanFrancisco, 1993.

Roof, Wade Clark. *Spiritual Marketplace: Baby Boomers and the Remaking of American Religion*. Princeton, NJ: Princeton University Press, 2001.

Ross, Mandy. *Naming Ceremonies*. Rites of Passage. Chicago: Heinemann Library, 2004.

Russell, Bertrand. *What I Believe*. Abingdon: Routledge, [1925] 2013.

Sands, Robert R., and Linda Sands. "Running Deep: Speculations on the Evolution of Running and Spirituality in the Genus Homo." *Journal for the Study of Religion, Nature, and Culture* 3, no. 4 (2009): 552–577.

Schmidt, Leigh Eric. *Hearing Things: Religion, Illusion, and the American Enlightenment*. Cambridge, MA: Harvard University Press, 2000.

Schmidt, Leigh Eric. *Restless Souls the Making of American Spirituality*. Berkeley: University of California Press, 2012.

Schneiders, S. M. "Spirituality in the Academy." *Theological Studies* 50, no. 4 (December 1, 1989): 676–697.

Schultz, Tom. "The Rise of the Dones." *Holy Soup*, November 12, 2014, http://holysoup.com/2014/11/12/the-rise-of-the-dones/. (accessed November 13, 2014).

Schwartz, Daniel. *Aquinas on Friendship*. Oxford; New York: Oxford University Press, 2012.

Scott, David, and Charles Hirschkind, eds. *Powers of the Secular Modern: Talal Asad and His Interlocutors*. Cultural Memory in the Present. Stanford, CA: Stanford University Press, 2006.

Searle, John R. *Speech Acts: An Essay in the Philosophy of Language*. London: Cambridge University Press, 1969.

Sentilles, Sarah. *Breaking Up with God: A Love Story*. New York: HarperOne, 2011.

Shaw, Sylvie, and Andrew Francis, eds. *Deep Blue: Critical Reflections on Nature, Religion and Water*. London; Oakville, CT: Equinox, 2008.

Silen, W., T. E. Machen, and J. G. Forte. "Acid-Base Balance in Amphibian Gastric Mucosa." *The American Journal of Physiology* 229, no. 3 (September 1975): 721–730.

Slote, Michael A. *From Enlightenment to Receptivity: Rethinking Our Values*. New York: Oxford University Press, 2013.

Smith, Christian. *Lost in Transition: The Dark Side of Emerging Adulthood*. New York: Oxford University Press, 2011.

Smith, Christian. *Souls in Transition: The Religious and Spiritual Lives of Emerging Adults*. Oxford; New York: Oxford University Press, 2009.

Smith, Christian, and Melinda Lundquist Denton. *Soul Searching: The Religious and Spiritual Lives of American Teenagers*. Oxford; New York: Oxford University Press, 2005.

Smith, Dinitia. "Dinitia Smith, Philosopher Gamely in Defense of His Ideas." *New York Times*, May 30, 1998, http://www.nytimes.com/1998/05/30/arts/philosopher-gamely-in-defense-of-his-ideas.html (accessed June 23, 2013).

Smith, Jonathan Z. *Imagining Religion: From Babylon to Jonestown*. Chicago: University of Chicago Press, 1982.

Smith, Jonathan Z. *Relating Religion: Essays in the Study of Religion*. Chicago: University of Chicago Press, 2004.

Smith, Wilfred Cantwell. *Faith and Belief: The Difference between Them*. Oxford: Oneworld Publications, 1998.

Smith, Wilfred Cantwell. *The Meaning and End of Religion*. Minneapolis, MN: Fortress Press, 1991.

Sober, Elliott, and David Sloan Wilson. *Unto Others: The Evolution and Psychology of Unselfish Behavior*. Cambridge, MA: Harvard University Press, 1998.

Solon, Olivia. "'Atheist Church' Seeks £500,000 in Crowdfunding to Build Online Platform." *Wired*, October 20, 2013, http://www.wired.co.uk/news/archive/2013-10/20/sunday-assembly-expansion.

Spivak, Gayatri Chakravorty. "Preface." In Jacques Derrida, *Of Grammatology*, lxxxix–xc. Baltimore, MD: Johns Hopkins University Press, 1976.

Spufford, Francis. *Unapologetic: Why, despite Everything, Christianity Can Still Make Surprising Emotional Sense.* San Francisco: HarperOne, 2013.

Stallybrass, Peter. *The Politics and Poetics of Transgression.* Ithaca, NY: Cornell University Press, 1986.

Star, Daniel. "Do Confucians Really Care? A Defense of the Distinctiveness of Care Ethics: A Reply to Chenyang Li." *Hypatia* 17, no. 1 (February 2002): 77–106.

Stark, Rodney. *What Americans Really Believe: New Findings from the Baylor Surveys of Religion.* Waco, TX: Baylor University Press, 2008.

Stedman, Chris. *Faitheist: How an Atheist Found Common Ground with the Religious.* Boston, MA: Beacon Press, 2012.

Stenger, Victor. "Quantum Quackery." *Skeptical Inquirer* 21, no. 2 (January–February 1997), http://www.csicop.org/si/show/quantum_quackery/ (accessed August 16, 2013).

Stevens, Jeffrey R., and Marc D. Hauser. "Why Be Nice? Psychological Constraints on the Evolution of Cooperation." *Trends in Cognitive Sciences* 8, no. 2 (February 2004): 60–65.

Stock, Brian. *The Implications of Literacy: Written Language and Models of Interpretation in the Eleventh and Twelfth Centuries.* Princeton, NJ: Princeton University Press, 1983.

Sunday Assembly Silicon Valley. "About," http://sundayassembly.com/about/ (accessed November 11, 2013).

Symons, Michael. "From Agape to Eucharist: Jesus Meals and the Early Church." *Food and Foodways* 8, no. 1 (January 1999): 33–54.

Tanner, Kathryn. "In Praise of Open Communion: A Rejoinder to James Farwell." *Anglican Theological Review* 86, no. 3 (Summer 2004): 473–485.

Taves, Ann. *Fits, Trances, and Visions: Experiencing Religion and Explaining Experience from Wesley to James.* Princeton, NJ: Princeton University Press, 1999.

Taylor, B. "Surfing into Spirituality and a New, Aquatic Nature Religion." *Journal of the American Academy of Religion* 75, no. 4 (October 17, 2007): 923–951.

Taylor, Charles. *A Secular Age.* Cambridge, MA: Belknap Press of Harvard University Press, 2007.

Taylor, Charles. *Modern Social Imaginaries.* Public Planet Books. Durham, NC: Duke University Press, 2004.

Taylor, Charles. *Sources of the Self: The Making of the Modern Identity.* Cambridge, MA: Harvard University Press, 1989.

Taylor, Jeremy. *Dream Work: Techniques for Discovering the Creative Power in Dreams.* New York: Paulist Press, 1983.

Taylor, Mark C. *After God.* Chicago: University of Chicago Press, 2009.

Taylor, Mark C., ed. *Critical Terms for Religious Studies.* Chicago: University of Chicago Press, 1998.

ThinkAtheist. Website, http://www.thinkatheist.com (accessed August 9, 2014).

Time. "Record High." September 16, 1957.

Tolle, Eckhart. *The Power of NOW: A Guide to Spiritual Enlightenment.* Revised edition. Vancouver; Novato, CA: Namaste; New World Library, 2004.

Tolle, Eckhart. Eckhart Tolle TV, http://www.eckharttolletv.com (accessed July 9, 2013).

Travis, Trysh. *The Language of the Heart: A Cultural History of the Recovery Movement from Alcoholics Anonymous to Oprah Winfrey.* Chapel Hill, NC: University of North Carolina Press, 2013.

Tronto, Joan C. *Moral Boundaries: A Political Argument for an Ethic of Care.* New York: Routledge, 1993.

Tugwell, Simon, ed. *Albert & Thomas: Selected Writings.* The Classics of Western Spirituality. New York: Paulist Press, 1988.

Ullman, Chana. *The Transformed Self: The Psychology of Religious Conversion.* Emotions, Personality, and Psychotherapy. New York: Plenum Press, 1989.

Ullman, Montague, and Claire Limmer, eds. *The Variety of Dream Experience: Expanding Our Ways of Working with Dreams.* 2nd edition. SUNY Series in Dream Studies. Albany: State University of New York Press, 1999.

Unruh, Anita, and Susan Hutchinson. "Embedded Spirituality: Gardening in Daily Life and Stressful Life Experiences: Embedded Spirituality." *Scandinavian Journal of Caring Sciences* 25, no. 3 (September 2011): 567–574.

US Bureau of Labor Statistics. "Number of Jobs Held, Labor Market Activity, and Growth among the Youngest Baby Bookers: Results from a Longitudinal Study," July 25, 2012, http://www.bls.gov/news.release/pdf/nlsoy.pdf (accessed November 2, 2014).

US Census Bureau. *Population: Religion—Self-Described Religious Identification of Adult Population: 1990, 2001, 2008.* The 2012 Statistical Abstract, https://www.census.gov/compendia/statab/cats/population/religion.html. (accessed January 14, 2013).

VandeCreek, Larry, Mark-David Janus, James W. Pennebaker, and Bradley Binau. "Praying about Difficult Experiences as Self-Disclosure to God." *International Journal for the Psychology of Religion* 12, no. 1 (January 2002): 29–39.

Vásquez, Manuel A. *More than Belief: A Materialist Theory of Religion.* Oxford; New York: Oxford University Press, 2011.

Vernon, Glenn M. "The Religious 'Nones': A Neglected Category." *Journal for the Scientific Study of Religion* 7, no. 2 (1968): 219.

Walsh, Froma. "Human-Animal Bonds I: The Relational Significance of Companion Animals." *Family Process* 48, no. 4 (December 2009): 462–480.

Walsh, Froma. "Human-Animal Bonds II: The Role of Pets in Family Systems and Family Therapy." *Family Process* 48, no. 4 (December 2009): 481–499.

Ward, Charlotte, and David Voas. "The Emergence of Conspirituality." *Journal of Contemporary Religion* 26, no. 1 (January 2011): 103–121.

Ward, Patricia A. *Experimental Theology in America: Madame Guyon, Fénelon, and Their Readers.* Waco, TX: Baylor University Press, 2009.

Warner, Michael, Jonathan VanAntwerpen, and Craig J Calhoun. *Varieties of Secularism in a Secular Age.* Cambridge, MA: Harvard University Press, 2013.

Warren, Rick. *The Purpose Driven Life Journal: Reflections on What on Earth Am I Here For?* Grand Rapids, MI: Zondervan, 2003.

Watters, Ethan. *Urban Tribes: Are Friends the New Family?* London: Bloomsbury, 2004.

Wattles, Jeffrey. *The Golden Rule.* New York: Oxford University Press, 1996.

Weber, Max. *The Protestant Ethic and the Spirit of Capitalism.* Routledge Classics. London; New York: Routledge, 2001.

West, Melissa Gayle. *Exploring the Labyrinth: A Guide for Healing and Spiritual Growth.* New York: Broadway Books, 2000.

Williamson, Marianne. "Monday Nights: Teachings Based on *A Course in Miracles,*" http://www.marianne.com/events.htm (accessed February 18, 2014).

Winston, Kimberley. "Meet the Nones: Unbelief Is Now the World's Third-Largest 'Religion.'" *Sojourners,* December 19, 2012, http://sojo.net/blogs/2012/12/19/unbelief-now-world's-third-largest-religion (accessed December 20, 2012).

Woolley, Jacqueline, and Katrina Phelps. "The Development of Children's Beliefs about Prayer." *Journal of Cognition and Culture* 1, no. 2 (June 1, 2001): 139–166.

Workman, Lance, and Will Reader. *Evolutionary Psychology: An Introduction.* Cambridge: Cambridge University Press, 2014.

Wright, Wendy M. "Babette's Feast: A Religious Film." *Journal of Religion and Film* 1, no. 2 (October 1997). http://www.unomaha.edu/jrf/BabetteWW.htm.

Wuthnow, Robert. *After Heaven: Spirituality in America since the 1950s.* Berkeley: University of California Press, 1998.

Wuthnow, Robert. *After the Baby Boomers: How Twenty- and Thirty-Somethings Are Shaping the Future of American Religion.* Princeton, NJ: Princeton University Press, 2007.

Wuthnow, Robert. *All in Sync: How Music and Art Are Revitalizing American Religion.* Berkeley: University of California Press, 2003.

Yogis, Jaimal. *Saltwater Buddha: A Surfer's Quest to Find Zen on the Sea.* Boston, MA: Wisdom Publications, 2009.

Zagzebski, Linda. "The Virtues of God and the Foundations of Ethics." In *Readings in the Philosophy of Religion,* edited by Kelly James Clark, 109–119. New York: Broadview Press, 2000.

Zaleski, Philip, and Carol Zaleski. *Prayer: A History.* New York: Mariner Books, 2005.

Zinnbauer, Brian J., Kenneth I. Pargament, Brenda Cole, Mark S. Rye, Eric M. Butter, Timothy G. Belavich, Kathleen M. Hipp, Allie B. Scott, and Jill L. Kadar. "Religion and Spirituality: Unfuzzying the Fuzzy." *Journal for the Scientific Study of Religion* 36, no. 4 (December 1997): 549.

Zuckerman, Phil. *Living the Secular Life: New Answers to Old Questions.* New York: Penguin Press, 2014.

Zuckerman, Phil. *Society without God: What the Least Religious Nations Can Tell Us about Contentment.* New York; Chesham: New York University Press, 2010.

INDEX

Figures and tables are indicated by "f" and "t" following page numbers.